Rice, Rutter and Co

The National Portrait Gallery of Distinguished Americans

Vol. IV

Rice, Rutter and Co

The National Portrait Gallery of Distinguished Americans
Vol. IV

ISBN/EAN: 9783744680943

Printed in Europe, USA, Canada, Australia, Japan

Cover: Foto ©ninafisch / pixelio.de

More available books at **www.hansebooks.com**

THE
NATIONAL
PORTRAIT GALLERY

OF

Distinguished Americans;

WITH

BIOGRAPHICAL SKETCHES

BY

CELEBRATED AUTHORS.

Illustrated by One Hundred and Sixty Fine Steel Engravings.

FROM THE MOST AUTHENTIC PORTRAITS.

COMPLETE IN FOUR VOLUMES.
VOL. IV.

PHILADELPHIA:
RICE, RUTTER & CO.,
No. 525 MINOR STREET.
1865.

CONTENTS OF VOLUME IV.

JOHN ADAMS, Second President of the United States.
ABIGAIL ADAMS, consort of John Adams.
SAMUEL ADAMS, Governor of Massachusetts, etc.
PHILIP H. SHERIDAN, Major-General United States Army.
CHARLES COTESWORTH PINCKNEY, Major-General, Minister to France, etc.
SAMUEL CHASE, Associate Justice of the Supreme Court of U. S.
OLIVER O. HOWARD, Major-General United States Army.
ROBERT R. LIVINGSTON, Chancellor of the State of New York.
JOHN QUINCY ADAMS, Sixth President of the United States.
LOUISA CATHARINE ADAMS, consort of John Quincy Adams.
EDWARD EVERETT, Secretary of State, Minister to England, etc.
NATHANIEL BOWDITCH, LL.D., F.R.S., Mathematician, etc.
THOMAS SAY, Naturalist.
JOHN W. FRANCIS, M.D., LL.D., Professor of Forensic Medicine, New York.
NATHANIEL GREENE, Major-General in the Continental Army.
EDMUND PENDLETON GAINES, Major-General U. S. A.
WILLIAM CHARLES COLE CLAIBORNE, Governor of Louisiana.
JOHN RANDOLPH, Minister to Russia, Senator from Va., etc.
JOHN McLEAN, Associate Justice of the Supreme Court of U. S.
LYDIA HUNTLEY SIGOURNEY, Authoress.
ISAAC SHELBY, First Governor of Kentucky.
EDWARD LIVINGSTON, Minister to France, etc.
BENJAMIN LINCOLN, Major-General and Secretary of War.
BENJAMIN RUSH, M.D., Professor in the University of Pa.
JOHN TYLER, Tenth President of the United States.
JAMES K. POLK, Eleventh President of the United States.
ZACHARY TAYLOR, Twelfth President of the United States.
WM. H. PRESCOTT, Historian.
MILLARD FILLMORE, Thirteenth President of the U. S.
FRANKLIN PIERCE, Fourteenth President of the U. S.
GEORGE M. DALLAS, Vice President of the United States.
DANIEL D. TOMPKINS, Vice President United States.
WILLIAM GASTON, Judge of the Supreme Court of N. C.
WILLIAM R. DAVIE, Major-General and Governor of N. C.
LUTHER MARTIN, Attorney-General of the State of Maryland.
PHILIP SYNG PHYSICK, M.D., Professor in the University of Pa.
JAMES BUCHANAN, Fifteenth President of the United States.

John Adams

JOHN ADAMS.

Among the earliest settlers of the English colonies in New England was a family by the name of Adams. One of the grantees of the charter of Charles the First to the London Company was named Thomas Adams, though it does not appear that he was of those who emigrated with Governor Winthrop, in 1630.

It appears by the Governor's journal, that in 1634 there came a considerable number of colonists, under the pastoral superintendence of the Rev. Thomas Parker, in a vessel from Ipswich, in the county of Suffolk, in the neighborhood of which is Braintree in Essex.

There was, it seems, after their arrival, some difficulty in deciding where they should be located. It was finally determined that Mount Wollaston, situated within the harbor, and distant about nine miles from the three mountains, and whence the intrusive merry mountaineer Morton had been expelled, should, with an enlarged boundary, be annexed to *Boston ;* and the lands within that boundary were granted in various proportions to individuals, chiefly, if not entirely, of the new company from Ipswich.

The settlement soon increased ; and feeling, like all the original settlements in New England, the want of religious instruction and social worship, found it a great inconvenience to travel nine or ten miles every Sunday to reach the place of their devotions. In 1636 they began to hold meetings, and to hear occasional preachers, at Mount Wollaston itself. Three years afterwards they associated themselves under a covenant as a Christian Church ; and in 1640 were incorporated as a separate town, by the name of *Braintree.*

Of this town Henry Adams, junior, was the first town-clerk ; and the first pages of the original town records, still extant, are in his handwriting. He was the oldest of eight sons, with whom his father, Henry Adams, had emigrated, probably from Braintree in England, and who had arrived in the vessel from Ipswich in 1634. Henry Adams the elder, died in 1646, leaving a widow, and a daughter named Ursula besides the eight sons above-mentioned. He had been a brewer in England, and had set up a brewery in his new habitation. This establishment was continued by the youngest but one of his sons, named Joseph. The other sons sought their fortunes in other towns, and chiefly among their first settlers. Henry, who had been the first town clerk of Braintree, removed, at the time of the incorporation of Medfield in 1652, to that place, and was again the first town-clerk there.

Joseph, the son who remained at Braintree, was born in 1626; was at the time of the emigration of the family from England, a boy of eight years old, and died at the age of sixty-eight in 1694, leaving ten children,—five sons and five daughters.

One of these sons, named John, settled in Boston, and was father of Samuel Adams, and grandfather of the revolutionary patriot of that name.

Another son, named also Joseph, was born in 1654; married Hannah Bass, a daughter of Ruth Alden, and grand-daughter of John Alden of the May Flower, and died in 1736 at the age of eighty-two.

His second son named John, born in 1689, was the father of JOHN ADAMS, the subject of the present memoir. His mother was Susanna, daughter of Peter Boylston, and niece of Dr. Zabdiel Boylston, renowned as the first introducer of inoculation for the small-pox in the British dominions.

This JOHN ADAMS was born on the 30th October, 1735, at Braintree. His father's elder brother, Joseph, had been educated at Harvard College; and was for upwards of sixty years minister of a Congregational church at Newington, New Hampshire.

John Adams, the father, was a farmer of small estate and a common school education. He lived and died, as his father and grandfather had done before him, in that mediocrity of condition between affluence and poverty, most propitious to the exercise of the ordinary duties of life, and to the enjoyment of individual happiness. He was for many years a deacon of the church, and a select man of the town, without enjoying or aspiring to any higher dignity. He was in his religious opinions, like most of the inhabitants of New England at that time, a rigid Calvinist, and was desirous of bestowing upon his eldest son the benefit of a classical education, to prepare him for the same profession with that of his elder brother, the minister of the gospel at Newington.

JOHN ADAMS, the son, had at that early age no vocation for the Church, nor even for a college education. Upon his father's asking him to what occupation in life he would prefer to be raised, he answered that he wished to be *a farmer*. His father, without attempting directly to control his inclination, replied that it should be as he desired. He accordingly took him out with himself the next day upon the farm, and gave him practical experience of the labors of the plough, the spade, and the scythe. At the close of the day the young farmer told his father that he would go to school. He retained, however, his fondness for farming to the last years of his life.

He was accordingly placed under the tuition of Mr. Marsh, the keeper of a school then residing at Braintree, and who, ten years afterwards, was also the instructor of Josiah Quincy, the celebrated patriot, who lived but to share the first trials and to face the impending terrors of the revolution.

In 1751, at the age of sixteen, JOHN ADAMS was admitted as a student at Harvard College, and in 1755 was graduated as Bachelor of Arts. The class to which he belonged stands eminent on the College catalogue, for the unusual number of men distinguished in after-life. Among them were Samuel Locke, some time President of the College; Moses Hemmenway, subsequently a divine of high reputation; Sir John Wentworth, Governor of the province of New Hampshire; William Browne, a judge of the Superior Court of the Province of Massachusetts Bay, and afterwards Governor of the island of Bermuda; David Sewall, many years judge of the District Court of the United States in the district, and afterwards State of Maine; and Tristram Dalton, a Senator of the United States. Three of these had so far distinguished themselves while under-graduates, that, in the traditions of the College, it was for many years afterwards known by the sons of Harvard as the class of Adams, Hemmenway, and Locke.

John Adams, the father, had thus given to his eldest son a liberal education to fit him for the gospel ministry. He had two other sons, Peter Boylston and Elihu, whom he was educating to the profession which JOHN had at first preferred, of *farmers*. In this profession Peter Boylston continued to the end of a long life, holding for many years a commission as a justice of the peace, and serving for some time the town of Quincy as their representative in the legislature of the Commonwealth. He died in 1822 at the age of eighty-four, leaving numerous descendants among the respectable inhabitants of Quincy and of Boston. Elihu, at the commencement of the Revolution, entered the army as a captain, and with multitudes of others fell a victim to the epidemic dysentery of 1775. He left two sons and one daughter, whose posterity reside in the towns of Randolph, (originally a part of

Braintree,) Abington, and Bridgewater. The daughter was the mother of Aaron Hobart, several years a member of the House of Representatives of the United States, and afterwards of the Council of the Commonwealth.

Among the usages of the primitive inhabitants of the villages of New England, a *liberal*, that is, a college education, was considered as an outfit for life, and equivalent to the double portion of an eldest son. Upon being graduated at the College in 1755, JOHN ADAMS, at the age of twenty, had received this double portion, and was thenceforth to provide for himself.

"The world was all before him, and Providence his guide."

At the commencement, when he was graduated, there were present one or more of the select-men of the town of Worcester, which was then in want of a teacher for the town school. They proposed to Mr. Adams to undertake this service, and he accepted the invitation. He repaired immediately to Worcester, and took upon him the arduous duties of his office; pursuing at the same time the studies which were to prepare him for the ministry.

His entrance thus upon the theatre of active life was at a period of great political excitement. Precisely at the time when he went to reside at Worcester, occurred the first incidents of the seven years' war, waged between France and Britain for the mastery of the North American continent. The disaster of Braddock's defeat and death happened precisely at that time, like the shock of an earthquake throughout the British colonies. Politics were the speculation of every mind—the prevailing topic of every conversation. It was then that he wrote to his kinsman, Nathaniel Webb, that prophetic letter which has been justly called a literary phenomenon, and which shadowed forth the future revolution of Independence, and the naval glories of this Union.

His father had fondly cherished the hope that he was raising, by the education of his son, a monumental pillar of the Calvinistic church; and he himself, reluctant at the thought of disappointing the hopes of his father, and unwilling to embrace a profession laboring then under strong prejudices unfavorable to it among the people of New England, had acquiesced in the purpose which had devoted him to the gospel ministry. But the progress of his theological studies soon gave him an irresistible distaste for the Calvinistic doctrines. The writings of Archbishop Tillotson, then at the summit of their reputation; the pro-

JOHN ADAMS.

found analysis of Bishop Butler, with his sermons upon human nature and upon the character of Balaam, took such hold upon his memory, his imagination, and his judgment, that they extirpated from his mind every root of Calvinism that had been implanted in it; and the philosophical works of Bolingbroke, then a dazzling novelty in the literary world, although wholly successless in their tendency to shake his faith in the sublime and eternal truths of the gospel, contributed effectively to wean him from the creed of the Genevan Reformer.

About one year after his first arrival at Worcester, after much anxious deliberation and consultation with confidential friends, he resolved to relinquish the study of divinity, and to undertake that of the law. He accordingly entered the office of Col. James Putnam, then a lawyer of reputation at Worcester, and became at the same time an inmate of his house. With him he lived in perfect harmony for the space of two years, pursuing, with indefatigable diligence, the study of the law, and keeping at the same time the town school. In 1758 he completed his preparatory professional studies; relinquished his school, and returned to his paternal mansion at Braintree. He applied, though a total stranger, to Jeremy Gridley, then the most eminent lawyer in New England, and Attorney-general of the Province, to present him to the judges of the Superior Court for admission to the Bar. Mr. Gridley examined him with regard to his proficiency in the studies appropriate to his profession, and warmly recommended him to the Court, securing thereby his admission.

He opened an office, and commenced the practice in his native town. Two years after, in 1760, he lost his father; but continued to reside with his mother and brother till 1764. His attendance upon the Courts in the counties of Suffolk, and of the old colony, was assiduous; but an accidental engagement in a private cause, before the Court at Plymouth, gave him the opportunity to display talents, which brought him immediately into large and profitable practice. In 1762 the seven years' war was concluded by the cession to Great Britain and Spain of all the possessions of France on the continent of North America; and at the same time commenced in England the system of policy, which terminated in the Revolution of Independence. It commenced by an increased rigor of exaction and of restriction in the execution of the laws of trade. For this purpose the officers of the customs were instructed by an order of the royal council, to apply, in cases when they suspected articles of merchandize upon which the duties had not been paid, were concealed, to the justices of the Superior Courts, for *writs of assistance*, such as were sometimes issued from the Court of Exchequer in England, authorizing them to enter the houses and warehouses of the merchants, to detect the unlawfully imported goods. This was a new and odious process, to which the merchants in the colonies had never before been subjected; and its legality was immediately contested before the Superior Court. It was substantially the same case as that of the general search warrants, which some years after kindled so fierce and inextinguishable a flame upon the prosecution of John Wilkes in London. The spirit of English liberty was as sensitive and as intractable in the colonies, as it ever had been in the mother country. The remark of Junius, that the dogs and horses of England lost their metal by removing to another hemisphere, but that patriotism was improved by *transportation*, meant by him for a sarcasm, was a truth too serious for the derision of a British statesman. The trial of John Peter Zenger, at New-York, had vindicated the freedom of the press, and the rights of juries, twenty years before they issued victorious from the re-considered opinions of Camden, and the prevaricating wisdom of Mansfield. And in the trial of the writs of assistance, at Boston, James Otis had

———"taught the age to quit their clogs
"By the known rules of ancient Liberty;"

while the search warrants for the Essay on Woman, and the 45th number of the North Briton, and the Letter of Junius to the King, were slumbering in the womb of futurity.

JOHN ADAMS, at the age of twenty-seven, attended as a member of the bar, the trial upon the writs of assistance, and witnessed the splendid exhibitions of genius and learning exerted in the cause of freedom by the pioneer of American Independence, James Otis. Small is the portion of mankind to whom it is given to discern the great events which control the destinies of nations in their seminal principles. The origin of the American Revolution has been usually ascribed to the Stamp Act; JOHN ADAMS had seen it in the first campaign of the seven years' war in 1755. He saw and marked its progress on the argument of James Otis upon writs of assistance in 1762; a cause which, although it produced great excitement at the time, would scarcely have been noticed among the historical incidents of the term, but for the minutes, which his curiosity induced him to take of the trial as it proceeded, and from an imperfect copy of which, taken afterwards by one of the law students in his office, the account of it in the subsequent histories of that period has been published.

On the 25th of October, 1764, he was married to Abigail Smith, second daughter of William Smith, minister of a congregational church at Weymouth, then in her twentieth year.

This was the memorable year of the Stamp Act, and from this year may be dated his first entrance upon political life. His friend and patron, Gridley, had just before that formed, with some other members of the bar and men of literary taste, a small social circle, who met once a week at each other's houses for the discussion of topics of literature and law, oral or in writing. Before this society Mr. Adams one evening read a short paper of Observations on the Feudal and Canon Law, which he afterwards published in the Patriotic newspaper. The sensation which it produced on the public mind was so great, that in the following year it was re-published in London, and there attributed to the pen of Gridley. It has been frequently since re-published, and even now may be considered as a worthy precursor to the declaration of Independence.

Popular commotions prevented the landing of the Stamp Act papers, which had been sent from England to be used in all processes before the judicial courts.

Thomas Hutchinson, at once the Lieut. Governor and Chief Justice of the Superior Court of the Province, had closed the sessions of the Court, on the pretence that they could not be lawfully held but by using the stamps.

The suspension of the Courts was severely felt throughout the Province; but especially in the town of Boston, where, after some time, a town meeting was held, at which it was determined to present a petition to the Governor and Council, that the Courts of justice might be forthwith re-opened; and they prayed to be heard by counsel in support of the petition. This was accorded, and the counsel appointed by the town were Jeremy Gridley, then Attorney-general, James Otis, and John Adams, then a young man of thirty, and not even an inhabitant of the town. The Governor and Council had not ventured to refuse hearing counsel in support of the town petition; but, perhaps, from the same timid policy, would hear them only with closed doors, and without admitting any supernumerary hearers. They suggested to the three gentlemen, who represented the town, the expediency of deciding between themselves the points upon which they proposed to support the petition. Mr. Gridley, the officer of the crown, without entering upon the question of right, represented only the general and severe distress suffered by all classes of the people, not only of the town, but of the whole province, by the suspension of all proceedings in the Judicial Courts. Mr. Otis argued, that from this unforeseen and unexampled state of things, the nature of the case gave a right of necessity, authorizing the Governor and Council to command the re-opening of the Court until the pleasure of the authority beyond the sea could be known. Mr. Adams assumed, as the basis of his argument, that the British Parliament had no right of taxation over the colonies. That the Stamp Act was an assumption of power, unwarranted by, and inconsistent with, the principles of the English constitution, and with the charter of the Province. That it was null and void; binding neither upon the people, nor upon the courts of justice in the colony; and that it was the duty of the Governor and Council to require of the judges of the Courts, that they should resume their judicial Courts, and proceed without exacting from suitors, or applying to their own records, the use of any stamps whatever. This, and a cotemporaneous resolution of the same import, introduced into the House of Representatives of the Province by Samuel Adams, are believed to have been the first direct denial of the unlimited right of legislation of Parliament over the colonies in the progress of that controversy. In the argument before the Governor and Council, it could be assumed only by Mr. Adams. Mr. Gridley being at that time the king's Attorney-general, and Mr. Otis having, in a celebrated pamphlet on the rights of the colonies, shortly before published, admitted the right of taxation to be among the lawful authorities of Parliament.

The Governor and Council deferred their decision upon the petition of the town, and before the period arrived for the next regular session of the Superior Court, the intelligence came of the repeal of the Stamp Act, and relieved them from the necessity of any decision upon it.

The selection of Mr. Adams as one of the law council of the town of Boston upon this memorable occasion, was at once an introduction to a career of political eminence, and a signal advancement of his professional reputation as a lawyer. He had already, as chairman of a committee of the town of Braintree, draughted instructions, on the subject of the Stamp Act, to the Representative of the town in the general court, which had been published, and attracted much notice; and he was shortly after elected one of the select-men of the town.

He had formed an intimate acquaintance and warm friendship with Jonathan Sewall, who had married a Miss Quincy, a relation of Mr. Adams. Sewall, a man of fine talents, distinguished as an orator and a writer, had commenced his career as a patriot; but had been drawn over by the artifices of Bernard and Hutchinson, and by lucrative and honorable offices, to the royal cause. Through him the office of advocate-general was offered to Mr. Adams, which he declined, though tendered with an assurance that no sacrifice of his political sentiments would be expected from him by his acceptance of the office. He was already known in that Court by the defence of Ansell Nickerson, an American seaman, who, in self-defence against a press-gang from a king's ship in the harbor of Boston, had killed, with the stroke of a harpoon, their commander, Lieut. Panton. MR. ADAMS's defence was, that the *usage* of impressment had never extended to the colonies; that the attempt to impress Nickerson was, on the part of Lieutenant Panton, unlawful; and that the act of Nickerson in killing him was justifiable homicide. Although the commander of the naval force on the American station, Captain Hood, afterwards Lord Hood, a name illustrious in the naval annals of Britain, was a member of the Court which decided the fate of Nickerson, he was acquitted and discharged; and thus, even before the question of Parliamentary taxation had been brought to its issue in blood, it was solemnly settled that the royal prerogative of impressment did not extend to the colonies. That prerogative, so utterly irreconcileable with the fundamental principle of the great charter, "*nullus homo capietur*," that dark spot on the snow-white standard of English freedom, that brand of servitude which Foster, from the judicial bench, stamped on the forehead of the British seaman; that shame to the legislation of the mother country, was, by the exertions of JOHN ADAMS, banished from the code of colonial law.

In the inimitable portrait of the just man drawn by the great Roman Lyric Poet, he is said to be equally immovable from his purpose by the flashing eye of the tyrant, and by the burning fury of a multitude commanding him to do wrong. Of all revolutions, ancient or modern, that of American Independence was pre-eminently popular. It was emphatically the revolution of the people. Not one noble name of the parent realm is found recorded upon its annals, as armed in the defence of the cause of freedom, or assisting in the councils of the confederacy; a few foreign nobles, La Fayette, De Kalb, Pulaski, Steuben, Du Portail, Du Coudray, and a single claimant of a British peerage, Lord Stirling, warmed by the spirit of freedom, and stimulated by the electric spark of military adventure, joined the standard of our country; and more than one of them laid down their lives in her cause. Of the natives of the land, not one—not Washington himself—could be justly styled the founder of Independence. The title of *Liberator*, since applied to an immeasurably inferior man in another continent of this hemisphere, could not be, and never was, applied to Washington. Of the nation, formed after the revolution was accomplished, he was by the *one people* placed at the head; of the revolution itself, he was but the *arm*.

North American Independence was achieved by a new phenomenon in the history of mankind,—by a self-formed, self-constituted, and self-governed Democracy. There were leaders of the people in the several colonies; there were representatives of the colonies, and afterwards of the States in the continental Congress; there was a continental army, a continental navy, and a continental currency; agents, factors, and soldiers; but the living soul, the vivifying spirit of the whole, was a steady, firm, resolute, inflexible will of the people, marching through fire and sword, and pestilence and famine, and bent to march, were it through the wreck of matter and the crush of worlds—to INDEPENDENCE.

The objections urged from time immemorial against the democracies of former ages were, the *instability* of the popular will—the impetuosity of their passions—the fluctuation of their counsels, and the impossibility of resisting their occasional and transitory animosities and resentments. Little of all this was seen in the course of the North American revolution. Even before its outset the people were trained to a spirit of self-control, well suited to prepare them for the trials that awaited them, and to carry them triumphantly through the fiery ordeal. No event contributed more to the formation of this spirit than the tragedy of the 5th of March, 1770, and its consequences. To suppress the popular commotions which the system of Parliamentary taxation had excited and could not fail to provoke, two regiments of soldiers were stationed at Boston; and becoming daily more odious to the inhabitants, were exposed to continual insults from the unguarded and indiscreet among them. On the 5th of March, a small party of the soldiers, under command of Lieut. Preston, were thus assailed and insulted by a crowd of people gathering round them, until they fired upon them, and killed and wounded several persons. The passions of the people were roused to the highest pitch of indignation, but manifested themselves by no violence or excess. Lieutenant Preston and six of the soldiers were arrested by the civil authority, and tried before the Superior Court for murder. They were so well advised as to apply to JOHN ADAMS and Josiah Quincy, known as among the most ardent among the patriots, to defend them; and they hesitated not to undertake the task. The momentary passions of the people identified the sufferings of the victims of that night with the cause of the country, and JOHN ADAMS and Josiah Quincy were signalized as deserters from the standard of freedom. How great was the load of public obloquy under which they labored, lives yet in the memory of surviving witnesses; and is recorded in the memoir of the life of Josiah Quincy, which the filial veneration of a son, worthy of such a father, has given to the world. Among the most affecting incidents related in that volume, and the most deeply interesting documents appended to it, are the recital of this event, and the correspondence between Josiah Quincy the defender of the soldiers and his father on that occasion. The fortitude of JOHN ADAMS was brought to a test equally severe; as the elder council for the prisoners on trial, it was his duty to close the argument in their defence. The writer of this article has often heard from individuals, who had been present among the crowd of spectators at the trial, the electrical effect produced upon the jury, and upon the immense and excited auditory, by the first sentence with which he opened his defence; which was the following citation from the then recently published work of Beccaria.

"May it please your Honors, and you, Gentlemen of the Jury.

"I am for the prisoners at the bar, and shall apologize for it only in the words of the Marquis Beccaria. 'If I can but be the instrument of preserving one life, his blessing and tears of transport shall be a sufficient consolation to me for the contempt of all mankind.'"

Captain Preston and the soldiers were acquitted, excepting two, who were found guilty of manslaughter, an offence which, being at that time entitled to the benefit of clergy, was subject to no sharper penalty than the gentle application of a cold iron to the hand, and, except as a warning for the future, was equivalent to an acquittal.

The town of Boston instituted an annual commemoration of the massacre of the 5th of March, by the delivery of an oration to the inhabitants assembled in town meeting. This anniversary was thus celebrated for a succession of thirteen years, until the close of the Revolutionary War, when that of the 4th of July, the day of national Independence, was substituted in its place. The Boston massacre is, however, memorable as the first example of those annual commemorations by public discourses ever since so acceptable to the people.

Within two months after the trial of the soldiers, MR. ADAMS received a new testimonial of the favor and confidence of his townsmen, by their election of him as one of their Representatives in the General Court or Colonial Legislature. In this body the conflict of principles between metropolitan authority and British colonial liberty was pertinaciously maintained. Sir Francis Bernard had just before closed his inglorious career, by seeking refuge in his own country from the indignation of the people over whom he had been sent to rule. He was succeeded by Thomas Hutchinson, a native of the province, a man of considerable talent, great industry, and of grasping ambition; who, in evil hour for himself, preferred the path of royal favor to that of patriotism for the ascent to power and fortune.

In times of civil commotion, the immediate subject of contention between the parties scarcely ever discloses to the superficial observer the great questions at issue between them. The first collision between Hutchinson and the two branches of the General Court was about the *place* where they were to hold their sessions.

Hutchinson, by instructions, secretly suggested by himself, convened the General Court at Cambridge, instead of Boston. They claimed it as a chartered right to meet at the town-house in Boston; and hence a long controversy between the Governor and the two houses, which, after three years of obstinate discussion, terminated by the restoration of the Legislature to their accustomed place of meeting.

By the charter of the colony, the members of the House of Representatives were annually elected by the people of the towns, and twenty-eight counsellors by the House of Representatives and council, with the approbation of the Governor. The judges of the Superior Court were appointed by the Governor and Council; and the Governor, Lieutenant-governor, and Judges were paid by annual grants from the General Court. In ordinary times the Council had always been more friendly to the Executive administration, and less disposed to resist the transatlantic authority than the House; but as the contest with the mother country grew warmer, and the country party in the House stronger, they dropped in their elections to the Council all the partizans of the Court, and elected none but the most determined patriots to the council board. The only resource of the Governor was to disapprove the most obnoxious of the persons elected, and thus to exclude a few of the most prominent leaders; but in their places the House always elected others of the same principles.

Among the devices to which, at the instigation of Hutchinson himself, the British Government resorted to remedy these disorders, was that of vacating the charter of the colony; of reserving to the King in council the appointment of the councillors, and of paying by Parliamentary authority the Governor and Judges, himself. The drift of these changes could not be mistaken. Hutchinson, who affected the character of a profound constitutional lawyer, entered into long and elaborate discussion of the rights and authority of Parliament in messages to the General Court, which were answered separately by reports of committees in both Houses. In the composition of these papers Mr. ADAMS was frequently employed, together with his distinguished relative, Samuel Adams. For the discussion of profound constitutional questions, the education of JOHN ADAMS as a lawyer, had pre-eminently qualified him to cope with Hutchinson in his black letter messages; and for the arguments on chartered rights and statutory law, he was relied upon beyond all others.

In 1772, having removed to his primitive residence at Braintree, he ceased to represent the town of Boston in the Legislature; but he was soon after elected to the council, and negatived by the Governor. In 1774 he was elected one of the members from the colony of Massachusetts Bay to the Continental Congress; and on the first meeting of that body, on the 5th of September of that year, took his seat among the founders of the North American Union. His service in Congress continued until November, 1777, when he was chosen by that body, in the place of Silas Deane, a joint commissioner at the Court of France, with Benjamin Franklin and Arthur Lee.

He embarked for France on the 13th of February, 1778, in the Boston frigate, commanded by Samuel Tucker; and, after a most tempestuous passage of forty-five days, landed at Bordeaux in France. The recognition by France of the Independence of the United States, and the conclusion of the treaties of commerce and of alliance between the two nations, had taken place between the appointment of MR. ADAMS and his arrival at Paris.

After the ratification of those treaties, Congress thought proper to substitute a single minister plenipotentiary at the court of France.

Dr. Benjamin Franklin was appointed the minister. Arthur Lee had previously received a separate commission as minister to the Court of Spain. MR. ADAMS, without waiting for a letter of recall, returned in the summer of 1779, in the French frigate La Sensible, to the United States. The French minister to the United States, the Chevalier de la Luzerne, together with his secretary of legation, since highly distinguished through all the scenes of the French Revolution, Barbe de Marbois, were passengers in the same frigate. They arrived at Boston on the 2d of August, 1779. Precisely at that time the convention which formed the constitution of the Commonwealth of Massachusetts was about to assemble, and MR. ADAMS was returned to it as a member from the town of Braintree.

The convention assembled at Cambridge on the 1st of September, 1779, and, after appointing a committee of thirty-one members to prepare a declaration of rights, and a constitution for the Commonwealth, adjourned over, on the 7th of that month, to the 28th of October ensuing, to receive the report of the committee. MR. ADAMS was a member of this committee, and made the first draught of the declaration of rights and of the constitution reported to the convention.

But, in the interval of the adjournment, MR. ADAMS had received from Congress a new commission for the negotiation of peace with Great Britain; in pursuance of which he embarked on the 14th of November, at Boston, in the same French frigate in which he had returned to the United States. Her destination was Brest; but having sprung a leak on her passage, and being in danger of foundering, she was obliged to make the first European port, which was that of Ferrol in Spain. There she arrived on the 7th of December, and thence MR. ADAMS travelled, in mid winter, by land to Paris.

The events of the Revolutionary war were not yet sufficiently matured for the negotiation of peace. Soon after the appointment of MR. ADAMS to this service, Henry Laurens of South Carolina, then President of Congress, was appointed minister plenipotentiary to negotiate a treaty of amity and commerce with the United Netherlands, with a separate commission to negotiate a loan of money in that country. On his passage to Europe, Mr. Laurens was captured by a British cruizer, and was lodged in the tower of London as a prisoner of state. MR. ADAMS then received a commission for the same service, and a new appointment was made of five commissioners for the negotiation of peace. These were JOHN ADAMS, Benjamin Franklin, John Jay, Henry Laurens, and Thomas Jefferson; the last of whom was, however, prevented by the circumstances of his family from proceeding to Europe until after the conclusion of the peace. In July, 1780, MR. ADAMS left Paris and went to Holland, where, as a preliminary to the negotiation of a treaty of amity and commerce, it was necessary to procure the recognition of the United States as an independent power. The negotiation for a loan was a separate power to contract with individuals. In both these negotiations MR. ADAMS was eminently successful. The condition of the United Netherlands at that time required a different mode of negotiation from that which was suitable with the other nations of Continental Europe. They constituted a free, confederated republic; with a prince allied to many of the European sovereigns, and especially to the Kings of Great Britain and of Prussia, at their head. The politics of the country were discussed in the Legislative Assemblies of the several provinces, and the freedom of the press opened avenues to the hearts of the people. In point of form, MR. ADAMS, as the representative of the United States claiming to be a sovereign and independent power, was to address the President of the States General, which he did in a memorial claiming to be received as a public minister; but setting forth all the arguments suited to produce an impression upon the minds of the people favorable to the objects of his mission. The President of the States General received the memorial, and laid it before the Assembly, who referred it to the Legislative Assemblies of the several provinces for consideration; Mr. ADAMS caused it forthwith to be published in the English, French, and Dutch languages in pamphlets; and it was re-published in many of the newspapers and other periodical journals of the country. No public document of the revolution was ever so widely circulated; for, as an extraordinary state paper, it was re-published in every country and every language of Europe. Its success was not less remarkable than the extent of its circulation. It set in motion the whole population of the Netherlands. Popular petitions, numerously signed, poured in upon the States of the provinces, praying for the recognition of the Independence of the United States, and the reception of Mr. ADAMS as their minister. The similarity of the condition of the United States to that of the Netherlands in their struggle for Independence against Spain, strongly urged in the memorial, became a favorite topic for popular feeling in all the provincial Assemblies. The Leyden Gazette, edited by John Luzac, one of the most accomplished scholars of the age, and one of the purest republican spirits of any age or clime, was engaged with deep and fervid interest in the cause of America, stimulated, even to enthusiasm, by the personal friendship formed with the kindred spirit of JOHN ADAMS. Another Frenchman of great ability, and highly distinguished as the author of the best history extant, in the French language, of the United Provinces, A. M. Cerisier, at the instance of MR. ADAMS, commenced a weekly journal under the title of " the Politique Hollandais," devoted exclusively to the communication of correct intelligence from America, and to set forth the community of principles and of interests between the new and the old republic. Having formed an intimate acquaintance with an eminent lawyer at Amsterdam, named Calkoen, that gentleman, who was a member of a political and literary society which held private weekly meetings, addressed sundry queries to MR. ADAMS respecting the state of the war, the condition of the people in the United States, and their dispositions with regard to the cause of Independence; which he answered in twenty-six letters, since frequently published. They were read and discussed at the meetings of the society, and furnished facts and argument for the friends of America and of freedom to counteract the influence and the misrepresentations of the English party or Anglomanes, always numerous and powerful in the United Netherlands. The armed neutrality of the north, and the insolent, domineering tone of Sir Joseph York, the British minister at the Hague, contributed to the excitement of the people in favor of the American cause; and after patiently waiting till the state of public opinion was sufficiently matured, MR. ADAMS ventured upon a step, the boldness of which could only be justified by success. He addressed a note to the States General, which he delivered in person to their President, referring to the memorial which he had twelve months before presented; proposing a treaty of amity and commerce between the two nations, and demanding a categorical answer which he might transmit to his sovereign.

With this demand the States General of the United Netherlands promptly complied. The Independence of the United States was formally recognized by the reception of MR. ADAMS as their minister. A commission, consisting of one member from each of the Provinces, was appointed to treat with him; and with them he concluded the treaty of amity, navigation, and commerce of 8th October, 1782; still recognized at this day by the United States, and by the present king of Holland, as the law of commercial intercourse between the two nations.

While conducting this political negotiation, MR. ADAMS had also contracted with three banking houses at Amsterdam, a loan of five millions of florins, at a yearly interest of five per cent.; furnishing, at a critical period of the war, a most seasonable supply to the exhausted treasury of the United States.

The day after the conclusion of the commercial treaty, and of a convention concerning maritime prizes of the same date, MR. ADAMS proceeded to Paris, where the negotiation for peace with Great Britain had already been commenced between his colleagues, Dr. Franklin and Mr. Jay; first with certain informal agents appointed by the British Government, and afterwards with Richard Oswald, formerly commissioned by George the Third to treat for peace with the commissioners of the United States of America. This negotiation terminated in the preliminary articles of peace of 30th November, 1782; succeeded by the definitive treaty also concluded at Paris on the 3rd of September, 1783.

The responsibilities of public men in stations of high dignity and trust in ordinary and prosperous times, are sufficiently arduous for the trial of the tempers of men; but the labors, the anxieties, the perturbations of mind incident to the condition of a man charged with the duty of maintaining, in a desperate conflict with oppressive power, not only his own character and honor, but the existence of his country, can scarcely be conceivable to an American of the present age. They stagger the firmness of the most intrepid soul. They prey upon a bodily frame hardy as the Nemæan lion's nerve. Blessed with an excellent natural constitution, Mr. Adams had in early youth ever plied it with intense study and indefatigable professional labor; from the time that he had become engaged in the service of his country, his days and nights had been devoted to the performance of his duties. In the midst of his negotiations in Holland he was brought within a hair's breadth of the grave by a typhus fever, in the summer of 1781, at Amsterdam; and a few days after the signature of the definitive treaty of peace, he was taken with a slow nervous fever, which again brought him to death's door. To promote his recovery, he was advised by his physician to indulge himself in a temporary relaxation from public business; and in October, 1783, he made his first visit to England, where, though in a private capacity, upon the meeting of Parliament, he heard the lips of George the Third on his throne, announce to his people, that he had concluded a definitive treaty of peace with the *United States of America.*

In January, 1784, he was suddenly called back to his post, in Holland, to negotiate a new loan of two millions of florins, which had become necessary for the punctual payment of the interest upon that which had been previously contracted, and which he effected upon terms equally advantageous. On his return to the Hague, he held conferences with the Baron de Thulemeyer, the minister of the great Frederic of Prussia, commissioned by him to conclude a treaty of amity and commerce with the United States. While engaged in this discussion, Congress had appointed John Adams, Benjamin Franklin, and Thomas Jefferson, commissioners to negotiate treaties of commerce with any of the European powers, or of the Barbary States, which might be inclined to form such engagements.

The commission met at Paris, in August, 1794, and communicated, through the ministers of the several powers of Europe, their powers to negotiate treaties of amity and commerce. But under this commission, the treaty which had been already nearly concluded by Mr. Adams and the Baron de Thulemeyer was the only one accomplished in Europe. In the spring of 1785, Doctor Franklin, at the age of nearly four-score, and laboring under the painful disease which finally closed his illustrious life, returned to the United States. Mr. Jefferson was appointed his successor at the Court of France, and Mr. Adams received a commission as the first minister plenipotentiary of the United

States at the Court of the British king. They still remained jointly charged with the commission for negotiating treaties of commerce, under which was concluded a treaty with the Emperor of Morocco, and a commercial treaty with Portugal; the ratification of which by the Portuguese Government was withheld, under the controling influence of Great Britain at that Court.

In May, 1785, Mr. ADAMS proceeded to London, where he was received by George the Third as the minister of the Independent States of North America. He was authorized to form a commercial treaty with Great Britain of the most liberal character; but a proud and mortified spirit had succeeded in the breast of the monarch, and a resentful and jealous rivalry in the temper of the nation, to the cruel and desolating war, which for seven years had been waged to subdue the North American people. In that people, too, an irritated and resentful temper still rankled long after the conflict for independence had closed. Mutual charges of bad faith in failing to execute the articles of the treaty of peace, but two well founded on both sides, continued the alienation of heart between the nations, which the contest and the separation had caused. The British Government had, indeed, more than plausible reasons for declining to conclude a commercial treaty with a Congress, which had not even authority to carry into execution the stipulations of the treaty of peace. After a residence in England of three years, in June, 1778, Mr. ADAMS returned to the United States, precisely at the moment when the ratification, by nine States, of the constitution, had established the form of government for the Union, under which we yet live.

During his residence in England he had composed and published, in three volumes, his Defence of the Constitutions of the United States,—a treatise upon Goverment, afterwards called the History of the principal Republics of the World; a work which has contributed more than any other ever written, to settle the opinions of mankind upon the great question, whether the legislative power of a free state should be vested in a single assembly, or in two separate co-ordinate branches; incidental to which is the question, not less important, of a single or a plural executive. Upon these points there is now scarcely any diversity of opinion among the enlightened theorists of Government.

Just before his return to the United States, Mr. ADAMS had been elected, by the Legislature of Massachusetts, a member of Congress, under the articles of Confederation; but that body was in a virtual state of dissolution. The constitution of the United States had received the sanction of the people. The times and places for holding the

JOHN ADAMS.

elections to organize the new government, had been fixed and the semblance of authority, which was all that the Confederation Congress had ever possessed, was vanishing even before the fabric of its more efficient substitute was completed.

In December, 1788, the first elections were held for carrying into execution the Constitution of the United States; at which George Washington was unanimously chosen President, and JOHN ADAMS was elected Vice-President of the Union; and four years afterwards they were both, in like manner, re-elected to the same offices. At the close of the second term, Washington declined a second re-election, and MR. ADAMS was chosen President of the United States.

During the eight years of Washington's administration, MR. ADAMS presided in the Senate. Throughout the whole of both those terms he gave to the administration a firm and efficient support.

Wherever there is Government, there must be councils of administration and collisions of opinion, concerning its mode and its measures. In all governments, therefore, there are parties which necessarily become braided, and, too often, entangled with the personal characters, principles, passions, and fortunes of individual men. No sooner had the founder of the Christian faith laid the corner-stone, for the establishment of the purest and most self-sacrificing of all religions, by the selection of the twelve apostles, than ambition and avarice, the thirst of place and treachery, were disclosed among them.

The Constitution of the United States was the result of a compromise between parties, which had existed from the first formation of the American Union. It drew together, by closer ties, the inhabitants of an extensive country, chiefly descended from one common stock, but greatly diversified by the varieties of climates, and of soils on which they had settled, and the oppositions of religious and political opinions in which they had originated. It made them permanently, and by political organization, what the enthusiasm of a common struggle for freedom, common sufferings and common dangers had made them for a time, in the war of Independence, but which the imbecility of the Articles of Confederation had failed to sustain, it made them *One People*. This stupendous monument of wisdom and virtue was accomplished by a party—then known by the denomination of *Federalists*; a name which, from various causes, has since become a term of reproach, but which, at that time, Washington and Madison were alike proud of bearing. In the disjointed condition of the confederacy, there was but one man whose talents and services had rivetted him in the gratitude and affections of all his countrymen, and that was, the leader of the armies of the Revolution. He presided in the convention which formed the Constitution; and no one can analyse that instrument without perceiving that much of its character, and expecially the construction of its executive power, was adapted to *him*, and fashioned upon the preconception that the office would be occupied by him.

Nor was this anticipation disappointed. He was twice elected by the unanimous suffrages of the electoral colleges President of the United States. But he was scarcely installed in office, and the wheels of the new machine of government had scarcely began to move, when the spirit of party, transferred from the confederacy to the constitution, sought, in the principal subordinate officers of the government, leaders for the succession, to be thereafter seated in the chair of Washington. These leaders immediately presented themselves in the persons of Thomas Jefferson, Secretary of State, and Alexander Hamilton, Secretary of the Treasury. In the diversity of the principles of these two men, conflict immediately sprung up, as to those which should govern the administration. Those of Hamilton were more congenial to the mind of Washington, and became the ruling principles of the administration; upon which Jefferson retired from public office, and was thenceforward looked up to as the head of the opposition to Washington's administration. Before the close of Washington's second term, Hamilton had also retired, but continued to support his administration.

At the time when MR. ADAMS was chosen President of the United States, he was supported by the party which had sustained the administration. Jefferson was his competitor, as the leader of the opposition. The contest was close. MR. ADAMS was elected by a bare majority of the electoral votes; and by the provision of the constitution then existing, that both candidates should be voted for as President, and that the person having the highest number of votes short of a majority should be Vice-President, Mr. Jefferson was elected to that office; and thus the head of the opposition became the presiding officer in the Senate of the United States, and at the next election, in December, 1800, was chosen President of the United States.

On the 3d of March, 1801, the official term of MR. ADAMS expired, and he retired to his residence at Quincy, where he passed the remainder of his days.

The administration of MR. ADAMS was but a continuation of that of his predecessor. It was the practical execution of the constitution, by the party which had formed and fashioned it, and had succeeded against a determined and persevering opposition in procuring its acceptance by the people. Mr. Jefferson had availed himself of the passions and prejudices of the people to obtain the possession of power, constantly modifying his opposition according to the fluctuations of public opinion, and taking advantage of every error, in the policy of the federal party, to which an odious imputation could be applied. In the course of their common service in Congress during the War of Independence, and in that of the joint commission in Europe after the peace, the most cordial harmony had subsisted between him and Mr. Adams. Their views of the French Revolution first divided them; and upon a re-publication in this country of one of Thomas Paine's revolutionary pamphlets, Mr. Jefferson, in a note to the printer, recommended it as a corrective to the *political heresies* then in circulation. The allusion was universally understood as intended to apply to the publication of certain essays, under the title of Discourses on Davila, and known to be written by Mr. Adams. Mr. Jefferson, in a letter to Mr. Adams, disclaimed all such intention; but his subsequent deportment, and the essential diversity of their opinions, gradually alienated them from each other, and dissolved the personal friendship which had subsisted between them. During the administration of Mr. Jefferson there was no personal intercourse between them; but when the great questions of the rights of neutral commerce, and the outrageous impressment of American seamen by the naval officers of Great Britain, brought the Government of the United States into imminent danger, Mr. Adams, though remaining in private life, sacrificed all his resentments and by numerous writings in the public journals, gave the most efficient support to the administration of his successor.

In 1809 Mr. Jefferson himself was succeeded by his friend and most faithful counsellor, James Madison. During his administration, the controversies with Great Britain, in the midst of which Mr. Jefferson had retired, rankled into a war, precisely at the time when the tide of victory and of triumph was turning in favor of Britain, against Napoleon, at the closing stage of that revolution by which France had passed from an absolute monarchy, through a brutal and sanguinary mock-democracy, to a military despotism, and thence to the transient resurrection of the dry bones of the Bourbons.

In the contests with Great Britain concerning neutral rights and impressment, which had preceded and led to the war, the interests of the commercial portion of the community were most immediately and deeply involved. But Mr. Jefferson's system of defence consisted in commercial restrictions, non-intercourse and embargoes, destructive to the very interest which it was the duty of the Government to maintain. The Cæsarian ambition of Napoleon, and his unparalleled suc cession of military triumphs, had alarmed the American politicians of the federal school, till they had frightened themselves into the belief that Napoleon Bonaparte was affecting universal empire, and about to become master of the world. They believed also, that Great Britain presented the only obstacle to the accomplishment of this design; and in this panic-terror, they lost all sense of the injustice and insolence of Great Britain exercised upon themselves. The restrictive system bore most impressively upon New England, to whose people, commerce, navigation, and the fisheries, were necessaries of life; and they felt the restrictive system as aggravation rather than relief. When the war came, it was a total annihilation of all their modes of industry, and of their principal resources of subsistence. They transferred their resentments from the foreign aggressor to their own Government, and became disaffected to the Union itself. The party in opposition to Mr. Madison's Administration prevailed throughout all the New England States; and had the war continued one year longer, there is little doubt that the floating projects of a separation, and of a northern confederacy, would have ripened into decisive action. Throughout the whole of this ordeal, Mr. Adams constantly supported the Administration of Mr. Madison, till the conclusion of the peace at Ghent, in December, 1814, scattered the projects of the northern confederacy to the winds, and restored, for a short and happy interval, *the era of good feelings.*

In December, 1820, Mr. Adams was chosen one of the electors of President and Vice-President of the United States; and, together with all his colleagues of the electoral College of Massachusetts, voted for the re-election of James Monroe and Daniel D. Tompkins to those offices.

The last public service in which Mr. Adams was engaged, was as a member of the convention to revise the Constitution of the Commonwealth of Massachusetts, of which body he was unanimously chosen President. Then in the 86th year of his age, he declined to assume the arduous duties of that station, but gave his attendance as a member throughout the sessions of the convention, and occasionally took part in their debates.

This election was communicated to Mr. Adams by a Committee of the Convention, with the following resolutions:—

" In Convention, November 15, 1820.

" Whereas, the Honorable John Adams, a member of this Convention, and elected the President thereof, has, for more than half a

JOHN ADAMS.

century, devoted the great powers of his mind, and his profound wisdom and learning, to the service of his country and mankind :

In fearlessly vindicating the rights of the North American provinces against the usurpations and encroachments of the superintendant government :

In diffusing a knowledge of the principles of civil liberty among his fellow subjects, and exciting them to a firm and resolute defence of the privileges of freemen :

In early conceiving, asserting, and maintaining the justice and practicability of establishing the independence of the United States of America :

In giving the powerful aid of his political knowledge in the formation of the Constitution of his native State, which constitution became in a great measure the model of those which were subsequently formed :

In conciliating the favor of foreign powers, and obtaining their countenance and support in the arduous struggle for independence :

In negotiating the treaty of peace, which secured forever the sovereignty of the United States, and in defeating all attempts to prevent it ; and especially in preserving in that treaty the vital interest of the New England States :

In demonstrating to the world, in his defence of the Constitutions of the several united States, the contested principle, since admitted as an axiom, that checks and balances in legislative power, are essential to true liberty :

In devoting his time and talents to the service of the nation, in the high and important trusts of Vice-President and President of the United States :

And lastly, in passing an honorable old age in dignified retirement, in the practice of all the domestic virtues, thus exhibiting to his countrymen and to posterity, an example of true greatness of mind and of genuine patriotism :—

Therefore, Resolved, That the members of this convention, representing the people of the commonwealth of Massachusetts, do joyfully avail themselves of this opportunity to testify their respect and gratitude to this eminent patriot and statesman, for the great services rendered by him to his country, and their high gratification that, at this late period of life, he is permitted by Divine Providence to assist them with his counsel in revising the constitution which, forty years ago, his wisdom and prudence assisted to form.

Resolved, That a committee of twelve be appointed by the chair, to communicate this proceeding to the honorable JOHN ADAMS, to inform him of his election to preside in this body, and to introduce him to the chair of this convention.

In this resolution, honorable alike to the people of the Commonwealth of Massachusetts, to their representatives by whom it was adopted, and to him whom it intended to honor, is contained a concentrated summary of the life, character, and services of JOHN ADAMS. It closes with appropriate dignity his career as a public man.

Nor was he less exemplary in all the relations of private and domestic life. As a son, a husband, a brother, a father, and a friend, his affections were ardent, disinterested and faithful. His filial piety not exclusively confined to his immediate parents, carefully preserved the memorials of their ancestors, for three preceding generations, to the patriarch, first settler of Braintree, Henry Adams, and he caused to be erected in the cemetery, where

> " Each in his narrow cell for ever laid,
> The rude fore-fathers of the hamlet sleep,"

monuments of the solid and simple granite from the soil on which they had settled, recording their names and years, spelt by no unlettered muse, but embracing in the inscription of little more than those dates, all that remains of their short and simple annals.

In the common experience of mankind, friendship, the pleasures of which are among the choicest enjoyments of life, is yet a sentiment of so delicate a texture, that it almost invariably sinks under the collision of adverse interests and conflicting opinions. With contests of opinion untainted with opposing interests, friendship may indeed subsist unimpaired; but in the discussion of religious or political opinions, which divide the minds of men, interest and opinion act and re-act upon each other, till the tender bloom of friendship withers and dies under their chilling frost. So fared it with the friendship formed by MR. ADAMS in early life with Jonathan Sewall. So fared it with the friendship formed in a common service, in the trying scenes of the war of Independence, with Thomas Jefferson. An affecting passage in his diary in 1774, records the pang with which he had parted from the friend of his youth, and an intercourse of mutual respect, and good-will was restored between them after the close of the revolutionary war. A reconciliation with Mr. Jefferson was, by the interposition of a common friend, effected, after all collisions of interests had subsided; and for the last ten years of their lives a friendly and frequent correspondence was maintained, with mutual satisfaction, between them. Many of those

JOHN ADAMS.

letters have been published, equally creditable to both; and that of Mr. Jefferson upon the decease of Mrs. Adams, in October, 1818, as an effusion of sympathy with the severest of earthly afflictions, in the administration of tender and delicate condolence, has never been surpassed.

They died on one and the same day, the jubilee of the day of Independence—a coincidence so remarkable, that men of a religious turn of mind, in days of more devoted faith, would have regarded it as a special interposition of Providence, to stamp on the hearts of their country, and of unnumbered future ages, a more indelible remembrance of that memorable event, and of the share which they had jointly taken in its imperishable deed.

The death of JOHN ADAMS occurred on the 4th of July, 1826, at the moment when his fellow-citizens, of his native town of Quincy, were celebrating in a social banquet, to which he had been invited, the anniversary of the Nation's Independence. His physical faculties had gradually declined in the lapse of years, leaving his intellect clear and bright to the last hour of his life.

Some years before his decease he had, by two several deeds of gift, conveyed to the inhabitants of the town of Quincy, his library and several valuable lots of land, the proceeds of the income of which were to be devoted to the erection of a stone temple for the worship of God. and of a school-house for a classical school.

Shortly after his death, the worshippers at the first Congregational church in Quincy, of which he had been a member, determined, with the aid of his donation to erect the temple, which was done in the year 1828; and after it was completed, his mortal remains, with those of the partner of his life, were deposited side by side in a vault beneath its walls.

Within the same house, a plain, white marble slab, on the right hand of the pulpit, surmounted by his bust, (the work of Horatio Greenough,) bears the following inscription, written by his eldest son.

Libertatem, Amicitiam, Fidem, Retinebis.

D. O. M.

Beneath these walls
Are deposited the mortal remains of
JOHN ADAMS,
Son of John and Susanna (Boylston) Adams,
Second President of the United States.
Born $\tfrac{19}{30}$ October, 1735.

NATIONAL PORTRAITS.

On the fourth of July, 1776,
He pledged his Life, Fortune, and sacred Honour
To the INDEPENDENCE OF HIS COUNTRY.
On the third of September, 1783,
He affixed his seal to the definitive treaty with Great Britain,
Which acknowledged that independence,
And consummated the redemption of his pledge.
On the fourth of July, 1826,
He was summoned
To the Independence of Immortality
And to the JUDGMENT OF HIS GOD.
This House will bear witness to his piety;
This Town, his birth-place, to his munificence;
History to his patriotism;
Posterity to the depth and compass of his mind.
At his side
Sleeps, till the trump shall sound,
A B I G A I L,
His beloved and only wife,
Daughter of William and Elizabeth (Quincy) Smith.
In every relation of life a pattern
Of filial, conjugal, maternal, and social virtue.
Born November $\frac{11}{22}$, 1744,
Deceased 28 October, 1818,
Aged 74.

Married 25 October, 1764.
During an union of more than half a century
They survived, in harmony of sentiment, principle and affection.
The tempests of civil commotion:
Meeting undaunted and surmounting
The terrors and trials of that revolution,
Which secured the freedom of their country;
Improved the condition of their times;
And brightened the prospects of futurity
To the race of man upon earth.

PILGRIM,
From lives thus spent thy earthly duties learn;
From fancy's dreams to active virtue turn:
Let freedom, friendship, faith, thy soul engage,
And serve, like them, thy country and thy age.

A Adams

MRS. ABIGAIL ADAMS.

Mrs. ABIGAIL ADAMS, wife of John Adams, second President of the United States, was one of three daughters of William Smith, minister of a Congregational church at Weymouth in the Colony of Massachusetts Bay; and of Elizabeth Quincy, a daughter of Colonel John Quincy, the proprietor of Mount Wollaston. This spot, situated on the sea-shore in the Bay of Boston, about seven miles south-east of that city, was the seat of a settlement by Thomas Wollaston and thirty of his associates in 1625, five years before that of the Massachusetts Colony. Wollaston abandoned his settlement the next year, and left part of his men under the command of Thomas Morton. The settlement itself was broken up by Governor Winthrop in the Summer of 1630, shortly after the landing of his Colony. Mount Wollaston was in 1634 made part of Boston, and the land was granted to William Coddington. He soon after sold it to William Ting, one of the principal merchants of Boston, and one of the four first representatives of the town in the General Court. Ting had four daughters, between whom, after his decease, his inheritance was divided. One of those daughters married Thomas Shepard, the celebrated minister of Charlestown; and in the distribution of the estates, the farm at Mount Wollaston was assigned to her. Her daughter, Anna, married Daniel Quincy, son of the second Edmund Quincy, and was the mother of Colonel John Quincy. Mrs. Anna Shepard survived her son-in-law, and at her decease bequeathed the estate at Mount Wollaston to his son John Quincy, then a student at Harvard College. In 1716 he married Elizabeth Norton, daughter of John Norton, minister of the first Congregational church at Hingham, a town distant about six miles south-east of Mount Wollaston. Elizabeth Quincy was the eldest daughter of this marriage, and in 1742 became the wife of William Smith.

Abigail Smith, second daughter of William and Elizabeth Smith, was born on the 11 of November, the day dedicated in the Roman calendar to Saint Cecilia, 1744. Her father, grandfather, and great grandfather, had all been educated at Harvard College. The Shepards and the Nortons are commemorated among the most learned and talented of the clergymen who held so conspicuous a place in the primitive settlement of New England. Thomas Shepard, the father of him who married Anna Tyng, is known from the Magnalia of Cotton Mather as one of the shining lights of the Reformation. His son was scarcely less distinguished, but died in the prime of life. That they are yet held in affectionate remembrance, is in evidence from the very recent fact, that a church adhering to the primitive Puritan doctrines, at Cambridge, has assumed and bears their name. John Norton, the minister of Hingham, was a nephew of his namesake, illustrious in the history of the Massachusetts Colony, and was himself many years eminent among the pastoral teachers of his age and country. The maternal grandfather of Abigail Smith, John Quincy, had been graduated at Harvard College in 1708. Her father, William Smith, in 1725. From this line of ancestry, it may justly be inferred that the family associations of Abigail Smith were from her infancy among those whose habits, feelings, and tastes are marked by the love and cultivation of literature and learning. The only learned profession in the first century of the settlement of New England was that of the clergy. The law formed no distinct profession, and the lawyers were little esteemed. Science was scarcely better cultivated by the practitioners of the medical art; but religion was esteemed among the most important of worldly concerns, and the controversial spirit with which it was taught, and which was at once the cause and effect of the Protestant reformation, stimulated the thirst for learning, and sharpened the appetite for the studies by which it is acquired.

The importance of learning and of literature to the cause of religion, and the entire dependence of practical morals upon religious principle, were so well understood by the first founders of New England, that the settlers of the Massachusetts Colony had scarcely thrown up sheds and piled log-houses to shelter their bodies from the storm, before their thoughts turned to the erection of the edifice which should serve them and their children for the habitation of the mind. In 1634 they made an appropriation for a school at Newtown, and in 1638 John Harvard, himself one of the most distinguished of their ministers, bequeathed at his decease the sum of £779. 17s. 2d. for the establishment of a college for the education of ministers of the Gospel. The bequest was immediately carried into effect. In 1642 the first

MRS. ABIGAIL ADAMS.

class was graduated—the town where the college was situated received the name of Cambridge from that in England, where all the religious teachers of the Colony had been educated; and the College of Harvard, made by the Constitution of the Commonwealth of Massachusetts an university, bears the name of its founder in glory from age to age down to the extinction of time.

But in providing for the education of learned ministers of the Gospel, the Puritan fathers of New England were not equally solicitous to cultivate and adorn the minds of their *daughters*. The education of women was not neglected, but was generally confined to the concerns of the household. The women, indeed, mingled in the religious controversies of the first Colonial age, more perhaps than was conducive to their own happiness or to the tranquillity of their relatives; but the example and the fate of Mrs. Hutchinson and of her doctrines, appears to have operated rather as a warning than as an example to the women of the succeeding age. For the *practice* of the learned professions, women are by their sex as effectually unfitted as for fighting battles, holding the plough, felling the forest, or navigating the ocean.

The education of the daughters of Mr. Smith was in their father's house, with such advantages as a country clergyman in a village of New England, towards the middle of the eighteenth century, could afford. It was about that time that Goldsmith, in his Deserted Village, and in his Vicar of Wakefield, painted to the life that condition in human society, and that class of characters formed by it, of which Mr. Smith and his family might have served as the originals.

On the 25th of October, 1764, in the twentieth year of her age, Miss Abigail Smith was married to John Adams, then an attorney at law residing in Braintree, the town adjoining to Weymouth, and then rising to great eminence at the bar. He had until then devoted himself, with the most indefatigable industry, to the studies and the practice of his profession for about seven years, taking little part in the politics of the time. The subject of politics, in its most comprehensive sense, had, however, furnished a source of profound meditation to his mind for many years before that of his marriage. His letter of —— September, 1755, from Worcester to Nathan Webb, has been called a literary phenomenon. A shorter and far more carelessly written letter, in December 1761, is perhaps not less characteristic.

In November 1762, Miss Smith's elder sister, Mary, had been married to Richard Cranch, a native of Devonshire in England, who had emigrated to this country in early youth, and was then settled at Germantown, part of the town of Braintree. In December 1761, Mr. Adams was upon a visit to Mr. Cranch at his house in Germantown; Mr. Cranch having an opportunity to enclose a letter which he had received the day before for Miss Mary Smith, put it under a cover thus addressed:—

"*Miss Polly Smith, Weymouth.*
"*Germantown, Dec. 30th.* 1761
"Dear Miss Polly,
"I was at Boston yesterday, and saw your brother, who was well. I have but a moment's notice of an opportunity of sending to you the enclosed, which I took at your uncle Edward's.
"I am, with compliments to your family,
"Your affectionate humble servant,
"R. Cranch."

Under which Mr. Adams wrote as follows:—

"Dear Ditto,
"Here we are, Dick and Jack, as happy as the wickedness and folly of this world will allow philosophers. Our good wishes are poured forth for the felicity of you, your family, and neighbors. My— I don't know what—to Miss Nabby; tell her I hear she's about commencing a most loyal subject to young George, and although my allegiance has been hitherto inviolate, I shall endeavor all in my power to foment rebellion.
"J. Adams."

To account for the preservation of this cover of a letter, not by the lady to whom it was addressed, but by her younger sister, then the loyal subject of young George, it may be necessary to remember that she was then just turned of seventeen; that it was shortly after the accession of George the Third to the throne; and that nearly three years after, on the 25th of October, 1764, she married the instigator to rebellion.

The year 1765 is memorable in the history of the world, and especially in that of the United States and that of Great Britain, as the year in which the British Parliament enacted the Stamp Act. Until that time Mr. Adams had taken little part in political affairs: his whole soul had been absorbed in the study and practice of his pro-

MRS. ABIGAIL ADAMS.

fession. But from the period of the Stamp Act he devoted himself to the cause of his country. In August of that year, in the midst of the violent fermentation occasioned by the resistance of the people to the execution of the Stamp Act, he published, in a Boston newspaper, the Dissertation on the Canon and Feudal Law, in which the right of popular resistance against oppression is laid down as distinctly as in the Declaration of Independence, and almost in the same terms The right and the determination of resistance was formed in the mind of John Adams from the first appearance of the Stamp Act, and his partner imbibed his principles, and prepared herself for all the trials and sacrifices which it was apparent must in such a contest be required of her. For ten years after their marriage Mr. Adams continued with increasing reputation in the practice of the law, residing alternately in the mansion descended to him from his father, and at Boston. In September, 1774, Mr. Adams was called to attend the meeting of the first Congress at Philadelphia. That session was short; but from the meeting of the second session in May, 1775, it was not again discontinued till the close of the war of the Revolution, and during the whole of that time she resided at Braintree, with a family of infant children, far from the partner of her heart, and exposed with her family, during a great part of the time, to continual dangers, scarcely less formidable than those which her husband, far distant from her, was on his part called to encounter.

The first deadly conflict of the war was in April 1775, at Lexington. The incident which gave occasion to it was the detachment of a body of troops from the British army at Boston, sent out to intercept John Hancock and Samuel Adams, then on their way to attend the meeting of this second Congress. John Adams was not with them, but had left his home for the same destination several days before. But his dwelling-house, his wife, and children, were within a shorter distance from Boston than Lexington or Concord; and the same spirit which had instigated the British commander to send a body of men to seize the persons of two members of the Continental Congress, might with a much smaller force have visited the dwelling-house, and destroyed or made prisoners of the family of the third. For several months this danger was so imminent, that the library, and all the most valuable furniture of the house, were removed to a distant part of the town; nor were they restored till after the British army had, in April 1776, evacuated Boston.

Soon after the close of this trial, aggravated by an epidemic dysentery, with which, in the Autumn of 1775, Mrs. ADAMS herself and every member of her family were severely afflicted, and to which her own mother, a brother of her husband, and a young woman living with her, in the course of two or three weeks fell victims, it was succeeded by another scarcely less distressing. After the removal of Congress from Philadelphia to Yorktown, in November, 1777, Mr. Adams made a short visit to his family, and, while absent, was appointed a joint Commissioner at the Court of France, with Dr. Benjamin Franklin and Arthur Lee, in the place of Silas Deane, who was recalled. In February, 1778, he sailed from Nantasket Roads in the Boston frigate, Captain Samuel Tucker; taking with him his eldest son, then a boy in the eleventh year of his age. It was the most perilous period of the war for a passage across the Atlantic. The Boston was an old brigantine converted into a small frigate of 28 guns, far inferior in force and weight of metal to the sloops of war of our present navy. While she was preparing for sea in the harbor of Boston, there was a British squadron anchored at no greater distance than Newport, Rhode Island, watching her departure; well informed of her destination, advised of the fact that a member of Congress was going out in her as a passenger, and eager in coveting possession both of the passenger and the ship. France had not then acknowledged the Independence of the United States, nor was it certain what reception the ship or Commissioner would find in that country. Mrs. ADAMS would for herself have been prepared to encounter every hazard with the partner of her life; but to expose her with three infant children, the whole family at once, was too much to undertake. She remained at Braintree, with three of the children.

In February, 1778, France acknowledged the Independence of the United States, and the treaties of commerce and of eventual alliance were concluded. Congress soon after determined to have, instead of three Commissioners at the Court of France, only one Minister Plenipotentiary, and the choice fell upon Dr. Franklin. Mr. Lee had another commission as Minister to Spain. Mr. Adams was left without being recalled, but without appointment to any other mission. He returned to the United States in August, 1779; but it had not been the intention of Congress to dispense with his further services in Europe. Soon after his return he received a commission to negotiate a peace with Great Britain; and in November, 1779, embarked again for France, taking with him his two elder sons, John Quincy and Charles—Mrs. ADAMS again remained with the two other children, a daughter and the youngest son, till after the conclusion of the peace. This was followed by a joint commission to Mr. Adams, with

MRS. ABIGAIL ADAMS.

Dr Franklin and Mr. Jefferson, to negotiate treaties of commerce with any of the European or Barbary Powers; and to this succeeded the appointment of Mr. Adams as Minister Plenipotentiary to the Court of Great Britain.

In May, 1784, Mrs. ADAMS embarked, with her only daughter, at Boston, to join her husband; she arrived at London in July. Mr. Adams was then at the Hague, in the discharge of the office of Minister Plenipotentiary to the United Netherlands, to which he had been appointed by Congress after the capture and imprisonment, in the tower of London, of Henry Laurens. About the same time of Mrs. ADAMS's arrival in England, Mr. Jefferson arrived in France, on the joint mission to negotiate commercial treaties, which negotiation was to be conducted at Paris. Mr. Adams, therefore, repaired to London to meet his family, and proceeded with them to Paris. They resided nearly a year at Auteuil, a village adjoining that of Passi, the residence of Doctor Franklin, until his final return to the United States, in 1785. He had, soon after the conclusion of the peace, requested of Congress permission to return, and to retire from the service of the Union. In the Spring of 1785 Mr. Jefferson was appointed his successor at the Court of France, and Mr. Adams was commissioned as Minister Plenipotentiary to Great Britain. He proceeded with his family to London. There he resided three years, and in the Summer of 1788, at his own request, received permission to return home. He arrived at Boston precisely at the time when, by the ratification of nine States, the Constitution of the United States was received as the Supreme law of the land.

During her absence in Europe, Mrs. ADAMS had resided one year in France and three years in England. She had made several excursions of several days, to visit some of the beautiful scenes and magnificent country-seats which abound in England; and before her return had, in company with her husband, visited the scarcely less magnificent scenery of the Netherlands. In her own country she had, from her childhood, been accustomed to view and to admire the scenery between her native village and Boston, scarcely surpassed for natural beauty by any object upon earth. In France, in England, in Holland, she had seen the highest attainments of art and the most unbounded profusion of wealth lavished to improve and adorn the simple beauties of nature. In the inspection and enjoyment of these beauties she had taken great delight; and in familiar letters to her friends in this country had given descriptions of them, exceed ingly interesting to her correspondents, and which, even at this day, might be read with pleasure by the public.

Her letters to her husband and children, and to friends of her own sex, during the Revolutionary war, among which Mrs. Mercy Warren, sister of James Otis and wife of General James Warren of Plymouth, deserves to be particularly remembered, have an interest of a higher character. These ladies, familiar with the Roman history, and living in times when the exercise of the virtues of lofty patriotism were as necessary and as useful to the cause of liberty among the daughters of the land, as among their husbands and their brothers, corresponded with each other throughout the Revolutionary war— Mrs. ADAMS assuming the signature of *Portia*, and Mrs. Warren that of *Marcia ;* and no correspondence of the Roman matrons bearing those names ever breathed a purer or more vivid spirit of patriotism. The letters of Mrs. ADAMS to her sons, while they were in Europe, were read and admired; and translations of more than one of them were made and published in some of the periodical journals of France.

The Government of the United States, under their present Constitution, was organized in April, 1789, and Mr. Adams was elected the first Vice President of the United States. He held that office during the eight years of President Washington's administration, and was elected his immediate successor. The sessions of the first Congress were held at the city of New York. In 1790 the seat of government was removed to Philadelphia, and continued there till December, 1800, when it was transferred to Washington, in the District of Columbia. During the sessions of Congress Mr. Adams usually resided with his family at New York, and afterwards at Philadelphia; and in the intervals between them, on his estate at Quincy, about eight miles distant from Boston. Mrs. ADAMS's health, as she advanced in years, became frequently infirm; but, with the exception of one or two sessions, when she was detained at home by indisposition, she resided with her husband at the seat of government.

In the administration of the first President of the United States two parties immediately disclosed themselves. They were at first merely the successors of those between which the struggle had been maintained for and against the establishment of the Constitution of the United States. The contest between persons and property, between the many and the few, inherent in the vitals of human society, was always fermenting in the community. These elements of contention, always acting and reacting upon the course of human events, and always modified by them, gave rise to two systems of administration, the leading minds of which were Alexander Hamilton and Thomas Jefferson. Washington endeavored to hold the balance between them; and Mr. Adams, in his station of Vice-President, gave his cordial and effective support to the general measures of his administration. The French Revolution breaking forth in the same year when the Constitution of the United States went into operation, and involving in its progress all the elements of contention incident to human society, produced a conflict of principles which not even the moderation, the spotless integrity, and the enduring fortitude of Washington himself could assuage. Jefferson and Hamilton both successively retired from the administration, but neither of them to quiet retirement. The spirit of party turned with a virulence, incredible at this day, against Washington himself; and upon his retirement, Mr. Adams was, by a bare majority of the electoral votes over Mr. Jefferson, chosen the successor to the Presidency, Mr. Jefferson himself being by the same election seated in the chair of the Vice-Presidency.

The party struggle continued during the administration of Mr. Adams; and the defection of Hamilton, with other leaders of the Federal party, turned the scale of the election of 1800. Thomas Jefferson and Aaron Burr were returned with an equal number and a majority of votes in the electoral colleges, and after a severe contest between them in the House of Representatives, Mr. Jefferson was elected President of the United States. Mr. Adams retired to private life, and spent the last twenty-five years of his life at his residence in Quincy, where, on the 4th of July 1826, he died.

Mr. Jefferson, in his Inaugural Address, alluded to the political intolerance which had marked the party conflicts of the preceding administrations, and urged his countrymen to *restore* harmony and affection to social intercourse. Of that intolerance, and of the bitter and rancorous imputations which are its most effective weapons, no man who had devoted his life to the service of his country ever endured more than Mr. Adams. From the day when he took his seat as President of the Senate, until that when his administration expired, he was assailed with unappeasable virulence; nor did it even cease with his retirement to private life. The exemplary deportment of Mrs. ADAMS towards persons of all parties during the twelve years of her husband's connexion with the government of the United States, disarmed even the demon of party spirit. She enjoyed universal esteem, as well for the endowments of her mind, as for the correctness of her deportment; and the only form in which personal malevolence or party malignity could assume to turn her virtues into weapons of annoyance to her husband, was that of occasional insinuations that she exercised over him an uncontrolable influence, extended even to measures of public concernment; a slander not less unjust than all the others with which Mr. Adams was incessantly pursued.

During the remainder of her life Mrs. ADAMS shared the retirement of her husband, in the exercise of all the virtues that adorn and dignify the female, and the Christian character. As the mistress of a household, she united the prudence of a rigid economy with the generous spirit of a liberal hospitality; faithful and affectionate in her friendships, bountiful to the indigent, kind and courteous to her dependents, cheerful, good-humoured and charitable in the intercourse of social life with her neighbors and acquaintance. She lived in the habitual practice of benevolence, and of sincere, unaffected piety. In the year 1813 she was called to endure one of the severest afflictions that can befall the lot of humanity, the death of her only daughter, wife of Colonel William Stephens Smith of New York, after a long, lingering, and painful disease. She had before, at earlier periods of her life, lost one infant daughter and one son, Charles Adams, in the prime of life and the thirtieth year of his age.

Mrs. ADAMS herself died of a typhus fever on the 28th of October, 1818, at the age of seventy-four; leaving to the women of her country an example which, could it be universally followed, would restore to mankind the state of paradise before the fall.

SAMUEL ADAMS.

SAMUEL ADAMS was born in Boston, Massachusetts, in September, 1722. His ancestors were amongst the early settlers of New England. The family has already been traced through its various branches, in the biographical sketch of President John Adams in this volume, and requires no further notice in this place. SAMUEL ADAMS was remarkable for steady application to his studies at the celebrated Latin school of Master Lovell. He entered Harvard university at an early age, and graduated in 1740, when he discussed the following question, " Whether it be lawful to resist the supreme magistrate, if the commonwealth cannot otherwise be preserved." He maintained the affirmative in the presence of the king's governor and council; and thus evinced, at that early period, his attachment to the liberties of the people. About the same time he published a pamphlet, called "Englishmen's Rights," the expense of which he paid out of the small stipend allowed him by his father while he was a student.

It has been stated that he intended to have devoted himself to the gospel ministry, but that his father designed him for the bar; the intentions of both were overruled by his mother, and the course of life adopted was that of commerce, to which he was neither inclined nor fitted; and although he was placed under the charge of an eminent merchant, Mr. Thomas Cushing, he acquired little knowledge of business, nor was he able to support himself when he commenced business on his own account. The capital given to him by his father, by imprudent credits and other losses was soon consumed. His father died soon after, and as he was the eldest son, the care of the family and the management of the estate devolved upon him.

It may be seen that Mr. ADAMS took an interest in political subjects at an early period of life, both from the choice of his subject when he took his degree at Cambridge, and of his first pamphlet. Similar subjects occupied his attention afterwards. While yet a clerk to Mr

Cushing, he formed a club, each member of which agreed to furnish a political essay for a newspaper called the Independent Advertiser. These essays brought the writers into notice, and they were dubbed, in derision, the " Whipping-post Club." During the administration of Governor Shirley, he was known as a political writer in opposition to the dangerous union of too much civil and military power in the hands of one man. His ingenuity, wit, and clear and cogent arguments, gained public confidence, and laid the foundation for that influence over his fellow-citizens, which made him afterwards a mark for the especial dislike of the royalists.

In 1763 the agent of Massachusetts in London transmitted intelligence that it was contemplated, by the ministry, to tax the colonies. This soon produced a great excitement. It was expected that Governor Bernard would immediately call the Massachusetts house of assembly together, and that such instructions would be sent to the agent as might have a tendency to prevent the contemplated proceedings; but to the surprise of the public, the governor took no notice of the subject.

In May, 1764, a new election was held of members of the assembly, and according to custom, written instructions were prepared by the people for their representatives. Mr. Adams was one of the five who were selected by the people of Boston on this occasion. The instructions were written by him, and were approved by the town. The document was published at the time in the Boston Gazette, and is said to be the first public document that denied the " supremacy of the British parliament, and their right to tax the colonies without their own consent."

It is well known that at this time a private club was formed in Boston for the purpose of deciding on the most proper measures to be taken at this important crisis. It was composed of the leading patriots of the day. It was the secret spring which set in motion the public body. Mr. Adams was one of that patriotic conclave, and went with all his heart into the measures determined on, to resist every infringement of the rights of the colonies. The Stamp Act was a flagrant violation of them; and to suffer it to be quietly carried into effect, would establish a precedent and encourage further proceedings. Mr. Adams was not averse to the manner in which the people evinced their determined opposition by destroying the stamp papers and office in Boston; but he highly disapproved the riots and disorders which followed, and personally aided the civil power in the suppression of them.

SAMUEL ADAMS.

He was elected a member of the general assembly of Massachusetts in 1765, in the place of Oxenbridge Thatcher, deceased. He was soon after chosen clerk to the House, and acquired influence in the Legislature, in which he continued nearly ten years. He was frequently upon important committees, and was the soul that animated their most decisive resolutions. In 1767 he suggested a plan to counteract the operation of the act imposing duties. It was agreed to by the merchants, and nearly all of them in the province bound themselves, if the duties were not repealed, not to import any but certain enumerated articles after the 1st of January, 1769.

He was chairman of the committee appointed by the people of Boston to wait upon Lieutenant-governor Hutchinson, and urge the withdrawal of the British troops from the town, after the fatal affray of the 5th of March, 1770. Mr. Adams, in a speech of some length, pressed the subject with great ability, and enumerated the fatal consequences which would ensue if the vote of the town was not immediately complied with. Hutchinson prevaricated, and denied that the troops were subject to his authority; but promised to direct the removal of the 29th regiment. Mr. Adams again rose. Filled with the magnitude of the subject, and irritated by the manner in which it had been treated by the Lieutenant-governor, he replied with indignation and boldness, " That it was well known that, acting as governor of the province, he was by its charter commander-in-chief of his Majesty's military and naval forces, and, as such, the troops were subject to his orders ; and if he had the power to remove one regiment, he had the power to remove both ; and nothing short of that would satisfy the people ; and it was at his peril if the vote of the town was not immediately complied with ; and if it be longer delayed, he alone must be answerable for the fatal consequences that would ensue." This produced a momentary silence. It was now dark, and the people were waiting for the report of their committee. After a short conference with Colonel Dalrymple, Hutchinson gave his consent to the removal of both regiments, which was accordingly effected the following day.

As early as 1766 Mr. Adams had been impressed with the importance of establishing committees of correspondence throughout the colonies; but the plan was not carried into operation until 1772, when it was first adopted by Massachusetts on his motion, at a public town meeting in Boston, and was soon after followed by all the provinces.

Every method had been tried to induce Mr. Adams to abandon the cause of his country, which he had supported with so much zeal, courage, and ability. Threats and caresses had proved equally un availing. Prior to this time there is no certain proof that any direct attempt was made upon his virtue and integrity, although a report had been publicly and freely circulated that it had been unsuccessfully tried by Governor Bernard. Hutchinson knew him too well to make the attempt. But Governor Gage was empowered to try the experiment. He sent to him a confidential and verbal message by Colonel Fenton, who waited upon Mr. Adams, and after the customary salutations, he stated the object of his visit. He said, that an adjustment of the disputes which existed between England and the colonies, and a reconciliation, was very desirable as well as important to the interest of both. That he was authorized from Governor Gage to assure him, that he had been empowered to confer upon him such benefits as would be satisfactory, upon the condition that he would engage to cease in his opposition to the measures of government. He also observed, that it was the advice of Governor Gage to him, not to incur the further displeasure of his Majesty; that his conduct had been such as made him liable to the penalties of an act of Henry VIII. by which persons could be sent to England for trial of treason or misprision of treason, at the discretion of a governor of a province; but by changing his political course, he would not only receive great personal advantages, but would thereby make his peace with the king. Mr. Adams listened with apparent interest to this recital. He asked Colonel Fenton if he would truly deliver his reply as it should be given. After some hesitation, he assented. Mr. Adams required his word of honor, which he pledged.

Then rising from his chair, and assuming a determined manner, he replied, "I trust I have long since made MY PEACE WITH THE KING OF KINGS. No personal consideration shall induce me to abandon the righteous cause of my country. Tell Governor Gage, IT IS THE ADVICE OF SAMUEL ADAMS TO HIM no longer to insult the feelings of an exasperated people."

With a full sense of his own perilous situation, marked as an object of ministerial vengeance, laboring under pecuniary embarrassment, but fearless of personal consequences, he steadily pursued the great object of his soul,—the liberty of the people.

The time required bold and inflexible measures. Common distress required common counsel. The aspect was appalling to some of the most decided patriots of the day. The severity of punishment, which was inflicted on the people of Boston by the power of England, produced a melancholy sadness on the friends of American freedom. The Massachusetts house of assembly was then in session at Salem

SAMUEL ADAMS.

A committee of that body was chosen to consider and report the state of the province. Mr. Adams, it is said, observed that some of the committee were for mild measures, which he judged no way suited to the present emergency. He conferred with Mr. Warren of Plymouth upon the necessity of sprited measures, and then said, " Do you keep the committee in play, and I will go and make a caucus by the time the evening arrives, and do you meet me." Mr. Adams secured a meeting of about five principal members of the house at the time specified, and repeated his endeavors for the second and third nights, when the number amounted to more than thirty. The friends of the administration knew nothing of the matter. The popular leaders took the sense of the members in a private way, and found that they would be able to carry their scheme by a sufficient majority. They had their whole plan completed, prepared their resolutions, and then determined to bring the business forward; but before they commenced, the door-keeper was ordered to let no person in, nor suffer any one to depart. The subjects for discussion were then introduced by Mr. Adams with his usual eloquence on such great occasions. He was chairman of the committee, and reported the resolutions for the appointment of delegates to a general congress to be convened at Philadelphia, to consult on the general safety of America. This report was received with surprise and astonishment by the administration party. Such was the apprehension of some, that they were apparently desirous to desert the question. The door-keeper seemed uneasy at his charge, and wavering with regard to the performance of the duty assigned to him. At this critical juncture, Mr. Adams relieved him by taking the key and keeping it himself. The resolutions were passed; five delegates, consisting of Samuel Adams, Thomas Cushing, Robert Treat Paine, John Adams, and James Bowdoin, were appointed, the expense was estimated, and funds were voted for the payment. Before the business was finally closed, a member made a plea of indisposition, and was allowed to leave the house. This person went directly to the Governor, and informed him of their high-handed proceedings. The Governor immediately sent his secretary to dissolve the assembly, who found the door locked. He demanded entrance; but was answered, that his desire could not be complied with until some important business, then before the house, was concluded. Finding every method to gain admission ineffectual, he read the order on the stairs for an immediate dissolution of the assembly. The order, however, was disregarded by the house. They continued their deliberations, passed all their intended measures, and then obeyed the mandate for dissolution.

NATIONAL PORTRAITS.

After many unavailing efforts, both by threats and promises, to allure this inflexible patriot from his devotion to the sacred cause of independence, Governor Gage at length, on the 12th of June, 1775, issued that memorable proclamation, of which the following is an extract :—" In this exigency of complicated calamities, I avail myself of the last efforts within the bounds of my duty to spare the further effusion of blood, to offer, and I do hereby in his Majesty's name offer and promise, his most gracious pardon to all persons who shall forthwith lay down their arms, and return to the duties of peaceable subjects, excepting only from the benefit of such pardon, SAMUEL ADAMS and John Hancock, whose offences are of too flagitious a nature to admit of any other consideration than that of condign punishment." This was a diploma, conferring greater honors on the individuals than any other which was within the power of his Britannic majesty to bestow.

In a letter, dated April, 1776, at Philadelphia, while he was in congress, to Major Hawley of Massachusetts, he said, " I am perfectly satisfied of the necessity of a public and explicit declaration of independence. I cannot conceive what good reason can be assigned against it. Will it widen the breach ? This would be a strange question after we have raised armies and fought battles with the British troops ; set up an American navy, permitted the inhabitants of these colonies to fit out armed vessels to capture the ships, &c. belonging to any of the inhabitants of Great Britain ; declaring them the enemies of the United Colonies, and torn into shivers their acts of trade, by allowing commerce, subject to regulations to be made by ourselves, with the people of all countries, except such as are subject to the British king. It cannot, surely, after all this, be imagined that we consider ourselves, or mean to be considered by others, in any other state than that of independence."

In another letter to James Warren, Esq. dated Baltimore, December 31, 1776, he said, " I assure you business has been done since we came to this place, more to my satisfaction than any or every thing done before, excepting the ' Declaration of Independence,' which should have been made immediately after the 19th of April, 1775."

Notwithstanding we had raised armies, built navies, fought battles, and had seen the public grievances still unredressed, yet the minds of many of the leading Whigs were not prepared for the great question of a final separation of the two countries till July 4, 1776.

The character of MR. ADAMS had become celebrated in foreign countries. In 1773 he had been chosen a member of the society of

SAMUEL ADAMS.

the bill of rights in London; and in 1774 John Adams and Doctor Joseph Warren were elected on his nomination.

Our patriots, in their progress to independence, had successfully encountered many formidable obstacles; but in the year 1777 still greater difficulties arose, at the prospect of which some of the stoutest hearts began to falter. It was at this critical juncture, after Congress had resolved to adjourn from Philadelphia to Lancaster, that some of the leading members accidentally met in company with each other. A conversation in mutual confidence ensued. Mr. Adams, who was one of the number, was cheerful and undismayed at the aspect of affairs; while the countenances of his friends were strongly marked with the desponding feelings of their hearts. The conversation naturally turned upon the subject which most engaged their feelings. Each took occasion to express his opinions on the situation of the public cause, and all were gloomy and sad. Mr. Adams listened in silence till they had finished. He then said, "Gentlemen, your spirits appear to be heavily oppressed with our public calamities. I hope you do not despair of our final success?" It was answered, "That the chance was desperate." Mr. Adams replied, "If this be our language, it is so, indeed. If we wear long faces, they will become fashionable. The people take their tone from ours; and if we despair, can it be expected that they will continue their efforts in what we conceive to be a hopeless cause? Let us banish such feelings, and show a spirit that will keep alive the confidence of the people rather than damp their courage. Better tidings will soon arrive. Our cause is just and righteous, and we shall never be abandoned by Heaven while we show ourselves worthy of its aid and protection."

At this time there were but twenty-eight of the members of Congress present at Philadelphia. Mr. Adams said, "That this was the smallest, but the truest Congress they ever had."

But a few days had elapsed when the news arrived of the glorious success at Saratoga, which gave a new complexion to our affairs and confidence to our hopes.

Soon after this, Lord Howe, the Earl of Carlisle, and Mr. Eden, arrived as commissioners to treat for peace under Lord North's conciliatory proposition. Mr. Adams was one of the committee chosen by Congress to draught an answer to their letter. In this it is stated, "That Congress will readily attend to such terms of peace as may consist with the honor of an independent nation."

At this time the enemies of our freedom were busily employed to create disunion among its friends. Reports were circulated of attempts to deprive General Washington of his command, in which, it was said, Mr. ADAMS was a principal leader. This was not true. It is possible that some warm expressions may have fallen from him when he spoke of the multiplied disasters which attended our military operations, and of the effects they produced on the public mind; and for political purposes, our opponents gave to them, probably, a different and distorted sense.

In a letter to his friend, Richard Henry Lee, Esq. dated in 1789, in speaking of executive appointments as provided for in the constitution of the United States, he thus notices the subject: "I need not tell you, who have known so thoroughly the sentiments of my heart, that I have always had a very high esteem for the late commander-in-chief of our armies; and I now most sincerely believe, that while President Washington continues in the chair, he will be able to give, to all good men, a satisfactory reason for every instance of his public conduct. I feel myself constrained, contrary to my usual manner, to make professions of sincerity on this occasion; because Doctor Gordon, in his History of the Revolution, has gravely said that I was concerned in an attempt to remove General Washington from command; and mentions an anonymous letter to your late Governor Henry, which I affirm I never saw, nor heard of, till I lately met with it in reading the history."

In 1779 SAMUEL ADAMS was placed by the state convention on a committee to prepare and report a form of government for Massachusetts. By this committee he and John Adams were appointed a subcommittee to furnish a draught of the constitution. The draught produced by them was reported to the convention, and, after some amendments, accepted. The address of the convention to the people was jointly written by them.

In 1781 he was elected a member of the Senate of Massachusetts, and was shortly afterwards elevated to the presidency of that body.

In 1787 he was chosen a member of the Massachusetts convention for the ratification of the constitution of the United States. He had some objections to it in its reported form; the principal of which was to that article which rendered the several States amenable to the Courts of the nation. He thought that this would reduce them to mere corporations. There was a very powerful opposition to it, and some of its most zealous friends and supporters were fearful that it would not be accepted.

MR. ADAMS had not then given his sentiments upon it in the convention; but regularly attended the debates.

Some of the leading advocates waited upon MR. ADAMS and Mr

SAMUEL ADAMS.

Hancock, to ascertain their opinions and wishes, in a private manner. Mr. Adams stated his objections, and said that he should not give it his support unless certain amendments were recommended to be adopted. These he enumerated. Mr. Hancock was president of the convention, and at that time confined to his house by indisposition. His opinion coincided with that of Mr. Adams; and he observed, that he would attend and give it his support upon the same condition expressed by Mr. Adams. This was mutually agreed to. Mr. Adams prepared his amendments, which were brought before the convention, and referred to a committee, who made some inconsiderable alterations, with which the constitution was accepted. Some of these were afterwards agreed to as amendments, and form, at present, a part of that instrument.

In 1789 he was elected Lieutenant-governor of the State of Massachusetts, and continued to fill that office till 1794, when he was chosen governor of that state. He was annually re-elected till 1797, when, oppressed with years and bodily infirmities, he declined being again a candidate, and retired to private life.

After many years of incessant exertions, employed in the establishment of the independence of America, he died on the 3d October, 1803, in the eighty-second year of his age, in indigent circumstances.

The person of Samuel Adams was of middle size. His countenance was a true index of his mind, and possessed those lofty and elevated characteristics which are always found to accompany true greatness.

He was a steady professor of the Christian religion, and uniformly attended public worship. His family devotions were regularly performed, and his morality was never impeached.

In his manners and deportment he was sincere and unaffected; in conversation, pleasing and instructive; and in his friendships, steadfast and affectionate.

His revolutionary labors were not surpassed by those of any individual. From the commencement of the dispute with Great Britain he was incessantly employed in public service; opposing, at one time, the doctrine of the supremacy of " parliament in all cases," taking the lead in questions of controverted policy with the royal governors, writing state papers from 1765 to 1774;—in planning and organizing clubs and committees, haranguing in town meetings, or filling the columns of public prints with essays adapted to the spirit and temper of the times. In addition to these occupations, he maintained an extensive and laborious correspondence with the friends of American freedom in Great Britain and in the provinces.

NATIONAL PORTRAITS.

No man was more intrepid and dauntless when encompassed by dangers, or more calm and unmoved amid public disasters and adverse fortune. His bold and daring conduct and language subjected him to great personal hazards. Had any fatal event occurred to our country, by which she had fallen in her struggle for liberty, SAMUEL ADAMS would have been the first victim of ministerial vengeance. His blood would have been first shed as a sacrifice on the altar of tyranny, for the noble magnanimity and independence with which he defended the cause of freedom. But such was his firmness, that he probably would have met death with as much composure as he regarded it with unconcern.

His writings were numerous, and much distinguished for their elegance and fervor; but, unfortunately, the greater part of them have been lost, or so distributed as to render their collection impossible.

He was the author of a letter to the Earl of Hillsborough;—of many political essays directed against the administration of Governor Shirley;—of a letter in answer to Thomas Paine in defence of Christianity, and of an oration published in the year 1776.

Four letters of his correspondence on government are extant, and were published in a pamphlet form in 1800.

MR. ADAMS's eloquence was of a peculiar character. His language was pure, concise, and impressive. He was more logical than figurative. His arguments were addressed rather to the understanding than to the feelings; yet he always engaged the deepest attention of his audience. On ordinary occasions there was nothing remarkable in his speeches; but on great questions, when his own feelings were interested, he would combine every thing great in oratory. In the language of an elegant writer, the great qualities of his mind were fully displayed in proportion as the field for their exertion was extended; and the energy of his language was not inferior to the depth of his mind. It was an eloquence admirably adapted to the age in which he flourished, and exactly calculated to attain the object of his pursuit. It may well be described in the language of the poet, " thoughts which breathe, and words which burn." An eloquence, not consisting of theatrical gesture or the pomp of words; but that which was a true picture of a heart glowing with the sublime enthusiasm and ardor of patriotism; an eloquence, to which his fellow-citizens listened with applause and rapture; and little inferior to the best models of antiquity, for simplicity majesty, and persuasion.

PHILIP HENRY SHERIDAN.

The name SHERIDAN, has long been a bright star of the Emerald Isle. Thomas, and his son Richard, have been celebrated in dramatic circles, wherever English literature is appreciated. But whether Sheridan, the immigrant, who left Ireland and landed in Boston, was any relative of theirs, we do not know; enough, that his now famous son, PHILIP HENRY, was born in Boston, in the year 1831. It was a long journey for little Philip, when he was borne into Perry County, Ohio, where his father located on the great thoroughfare of western travel. With his Catholic neighbors, he was often taken to the church of St. Joseph, at Somerset, said to be the oldest house of public worship in the State.

Fondness for the noble horse was his early passion. When five years of age, he was one day met by some older lads, who sought amusement, and proposed that Philip should take his first grand ride. It pleased him. They placed him upon an unbridled horse, that was grazing in the pasture, and, to their astonishment, away went the steed over the fence, and out of sight. The child clung fast, and was carried into a tavern shed, more than a mile distant, where the horse was recognized, and the rider pronounced brave enough for an Indian hunter. Philip was thenceforth a hero in the neighborhood; for the horse was known to be vicious, and to have unsaddled excellent riders. They were prepared for the later exploits of "Cavalry SHERIDAN."

When old enough to leave home, he appeared in Zanesville with his horse and cart, making his own way in the world. Faithful, active, frank, and intelligent, he attracted the attention of a member of Congress, whose home was in the town. An elder brother, and other friends, spoke of a cadetship in the military academy, at West Point, for the young cartman: the Congressman secured the appointment. In 1848, Philip passed the examinations, and was enrolled in that institution. He ranked high, even among such class-mates as McPherson,

Schofield, and Terrill. He was graduated brevet second-lieutenant in the United States infantry.

There was a defence to be maintained against Mexico, and in 1853, young SHERIDAN was sent to Fort Duncan, on the Rio Grande, to render his first practical military service in a perilous country, exposed to the savageness of the Apache and Comanche Indians. There was soon an occasion to test his valor. He and two comrades were one day outside the fort, when a band of Apache Indians appeared; the chief leaped from his "fiery mustang" to seize his prisoners. In an instant SHERIDAN's eye kindled into admiration for the horse, and springing upon him, he galloped away to Fort Duncan. Summoning the troops, ordering his pistols, without dismounting, he hastened back, as a true cavalryman, to rescue his two companions, who were heroically fighting for their lives. One shot, and an Indian fell dead at the feet of the Lieutenant's horse. The soldiers came up, and the savages were ridden down, until few escaped. This valiant deed was, however, rebuked by the commandant of the fort, on the ground that the Lieutenant was away from his command. That jealous, irritated officer, was afterwards a general in the Confederate army. For two years SHERIDAN endured his displeasure, doing good service in making defences and explorations, when he at length sought a different post of duty. Promoted to a full lieutenant, he was, for a time, assigned to the command of Fort Wood, in New York harbor. Next he was sent to the Pacific coast, where he commanded an escort of men who were surveying the route for a railway connecting San Francisco with the Columbia river. This service won him a mention in Congress in the highest terms. We follow him to Fort Vancouver, displaying his dashing courage against the Yokima Indians, and winning admiration from them, as well as worthier praise from his superior officers. After the "Yokima Reservation" was formed, he was appointed to command this Indian domain; and gaining the confidence of his wild subjects, he administered their affairs to the entire satisfaction of the government. He created a new military post at Yamhill, southwest of Fort Vancouver, where he lived on the coarsest fare, passed days of danger, made bronzing marches, and prepared himself for activity in the greatest war of modern times.

With the rank of Captain, he was sent to Jefferson Barracks, St. Louis, Missouri, in the autumn of 1861. On his arrival, he was appointed president of the board which audited the claims that arose under the administration of General Fremont, in the west. It was a practical business affair, performed with such courtesy and ability, that he was given the position of Chief Quartermaster and Commissary of the Western army. An appreciative staff officer thus wrote of him: "A modest, quiet little man was our Quartermaster. Yet nobody could deny the vitalizing energy and masterly force of his presence, when he had occasion to exert himself. Neat in person, courteous in demeanor, exact in the transaction of business, and most accurate in matters appertaining to the regulations, orders, and general military custom, it was no wonder that our acting Chief Quartermaster should have been universally liked. Especially was he in favor socially, for it soon became known that he was, off duty, a most genial companion. Whenever he did allow his ambition to appear, it appeared to be of a moderate cast. 'He was the sixty-fourth captain on the list, and with the chances of war, he thought he might soon be major.' Such were the terms in which the future Major-General spoke of his promotion. No visions of brilliant stars, single or dual, glittered on the horizon of his life. If he could pluck an old leaf, and gild the same for his shoulders' wear, he was satisfied. If any one had suggested the possibility of a brigadiership, our Quartermaster would have supposed it meant in irony. Yet he was even then recognized as a man of vigorous character. . . . Not a clerk or orderly, but treasured some act of kindness done by Captain SHERIDAN."

His labors were very arduous. Everything, at that period of the war, needed organizing. The system of obtaining and forwarding supplies was imperfect. It was not strange, therefore, if the army that in the spring of 1862 was fighting terribly for the salvation of Missouri, could not be supplied perfectly with all that was needed. Nor was it surprising that there was a slight collision between him and General Curtis. But the affair was soon settled, and after making purchases of horses in Wisconsin for the army, Captain SHERIDAN was appointed Chief Quartermaster of the department, under General Halleck, then at Corinth, Mississippi. After the retreat of the Confederate forces from that place, there was a demand for officers in the cavalry service, that swift pursuit might be made. The attention of the superior officers was turned to SHERIDAN. He was at once commissioned Colonel of the second regiment of Michigan cavalry, and proved "the right man in the right place." He was in his field of success when attached to Elliot's cavalry force, enduring hardships, making raids into dangerous regions, destroying rail-roads and stores of the enemy, gaining a victory over Forest's bold riders, and soon finding Chalmers with nine regiments, facing him with but two. It was a perilous hour, but it suggested an admirable strategy. Colonel SHERIDAN sent ninety men around to fall on the rear of the enemy, while he would attack the front. The daring plan was successful. The enemy, surprised, terrified, and routed, fled in confusion, while the victors pursued him for twenty miles. General Grant, ever ready to crown merit, commended him; and on the first day of July, 1862, he was deservedly made a Brigadier-General. He rendered signal services, during the summer, in Mississippi and Kentucky, defending Louisville from capture and pillage.

In the organization of the Army of the Cumberland, General SHERIDAN was assigned to the command of the division of McCook's corps which constituted the right wing of the army. After the terrific battle of Murfreesboro', where all seemed for so long doubtful, but where the result was one of the grandest triumphs, at the very hour that President Lincoln was signing the Emancipation Proclamation of January, 1863, our cavalry hero was one of the eleven brigadiers of whom General Rosecranz said, in his report: "They ought to be made major-generals in our service." SHERIDAN received the appointment of Major-General, dated from the last day of 1862.

It is quite impossible to separate biography from history, during such eventful times as those in which were fought the many battles that gained Chattanooga, and held it for the Union. In some of those fierce engagements among the mountains, "the divisions of Wood and SHERIDAN were wading breast deep in the valley of death." Victory followed victory. The eyes of the generals were looking toward Atlanta.

General Grant was summoned to Washington in March, 1864, to receive the commission of Lieutenant-General of the armies of the United States. He would thenceforth be in the eastern department. He had already marked General SHERIDAN as one of the few great leaders in the future campaigns. SHERIDAN was relieved of his command (he knew not why), and ordered to report at Washington. To his surprise, he found himself placed in command of all the cavalry on the Potomac, in place of General Pleasanton, who was ordered into Missouri, where brave service was needed. SHERIDAN had now a large field, suited to his genius. Organizing his corps into three divisions, each commanded by able generals, he soon reported himself ready for duty. On the fourth of March, the Rapidan was crossed by the entire Army of the Potomac. The march began toward the tangled, swampy wilderness, near Spottsylvania, where the forces of General Lee were waiting for battle. The plan of General Grant was not to hurl his battalions on the enemy's intrenchments, but to manœuvre sufficiently to keep him in check, and then move in between him and the Confederate capital. General SHERIDAN was protecting the flanks of the great army, and reconnoitring the position and movements of the enemy. On the fifth, as the splendid columns were about to turn the lines of the enemy, General Meade received a despatch from SHERIDAN. Breaking the seal, and reading it, he said: "They say that Lee intends to fight us here." "Very well," replied the imperturbable Grant. The plan of battle was soon matured. Then followed the terrific scenes of blood in the Wilderness. For three days, the carnage was frightful. It devolved upon SHERIDAN's cavalry to protect the army trains, and the ambulances containing the sick and wounded. On the ninth of March, the enemy began to fall deliberately back, still in a challenging attitude. Then commenced the chase for Spottsylvania Court House, both armies anxious to secure the position. Grant did not gain it; but he reported that all was prosperous, saying: "I propose to fight it out on this line, if it takes all summer."

To clear up "this line," General SHERIDAN was ordered, on the ninth, to select his best mounted troops, and start out on an expedition to the rear of Lee's army, to cut off his communications and supplies. He was given full discretion as to his plans. He ordered three days' rations to be given to his men, leaving behind everything that was not actually needed upon a great march. In a somewhat circuitous route, he appeared at the fords of the North Anna river, and at Beaver Dam. There he came upon a provost-guard of the enemy, having charge of more than three hundred union prisoners, who had been captured the day before, at Spottsylvania. The union prisoners were released, and their guard captured. Thence, pushing on toward Richmond, a detachment destroyed the rail-road track and Confederate property at Ashland. On the eleventh, SHERIDAN'S command reached a point within six miles of Richmond, where they encountered the Confederate cavalry, under General J. E. B. Stuart. A severe battle was fought; Stuart was killed, several guns were captured, and the Federal forces gained the day. Before daybreak, the next morning, a detachment moved forward to reconnoitre, and penetrated the second line of defences around Richmond, approaching within two miles of that city. After capturing a Confederate courier, they withdrew. Early the next morning, SHERIDAN'S advance appeared at Meadow Bridge, where the enemy had destroyed the bridge, and constructed defences which commanded the rail-road bridge, over which the Union troops might attempt to cross. It was a way of great peril; but, nothing daunted, SHERIDAN'S gallant soldiers dashed across, and rushing through about half a mile of marshy ground, charged upon the enemy, and carried the works, after a most determined resistance.

In the meantime, another force of the enemy had come up in his rear, and almost surrounded SHERIDAN'S wearied army. To retreat would be fatal; the railroad-bridge could not be gained. To go forward would lead them upon a force greatly outnumbering the Union troops. To cross the river Chickahominy, the Meadow Bridge must be reconstructed and crossed under the concentrated fire of the enemy. Here was a position to task the finest energies of generalship. SHERIDAN'S decision was quickly made. The bridge must be rebuilt. It was done amid the constant fire of the Confederates, who were bravely kept at bay. Tremendous work was done by the Union artillery; charges were repelled by fierce counter-charges. Once or twice, the men were slowly pressed back; but the calm, self-possessed SHERIDAN encouraged them by his presence, and they regained their position. At length the bridge was completed. The ammunition train must pass over it. If the firing continued, it was scarcely possible to avoid the horrors of an explosion, and the risk of a capture of his forces. The peril only added to the resources of the cool commander. He put himself at the head of some picked men, and when the ammunition train was ready to be moved, he pointed his followers to the enemy, and said: "Boys, do you see those fellows, yonder? They are green recruits, just from Richmond. There's not a veteran among them. You have fought them well, to-day; but we have got to whip them. We can do it, and we will." A rousing cheer went up from the men, who were proud of their leader; and in clear, ringing tones, he gave the order: "Forward! Charge!" Onward they dashed; the foe went flying before them to the intrenchments. Then the artillery opened upon the Confederates, increasing their terror. Under cover of this brilliant charge, the train crossed the bridge in safety. The Union forces marched forward, with a heavy rain upon them, driving the enemy to Mechanicsville, and thence to Cold Harbor, taking many prisoners, and encamping near Gaines' Mills. Two days after, he brought his command to General Butler's head-quarters, without molestation, and opened communication with Washington. It was said, not long after: "Other expeditions may have resulted in a larger destruction of property, the capture of more prisoners, or the traversing of a larger region of territory; but none, during the war, has carried greater terror into the hearts of the enemy, or more gallantly extricated itself from a position of extraordinary difficulty."

General SHERIDAN made his head-quarters, for a few days, at White House, on the Pamunky river; but most of the time he was at the head of his troops, aiding the main army, on its way to the Chickahominy. He was frequently in conflict with the Confederate cavalry, under Fitzhugh Lee. Various engagements at different points occurred, after which, he guarded the flank of General Grant's army, in its movement across the James river. While the main army was pushing on to Petersburg, General SHERIDAN set out, on the eighth of June, for a second cavalry expedition into the heart of Virginia. The object was to cut off the northward and westward lines of the enemy, and prevent him from receiving supplies or troops over the rail-roads. The points aimed at were Gordonsville and Charlottesville. Had his movements been properly sustained, he would have realized his hopes. Yet he did a noble work.

A third invasion of Maryland and Pennsylvania was planned, and already on foot, by the Confederates, marching through the valley of the Shenandoah. The national capital was more seriously threatened than ever before. Baltimore was endangered. Chambersburg was desolated. The North was filled with alarm. The design was to draw General Grant and all his forces from Petersburg and Richmond. But "Grant was a very obstinate man." He knew, too, of an unwearied, persistent trooper, whose soldiers could be trusted for the routing of the invaders. The Military Division of the Shenandoah was organized. The command of it was given to General SHERIDAN, although he was the youngest of all the major-generals; for "he had already exhibited a skill and tact in the handling of troops, a combination of caution and audacity, a celerity of movement, and a fertility of resource, which indicated him as the man for the place." General Grant knew his man, and the result proved that he was not mistaken.

General SHERIDAN was soon at Harper's Ferry, making that his head-quarters. Already had the Confederate General Early gathered large plunder, fallen back, and prepared to forward it to Richmond. He probably intended to return into the rich valleys of the loyalists. SHERIDAN united his troops at the entrance of the valley, and began to press Early from the important positions which he held at such places as Martinsburg and Williamsport. He made feints of an advance, in order to discover the strength of his enemy. Early, priding himself on his acuteness, imagined that he was luring on the young pursuer, and that he would soon get him where he could finish him. Both generals were wary. SHERIDAN secured Winchester on the twelfth of August. Finding that there was some prospect of the enemy moving southward, to join General Lee, he arrested his progress, and drew back to Charlestown, in order to attract Early nearer to the Potomac. Early thought that SHERIDAN was afraid, and that by good management he might flank him, re-enter Maryland, and reap another harvest of plunder. He therefore moved to Berryville. But his opponent was ready for meeting him. After some fighting and marching, he crowded Early west of Opequan creek, and got between him and Richmond. A severe battle began, on September 19, when the Confederates were "sent whirling through Winchester," as SHERIDAN expressed it. They lost three of their ablest generals, one of whom was Fitzhugh Lee, their cavalry leader, and about 12,000 men, in killed, wounded, and prisoners. With his usual rapidity, SHERIDAN led on his army, and encountered the enemy, strongly fortified, on Fisher's Hill. By dividing his forces, and making an attack in front and in the rear, he drove him from his intrenchments. Confused, disorganized, losing the munitions of war, and greatly scattered; many of the enemy fled to the mountains, and determined to abandon the conflict. A terrible work of devastation was begun, to avenge the ravages of the enemy in the northern valleys, and to make the Shenandoah unfit for being any longer the avenue to invasion. General Early again rallied his forces, and intrenched them on Fisher's Hill, at a time when SHERIDAN was absent in Washington. A fierce battle ensued. The tidings reached SHERIDAN that his noble army was yielding to the foe. One man — one moment of his presence, might turn the tide of war. He hastened to Winchester, and mounted his horse for a ride that has been thrillingly described by the distinguished poet, Thomas Buchanan Read:

> UP from the South, at break of day,
> Bringing to Winchester fresh dismay,
> The affrighted air with a shudder bore,
> Like a herald in haste to the chieftain's door,
> The terrible grumble, and rumble, and roar,
> Telling the battle was on once more,
> And SHERIDAN twenty miles away.
>
> And wider still those billows of war
> Thundered along the horizon's bar;
> And louder yet into Winchester rolled
> The roar of that red sea uncontrolled,
> Making the blood of the listener cold
> As he thought of the stake in that fiery fray,
> And SHERIDAN twenty miles away.
>
> But there is a road from Winchester town,
> A good broad highway, leading down;
> And there, through the flush of the morning light,
> A steed, as black as the steeds of night,
> Was seen to pass, as with eagle flight —
> As if he knew the terrible need,
> He stretched away with his utmost speed;
> Hill rose and fell — but his heart was gay,
> With SHERIDAN fifteen miles away.
>
> Still sprung from those swift hoofs, thundering south,
> The dust, like the smoke from the cannon's mouth;
> Or the trail of a comet, sweeping faster and faster,
> Foreboding to traitors the doom of disaster;
> The heart of the steed and the heart of the master,
> Were beating like prisoners assaulting their walls,
> Impatient to be where the battle-field calls;
> Every nerve of the charger was strained to full play,
> With SHERIDAN only ten miles away.

NATIONAL PORTRAITS.

Under his spurring feet, the road
Like an arrowy Alpine river flowed,
And the landscape sped away behind
Like an ocean flying before the wind;
And the steed, like a bark fed with furnace ire,
Swept on, with his wild eyes full of fire.
But, lo! he is nearing his heart's desire —
He is snuffing the smoke of the roaring fray
With SHERIDAN only five miles away.

The first that the General saw, were the groups
Of stragglers, and then the retreating troops;
What was done — what to do — a glance told him both,
Then, striking his spurs with a terrible oath,
He dashed down the line 'mid a storm of huzzas,
And the wave of retreat checked its course there, because
The sight of the master compelled it to pause.
With foam and with dust, the black charger was gray;
By the flash of his eye, and his red nostrils' play,
He seemed to the whole great army to say:
"I have brought you SHERIDAN all the way
From Winchester, down to save the day!"

Hurrah! hurrah for SHERIDAN!
Hurrah! hurrah for horse and man!
And when their statues are placed on high,
Under the dome of the Union sky —
The American soldiers' temple of Fame —
There, with the glorious General's name,
Be it said, in letters both bold and bright:
"Here is the steed that saved the day
By carrying SHERIDAN into the fight
From Winchester — twenty miles away!"

The losses on each side were heavy. The victory over the Confederates was so decisive, that Early's army never recovered from this stunning blow. It was said that "the only reinforcement which the Army of the Shenandoah received, or needed to recover its lost field of battle, camps, intrenchments, and cannon, was one man — SHERIDAN."

General SHERIDAN had been promoted to a Brigadier-General of the regular army, in place of the lamented McPherson. He was now made a Major-General in the regular army, in place of George B. McClellan, who had resigned.

About the first of March, 1865, SHERIDAN moved his splendid cavalry through the country, routing Early, taking over 1,200 prisoners, several staff-officers, much material of war, and some

PHILIP HENRY SHERIDAN.

of Early's baggage. The General himself barely escaped. The James River Canal, and two railroads were destroyed, thus greatly injuring the Confederate cause. SHERIDAN seems to have been almost everywhere in the vicinity of Richmond, during the next few days. On Saturday, April 1st, he was at Five Forks, nearly west from Richmond, fighting a severe battle, while the main Army of the Potomac was attacking the forces of Lee. His masterly movements, with the simultaneous onset along the whole lines on Sunday, compelled the enemy to speedily evacuate Petersburg and Richmond. The whole country shouted in exultation; but the work was not all yet done. It was feared that the most terrific battle of modern times was still to be fought. Lee moved in haste, but dared not cross the Appomattox river; he pressed on to the neighborhood of Amelia Court House, and there was SHERIDAN, whose cavalry seemed to have an almost ubiquitous power. We relate, in SHERIDAN's own words, what occurred on the sixth, as he pursued the Confederate forces:

"It was apparent, from the absence of artillery fire, and the manner in which they gave way when pressed, that the force of the enemy opposed to us was a heavy rear-guard. The enemy was driven until our lines reached Sailor's creek; and from the north, I could see our cavalry on the high ground above the creek and south of it, and the long line of smoke from the burning wagons. A cavalryman, who in a charge cleared the enemy's works and came through their lines, reported to me what was in their front. I regret that I have forgotten the name of this gallant young soldier." He then ordered an attack to be made on both the right and left wings, and he says: "The cavalry in rear of the enemy attacked simultaneously; and the enemy, after a gallant resistance, was completely surrounded, and nearly all threw down their arms and surrendered. General Ewell, commanding the enemy's forces, and a number of other general officers, fell into our hands, and a very large number of prisoners."

It was during some of these anxious and eventful hours, that SHERIDAN sent word to Lieutenant-General Grant, whose forces had been crowding hard upon the enemy: "I wish you were here yourself; if things are pressed, I think Lee will surrender." A nobler compliment was never paid to a General-in-chief. And a less jealous man than Grant did not breathe, as he sent back the order: "Press th'ngs." SHERIDAN was already striking right and left. He knew that Grant and Lee were in correspondence in regard to a cessation of the war. He heard of a white flag on the ninth, and before long was talking face to face with the Confederate General Gordon, at Appomattox Court House, about a suspension of hostilities. "I notified him that I desired to prevent the unnecessary effusion of blood, but as there was nothing definitely settled in the correspondence, and as an attack had been made on my lines with the view to escape, under the impression that our force was only cavalry, I must have some assurance of an intended surrender." He was assured " that there was no doubt of the surrender of General Lee's army . . . . . and hostilities ceased until the arrival of Lieutenant-General Grant." Thus was the Confederate chieftain brought fairly at bay by the Hero of the Shenandoah.

On the ninth of April, 1865, the surrender was accomplished. The vast plans of General Grant had been successful, and would soon be crowned with complete victory. On the evening of the twentieth, Generals Grant and SHERIDAN were in Washington talking—not only of the murdered President, but of the enemy's forces yet in the southwest. They must surrender. SHERIDAN left the next day, to restore order and law in Texas.

It has been said: "Grant, Sherman, and Thomas are great in strategy, and calm in execution. SHERIDAN has never failed in his plans, but has won his victories chiefly through his sublime heroism—on fire with martial daring and glory . . . . He heartily despises a council of war, and never forms part of one if he can avoid it. He executes, not originates plans; or, as Rosecranz once expressed it: 'He fights — he fights.' His care for the reputation of his subordinates, his freedom from all petty jealousy, his honesty of purpose, and the nobleness of his ambition to serve the country and not himself, his geniality and general good-humor, and the brevity of his black storms of anger, make him, like Grant, not only a well-beloved leader, but one that the country can safely trust to guard its honor and preserve its existence."

MAJOR GENERAL

Charles Cotesworth Pinckney

CHARLES COTESWORTH PINCKNEY.

"For these are the men, that when they have played their parts and had their exits, must step out, and give the moral of their scenes: and deliver unto posterity an inventory of their virtues and vices." SIR THOMAS BROWNE.

GENERAL CHARLES COTESWORTH PINCKNEY was one of that race, or order of men, who are now nearly, if not quite, extinct in South Carolina. He lived at that fortunate period when a classical and highly-finished education was deemed indispensable, not only for him who had his own fortune to build up, but also for him who had a fortune to spend. The direct trade between the Mother country and the Province, created by the valuable staple products of Rice and Indigo, put it in the power of the planters of South Carolina to send their sons to England with remarkable facility. In proportion, therefore, to population and extent of territory, the number of her young men educated in the English universities far exceeded that of any other of the Colonies. Thus, at the very commencement of our disputes with the Mother country she possessed a band of learned, intelligent, and accomplished gentlemen, fit either for the council or the field; and whose knowledge of the true principles of constitutional liberty gave that high tone to public sentiment, which mainly contributed to bear the people triumphant through that terrible period, which was truly and emphatically said to have "tried men's souls." Among those patriotic men, the subject of this memoir stood in the very first rank; and we shall now attempt to give a brief sketch of his life, which was long, useful, and honorable to his country.

The ancestor of General PINCKNEY came over to South Carolina in the year 1692. From him descended CHARLES, commonly known by the name of Chief Justice Pinckney, a man of great integrity, and of considerable eminence under the Provincial government. The Chief Justice was twice married. His second wife was Eliza Lucas, daughter of George Lucas, a Colonel in the British army and Governor of Antigua; and on the 25th day of February, 1746, she gave birth to General PINCKNEY at Charleston. In the year 1753, being then seven years old, he was taken over to England by his father, with his brother, the late Major-general Thomas Pinckney. The Chief Justice was one of those sensible men who valued education and moral discipline as far beyond the mere advantages of wealth, and he resolved, even though it might impair the patrimony of his sons, to buy it for them at the highest cost. Accordingly, in his will he enjoins that they shall be thoroughly educated before returning to America; and that in case the income of his estate proved inadequate, a portion of the estate itself must be sold to accomplish this great object of his parental solicitude.

After five years of private tuition, General PINCKNEY was considered as well fitted for Westminster, and in 1758 he was placed by his father at that celebrated school, then under the care of a very distinguished scholar, Doctor Markham, who was afterwards advanced to the See of York. There his industry and good conduct won the esteem of the master; while he there, too, imbibed that classical taste and love of study, which, during an unusually long and eventful life, constituted both its ornament and its solace. That he stood high in the estimation of the master, may be inferred from the following fact. An occurrence in the school having, on investigation, produced much contradictory evidence, Doctor Markham, addressing young PINCKNEY, said, "I know the strictness of your principles and your attachment to truth: speak, PINCKNEY! my decision shall be guided by your sentiment." From Westminster he was removed, in due course, to *Christ Church*, Oxford, where he had the acute Doctor Cyril Jackson as his private tutor. Judge Blackstone was then the Law lecturer; and as the best evidence of General PINCKNEY's attention and assiduity to that branch of his studies, he has left behind him four large volumes of manuscript, containing those celebrated lectures, which, with a diligence extraordinary in so young a man, he had written down at the time. With so much application and perseverance, knowledge could not be wooed in vain; and he consequently left Oxford with the reputation of being a fine scholar at the early age of eighteen. From that ancient university he entered as a law student at the Temple, where, having done something more than eat the usual number of dinners, he returned to South Carolina in 1769, having, during the last year, visited France and Germany, and devoting nine months to military studies at the Royal Academy of Caen in Normandy.

CHARLES C. PINCKNEY.

Sixteen years of absence had not impaired, or in the slightest degree weakened, his affection for his native soil. While in England he had keenly participated in the indignation felt at the passage of the Stamp Act; and a portrait taken of him at that time for his friend Sir Matthew Ridley, represents him in the act of arguing vehemently against that arbitrary measure. It has been declared by his contemporaries, that on his return from England he appeared before them at once as a remarkable young man. His elegant literary attainment—his sound legal knowledge—his high sense of all that was held honorable in the eyes of men, united to the most distinguished manners, impressed on those who knew him the certainty of his future success and elevation.

His commission to practise in the Provincial Courts is dated January 19th, 1770, and he very soon began to acquire business and reputation. It is worthy of notice, as showing the estimation in which he was held by his legal brethren, that he was appointed by Sir Egerton Lee, (his Majesty's Attorney General of the Province,) under a full and formal commission, to act as his substitute on Circuit in the District and Precinct courts of Camden, Georgetown, and Cheraws. This was in 1773, when General PINCKNEY was still a young man: and when we consider the high estimate of their profession by the English lawyers of that day, most of them being not only men of learning and accomplishments, but likewise of high birth and descent, this appointment may be taken as evidence of extraordinary merit. His professional pursuits, with all its emoluments and the expectation of its high reward, was, however, doomed to a sudden blight. The gathering storm of the Revolutionary war burst on the plains of Lexington. It struck on the ear of the patriots of South Carolina, and they at once resolved to prepare for that bloody and unnatural conflict with England, which was now seen to be inevitable.

Accordingly a meeting of the Provincial Congress was summoned by the Committee of Safety to be held in the city of Charleston. It assembled on the first day of June, 1775, and it was almost instantly decided to raise two regiments of infantry, of five hundred men each. The military ardor at this moment was so great, that the first families of the Province eagerly contended for appointments, and the number of candidates far exceeded the demand. In the midst of this band of gallant spirits, the abilities of General PINCKNEY were seen and acknowledged, and he was elected captain in the first regiment, appearing highest on the list. His Colonel was that firm republican, old Christopher Gadsden. He immediately proceeded on the recruiting service, and fixed his quarters at Newbern in North Carolina. Whilst there, he proved his discernment and intrepidity of purpose, by advising the arrest of two suspicious persons, who came under the assumed garb of *settlers*. Their personal appearance and easy address convinced him that they were not what they would seem to be. He waited on the Committee of Public Safety, and having declared his reasons for believing that the strangers were hostile to the interests of the country, recommended their instant arrest. Unfortunately, the members of the Committee were timid, and refused to follow his advice. The event proved the soundness of his judgment. The strangers left Newbern for Cross Creek, and almost immediately excited the Scotch settlers, their countrymen, to arm in support of the Royal Government. General Moore was sent against them, and they were defeated. The younger of the strangers escaped; his name was McDonald. The other, who proved to be a veteran officer, of the name of McLeod, was killed. Having completed the recruiting service, he joined his regiment in Charleston, which was soon after placed on the *Continental* establishment by a resolution of Congress. In a short time General PINCKNEY obtained the command of the first regiment—its Colonel, Christopher Gadsden, being made a Brigadier, and its Lieutenant-Colonel and Major having been transferred to the command of other regiments.

The glorious defence of Fort Moultrie, and the signal defeat of the British fleet in its attack on that post, gave a calm, and long respite to the people of South Carolina from the horrors of war. The power of England then bore heavily on the States of New-York and Pennsylvania. Burning with ardor to distinguish himself in the field, General PINCKNEY hastened to join the Northern army. He was cordially received by General Washington, who appointed him an aid-de-camp; and in this capacity he was present at the battle of Brandywine, and the bloody affair at Germantown. The impression then made by him on the mind of the Commander-in-chief was of the most durable kind. It was exhibited throughout many years of friendship and of confidence, and on many interesting occasions, and only ceased with life itself. To one of his quick and energetic spirit, the opportunity which he now possessed of increasing his military knowledge, both as to science and discipline, it is reasonable to suppose was not allowed to escape unimproved.

On the first intimation of danger to the South, General PINCKNEY returned to take the command of his regiment. The State of Georgia about this period was greatly harassed by Tories, and repeated inroads of vagabonds from Florida. It was indispensable to make an effort to save her from total ruin. Major-general Howe, of North Carolina, who commanded the Southern Division, required the aid of the South Carolina forces, and General PINCKNEY was ordered on to join Howe in Georgia. This service was short, but severe. The army had to move about, and drive the enemy at a season of the year when exposure to the climate was sure to produce sickness, if not death. The soldiers were wretchedly provided, not only as to camp equipage, but even as to food. In a letter written at Fort Howe on the Altamaha, addressed to General Moultrie at Charleston, General PINCKNEY describes the sufferings of the men as almost intolerable. Ten and twelve were crowded into one small tent, and many were left uncovered, to sleep under the heavy and deadly dews of the Georgia skies. The Continental troops, which, at the beginning, counted eleven hundred strong, were in the course of two months reduced to only three hundred and fifty men fit for duty. About midsummer General PINCKNEY got back to Charleston, after three months of the hardest service, rendered more acute by the reflection, that disease, and not the weapons of their enemies, had destroyed his soldiers. The sudden dash of Provost at Charleston, the subsequent invasion of Georgia, and the assault on the lines of Savannah, all contributed to bring out into bold relief General PINCKNEY's fine qualities as a soldier. In the language of a brother officer, " his patient submission to the severities of service, his determined resolution and calm intrepidity, gave decided increase to his military reputation."

The campaigns of 1778 and '79, in the North, having reflected but little lustre on the British arms, Sir Henry Clinton consoled himself with the idea of making easy and brilliant conquests in the Southern and weaker States. Accordingly he prepared and fitted out a very powerful land and naval force for the capture of Charleston. The Royal army, in great strength, on the 11th of February, 1780, landed about thirty miles from the city. So feeble was the garrison at that moment, that, had the British army pushed on immediately to the city, it must have fallen almost without a blow; but Sir Henry Clinton preferred the slow method of a siege. The six Continental regiments in the Carolina establishment were at this time reduced to eight hundred men. The North Carolina and Virginia Continentals, about fifteen hundred strong, were ordered on by Congress: but of this number not more than seven hundred entered the city. Nevertheless, with this feeble garrison, and besieged both by land and water, it was unanimously determined, in a full house of assembly, to defend the town to the last extremity.

General PINCKNEY at this critical period, with three hundred men, was stationed in command at Fort Moultrie. It was a post of honor, and his heart must have throbbed with exultation as he thought of Moultrie's victory in June, '76; and that now fortune had brought him his turn, either to show the flag of his country waving in triumph, or to make it his winding-sheet. But his eager anticipations were disappointed. The British admiral Arbuthnot, taking advantage of a strong southerly wind and flood tide, swept rapidly by Fort Moultrie without stopping to engage it.

General PINCKNEY, however, opened a heavy and brisk fire on the ships as they passed under full sail, by which they received considerable damage, and twenty seamen were killed and wounded. Determined to share the fate of Charleston, he soon afterwards withdrew with a part of his garrison, and entered the city. A council of war was assembled for the purpose of deliberating on a capitulation, and it was then that General PINCKNEY displayed that boldness and decision of mind which belongs only to a man of great character. Rising with great composure and dignity of manner, he exclaimed, "I will not say, if the enemy attempt to carry our lines by storm, that we shall be able to resist them successfully: but am convinced we shall so cripple the army before us, that although we may not live to enjoy the benefits ourselves, yet to the United States they will prove incalculably great. Considerations of self are out of the question. They cannot influence any member of this council. My voice is for rejecting all terms of capitulation, and for continuing hostilities to the last extremity." This magnanimous proposition, although supported by Lieut. Colonel Laurens, was not adopted.

Charleston finally capitulated in May 1780, after a close investiture both by land and water of three months. General PINCKNEY was then removed to Haddrel's Point, about two miles from the city, with a large number of other prisoners. At this post they bore incredible privations. Without clothing, credit, or money, their sufferings became so extreme, that the Continental officers of the South Carolina and Georgia lines appointed General PINCKNEY to draw a memorial to Congress describing their condition. It is stated in this paper, that during their long captivity they had never received more than *nine* days' pay from their country.

The well-known influence of General PINCKNEY—his abilities— his zeal in the cause of liberty, and the boldness displayed in maintaining his principles, made him in a peculiar degree the object of British severity. After enduring an obstinate intermittent fever for several months, he was at last allowed by the Commandant of Charleston, to come over to the city, on the declaration of the British physician, Doctor McNamara Hayes, that it was indispensable for the restoration of his health. Yet, *four* days after the permission had been granted, the same officer suddenly ordered him to return to Haddrel's Point, although his only son was at that instant lying dead in the house; and he was forced to compliance.

Nothing, however, could shake the firmness of his soul—oppression might drive the iron into it, but could not weaken its integrity. Threats and temptations were alternately used, but in vain. To Major Money of the British army, he wrote in the following bold and eloquent strain. "I entered into this cause after reflection, and through principle. My heart is altogether American, and neither severity, nor favor, nor poverty, nor affluence, can ever induce me to swerve from it." To Captain McMahon, another British officer, he emphatically says, "The freedom and independence of my country are the gods of my idolatry."

It was during this period that the discussion between Major Barry, of the British army, and himself occurred on some points relating to the exchange of prisoners. Barry having quoted Grotius in support of his side of the question, General PINCKNEY promptly declared, that the opinions of that great jurist were in direct opposition to what had been stated. Reference was made to the author, when Major Barry was obliged to confess his error, lamenting "that he had not studied the passage with his usual accuracy."

At length he received the intelligence of his exchange, when it was too late to be of much value to him, in a letter from General McIntosh, dated at Philadelphia, 19th February, 1782. The war was then really at an end by the capture of Lord Cornwallis. Soon after he was raised to brevet rank as Brigadier; his commission is dated at Princeton, 1783, General Lincoln then acting as Secretary at War. On the return of peace, General PINCKNEY resumed the practice of law, his fortune having been much impaired. Time and casualties had swept away most of the old and learned members of the bar. He found in their place a new set of young men, clever, but of imperfect education—the war having broken the regular course of study. He, with a few more, might have ruled as monarchs of the bar; but his generous spirit disdained to profit by the weakness of others. He preferred to introduce a simple, liberal, and intelligible mode of practice, stripping off all useless subtleties and technical rules, and endeavoured to make the profession what it should be, enlightened and honorable in the eyes of the community. His business was large, and its profits commensurate,—reaching in one year the amount of four thousand guineas, a considerable sum for that day. A nice sense of honor made him discriminate in his cases, and it was not every one that offered, that he would take. He never forgot the injunction of his venerable father, to which his own generous heart involuntarily responded, to be the friend of the widow and the fatherless. From these he never would take compensation; and he carried into his profession the spirit of chivalry itself, which he exhibited on one remarkable occasion, and to which the writer of this sketch is not at liberty to do more than to allude. During this period he was more than once solicited by General Washington to enter into his cabinet. He was offered a place on the Supreme Bench; then the post of Secretary at War, as the successor of General Knox; afterwards that of Secretary of State, on the removal of Mr. Randolph. He steadily and consistently, for reasons satisfactory to his own mind, declined these honors, and stated finally in reply, "That whenever the President should call him to the performance of any public duty, to which private considerations ought to yield, and should say to him 'that he must accept,' all private obligations should cease."

This pledge he redeemed by accepting the mission to France, which General Washington, in a letter from Mount Vernon, July 8th, 1796, pressed on him in language that did honor to both. On this occasion his characteristic energy and decision was manifested. In a very few days after having notified his acceptance of the appointment, he embarked for Philadelphia and thence for Bordeaux. He arrived in Paris the 5th day of December; but on the way had to submit to the national *welcome* of the Poissardes, who, a post and a half from the city, stopped his carriage, and opening the door, insisted on the American ambassador's giving them the fraternal embrace.

On the next day he transmitted, by his Secretary of Legation, Major Henry Rutledge, to Mr. Monroe, his letters of recal; and a few days afterwards made his first and only visit to the Secretary of Foreign Affairs, Monsieur De La Croix, whose reception of him was cold and inauspicious.

The Directory had already determined not to receive him as minister of the United States, and accordingly Monsieur De La Croix addressed a note to Mr. Monroe, with whom the French government was still in correspondence, in these terms:—" The Directory has charged me to notify you, that it will not acknowledge nor receive another Minister Plenipotentiary from the United States until after the redress of the grievances demanded of the American government." This official insult, which must have been galling in the extreme, was borne with a serenity and dignity of mind that proved him fit to be an ambassador.

General Pinckney's sound judgment warned him, that on the very threshold of his embassy, prudence and duty both required that he should show the temper of forbearance. The interests of his country, her attachment, and proper feeling of gratitude towards an ancient ally, whose powerful arm had stretched across the Atlantic, and supported her in the dark hour of trial—all united to impress upon him the strongest disposition for peace. The moment had not yet arrived for him to vindicate his own high courage and the American people, in that noble sentiment which afterwards burst from his lips, and has become familiar as our household words.

"MILLIONS FOR DEFENCE, NOT A CENT FOR TRIBUTE."

The position of General Pinckney in the French capital was critical, and was well calculated to fill him with anxiety. He thus speaks of it in a letter to Colonel Pickering—"My situation, as you may easily conceive, is unpleasant; but if I can ultimately render any services to my country, I shall be fully compensated: at all events it shall be my study to avoid increasing the discontent of this government, without committing the honor, dignity, and respect, due to my own."

On the 5th of February, after being two months in Paris, he left it by an order from the Directory, having, by his patience and firmness, finally compelled them to address a note to himself, of which the following is an extract:—"Le Directoire executif Monsieur m'a chargé de vous faire savoir que n'ayant point obtenu de permission particulier, pour resider à Paris vous etes soumis à la loi qui oblige les etrangers à quitter le territoire de la Republique."

DE LA CROIX.

General Pinckney having obtained what he desired in this peremptory mandate, immediately left the territory of France, and retired to Holland to await the instructions of the American government. President Washington empowered Judge Marshall and Elbridge Gerry to join General Pinckney in Holland, and forthwith proceed with him to Paris; and there, as Envoys Extraordinary, endeavor to settle all existing difficulties. Success did not follow this new and sincere effort towards reconciliation. Our limits forbid enlarging on this portion of General Pinckney's diplomatic career. It is sufficient to remark, that it was satisfactory to the government and the country. His colleague, General Marshall, and himself, returned to the United States, leaving Mr. Gerry in France, who, as it appears from the correspondence of the day, was persuaded to this step by citizen Talleyrand, for the purpose of conducting a separate negotiation between the two nations. President Adams, however, did not sanction this conduct on the part of Gerry, and he received a positive letter of recal from the Secretary of State, dated Jan. 25, 1798.

The spirit of the nation was now justly excited, and when General Pinckney arrived in America, he found the tone of public sentiment strong for hostilities. On the 12th of October, 1798, he landed at Paulus Hook, where he was received by a large concourse of citizens, who greeted him with enthusiastic cheers. The yellow fever was then raging in New-York, and he was compelled to proceed to the town of Newark with his family. He there received a letter from James McIIenry, dated October 17th, 1798, enclosing his commission as a Major-general in the army of the United States, which was being put on the war establishment. It contained the following well-merited and just compliment to his patriotism: "The readiness you have expressed to accept of your appointment, after so long an absence from home and your private affairs, is extremely satisfactory; and will, I am sure, be fully estimated by the President and your country."

When President Adams appointed Washington to the command of the army, he also left to his judgment the selection of the other superior officers. The appointment, therefore, of General Pinckney is another strong proof of the continued friendship and confidence of Washington in his patriotism and abilities. The relative rank of the Major-generals stood thus: Washington—Alexander Hamilton—Charles Cotesworth Pinckney—Henry Knox. Hamilton, during the war of the Revolution, was the junior of General Pinckney. This circumstance being pointed out to him by a gentleman of his acquaintance, who laid much stress on the injustice and partiality of this preference, General Pinckney gave this memorable reply, worthy of a Themistocles or a Scipio:—"I am confident that General Washington had sufficient reasons for this preference. Let us first dispose of our enemies, we shall then have leisure to settle the question of rank."

Hostilities did not break out, and he once more retired to the calm and elegant enjoyments of a home, of which his social powers and polished manners formed one of the most graceful ornaments.

CHARLES C. PINCKNEY.

It is fact well understood, that if General PINCKNEY, in the year 1800, when the great struggle of parties happened, could have consented to unite his name with that of Mr. Jefferson, he would have been either President or Vice President of the United States. But, true to himself, true to his principles, consistent in all things, he would not, even to win the first office in the gift of the people, and gratify the inclination of his native State, agree to a measure that might seem to compromise his integrity. General PINCKNEY was a member of the enlightened assembly that formed the Constitution of the United States. Again his was one of the leading minds in the *State* Convention that framed the Constitution of 1790.

In the South Carolina State Convention of 1778 he exhibited not only very vigorous, but likewise liberal powers of mind. He forcibly and successfully sustained, in that convention, a proposition of the Rev. William Tennant to secure liberty and equality to all Protestant sects; and as he was a strict Episcopalian, it is but just to infer that he acted or argued from conviction, and not indifference. The uniform respect with which he treated the clergy of all denominations endeared him to them; and is evinced in the fact, that Christians of every sect united in choosing him the first President of the Bible Society of Charleston, and they continued him in that honorable station for fifteen years, to the period of his death.

General PINCKNEY was a considerable landholder in the city of Charleston. He had numerous tenants living on his property, and to all of them he was forbearing and compassionate; often submitting to the loss of his just dues rather than resort to the rigors of the law. Indeed, his benevolence was of the most enlarged character, and was experienced not only by the poor, and such as were dependent on him, but in his liberal support of churches, seminaries of learning, and every object of public utility. His hospitality was unbounded, and was of that princely sort, that it did honor to South Carolina. How many foreigners, how many Americans, are now living to whom such a reminiscence ought to be familiar? His conversation was singularly instructive and amusing, for he had both seen and thought much; and the ease and frankness of his manners invited the approach of all who chose to participate in its pleasures. His own library was extensive; but the valuable collection of his father, together with many manuscripts and interesting family documents, were burnt by the army of General Provost at a country-seat near Charleston, at the time of his forced march on the city—a loss which General PINCKNEY oftentimes lamented. His appetite for reading was great. Nothing in the shape of a book escaped his attention. He read from the moment he arose in the morning; that is, a page or a few sentences at a time, while he walked about his chamber and dressed; his intellect was constantly exercised.

General PINCKNEY, as he advanced in life, applied himself to the sciences—Chemistry and Botany became his favorite pursuits; and such was his thirst for knowledge, that, while on his embassy to France, he seized that opportunity of listening to the lectures of the celebrated Fourcroy. At his country residence (Pinckney Island, a most enchanting spot) he had an apartment fitted up as a laboratory, containing an excellent Philosophical apparatus; and there he amused himself during several hours of every morning in winter.

In person General PINCKNEY did not exceed the ordinary stature. His form was round, muscular, and closely knit; and admirably constructed for exercise and durability. His countenance was marked, and highly expressive of almost every variety of emotion; but in repose, particularly towards the close of his life, it wore the character of majesty; and no one could look upon it without feeling the inspiration of the profoundest veneration.

If the eye, as has been beautifully said, be the mirror of the soul, in *his* might have been clearly read—courage—benevolence—honor—truth; and, indeed, all these were the predominant qualities illustrated in his life. No man ever enjoyed in a higher degree the confidence of his fellow-citizens. His acknowledged gallantry of spirit—his disdain of all selfish, narrow, and dishonorable conduct—his public and private munificence—his readiness at all times to maintain the common-weal, and those great principles of constitutional liberty for which he had fought and suffered so much, endeared him to all men; and during the bitter conflicts of party, like the bright and impenetrable helmet of Minerva, preserved his head from every hostile touch.

Such is the brief and imperfect narrative of the *career* of this wise and virtuous man, who was honored in his generation, and is now gratefully remembered by posterity. General PINCKNEY was twice married. His first wife was Sarah, daughter of Henry Middleton, second President of Congress. Of this marriage three daughters survived him. The second wife was a descendant of Sir Nathaniel Johnson, one of the Proprietory Governors of South Carolina. She died without children. General PINCKNEY expired in Charleston on the 16th August 1825, with the fortitude of a Christian philosopher, in his eightieth year.

SAMUEL CHASE.

THE REV. THOMAS CHASE, the father of the subject of these pages, was the only son of Samuel Chase, of a highly respectable family in Great Britain. At the age of eighteen Thomas was sent to Eaton College, where, by his close application and untiring zeal, he became a proficient in the Latin and Hebrew languages, and soon after he received the honors of the College. The professorship of those languages was tendered to him, which he gladly accepted, as his father had lately suffered some loss in his pecuniary affairs.

In 1738 he fled from the persecution of Cromwell to the Island of Jamaica, where he practised physic, which science he had studied during his leisure hours at Eaton. He remained in Jamaica but a few months, whence he sailed to the American Colonies; and Somerset County, Maryland, was the place he chose for his residence.

In January, 1740, he was married to Matilda Walker, the daughter of a respectable farmer. The fruit of this union was one son; and the day that presented Mr. CHASE an heir deprived him of his amiable helpmeet.

In 1743 Mr. T. Chase was honored with the appointment of rector of St. Paul's parish in Baltimore, whither he removed with his infant son, who had received the name of SAMUEL.

Deprived of the tender care of a mother, SAMUEL was the sole object of his father's love, and under the direction of this kind parent he received his education.

At the age of eighteen he went to Annapolis, where he studied law under the direction of John Hammond and John Hall; and in 1761 he was admitted to the Provincial Courts.

The year following he was married to Miss Anne Baldwin of Annapolis, a lady of distinguished merit, pious, amiable, affable and courteous. This union was blessed with six children, the objects of the love and pride of their parents. Samuel Chase, his second son, became a judge in the District of Columbia, and was very highly esteemed.

Mr. CHASE soon became distinguished as a lawyer, and engaged with great zeal in opposing the odious and oppressive measures of Great Britain.

In 1794 he commenced his public life in the General Assembly of Maryland, and was an active member of that body for upwards of twenty years.

He was among the first opposers of the Stamp Act, and engaged, in the most decisive manner, to frustrate its malignant effects. He was one of the framers of the famous "Declaration of Rights of Maryland," and its firm supporter.

His leisure hours were also devoted to his country, in arousing the people to a sense of their wrongs by essays and pamphlets.

In 1774 he was chosen a delegate to the first Congress.

In 1776 he was again chosen to represent Maryland in the general Congress; and it may be said that Maryland, who had refused her consent, was induced by his entreaties to unite in declaring the United States free and independent.

His whole conduct in this Assembly was marked by activity and zeal, and a firm adherence to the principles of liberty breathed forth in the Declaration of Independence.

The name of CHASE is found on many of the most important committees, and he was always at his post.

In 1782 he was appointed by the Governor of Maryland, Agent and Trustee of the State of Maryland to recover the stock in the Bank of England owned by the State; and for this purpose he proceeded to England, where he remained one year, enjoying the intimacy of Fox, Pitt, Burke, and other great luminaries of the day. It would not be amiss here to state that the late William Pinckney was a student in his office at this time. Young Pinckney styled Mr. CHASE his "Patron and his Friend."

In March, 1783, Mr. CHASE was married to Miss Hannah Kilty Giles, of London, by whom he had two daughters; the eldest, Eliza, the widow of Dr. Skipwith Coale, afterwards resided in Baltimore; and Mary, his second daughter, was married to the eldest son of Commodore Barney, and proved herself an American matron, worthy to be the daughter of Judge CHASE and daughter-in-law of a hero.

In 1786 the liberality of the late Col. John Eager Howard induced him to remove to Baltimore.

In 1791 he was appointed Judge of the General Court of Maryland,

SAMUEL CHASE.

and in 1793 he received the appointment of Judge of the Criminal Court for Baltimore County; but it being thought unconstitutional to hold these two offices, he resigned his seat in the General Court.

In 1796 General Washington offered him a seat on the Bench of the Supreme Court of the United States. It was in the discharge of his duties in this Court that faction armed his opponents, and he was arraigned at the bar of his country to defend his slandered character. His defence on this occasion has been pronounced the most able production of the bar of this country; Aaron Burr, then Vice-President of the United States, presided at this trial; and the even-handed justice he dealt out was always a subject of praise by Mr. CHASE.

The late Chief Justice Marshall, in a letter dated May 6th, 1834, to one of Judge CHASE's descendants, writes of Judge CHASE:—

"He possessed a strong mind, great legal knowledge, and was a valuable judge, whose loss was seriously felt by his survivors.

"He was remarkable also for his vivacity and companionable qualities. He said many things which were much admired at the time, but I have not treasured them in my memory so as to be able to communicate them."

Judge Duvall, in a letter of the same date, writes:—

"I knew Judge CHASE intimately, from the year 1775 until the time of his decease. At the commencement of the revolution, Mr. CHASE, as an advocate at the bar, was at least on a level with the ablest lawyers in Maryland, and in my judgment he never had a superior.

"He was constantly engaged in public life, and in legislative assemblies he was more able and powerful than at the bar.

"The late Chancellor Hanson always said that Mr. CHASE was the ablest speaker he ever heard in a legislative assembly; and Mr. Hanson was capable of forming a correct opinion.

"His knowledge increased with his years. During the Revolutionary contest it may be said with truth, that in Maryland he was the foremost in supporting American rights. Always at his post in the legislature, he took the lead: and his talents enabled him to be formidable and influential. His zeal and patriotism led him into many political controversies, all of which he maintained with ability.

"Mr. CHASE's opinions as a Judge of the Supreme Court are held in high estimation. Whilst on the bench of the General Court of Maryland, his opinions were applauded. He was an able civilian and jurist.

"The truth of these general remarks, as to Mr. CHASE's character is known to every man who lived in his time and during the revolution."

In his private life he was a kind husband, a fond parent, and a lenient master. For many months he had suffered under a severe disease, ossification of the heart, and had purposed a journey to the North for the benefit of his health; but on the day previous he was taken suddenly ill, he called for writing materials, but it was too late; and he died without making a will, on the 19th of June, 1811, at the mature age of seventy years, a great and good man.

OLIVER OTIS HOWARD.

OLIVER OTIS HOWARD was born in Leeds, Kennebec County, Maine, on the eighth of November, 1830. Like most New England boys who have become distinguished in the history of their country, he inherited the care and training of educated parents, whose estate was sufficient to render them independent without the enervating influences that sometimes accompany wealth. To the privileges of home were added those of the common school in an enlightened community. When nine years of age, he was left fatherless. Being the eldest of three sons, he shared with his discreet and Christian mother the responsibilities of the family.

He had inherited unusual energy of character, which was strengthened and developed by the circumstances of his youth. For a time he lived with his maternal uncle, the Hon. John Otis, of Hallowell, where he enjoyed ampler means of education. If his rustic independence sometimes brought him into collision with the haughty lads of the city, his courage did not suffer in the school of scorn. Whatever he undertook he pursued with an obstinate perseverance. When he had decided to enter college, he completed his preparations in six months, and was enrolled at Bowdoin at the age of sixteen. To meet his expenses, he won time enough, from the college terms, to teach school, still maintaining a high standing in his class, especially in Mathematics.

Graduated at the age of twenty, he received an unsolicited appointment as a cadet in the Military Academy at West Point. It was secured to him by his uncle, then a member of Congress. After much deliberation, and with due respect to his mother's dread of the military service, even in those times of peace, he took his place among the cadets, standing at the head of his class the first year, and finally graduating the fourth on the list. Despite all reproaches, he exhibited a moral earnestness in adhering to the highest principles of conduct. He married the accomplished Miss E. A. Waite, of Portland. He was assigned to the Ordnance Department, and for several years he served at various arsenals with honor to himself. While at the Kennebec Arsenal, he procured for the residents of the post the advantages of a public-school system.

In 1856 he was ordered to Florida, as the Ordnance Officer of the Department. General Harney was then prosecuting a campaign against the Indians, and there Lieutenant HOWARD had his first experience with an army in the field. He was afterwards called to West Point, to take the office of Assistant Professor of Mathematics, where he remained until the breaking out of the war. At West Point he won the respect of the Academic Board, as well as of his fellow-officers and all who knew him, by the consistent Christian character which he maintained. He was untiring in his benevolent labors among the poor at West Point and vicinity. He organized Mission Sunday-Schools, and in every manner possible promoted their religious welfare. He instituted semi-weekly meetings, for prayer and reading, among the cadets, in his leisure hours, thus winning esteem for his earnest Christianity.

When the call to arms first sounded through the land, in 1861, he believed it to be his duty to respond, although his position was most pleasant at West Point, and his family a treasure of bliss. Early in May he offered his services to the Governor of Maine. Scarcely waiting for an answer, he went to his native State, and was appointed Colonel of the Third Maine Regiment of Volunteers. By the fifth of June he was on his way to the seat of war, with his regiment complete in men.

In the first battle of Bull Run he commanded a brigade of four regiments. Held for some time as a reserve, he was among the latest to go into action. He led forward his brigade in two lines, under a severe fire, and displayed a coolness and courage remarkable for one in his first severe experience of war. He attempted to dislodge the enemy from a thickly wooded height, but was compelled to withdraw his brave men, because the flanking force of Johnston was pressing toward the rear.

In the following September he was commissioned a Brigadier-General of Volunteers. In the first advance to the Rappahannock he bore an active part, commanding a force in a reconnoissance, and driving before him the troops of the Confederate General Stuart, who had been his classmate and intimate friend at

OLIVER OTIS HOWARD.

West Point. The expedition was so conducted as to elicit the commendation of General Sumner.

In the Peninsular campaign, General HOWARD's brigade was the first to land at Ship Point, whence he moved up and joined the main army at Yorktown. It was his desire, after examining the works, to lead an assaulting column against them, believing that it would be successful, if done without delay. But other counsels prevailed. The first battle in which his brigade was thoroughly engaged, was that of Fair Oaks, June 1st, 1862, where the enemy, flushed with partial successes on the previous day, came furiously upon one of his regiments, in order to break through the lines. General HOWARD, in person, rallied his men, and re-established their position, which they gallantly held all the day. Soon after, he rapidly advanced under "a hail-storm of bullets," leading the brigade in person, and relieving a part of General French's line. Still pushing on, riding in front, and cheering the enthusiastic troops, he ordered a charge. They swept all before them. A musket-ball struck through his forearm, but he did not falter. Binding the severe wound with a handkerchief, given him by his aide and brother, Lieutenant C. H. Howard, he dashed forward on the second horse that had been wounded under him. His brother was soon disabled by a shot. Many gallant officers fell; many a brave soldier was slain. General HOWARD's horse was killed, and at almost that instant another ball broke through the elbow of the bandaged arm. He held up his wounded arm, and pointed forward; the troops raised the shout, and pushed onward. But the shattered arm fell like a dead weight at his side, and he was compelled to turn his command over to Colonel Barlow. The brigade had done its noble work, advancing considerably beyond the line of battle, and its progress was voluntarily stayed.

Without a horse, General HOWARD walked back until he found a surgeon, who began to afford some relief to his wound. Then seeing his wounded brother coming, leaning upon two soldiers, he seemed to say, as did the hero of Sutphen, "Thy necessity is yet greater than mine," and directed that attention should first be given to the Lieutenant. Toward evening, the General submitted to an amputation of his right arm, and the next day the two HOWARDS started for their home in Maine. Such was his persistent courage. It had some reward. All along the homeward route he was hailed as "the hero of Fair Oaks," and the citizens of his own town gave him a distinguished reception. His temperate habits promoted a rapid recovery. On the Fourth of July he delivered a patriotic oration of two hours' length, the first of those eloquent speeches which thrilled the hearts of a loyal people. During his sixty days' leave he contributed largely to enable Maine to raise its full quota of troops before any other State.

General Howard was again in the field at the second Bull Run battle, commanding the rear-guard of the army on the retreat from Centreville. In the Maryland campaign he performed valiant service at South Mountain; and after General Sedgwick was wounded at Antietam, he was given command of the second division. He restored the lines in conjunction with his artillery, and held the ground until victory decided the day against the enemy. Commanding this division at Fredericksburg, in December, he was the first to enter the town. After a severe fight in the streets, the enemy was driven from it to the heights. In the famous assault afterwards, his division was hotly engaged, gaining new ground, lying down and holding it until dark, and then intrenching.

General Howard's commission as Major-General dates November 29th, 1862. In April, the next year, he was assigned to the command of the Eleventh Army Corps, which met the brunt of the attack at Chancellorsville. His nine thousand men, in an advanced and exposed position, were overwhelmingly attacked by twenty-five thousand (according to the official reports of the enemy), and compelled to retire. The next great occasion in which General Howard was prominent, was the battle of Gettysburg. After General Reynolds was mortally wounded, his command was given over to General Howard, whose valor was often signally displayed. During one of the fiercest engagements, when it required the personal energy and moral power of both officers and men to maintain their lines and resist the advance of an encouraged enemy, and when the shot fell in showers, General Howard was recognized by his badge of the empty sleeve, galloping in front of a regiment, and shouting "Forward!" The soldiers raised a cheer of assent, pushed forward, and gained a position behind the stone walls or fences, where they resisted the advance of the foe.

When General Meade arrived, he rode with General Howard along his lines, examining by moonlight the grounds, and finally determining to bring the whole army forward and put it in position at that point. It was thus prepared, by having a well chosen position, for one of the grandest battles of modern times. General HOWARD occupied Cemetery Hill during the terrific cannonade of the two following days, when a hundred guns poured their fire upon the devoted spot. On the third day the enemy made an assault, advancing upon the very slope of the hill; and great credit was given to HOWARD's corps for their obstinacy in holding their ground, which was "the key to General Meade's position." The enemy could not dislodge them. Even when it was suggested that the troops must be withdrawn in order to save a remnant, General HOWARD persisted in defying the enemy. At his request General Meade came, inspected the ground, and assented to HOWARD's plan. This was one of the displays of courage on the part of the heroes who won the day at Gettysburg.

The Eleventh Corps was transferred to the Southwest, and was led by General Howard in the relief of Tennessee. His troops made the celebrated charge in the night engagement at Lookout Valley, which may be considered the initiative of the succeeding glorious charges up the steeps of Lookout Mountain and of Missionary Ridge. Those were heroic deeds amid romantic scenes; in one of them the battle was above the clouds. In the relief of Knoxville, this corps and its commander received the warmest private and official commendations of General Sherman. On the consolidation of the Eleventh and Twelfth corps, in April, 1864, General HOWARD was assigned to the command of the Fourth Army Corps, consisting of twenty-five thousand effective men, who bore an active part in all the operations of the Army of the Cumberland, and whose various successes were largely attributable to the energy of their leader, and his promptness in obeying orders. He was much younger than the three division-commanders, Stanley, Newton, and Wood, who were officers in the regular army, but they evinced the fullest confidence in the judgment and ability of their superior officer. The Fourth Corps did its full share of labor and fighting at various points on the contested route to Atlanta, rejoicing with General HOWARD in the confidence bestowed upon him by Generals Thomas and Sherman. At their recommendation, the President telegraphed his appointment as the successor of the fallen hero, General McPherson, and on the twenty-sixth of July he assumed the command of the Army of the Tennessee. Two days later he fought successfully the Confederate General Hood, defeating him in every assault. After brave conduct at Atlanta, he and his army spent a month of hard marching and fighting among the mountains in defeating Hood's attempts to get in the rear of General Sherman and destroy his communications.

In the grand march from Atlanta to the sea, General HOWARD's army composed the right wing, moving independently for the first two weeks, and Kilpatrick's cavalry reporting to him. He threatened Macon, while the left wing, attended by General Sherman, moved to Milledgeville. All went forward harmoniously and with triumph, as the whole world knows.

As there were no remarkable battles in this march, many have supposed that there were scarcely any conflicts with the enemy, or exposure to his fire. But collisions by heads of columns were of daily occurrence, and frequently the enemy was forced back step by step, having selected some advantageous spot, and disputing the ground obstinately for hours. General HOWARD was therefore daily exposed to musketry or artillery fire, before the fall of Savannah. The Confederates were particularly stubborn in disputing the passage of the rivers, always burning the bridges, and then posting themselves upon the opposite banks to annoy the Federal troops when they were attempting to lay their pontoon boats. New devices were often needed to meet the unexpected obstacles which an unknown topography presented. General HOWARD seems to have had a peculiar constitutional fitness for his position and duties in these campaigns. Regular and methodical in personal habits, he never failed to be punctual and prompt in carrying out his part of any plan. To this end he would bring to bear the whole force of his character, shrinking from no amount of exposure or labor; diligent, watchful, and untiring. Although small in stature, and not unusually hardy in constitution, yet his inviolate temperance in all things secured a physical strength and endurance equal to every occasion. And for the same reason there were never times of relaxation or reaction when he must be excused from duty or dangers.

The general features of the Carolina campaign were very similar to those of the march to Savannah. The heavy rains, and the more numerous streams, made it somewhat more difficult.

OLIVER OTIS HOWARD.

The burning of Columbia will always be regarded as the marked incident of this campaign. And as General HOWARD's troops occupied the city, and the General himself was present, it is proper to add a word upon this subject.

No one, it is believed, not even the greatest sufferers at Columbia, have ever held General HOWARD responsible for the burning of their city. There was cotton burning in the streets when the Union troops entered the town, set on fire by the Confederates on their retreat. One brigade was established by General HOWARD in the city, to preserve order and hold the town. Liquor was given to these soldiers on every hand — probably to conciliate them, as the inhabitants were wofully affrighted. A high wind afterwards sprang up, and very soon the fires began to break out. General HOWARD was soon in the streets, and meeting many drunken men, he decided to have that brigade removed from the city; and bringing in a fresh division of troops, he employed them all the night in endeavoring to stay the flames. In spite of every effort, the fire raged, and eighty-one squares were almost completely consumed.

Many of the citizens of Columbia, and of other towns along the route of the army, speak in terms of commendation of General HOWARD, because of his acts of kindness. If it were beyond his power to aid any worthy person who appealed to him, his whole demeanor was kindly, and every such person went away with a grateful remembrance of the interview.

He never lost sight of his duty as a Christian, although his time was devoted to the practices of war. In fact, his character was so permeated and lighted up by the Christian spirit, that it appeared in nearly all his acts and conversation.

His religion was a part of himself, and yet it found expression in habitual practices and exercises positively and exclusively religious. For instance, no matter how early the day's march commenced, or how late he was in the saddle at night, the day was begun and ended by prayer; and no matter what the circumstances of eating a meal, it was always preceded by an offer of thanks to the great Giver. It was his habit on Sundays, when not in battle or on the march, to summon a chaplain, assemble the various detachments of troops belonging to his head-quarters, and have a brief religious service. On these occasions he would sometimes himself address a few remarks, suggested by the service, to the soldiers and officers present.

Such words were eagerly listened to, and often these Sabbath services were deeply interesting and touching, and left an abiding impression upon those present. He also was accustomed to visit the hospitals on Sunday, when practicable, and not only spoke words of cheer and comfort to the sick and wounded, but was often strengthened and encouraged in turn by the heroic utterances and behavior of those brave men.

Soon after Lee's surrender, when he had arrived at Richmond with his army, having marched from North Carolina, General HOWARD was summoned to Washington by the Secretary of War, and, on his arrival, requested to take charge of the Bureau of Refugees, Freedmen, and Abandoned Lands. After a few hours' consideration he accepted the position, not without misgivings as to his own fitness and abilities for it, but with a firm reliance upon Divine help to aid him in its difficult and delicate duties, and sustain him in the arduous and untried responsibilities.

The appointment seemed to meet the approbation of the entire country. He was known to be humane, and at the same time to have proved himself able and efficient as an officer in every position held during the war.

Nothing had been done in the organization of this Bureau except the passage of the bill by Congress, and even this was found to be quite inadequate in some respects for practical operations. The work was almost superhuman, but the Commissioner gave his whole mind and might to his duties; and it is believed no one could have given better satisfaction to the Government or the people. In his tours of inspection he addressed both white and colored audiences, and by his conciliatory words and measures did much to reconcile the property owners and the freed laborers to their condition. Providence, who raised him up for victories in war, has committed to him the greater work of promoting peace, humanity, and happiness. In admiration of his noble character, he has been called the Havelock of the American army.

ROBERT R. LIVINGSTON.

ROBERT R. LIVINGSTON was descended from a family of historical celebrity in the annals of Scotland. Kings, regents, and nobles appear in the line of his ancestors, and probably no individual ever emigrated to the new world who could boast more numerous or more distinguished evidences of rank and title. James Livingston, in the middle of the fifteenth century, was appointed regent of Scotland during the minority of James I; his grand-daughter married Donald, king of the Hebrides, one of whose descendants is celebrated by the immortal pen of Sir Walter Scott, in his poem, the Lord of the Isles.

The titles of Earl of Newburgh, Earl of Linlithgow, Earl of Callander, and Earl Livingstone, given to several distinct members of this family, attest its standing and importance in the state, and add lustre to the honors of its name. Nor were they undistinguished in the early literature of their native country; and the name of Rollock, of kindred origin, occurs at the close of the sixteenth century as first principal of the celebrated University of Edinburgh.

Lord Livingstone was the common ancestor of that branch of the Livingstons, which emigrated to this country in the middle of the seventeenth century. He was hereditary governor of Linlithgow castle, in which Mary Queen of Scots was born, and in which she was placed for safety during the invasion of Scotland by the Duke of Somerset. His daughter was one of the four ladies who attended this princess to France as her companion. His great grandson, John Livingston, an eminent, learned, and pious minister of the Gospel, emigrated to Rotterdam in 1663, the victim of religious persecution, and was one of the commissioners of Scotland in the negotiations which eventuated in a general peace, and in the transfer of the colony of New York from the states of Holland to England.

Robert Livingston, his son, about the period of his father's death, in 1678, emigrated to America; and in 1686, obtained a patent for the manor of Livingston. The banks of the noble Hudson, on which it is situate, attest in its ornaments their taste and opulence. He was a member of the convention at Albany in 1689, which threw off, on the part of New York, the oppressive government of James II. In a visit to England, he held a conference with King William, Lord Chancellor Somers, and others, and prompted the enterprise against the pirates who then infested various parts of the American coast. The agent employed to effect this purpose proved treacherous to the trust, and, as is supposed, with the connivance of Robert Fletcher, the governor of the state. This agent afterwards became chief among the pirates, and is known in the popular traditions of the country by the name of Captain Kidd. The grandsons of Robert were, Philip Livingston, one of the signers of the Declaration of Independence, on the part of the state of New York; William Livingston, governor of New Jersey, known as a poet of high order, and still more estimable for his vigorous defence of the civil and religious rights of the colonies in council and by the pen. Robert Livingston's great-grandsons were, John H. Livingston, the father of the Reformed Dutch Church in America, and president of Queen's college, New Jersey; Brockholst Livingston, late one of the justices of the Supreme court of the United States; Edward Livingston, formerly secretary of the department of state; and ROBERT R. LIVINGSTON, the subject of our present memoir. The talents of this highly gifted family have had an ample field for their display and exertion. The colonial history of the state of New York records their elevated standing in its political affairs, and their noble resistance to those measures of oppression which arrived at their height during the early reign of George III, and which resulted in the independent sovereignty of America.

Chancellor LIVINGSTON was born in the city of New York, in 1747, and was educated in King's, now Columbia college, where he was graduated in 1764. He entered upon the study of the law in 1765, under the direction of William Smith, the historian of New York, at that time an eminent counsellor of law, and subsequently chief justice of Canada. Shortly after having obtained his license in that profession, he was appointed recorder of his native city. The trying question of the rights of the British parliament, in which we were unrepresented, to impose exactions on our citizens, then first began to be agitated; and the subject of our memoir, as well as his illustrious father, were both ejected from their official stations, the latter as one of the justices of the court of Oyer and Terminer, for adherence to the rights of their countrymen.

ROBERT R. LIVINGSTON.

In return for royal persecution, Chancellor LIVINGSTON was rewarded by popular favor and the confidence of his country. In the immortal congress of 1776, Mr. LIVINGSTON represented the feelings and interests of the people of the state of New York. In this consecrated assembly, his zeal and patriotism were universally acknowledged.

When, at the recommendation of congress, each state proceeded to frame a constitution of government, Mr. LIVINGSTON was elected a member of the convention of New York, and was the chairman of the committee who presented the draught of that instrument, which was subsequently adopted.

On the formation of the department of foreign affairs, in 1781, under the articles of confederation, he accepted the appointment of secretary, and served in that capacity with great diligence, promptness, and impartiality, until 1783, when, on retiring from office, he received the thanks of congress, and an assurance of the high sense they entertained of the ability, zeal, and fidelity with which he had discharged the important trusts reposed in him. The diplomatic correspondence of the revolutionary war, which has been published by Mr. Sparks, may be here referred to as documentary testimony to his cabinet services in our great contest.

Mr. LIVINGSTON was appointed chancellor of the state of New York in 1783, being the first who held that office under the state constitution; and he continued in this highest legal station in the state until his mission to France, in 1801. No published documents record the evidences of his laborious research and accurate discrimination. But we assert, on the testimony of a most distinguished successor to his office (Chancellor Jones), that the august tribunal, whose justice he dispensed, though since covered with a halo of glory, never boasted a more prompt, more able, or more faithful officer.

When at length the valor of our ancestors had borne them successfully through the revolutionary contest, and redeemed those pledges which had been offered on the altar of their country, another and a still more arduous task remained. In vain had our patriots moistened the soil with their blood, had our countrymen been left the victims to their own tormenting feuds and passions. The bond of union which united us during the period that tried men's souls, was almost rent asunder during the trials of peace. The legislature of Virginia, so early as in 1785, at the instance of Mr. Madison, who then first gave presages of his future greatness, had appointed commissioners, with a view to form commercial regulations for the general control of the states. Commissioners from several states met accordingly at Annapolis, the following year. From the want of adequate powers, they separated without effecting the object for which they were delegated. In 1787, on the recommendation of the Massachusetts delegation, composed of Francis Dana and Rufus King, was convened, at Philadelphia, that memorable assemblage of heroes and statesmen, who met to devise a plan of government which should convey the blessings of liberty to the latest generations. Of the plan of that national compact which now binds these states, Hamilton and Madison were the principal authors.

Of the convention which assembled at Poughkeepsie in 1788, Chancellor LIVINGSTON was one of the most efficient members, and prevailed in effecting its ratification by his native state; thus securing its adoption by the United States. We are now in the full enjoyment of its blessings. May no vaulting ambition on the part of our statesmen, or madness on the part of our people, ever put it in jeopardy for a moment. May it never be rendered oppressive by too liberal a construction of its powers: may it never be nullified by metaphysical refinement.

In April, 1789, the city of New York was the scene of one of the most solemn ceremonies recorded in the annals of America. The great Washington having conducted, to a successful issue, the momentous contest for independence, and the sages of our nation having elaborated a constitutional code of government, all eyes were directed to the illustrious hero, whose wise and sagacious counsels, no less than his valor, pointed him out as the most competent, under Providence, to guide the vessel of state in safety. When that venerated patriot was about to enter upon the duties of the highest office known to freemen, Chancellor LIVINGSTON became the witness of his solemn appeal to heaven, that the laws should be faithfully administered.

The appointment of Chancellor LIVINGSTON to the court of France, was one of the first acts of the new administration of Jefferson. Napoleon Bonaparte, the youthful conqueror of Italy, was at this time first consul of the French republic. At his court, which excelled in magnificence and splendor the most august courts of Europe, the chancellor at once conciliated the good feelings of that extraordinary man by the amenity of his manners, and promoted the best interests of his country by persevering and enlightened exertions. During the short-lived peace of Amiens, Paris was visited by the refined and intelligent from every part of the civilized world; and here the chancellor found leisure, amidst the duties of official station, to cultivate those ornate studies, for which that capital furnishes every facility. On the

ROBERT R. LIVINGSTON.

day of a great levée, which assembled at the Tuilleries, says the biographer of Fox, the numerous representatives of nations and strangers from every country, to pay their respects to the first consul of France, now established as the sole head of the government, the American ambassador, Mr. LIVINGSTON, plain and simple in manners and dress, represented his republic with propriety and dignity.

In that important negotiation with the government of France, which resulted in the acquisition of Louisiana, Chancellor LIVINGSTON was the prominent and efficient agent. Its transfer by the Spanish government to France, in 1802, had excited the most lively feelings of the American republic. By this unexpected measure, they were made the neighbors to a power, which, under the giant energies of the first consul, threatened, in case of rupture, the very existence of our republic. Immediately preceding the entrance into it of the French authorities, the Spanish powers prohibited the inhabitants of the western country the use of New Orleans as a place of deposite for their productions, contrary to the treaty with his Catholic Majesty. A universal spirit of indignation animated the American people; and there were not wanting those who recommended an immediate recourse to arms. The discussions on this question in the congress of the United States elicited debates, in which De Witt Clinton and Gouverneur Morris, representatives of the state of New York in the American senate, sustained the different views of the rival parties of this country. In pursuance of the sound counsels of those who urged the propriety of negotiation and peace, the executive of the United States deputed, as minister to the court of France, the late President Monroe; but previous to his arrival, Mr. LIVINGSTON, in an elaborate and interesting memoir, addressed to the French government, had prepared them for the cession of the greater part of Louisiana.

The result of Chancellor LIVINGSTON's efforts was prompt and successful. On the 5th April, the first consul announced to his bureau of state his determination to sell whatever of American territory he had obtained from Spain. Seven days afterwards, Mr. Monroe arrived in Paris, and gave the consent of the American government to this negotiation. The menacing posture of affairs between France and England facilitated the objects of these arrangements, and resulted in the transfer of the entire country to the American republic, for a sum less than was adequate for the preparation of a single campaign.

By this important treaty, contrary to the anticipations of the timid or interested, the confederacy of our states was placed on an invulnerable basis; territory was added to our country, nearly equal in extent to that of the original states of our union; and the blessings of free government secured to millions, who had otherwise groaned under the vassalage of foreign dominion. The vast deserts of Louisiana are daily becoming the cheerful residence of an intelligent and christian population, with American blood flowing in their veins, and beating responsive to republican feelings; and the field of New Orleans is now added to those of Bunker Hill, Stillwater, and Chippeway, as trophies of American valor and patriotism.

After the signing of this eventful treaty, the three ministers arose, says one of them (the Count Marbois), when Mr. LIVINGSTON, expressing the general satisfaction, said, with prophetic sagacity, " We have lived long, but this is the noblest work of our whole lives. The treaty which we have just signed has not been obtained by art, or dictated by force; equally advantageous to the two contracting parties, it will change vast solitudes into flourishing districts. From this day, the United States take their place among the powers of the first rank; the English lose all exclusive influence in the affairs of America. Thus one of the principal causes of European rivalries and animosities is about to cease. The United States will reëstablish the maritime rights of all the world, which are now usurped by a single nation. These treaties will thus be a guarantee of peace and concord among commercial states. The instruments which we have just signed, will cause no tears to be shed; they prepare ages of happiness for innumerable generations of human creatures. The Mississippi and Missouri will see them succeed one another, and multiply, truly worthy of the regard of Providence, in the bosom of equality, under just laws, freed from the errors of superstition and the scourges of bad government."

The consequences of this act did not escape the penetration of the first consul. " This accession of territory," said he, " strengthens for ever the power of the United States, and I have just given to England a maritime rival, that will sooner or later humble her pride."

The official duties of resident minister at Paris did not prevent Chancellor LIVINGSTON from bestowing his attention to those objects of taste congenial to his feelings, and beneficial to his country. To the American Academy of Fine Arts, established in New York, in 1801, he added the excellent collection of busts and statues which are now the boast of that institution, and was instrumental in procuring, from the liberality of the first consul, its rich paintings and prints. He continued through life devoted to its interests, and was for many years its chief officer. To the Transactions of the Society for the

ROBERT R. LIVINGSTON.

Promotion of Useful Arts, established in 1793, chiefly through his exertions, he contributed many appropriate papers, and, during his residence abroad, enriched our agriculture with the improvements of French husbandry.

The last effort of his pen was his paper on Agriculture, written but a few days before his fatal illness. In this spirited essay, he vindicates the climate, soil, and capabilities of his native country. He shows the value of horticultural labor, and demonstrates the reciprocal connections between agriculture and manufactures. The inherent fertility and the indigenous resource of the country, are the themes of his admiration and eulogy. He was among the earliest, with Judge Peters, to employ gypsum as the means of fertilizing soils; and the introduction of clover, and a better breed of domestic cattle, attest his vigilant and enlightened zeal.

One other benefit conferred on mankind, will, of itself, convey the name of Chancellor LIVINGSTON to the remotest posterity; his coöperation with Robert Fulton, in effecting the successful application of steam navigation, the most important improvement since the invention of printing.

"The connection between Livingston and Fulton," says the late lamented Clinton, "realized, to a great degree, the vision of the poet. All former experiments had failed, and the genius of Fulton, aided and fostered by the public spirit and discernment of LIVINGSTON, created one of the greatest accommodations for the benefit of mankind. These illustrious men will be considered, through all time, as the benefactors of the world."[*]

The leisure hours of Chancellor LIVINGSTON were devoted to every variety of science, arts, and literature. The heroic authors of antiquity, Homer and Virgil, Demosthenes and Cicero, were among those which contributed to improve his taste and expand his thought and feeling. His historical researches were various and extensive. All this was not effected without unremitting industry. Every interval of time afforded from the duties and cares of public life, was devoted, with scrupulous fidelity, to add to his stores of knowledge. Like the Chancellor D'Aguesseau, in variety of pursuit he found that relaxation which others seek in pleasure and amusement.

The style of his oratory was chaste and classical, and of that persuasive kind which the father of poetry ascribes to Nestor. All who were witnesses, testify to the mute attention with which he riveted his

---

[*] Clinton's Discourse before the American Academy of Fine Arts.

auditors. But he chiefly delighted in the pathetic, and often, by his appeals to the sympathies of his hearers, counteracted the most powerful prejudices. His acknowledged integrity and patriotism doubtless added force to all he uttered. Franklin termed him the American Cicero: in him were united all those qualities which, according to bat illustrious Roman, are necessary in the perfect orator.

After a life, every portion of which was devoted to the benefit of his fellow-man, he paid the last debt to nature, at his seat, at Clermont, on the 26th of February, 1813.

Thus it appears, from this imperfect tribute, that the late Chancellor LIVINGSTON was an active agent in the most momentous events that have influenced the destinies of mankind. Of the congress of 1776, which resolved that these states were free and independent, he was a distinguished member, and belonged to that committee which framed the declaration of our grievances and rights, — and which will transmit their names to the latest posterity; of the convention of New York which formed the constitution of that state — the best devised scheme of polity then known to the world; of a subsequent convention, which ratified the constitution of the United States, devised by the wisdom of Hamilton and Madison; the important actor in a negotiation, which doubled our country in extent, and rendered it for ever secure from foreign intrusion; the coadjutor in that noblest of all improvements in mechanics, by which time and space are annihilated—the invention of steam navigation.

In Mr. LIVINGSTON, to the proud character of integrity, honor, and disinterestedness, were added the mild, yet ennobling features of religion. An inquiring believer in its truth, an exemplar of its gentle effects on the character, he daily sought its consolations, and strengthened his pious resolutions in the rich inheritance it promises. He was devoted to the Protestant Episcopal Church, from an enlightened preference of its doctrines and discipline, without hostile feelings to those who trust to other guides in religion than Chillingworth and Hooker.

Chancellor LIVINGSTON, at the time of his death, was in the 66th year of his age. His person was tall and commanding, and of patrician dignity. Gentle and courteous in his manners, pure and upright in his morals. His benefactions to the poor were numerous and unostentatious. In his life, without reproach; victorious in death over its terrors.

J. Q. Adams

JOHN QUINCY ADAMS.

In giving a sketch of the career of JOHN QUINCY ADAMS, the limits of our work require us almost entirely to confine the narrative to a bare recital of the successive leading events of his life. It is difficult to contemplate his history, without yielding to the impulses of the feelings and the imagination, and expatiating on the interesting reflections and meditations which, at every stage of his course, crowd into the mind, and demand expression. So protracted, however, was his public life, so full was it of important services, and so various were the stations in which his great talents were displayed, that the concisest narration of them will be kept, with difficulty, from too fully occupying our pages. His illustrious parents have been already duly commemorated in our work; and it will therefore be unnecessary to dwell upon their merits. He was born in Braintree, in Massachusetts, in that part of the town since incorporated by the name of Quincy, on Saturday, July 11, 1767, and was baptised the next day, in the congregational church of the first Parish of Braintree. He was named John Quincy, in consequence of the interesting circumstance that his maternal great-grandfather of that name, who was the owner of Mount Wollaston, and a leading civil and military character of his times, in honor of whom the town of Quincy received its name, was actually dying at the time of his birth.

In the eleventh year of his age he accompanied his father to France, who was sent by Congress, as joint commissioner, with Benjamin Franklin and Arthur Lee, to the court of Versailles. They sailed from Boston in February, 1778, and arrived at Bourdeaux early in April. While in France, he was, of course, put to school, and instructed in the language of that country as well as in the Latin. After about eighteen months, they returned to America in the French frigate La Sensible, in company with the Chevalier de la Luzerne, who came out as the minister of France to the United States. They arrived in Boston on the first of August, 1779. In November of the same year his father was again despatched to Europe, for the discharge of diplomatic services, which he rendered to the cause of America with such signal and memorable ability and success. He again took his son out with him. It seemed to be the determination of that great patriot, not only to do and to dare every thing himself for his struggling country, but to keep his son continually at his side ; so that, by sharing his perils and witnessing his toils, he might become imbued with his own exalted enthusiasm in the cause of liberty, and be prepared to promote and vindicate it with all the energies of his genius and all the sensibility of his soul. It is easy to imagine the exciting influences which must have operated upon the character of a youth at that susceptible and impressible age, accompanying such a father through the scenes in which he acted while in Europe, and the dangers he encountered in his voyages across the Atlantic. In one of these voyages, the ship in which they were embarked was under the command of the famous naval hero Commodore Tucker, and the whole passage was a succession of hazardous exposures and hair-breadth escapes from hostile squadrons and tempestuous gales.

While the younger Adams was receiving the impressions made upon him by a participation in the patriotic adventures and exertions of his father, and imbibing the wisdom and intrepid energy of spirit for which he was so distinguished, the same effect was still more heightened and deepened by the influence exerted upon him by the inculcations and exhortations to every public and private virtue contained in the letters of his mother. When he was thirteen years of age, while in France with his father, she addressed him in the following noble strains :—" It is your lot, my son, to owe your existence among a people who have made a glorious defence of their invaded liberties, and who, aided by a generous and powerful ally, with the blessing of heaven, will transmit this inheritance to ages yet unborn; nor ought it to be one of the least of your excitements towards exerting every power and faculty of your mind, that you have a parent who has taken so large a share in this contest, and discharged the trust reposed in him with so much satisfaction as to be honored with the important embassy that at present calls him abroad. The strict and inviolate regard you have ever paid to truth, gives me pleasing hopes that you will not swerve from her dictates ; but add justice, fortitude, and every manly virtue which can adorn a good citizen, do honor to your country, and render your parents supremely happy particularly your ever affectionate mother."

The opportunities and privileges of an education, under such au

JOHN QUINCY ADAMS.

spices, were not thrown away upon him, as the incidents of his subsequent career most amply prove.

In going to Europe this second time, he embarked with his father at Boston, in the same French frigate, La Sensible, bound to Brest; but as the ship sprung a leak in a gale of wind, it was necessary to make the first port they could, which was Ferrol in Spain. They traveled from that place to Paris by land, and arrived there in January, 1780.

The son, of course, was immediately placed at school. In July of that year, Mr. Adams removed to Holland. There his son was introduced to the public city school at Amsterdam, and afterwards to the University at Leyden. In July, 1781, Mr. Francis Dane, who had accompanied John Adams as Secretary of the embassy with which he was charged, received the commission of minister plenipotentiary to the Empress of Russia, and took JOHN QUINCY ADAMS, then fourteen years of age, with him as his private Secretary. Here the younger Adams remained until October 1782, when he left Mr. Dane at St. Petersburg, and returned through Sweden, Denmark, Hamburg, and Bremen, to Holland. Upon this journey he employed the whole winter, spending considerable time by the way, in Stockholm, Copenhagen, and Hamburg. He reached the Hague in April, 1783, and continued several months in Holland, until his father took him to Paris, where he was at the signing of the treaty of peace, which took place in September of that year, and from that time to May, 1785, he was, for the most part, with his father in England, Holland, and France.

At his own solicitations, his father permitted him, when eighteen years of age, to return to his native country. Soon after reaching America, he entered Harvard University, at an advanced standing, and was graduated with distingiushed honor, as Bachelor of Arts, in 1787. He then entered the office of the celebrated Theophilus Parsons, at Newbury Port, afterwards chief justice of Massachusetts; and after the usual period of three years spent in the study of the law, he entered the profession, and established himself in Boston.

He remained in that situation four years, occupying himself industriously in his office, extending his acquaintance with the great principles of law, and also taking part in the public questions which then occupied the attention of his countrymen. In the summer of 1791 he published a series of papers in the Boston Centinel, under the signature of Publicola, containing remarks upon the first part of Paine's Rights of Man. They suggested doubts in reference to the favorable issue of the French Revolution, at a time when most other men saw nothing but good in that awakening event. The issue proved the sa gacity of Publicola. These pieces were at first ascribed to his father. They were reprinted in England.

In April, 1793, on the first information of war between Great Britain and France, and before Washington had published his proclamation of neutrality, or it was known that such a step was contemplated by him, Mr. ADAMS published in the Boston Centinel three articles signed Marcellus, the object of which was to prove that the duty and interest of the United States required them to remain neutral in that war. In these papers he developed the two principles, which have ever been the basis of his creed as a statesman; the one is UNION at home, the other INDEPENDENCE of all entangling alliances with any foreign states whatever.

In the winter of 1793–4 he published another series of political essays, confirming, and more fully developing these views, and vindicating the course of President Washington in reference to the proceedings of the French minister, Genet.

In May, 1794, he was appointed by Washington, without any intimation of such a design, made either to him or to his father, minister resident to the United Netherlands. It was supposed at the time that he was selected in consequence of his having been commended to the favorable notice of Washington, as a suitable person for such an employment, by Mr. Jefferson.

From 1794 to 1801 he was in Europe, employed in diplomatic business, and as a public minister, in Holland, England, and Prussia. Just as President Washington was retiring from office, he appointed him minister plenipotentiary to the court of Portugal. While on his way to Lisbon, he received a new commission, changing his destination to Berlin. He resided in Berlin from November 1797 to April 1801, and while there concluded a highly important treaty of commerce with Prussia, thus accomplishing the object of his mission. He was then recalled, just before the close of his father's administration, and arrived in Philadelphia in September, 1801.

In 1802 he was elected, from the Boston district, a member of the Massachusetts Senate, and was soon after appointed, by the legislature of that state, a senator in the Congress of the United States for six years, from the 4th of March, 1803. As his views of public duty led him to adopt a course which he had reason to believe was disagreeable to the legislature of the State he represented, he resigned his seat in March, 1808. In March, 1809, President Madison nominated him Envoy Extraordinary and Minister Plenipotentiary to the Court of Russia.

JOHN QUINCY ADAMS.

Some time previous to this, however, in 1806, he had been appointed Professor of Rhetoric in Harvard University, at Cambridge in Massachusetts. So extraordinary were his powers of elocution, so fervid his imaginative faculties, and so rich his resources of literature and language, that his lectures, which were afterwards published in two octavo volumes, were thronged not only by the students of the university, but by large numbers of the admirers of eloquence and genius, who came from Boston and the neighboring towns to listen to them. During his whole life Mr. ADAMS cultivated the graces of elocution, and, in addition to his profound and varied knowledge of the sciences, of the ancient and modern languages, and of the literature and history of all nations, he was an eminent Orator as well as Poet.

While in Prussia, he furnished to the Port Folio, printed in Philadelphia, and to which, from the beginning to the end, he was an industrious anonymous contributor, a series of letters, entitled a "Journal of a Tour through Silesia." These letters were republished in London, without the permission of the proprietor of the Port Folio, in one volume octavo. They were reviewed in the journals of the day, and translated into French and German.

Mr. ADAMS signalized himself while in Russia, by an energetic, faithful, and wise discharge of the trust committed to him. He succeeded in making such an impression upon that government, by his reasonings and influence, that it has ever since been actuated by a feeling of kindness towards the United States, which has been of incalculable benefit to this country. It was through his instrumentality that the Russian Court was induced to take active measures to promote a pacification between England and the United States during the last war. When the proper time came, he was named at the head of the five commissioners who were appointed by President Madison to negotiate a treaty of peace with Great Britain. This celebrated diplomatic transaction took place at Ghent, in December, 1814. Mr. Adams then proceeded, in conjunction with Henry Clay and Albert Gallatin, who had also been associated with him in concluding the treaty of peace, to negotiate a convention of commerce with Great Britain; and he was forthwith appointed by President Madison minister plenipotentiary at the Court of St. James.

It is a most remarkable coincidence that, as his father took the leading part in negotiating the treaty that terminated the Revolutionary war with Great Britain, and first discharged the office of American ambassador to London, so he was at the head of the commission that negotiated the treaty that brought the second war with Great Britain to a close, and sustained the first mission to that country upon the return of peace. After having occupied that post until the close of President Madison's administration, he was at length called home, in 1817, to the head of the department of State, at the formation of the cabinet of President Monroe.

Mr. ADAMS's career as a foreign minister terminated at this point. It has never been paralleled, or at all approached, either in the length of time it covered, the number of courts at which he represented his country, or the variety and importance of the services he rendered. His first appointment to the office of a minister plenipotentiary was received at the hands of George Washington, who, in nominating him, acted in accordance with the suggestion of Thomas Jefferson. James Madison employed him in the weightiest and most responsible trusts during his whole administration, selected him to represent the United States at the two most powerful courts in the world, St. Petersburg and London, and committed to his leading agency the momentous duty of arranging a treaty of peace with Great Britain. It is enough to say, that throughout this long and brilliant career of foreign public service, he deserved, and received from his country, the encomium which Washington pronounced upon him, when, in 1797, he declared him "the most valuable public character we have abroad, and the ablest of all our diplomatic corps."

The public approbation of Mr. Monroe's act in placing him at the head of his cabinet, was well expressed by General Jackson, at the time, when he said that he was " the fittest person for the office; a man who would stand by the country in the hour of danger." While Secretary of State, an office which he held during the eight years of President Monroe's administration, he discharged his duties in such a manner as to increase the confidence of his countrymen in his ability and patriotism. Under his influence, the claims on Spain were adjusted, Florida ceded to the Union, and the republics of South America recognised. It will be the more appropriate duty of his future biographer to present a full view of the vast amount of labor which he expended, in the public service, while managing the department of state.

In the Presidential election, which took place in the fall of 1824, Mr. ADAMS was one of the candidates. No candidate received a majority of electoral votes. When, on the 9th of February, 1825, the two houses of Congress met in convention, in the hall of the House of Representatives, to open, and count, and declare the electoral votes, it was found that *Andrew Jackson* had 99 votes, JOHN QUINCY ADAMS, 84 votes, *William H. Crawford*, 41 votes, and *Henry Clay*

37 votes. According to the requirements of the constitution, the Senate then withdrew, and the House remained to ballot for a President until a choice should be effected. They were to vote by States; the election was limited to the three candidates who had the highest electoral votes, and the ballotting was to continue without adjournment until some one of the three had received the votes of a majority of the States. As Mr. ADAMS had received as many popular votes as General Jackson, the circumstance that the latter had obtained a large electoral vote had not so much weight as it otherwise might have had; and when the ballotting was about to begin, it was wholly uncertain which would be the successful candidate. The whole number of States was twenty-four. The votes of thirteen States were necessary for a choice. At the first ballot, it was found that *Maine, New Hampshire, Massachusetts, Rhode Island, Connecticut, Vermont, New-York, Maryland, Ohio, Kentucky, Illinois, Missouri,* and *Louisiana,* thirteen states, had voted for " JOHN QUINCY ADAMS, OF MASSACHUSETTS ;" and he was accordingly elected PRESIDENT OF THE UNITED STATES for four years from the 4th of March, 1825. A committee was appointed forthwith to inform him of his election, who, the next day, reported the following letter in reply to the communication :

" GENTLEMEN,

" In receiving this testimonial from the Representatives of the people and states of this Union, I am deeply sensible to the circumstances under which it has been given. All my predecessors in the high station, to which the favor of the House now calls me, have been honored with majorities of the electoral voices in their primary colleges. It has been my fortune to be placed, by the divisions of sentiment prevailing among our countrymen on this occasion, in competition, friendly and honorable, with three of my fellow-citizens, all justly enjoying, in eminent degrees, the public favor: and of whose worth, talents, and services, no one entertains a higher and more respectful sense than myself. The names of two of them were, in the fulfilment of the provisions of the constitution, presented to the selection of the House in concurrence with my own; names closely associated with the glory of the nation, and one of them further recommended by a larger minority of the primary electoral suffrages than mine. In this state of things, could my refusal to accept the trust, thus delegated to me, give an immediate opportunity to the people to form and to express, with a nearer approach to unanimity, the object of their preference, I should not hesitate to decline the acceptance of this eminent charge, and to submit the decision of this momentous question again to their determination. But the constitution itself has not so disposed of the contingency which would arise in the event of my refusal; I shall therefore repair to the post assigned me by the call of my country, signified through her constitutional organs; oppressed with the magnitude of the task before me, but cheered with the hope of that generous support from my fellow-citizens, which, in the vicissitudes of a life devoted to their service, has never failed to sustain me—confident in the trust, that the wisdom of the Legislative Councils will guide and direct me in the path of my official duty, and relying, above all, upon the superintending Providence of that Being 'in whose hand our breath is, and whose are all our ways.'

"Gentlemen: I pray you to make acceptable to the House, the assurance of my profound gratitude for their confidence, and to accep yourselves my thanks for the friendly terms in which you have communicated their decision.

"JOHN QUINCY ADAMS."

"*Washington*, 10*th* Feb. 1825."

The time is approaching when justice will be done to the administration of JOHN QUINCY ADAMS. The passions of that day are already fast subsiding, and the parties and combinations that arose under the exciting influences of the times, have long since been dissolved and scattered. The clear verdict of posterity may almost be heard, even now, in the general acknowledgment of its merits by the people of the country, in all its various sections. In the relations he sustained to the members of his cabinet, in his communications to the two houses, and in all his proceedings, there is a uniform manifestation of wisdom, industry, moderation, and devoted patriotism. Of course we do not speak of party questions, or refer to the operations or bearings of the parties of that period; but say only what we conscientiously believe will be assented to heartily by candid and honorable men of all parties. The great effort of his administration was to mature, into a permanent system, the application of all the superfluous revenue of the Union to internal improvement. This policy was first suggested in a resolution introduced by him, and adopted by the Senate of the United States in 1806; and was fully unfolded in his first message to Congress in 1825. It will be the duty of the philosophical historian of the country, a half century hence, to contrast the probable effects upon the general prosperity, which would have been produced by such a system of administration, regularly and comprehensively carried out, during the intermediate time, by the government of the Union, with what will then be seen to be the results of the policy which has prevailed over it.

In retiring from the Presidency in 1829, Mr. ADAMS returned to his family mansion in Quincy, where he remained, in quiet retirement, until he was called into public life, once more, by the people of the congressional district to which he belonged. He took his seat in the House of Representatives of the United States in 1831, where he continued till his death in the most indefatigable discharge of the duties of his station. However much some of his opinions might be disliked by large numbers of his countrymen; however strenuous the collision into which he was, from time to time, brought with those whose policy or views he might oppose; there was but one sentiment of admiration, throughout the entire Union, of the vigor, the activity, the intrepidity, the patience and perseverance of labor, the talent, the learning, and the eloquence which he continually exhibited. He knew neither fear nor fatigue; prompt, full, and fervid in debate, he was ever at his post; no subject arose upon which he did not throw light, and few discussions occurred which were not enlivened by the flashings of his genius and invigorated by the energy of his spirit. While he belonged to no party, all parties in turn felt the power of his talents; and all it is probable, recognized him as an extremely useful as well as interesting member of the great legislative assembly of the nation.

When he resumed his senatorial duties, he had reached the period of life when most men begin, if not to lose their power to engage in the arduous struggles of life, at least to lose their interest in them. But it was not so with him. Neither his natural force nor his natural fervor abated. His speeches and writings continued as full of fancy and of feeling as they were in his early manhood. As a scholar, his attainments were various, we might almost say universal, and profound. As a political controversial writer, he never found his equal; and his services as a public orator were called for on great occasions even to the last, when he came forward in all the strength of his intellectual energy, and with the imperishable richness and inexhaustible abundance of his rhetorical stores. When Congress were apprized of the death of General Lafayette, the unanimous voice of both Houses summoned him to the high and memorable duty of pronouncing their grateful eulogium upon that friend of America and champion of mankind. And at the call of the municipal authorities of the city of Boston, he pronounced funeral orations in commemoration of the departed worth of Presidents Monroe and Madison.

NATIONAL PORTRAITS.

At the time of Mr. Adams' first acceptance of a seat in the Senate, there were those among his best friends who doubted the policy of the step, and who feared the consequences to himself of a voluntary exposure at his age, to collision with the turbulent men more or less generally found there. They all lived to confess their mistake, as well as to acknowledge that without the latter portion of his career, Mr. Adams' fame would have lost an essential element. With no personal party, with no inducements of self-interest to hold out to others to follow him, and with strong prejudices, growing out of past contests, to overcome, he nevertheless made good his attitude of independence, and at times wielded a controlling influence over the House. One of his eulogists has marked out as the greatest event in his life, that decisive stroke of his which evoked order out of chaos at the opening of the twenty-sixth Congress. But others will be more inclined to believe that his steady and determined maintenance of a fundamental principle of republican government in the freedom of petition, in opposition to all the power of the House and the interests of both the great parties, until he actually succeeded in procuring the formal rescinding of the obnoxious rule of the House which had denied it, furnishes the most useful as well as the most noble example of moral heroism in politics which has yet been given in America. Neither did he in the end suffer in the popular estimation by his action. The tides of feeling in a republic flow swiftly, no matter how often they change their direction. He, who in 1837 narrowly escaped a vote of censure, if not a formal expulsion from an excited majority, whom at first the press and the people alike appeared to deplore, if not to condemn, but six years afterwards, when undertaking a private excursion for the gratification of once seeing the falls of Niagara before his death, became, most unexpectedly to himself, the hero of a species of ovation. Crowds every where turned out to meet him on his way, and to testify their admiration of the qualities he had shown in the great struggle. Nothing of the kind had happened since the reception of La Fayette. The people lauded in him a virtue valued in America for its rarity in public life quite as much as for its intrinsic worth. Like a plant which has survived and grown up from among thousands trodden under foot, firmness is estimated by the success it has met with in resisting. It can never be an attribute of the popular favorite of an hour, who lives only in sunshine, and whose self-reliance is never strong enough to fortify both his will and his power to outride a storm. Yet the intimate friends of Mr. Adams had good reason to suspect that he valued the applause of men quite as highly as he ought, and as the commonest demagogues do. The difference was in his mode of reaching it, which was never like theirs, graduated by a fear of the popular censure. He delighted in bold methods of *forcing* their approbation, by appealing to high principles, the power of which they could not fail to bow to in the long run, however disposed they might be for the moment to resist their application. He was fond of the position of a champion of a good cause against great odds, as well because it afforded a broad field for the exercise of his extraordinary dialectics, as because he felt sure that ultimately the victory would rest with the right.

Time wore on; and the bonds which unite the soul with the body were gradually but perceptibly losing their elasticity, though the spirit continued unconquered and vigorous as ever. It was not until the month of November, 1846, that a distinct notion of his mortality was presented to the mind of Mr. ADAMS. As he was leaving the house of his son in Boston, to make a visit in company with a friend, the late Dr. Parkman, to the spot which was not very long afterwards destined to witness that friend's singular and lamented murder, a shock of paralysis suddenly deprived him of all power of motion. But when he recovered his senses, so little conscious was he of the evil which afflicted him, that he was searching for causes entirely of a temporary nature to account for it. Slowly did the painful truth force itself upon his mind. But when at last it came, he immediately prepared himself to meet it, first, by perfecting his final disposition of all worldly matters, secondly, by resolutely setting about a plan of recovery. Day after day, as he accurately measured his returning strength, his chief regret seemed to be that it did not come up to his expectations, or respond to his exertions. Yet he did wonders with his exhausted frame. In the middle of November, he was lying in Boston hovering between life and death, with his physicians daring only to hope a partial restoration after a long period of prostration. In the middle of February succeeding, he had so far conquered the enemy as to resume his seat in the House of Representatives at Washington, with a return of thanks, for the cordial and warm greeting that immediately on his showing himself interrupted the formal proceedings of the day. From that date he fell into his usual habits of life, conceding as little as possible to the serious inroad that had been made on his vigor. And for a time his constitution seemed to respond to the demands he was making on it. He returned to the excitement of politics, and to the irregular hours of Washington life, which had become to him a second nature, instead of seeking to form new habits of mental repose and regular sustenance of a physical system so nearly worn out. The consequence was not immediate, but when it came it was decisive. As he rose in his place in the House of Representatives on the 21st of February, 1848, apparently with the design of making some motion or remark, he was observed first to hesitate and then to fall. The fatal bolt had sped. He was borne off to the Speaker's room, and was heard to utter the words "the last of earth," after which he never spoke more. The vital powers continued partially to act until the 23d, when Mr. ADAMS ceased to breathe. He had not been removed from the capitol.

The suddenness of this event, the place in which it occurred, the circumstances attending it, the high character and long public services of the deceased, all conspired strongly to excite the public attention. For several days little was done in either House of Congress. Not only were the funeral obsequies among the most impressive ever witnessed in Washington, but they were in one sense extended to great length by a formal vote of the House of Representatives, organizing a committee of one member from each state, for the purpose of following the remains to their last resting place at Quincy. As the procession passed through the three great cities, crowds followed it in each, and when it reached Boston, Faneuil Hall was thrown open as the fitting place temporarily to receive the body. At last on the 11th of March, they were transferred to and finally deposited at Quincy, with appropriate ceremonies in presence of the committee, and an eloquent sermon from Dr. Lunt, the pastor of the church of which Mr. ADAMS had been a member. Numerous tributes were paid to his memory in all parts of the Union, in the form of eulogies and resolutions of public bodies, all going to show the sense of the nation, that one of its greatest and purest characters had ended his course with honor and been gathered to his reward.

During his long life of almost eighty-one years, Mr. ADAMS was distinguished not only by faithful attention to all the great duties of the high stations he was called to fill, but to all their minor ones. As president, as member of the cabinet, as minister abroad, he examined all questions that came before him, and examined all, in all the minutiæ of their detail, as well as in all the vastness of their comprehension.

In the observance of all the proprieties of life, Mr. ADAMS was a noble example. In the exercises of the school and of the college—in the meetings of the agricultural, mechanical, and commercial societies, —in attendance upon Divine worship,—he gave the punctual attendance rarely seen but in those who are free from the weight of public cares. It is believed to have been the wish of his heart to die, like Chatham, in the midst of his labors, and the wish was gratified.

Louisa Catherine Adams

LOUISA CATHERINE ADAMS.

IN our Republic, where the principle of distribution is perpetually at work against the long continuance of property in the hands of any race of individuals, the duties of the female sex may be generally expected to prove too burdensome to admit of great devotion to pursuits exclusively literary or political, or even to that species of social influence which, in other countries, has not unfrequently made women the arbiters of weal or woe to a nation. The position in life of the greater number, is determined by the accident of marriage, and depends upon the success of exertions more often made by their partners after than before that event. Mere wealth is rather an obstacle than an aid to the acquirement of the distinction most coveted in America, while political success often attends him in advanced age, who has, in early days, struggled hard with poverty, and devolved upon a wife, selected perhaps with sole reference to the most ordinary duties of life, all the drudgery of domestic cares. The duties of a housekeeper, a wife, and a mother, while they make every woman who faithfully executes them respectable in the eyes of the world, do not, when exclusively pursued, so well fit her to shine upon that brilliant theatre of politics and fashion to which she may yet be called. This may in part account for the somewhat remarkable absence of female biography in the annals of our nation, and for the little power which appears hitherto to have been exerted by individuals of that sex in the circles of American society. At the same time it ought never to be forgotten that the greatest praise is due to those, who have been by circumstances distinguished above the rest, for having, as well by example as by precept, so rigidly preserved the standard of our morality pure; in this manner earning for themselves a far more substantial claim to the public gratitude, than all the fame which ever grew out of the brilliant salons of the corrupt society in the French metropolis.

Mrs. LOUISA CATHERINE ADAMS in early life enjoyed advantages not usual at that period to American ladies. The daughter of Joshua

Johnson, a citizen of the colony of Maryland, engaged in commercial pursuits in London, she was born in that city on the 12th of February, 1775. Mr. Johnson, although established in the mother country when the Revolution commmenced, was not one of those who took sides with her, and settled into the character of refugees and exiles from their native land. While his brother, Thomas Johnson, took a leading part at home, both in the Colony and as a delegate to the first Congress, and the remaining members of a numerous family were actively engaged in the war which ensued; he, himself, retired from Great Britain to Nantes in France. There he received, from the federal congress, an appointment as commissioner to examine the accounts of all the American functionaries then entrusted with the public money of the United States in Europe; in the exercise of the duties of which he continued until the peace of 1782. Our National Independence having then been recognised, he returned to London, where he continued to reside, and where he acted as consular agent for the United States, until his final return, in 1797, to his native soil.

It thus happened that the early years of Mrs. ADAMS were passed partly in Great Britain and partly in France, from each of which she derived advantages of observation, and opportunities for accomplishment in mind and manners, not very common with her countrywomen of that day. These eminently fitted her for the part she was in after-life called to perform. In the house of her father in London, then a general resort of all Americans, who, whether for business or pleasure, frequented that metropolis, she was introduced into society; and it was here that Mr. John Quincy Adams, when commissioned by President Washington to exchange the ratifications of the Treaty of 19th November, 1794, and to agree upon arrangements for carrying some of its provisions into execution, found her. The dry details of diplomatic conference were relieved by evenings of social intercourse, and the formalities of British negotiation made less tedious by the awakening of the most agreeable sympathies. Mr. Pinkney arrived, and Mr. Adams became released from his official duties; but in the mean time a matrimonial engagement had been contracted, which, on the 26th day of July, 1797, that is, the year following these events, terminated in a marriage, at the church of All-Hallows, where Miss Johnson became Mrs. ADAMS.

The discriminating eye of President Washington marked out Mr. Adams, while a young lawyer, in Boston, writing political essays upon the leading topics of that day, as fit for the public service. For some years prior to this marriage, he had been occupying the station of minister resident at the Hague, and the eminent ability of his official despatches confirmed the impression he had previously made. It procured for him the very honorable and confidential trust which carried him to London, as well as a subsequent promotion to be Minister Plenipotentiary to Lisbon. He was upon the eve of departure at the period of his marriage, when the accession of his father, John Adams, to the Presidency, occurred. This was productive of no advancement, but simply of a transfer from Lisbon in Portugal, to a similar station at Berlin in Prussia.

Perhaps it is not easy at this time to form a just estimate of the position occupied by representatives of the United States at the Courts of the sovereigns of Europe at the period now referred to. We were regarded as hardly more than successful rebels, whose example was not entirely of good omen, and as yet manifesting in our local discord and disorganization, rather an incapacity for regulating a well-ordered State, than any prospect of arriving at a station of much political weight. Under such circumstances, the appearance of representatives at courts, to which none had before been sent, was an event not merely to excite curiosity. It was known that a new government, having some appearance of stability, had been organised, at the head of which had been placed General Washington; and the first impressions obtained from his administration were to be strengthened or not, according to the efficiency of the agents he might think proper to employ. To Berlin, where no minister had before been acknowledged, Mr. Adams repaired, conducting his wife, as a bride, at once to play her part in the higher circles of social and political life. It need scarcely be added, that she proved perfectly competent to this; and that during four years, which comprised the period of her stay at that court, notwithstanding almost continual ill-health, she succeeded in making friends and conciliating a degree of good will, the recollection of which was, till the time of her death, believed to be among the most agreeable of the associations with her varied life.

In 1801, after the birth of her eldest child, she embarked with Mr. Adams on his return to the United States. The revolution which had taken place in the political affairs of the country, determined him to resume the practice of the law in Boston, to which place she came, a stranger to the habits and manners, though not to the feelings, of the people about her. Scarcely had sufficient time elapsed to become at home, before she was called upon to follow the wandering fortunes of the wife of a United States' senator. Very fortunately for her, a sister had become established at Washington, in whose house she again met the members of her own family, and thus found an agreeable home for those winter months, which other ladies, similarly situated, are rarely so happy as to enjoy. Almost always accompanying Mr. Adams, the alternative of Boston in summer and Washington in winter, continued with little intermission until the year 1808, when he resigned his seat in the senate of the United States. But in the ensuing year, 1809, a new revolution in her prospects and another scene awaited her. Mr. Adams was appointed by President Madison the first accredited minister to the empire of Russia; and as he was required to embark forthwith, she decided upon going with him, even at the cost of leaving with their grand-parents two of her children, to pursue their education at home, and taking only the third and youngest, then an infant of about two years old. They sailed from Boston early in August, and after a long and somewhat hazardous passage, arrived in St. Petersburg towards the close of October.

Here, again, Mrs. ADAMS was destined to be the first lady presented to the notice of the Russian court as a representative of American female manners and character, and here again she succeeded in making a favorable impression. But there were circumstances which rendered her abode at St. Petersburg much less agreeable to herself than it had been at Berlin. The great distance from America was not the only obstacle to communication. The extraordinary events which occurred in Europe at this period, rendered the difficulties much greater than usual in obtaining that information respecting those whom she had left behind, which was essentially necessary to cheerfulness; and the severity of the winter climate, together with the more formal and less friendly character of Russian society, did not contribute to its acquisition. Domestic sorrow, too, in the loss of an infant daughter, born during her stay there, threw its shadow over the scene. What universal anxiety marked the era, it is difficult in these quiet times to realise! For the civilized world was in arms; and while at one moment the desolating progress of Napoleon had almost touched the city in which she was then dwelling, and from which its own sovereign, the Emperor Alexander, was meditating a retreat; at another, the thunders of the British cannon were resounding from the walls of the American capital, within which her friends resided. Here were lessons of human vicissitude, in different quarters of the globe, which might well fix the mind in the contemplation of dark views of fortune, as well as the insecurity even of existence.

In this connection it is not unworthy of remark, that of all those persons sent from the United States as envoys to the court of St. Petersburg since Mr. Adams, whose stay was of nearly six years, but one (Mr. Middleton) has been content to remain for any period of considerable duration. The reason may probably be traced to the diametrical opposition of the Russian habits to those of our own country, the harshness of the climate, and to the exclusion, for so many of the winter months, from any thing approaching to social communication with home. Hence, high as this mission is held in the rank of political distinctions, it comes in no very long time to be felt by the incumbent as an expulsion from American society little short of an honorable exile. Mr. and Mrs. ADAMS were themselves anxious to return home long before they did, but were prevented by circumstances, which made their stay even more disagreeable. The principal of these was the general war. The offer made by Alexander, of mediation between Great Britain and the United States, promised at one moment to make St. Petersburg the seat of negotiation, but it was subsequently transferred to Ghent; and thither Mr. Adams was directed to proceed, to take his part as one of the commissioners. This was in April, 1814, and the fate of the attempt at reconciliation appeared so doubtful, and the state of Europe so unsettled, that it was deemed best he should go alone. Thus, in addition to all the causes of a general or temporary character, which make a Russian winter, in ordinary cases, something of a trial, Mrs. ADAMS was destined to pass her sixth season alone—separated from her husband, and from all the other relatives or friends who had accompanied her out, but who had one by one dropped off to find their way home. This was not agreeable, but there was no alternative.

Spring, however, brought with it cheerful tidings of the probability of peace and of departure. The general pacification preceded the particular treaty between Great Britain and the United States concluded at Ghent but a short time; and upon this Mrs. ADAMS received a proposition to proceed at once by a land journey to Paris there to rejoin her husband. To accept it, notwithstanding the difficulties which might be in the way of execution, was the work but of a moment. For to her mind, what could be the terror of a solitary journey through the late theatre of a furious and bloody war, the plains and villages still bearing palpable evidence of its horrors, compared with that charming prospect of a return to more genial climes, to the company of an affectionate husband, and an approximation towards her long-absent children.

Those who knew Mrs. ADAMS in her later days only, will not be likely to imagine her as by nature robust, or by education bold. And yet few women of the age ever underwent more extraordinary fatigue in her various journeys, or displayed more energy in the accomplishment of her undertakings. None, however, was so well calculated to test the strength of her nerves as that now in question. The passports of the Russian Government, however strong, and the reflection upon herself of the diplomatic character of her husband, however sacred, would, even in the most quiet times, have scarcely overcome, with many of the delicately nurtured female sex, the apprehensions of a departure in a carriage, alone, at a season still early for travelling, with a son eight years of age to take care of, and only menial servants of untried, and, as it proved, of very doubtful fidelity for her guard. In such circumstances, to be fastened in a snow-drift with night coming on, and to be forced to rouse the peasants of the surrounding country to dig them out, which happened in Courland, was no slight matter. But it was of little significance compared to the complicated anxieties incident to the listening, at every stopping place, to the tales of robbery and murder just committed on the proposed route, so perpetually repeated at that time to the traveller; and to the warnings given by apparently friendly persons of the character of her own servants, corroborated by the loss of several articles of value; and, most of all, to the observation of the restless contention between jarring political passions, under which the whole continent of Europe was heaving until it burst forth at the return of Napoleon from Elba. Hardly a day passed that did not require of Mrs. ADAMS some presence of mind to avoid becoming implicated in the consequences of party fury. For even the slight symbol of a Polish cap on the head of her servant came near making food for popular quarrel. Such was the sensibility of the public mind at the time.

A less determined woman, upon hearing of the condition into which France was thrown by Napoleon's return, would have stopped short at some intermediate point, without venturing to complete her undertaking. Not so with Mrs. ADAMS. She dismissed her servants, both of whom professed to be themselves afraid of going further, procured others, and went on. But she had not gone very far before she unluckily found herself entangled with a considerable detachment of the wild soldiery, elated to excess by the arrival of their great chief, and then on its way to Paris to prepare, under his inspection, for that last scene of slaughter, the field of Waterloo. This was a very awkward position, as the troops seemed disposed to require from all around them the most unequivocal declaration of political faith. Mrs. ADAMS at once appealed to the commander of the detachment, and by his advice she was enabled to fall back, although not without the exercise of considerable prudence, until the last of the men had passed, when she diverged into another road, and by making a considerable circuit, avoided any further meeting. Having proved in this manner that calmness and presence of mind render many things perfectly practicable which imagination at first invests with insuperable difficulties, she arrived in Paris safe and well, there to be greeted by her husband, on the evening of the 21st of March, 1815, immediately after that of the memorable arrival of Napoleon and the flight of the Bourbons.

The beginning of the celebrated hundred days! What an exciting moment to reach the French capital! crowded as it was with troops, collecting for the impending trial at arms, and its streets alive with that enthusiasm which, in its highest degree, it appears to be only within the scope of military heroism to excite. Whatever may have been the feeling throughout the country, there could not be a shadow of doubt in the mind of any spectator, that in the affections of the populace of Paris, as well as of the army, Napoleon was an idol. While, on the one hand, his appearance but for a few instants upon one of the balconies of the palace of the Tuilleries, was a signal for acclamation from the thousands who frequented its gardens to gain a glimpse of him; on the other, curses loud and deep, not unmingled with ridicule and contempt, were every where to be heard uttered against Louis and the allies. Here was room for observation to last a lifetime! Here was room for testing even the contrasts of this world; for at one and the same moment the splendid reviews of a cavalry force rarely surpassed, were filling the square of the Place Carousel with its loudest and most spirit-stirring notes, and the yet unremoved collections of what the genius of centuries had hallowed, were spreading around them in the halls of the Louvre a sense of the solemn stillness and repose of the highest walk of art. Mrs. ADAMS was capable of appreciating the advantages thus thrown in her way; and to her, whose European life had carried her very little to the great French metropolis, this opportunity of seeing it at such a period, well rewarded her effort to reach it, and was ever considered among the most fortunate events in her existence.

But, however interesting Paris might be, there were ties in Great Britain to Mrs. ADAMS, where her husband's new duty as the Minister from the United States called him, which made her leave France with little regret. These ties were her children, who had come out from America to join her, and whose arrival afforded her a joy, for the absence of which no brilliant scenes could compensate. In itself, a residence in England so immediately after a war between the two countries, which had terminated not quite to the satisfaction of her pride, was not calculated to be productive of much pleasure; yet it may fairly be questioned whether, in the bosom of her reunited family, and in the sweet and modest country-seat in the vicinity of London selected for their habitation, Mrs. ADAMS did not draw as much enjoyment from her domestic feelings, as she ever did from witnessing any of the more busy and exciting scenes in which she had been called to participate.

Two years thus elapsed, when the election of Mr. Monroe to the Presidency became the precursor of another change. One of his first official acts was the appointment of Mr. Adams to the responsible station of Secretary of State in his administration, and this, of course, required his immediate return to the United States. Upon receiving the intelligence, he took passage with his family in a vessel bound from London to New-York, where he arrived on the 6th of August, 1817, after just eight years of absence from his native country. Mrs. ADAMS thus took leave of Europe, after having passed in it the greater portion of her life, and that during a period, perhaps, as remarkable for a crowded succession of astonishing events as any in the history of man. To have lived in such times, so distinguished for the presence of all that exalts, adorns, or merely gives lustre to human action, was something of a privilege; but to have moved in scenes so various and so distant from each other, among the principal agents in all the great events at different points, was the lot among American ladies of scarcely any, excepting Mrs. ADAMS. Nevertheless she returned to our republican circles unwedded to the habits of a court, her mind unawed by the splendor either of civil or military monarchy.

The performance of the duties of the State department necessarily required a residence at Washington, and the manner in which Mr. Adams thought proper to devote himself to them, devolved upon his lady the entire task of making his house an agreeable resort to the multitudes of visiters who crowd to the capital on errands of business, or curiosity, or pleasure, from the various sections of the United States, during the winter season. A large diplomatic corps from foreign countries, who feel themselves in more immediate relations with the Secretary of State, and a distinguished set of public men, not then divided by party lines in the manner which usually prevails, rendered the society of that time, and Mrs. Adams's house, where it most often concentrated, among the most agreeable recorded in our annals. Much as it has been ridiculed since, the "era of good feelings" had some characteristics peculiar to itself. For an instant, sectional animosities relented, the tone of personal denunciation and angry crimination, too generally prevailing in extremes, yielded; and even where the jealous rivalry for political honors still predominated in the hearts of men, the easy polish of general society removed from casual spectators any sense of its roughness, or inconvenience from its impetuosity. Washington may have presented more brilliant spectacles since, but the rancor of party spirit has ever mingled its baneful force too strongly, not to be perceptible in the personal relations which have existed between the most distinguished of our political men.

During the eight years in which Mrs. Adams presided in the house of the Secretary of State, no exclusions were made in her invitations, merely on account of any real or imagined political hostility; nor, though keenly alive to the reputation of her husband, was any disposition manifested to do more than to amuse and enliven society. In this, the success was admitted to be complete, as all will remember who were then in the habit of frequenting her dwelling. But in proportion as the great contest for the Presidency, in which Mr. Adams was involved, approached, the violence of partisan warfare began to manifest its usual bad effects, and Mrs. Adams became inclined to adopt habits of greater seclusion. When, at last, the result had placed her in the President's mansion, her health began to fail her so much, that though she continued to preside upon occasions of public reception, she ceased to appear at any other times, and she began to seek the retirement, which after her return to private life she always preferred. Mr. Adams continued till the time of his death, a representative in Congress from the State of Massachusetts, and this rendered necessary an annual migration from that State to Washington, and back again, as well as a winter residence within the sound of the gaieties of that place; but while her age and health exempted her from the necessities of attending them, severe domestic afflictions soon contributed to remove the disposition. Thus the attractions of great European capitals, and the dissipation consequent upon high official station at home, though continued through that part of life when habits become most fixed, contributed nothing to change the natural elegance of her manners nor the simplicity of her tastes. In the society of a few friends and near relatives, and in the cultivation of the religious affections without display, she derived all the consolation which can in this world be afforded for her privations. To the world Mrs. Adams presented a fine example of the possibility of retiring from the circles of fashion, and the external fascinations of life, in time still to retain taste for the more quiet, though less showy attractions of the domestic fireside. A strong literary taste, which had led her to read much, and a capacity for composition in prose and verse, furnished resources for her leisure moments, not with a view to that exhibition which renders such accomplishments too often fatal to the more delicate shades of feminine character, but for her own gratification, and that of a few relations and friends. The late President Adams used to draw much amusement in his latest years at Quincy, from the accurate delineation of Washington manners and character, which was regularly transmitted, for a considerable period, in letters from her pen. And if, as time advanced, she became gradually less able to devote her sense of sight to reading and writing, her practice of the more homely female virtues of manual industry, so highly commended in the final chapter of the book of Solomon, still amused the declining days of her varied career.

Mrs. ADAMS survived the shock occasioned by the demise of her husband, with whom she had celebrated the golden wedding day,— the fiftieth anniversary of their union,—more than one year, when on the 12th of April, 1849, she also experienced a severe paralytic affection not unlike that by which he had been first stricken down. She partially recovered, remaining disabled, in the power of active exertion. The city of Washington, where she had been attacked, now became her permanent place of residence, and she remained in retirement from the world, seeing and seen by only a few intimate friends and relatives, who could still rejoice in the cheerfulness and the patient resignation which she manifested under her privations. Blessed with the retention of her intellectual faculties to an unusual degree in that disease, at her advanced age, she continued for three years more to present an example of quiet and contented infirmity, as touching as it was beautiful, and a religious submission which shed a softened glow over the close of her brilliant day. Life terminated on the 15th of May, 1852, when she calmly passed away, just as the clock which she especially valued as a memorial of her departed companion, was striking twelve.

Such was the respect entertained for the character of Mrs. ADAMS in Washington, where, from having spent in it the greater part of the last five and thirty years, she was the most known, that both Houses of Congress spontaneously voted to adjourn over for the sake of attending her funeral, an honor never before paid to an American matron. The number of citizens who voluntarily followed her remains to their resting place, more strikingly testified her worth, than can do all the pomp and circumstance of woe not unfrequently lavished upon such as office has clothed with power, or wealth has supplied with favors to bestow.

Edward Everett

EDWARD EVERETT.

EDWARD EVERETT was born in Dorchester, Norfolk County, Massachusetts. His father, Oliver Everett, was the son of a farmer in the town of Dedham in the same county, and descended from one of the original settlers of that place, who came to this country about the year 1635. The family still remains in Dedham, like their predecessors for five generations, respectable cultivators of the soil. Deprived by the narrow circumstances of the family of early opportunities of education, Oliver Everett succeeded in preparing himself for college after he came of age. He graduated at Cambridge in 1779, at the age of twenty-eight, was settled at the New South Church in Boston in 1782, and left the ministry in 1792 on account of ill health. President Allen in his Biographical Dictionary speaks of his "high reputation" and of "the very extraordinary powers of his mind." He retired to a small farm in Dorchester, and was made a judge of the court of common pleas for Norfolk county. He died on the 19th of December 1802, at the age of fifty-one

EDWARD EVERETT, the subject of this memoir, was the fourth in a family of eight children. The late Alexander H. Everett, minister to Spain, and afterwards commissioner to China, was an older brother. EDWARD was born on the 11th of April, 1794. His education, till he was thirteen years of age, was obtained almost exclusively at the public schools in Dorchester and Boston, to which latter place the family removed after his father's decease. He mentions, however, in his speech in Faneuil Hall, on occasion of the death of Mr. Webster, that he was for a short time a pupil of the distinguished statesman, who took the place of his brother, Ezekiel Webster, for a few weeks at a private school kept by the latter in Boston. In February, 1807, he was sent to the Academy at Exeter, in New Hampshire. Here, under the tuition of the celebrated Dr. Abbott, he completed his preparation for college. He entered Harvard University in August of that year, and graduated in 1811, with the highest honors of his class, and with a reputation which has seldom been attained at so early an age. After leaving college, he continued at Cambridge in the pursuit of theological studies. He filled the place of Latin tutor for about a year, and at the age of nineteen was settled for a short time in the ministry at Boston, during which time he wrote and published a "Defence of Christianity," an elaborate and most able work, displaying an extent of erudition which would be thought worthy of admiration in a scholar of mature age. In 1815, he was chosen professor of Greek Literature in Harvard University, and was permitted, for the improvement of his health and preparation for his new duties, to visit Europe, and pass some time at the principal foreign universities.

He embarked in one of the first vessels which sailed from Boston after the peace with England. Remaining in London till after the battle of Waterloo, he then left for Germany with his friend and townsman, Mr. George Ticknor, the distinguished author of the History of Spanish Literature. After passing a short time in the principal Dutch cities, they went to Göttingen, at that time the most celebrated of the German universities, where they remained two or three years. The vacations were employed in excursions to the principal cities and universities of the North of Germany. During his residence in Germany, Mr. EVERETT became acquainted with a considerable number of the most eminent literary and scientific men of the day, including Goethe, Blumenbach, Gauss, Heeren, Wolf, Hermann, Boeckh, Eichhorn, Hugo, and other celebrities.

Having completed his residence in Germany, he spent the winter of 1817–18 in Paris, engaged in philological pursuits, with free access to the immense treasures contained in the Royal library. He enjoyed the society of such men as Visconti, Alexander Humboldt, Benjamin Constant, Sismondi, Koray, and General Lafayette. In the spring of 1818, he went over to England, passed some time at the universities of Cambridge and Oxford, visited Wales, the Lakes, and Scotland, and passed a few days with Sir Walter Scott at Abbotsford, and with Dugald Stewart. During this visit to England, he became acquainted with many of the most distinguished literary and political characters, besides those just named, such as Sir James Mackintosh, Lord Jeffrey, Lord Holland, Lord Byron, Sir Humphrey Davy, and William Gifford.

In the fall of 1818 he returned to France, and in company with his friend and townsman, the late Hon. Theodore Lyman, commenced an extensive tour. They went first to Switzerland, and after making the usual tour through the Cantons, crossed the Simplon to Milan, passed through Lombardy to Venice, and thence to Florence and Rome. The winter was spent at Rome in careful study of the antiquities of the city and neighborhood. While at Rome he saw much of Canova, of the mother of Napoleon and the other members of the Bonaparte family, including the ex-king of Holland, and his son the present emperor, then a lad of twelve or fourteen years of age.

In the latter part of the winter of 1818–19, still accompanied by General Lyman, he went to Naples; and after visiting the places of interest in the neighborhood, including Pestum, they crossed to Bari on the Adriatic, and thence traveled on horseback through a country little visited, without carriage-roads or public conveyances, and much infested by brigands, by the way of Lecce to Otranto. From this place they took passage to Corfu, and thence crossed to the coast of Albania. At Yanina they were received with great kindness by the aged vizier Ali Pacha and his son Muctar. Mr. EVERETT bore letters to the famous Albanian chief from Lord Byron. Crossing Mount Pindus and penetrating the vale of Tempe, after a visit to Veli Pacha at Turnavo the capital of Thessally, they went to Thermopylæ, and took the road over Parnassus to Delphi, Thebes and Athens. They then made an excursion into the Morea, and returning to the North, embarked in the Gulf of Volo for Constantinople, stopping by the way at the plain of Troy. This tour took place about ten months before the war with Ali Pacha which brought on the Greek revolution.

Towards the end of June they left Constantinople to return homeward, passing the Balkan mountain not far from the route afterwards taken by the Russian army. Crossing the Danube at Nicopol, they went to Bucharest, the capital of Wallachia, and entered the Austrian dominions at the pass of Rothenturn. Having passed a week's quarantine in the secluded vale of the Aluda, at the foot of the Carpathian mountains, they proceeded to Hermanstadt the capital of Transylvania, and thence through the Banat of Temeswar, across Hungary to Vienna. After a short residence at the capital of the Austrian empire, they traversed the Tyrol and Bavaria, and returning by the way of Paris and London, took passage for America in September, 1819. The whole time spent by Mr. EVERETT in his studies and travels in Europe and Asia was above four years and a half, more than half of which was passed at the university of Göttingen.

Shortly after his arrival in Boston, he was solicited to assume the editorial charge of the North American Review. Its number of subscribers, at that time, was inconsiderable. The effect produced by him upon its circulation was instantaneous, and great beyond parallel in our literary history. Many of its numbers passed into a second and even a third edition. He gave it an American character and spirit; and such was the tone he imparted to it, that it commanded, not only the admiration and applause of his own countrymen, but the respect and acknowledgments of foreign critics and scholars. He defended our institutions and character with so much spirit and power, that the voice of transatlantic detraction was silenced; and in one memorable instance, an apology to the people of the United States was drawn from Campbell the poet, at that time, the editor of a British periodical. His editorial connection with the North American Review lasted four years, from 1819 to the close of 1823; but he continued to contribute to its pages for several years. It has been enriched by the contributions of many of our ablest scholars, but no single writer did so much in its earlier stages, to secure and maintain its high stand and widespread influence as EDWARD EVERETT. If he had written nothing else, his articles in that journal would constitute a monument of genius, eloquence, erudition and patriotism, which would secure to him an enviable reputation. His lectures on Greek literature, delivered to the students of Harvard University, are remembered with respectful gratitude by all whose privilege it was to be connected with the college during his continuance in office there.

While residing at Cambridge he kept up a correspondence with his learned friends abroad, and particularly with the scholars and patriots of Greece. It was at his solicitation that Mr. Webster brought the subject of the Greek revolution before congress, in December, 1823. His articles in the North American Review, and other public appeals, did much to awaken the interest which was felt throughout the country in the struggle for Grecian independence.

In the year 1824, he delivered an oration before a literary society at Harvard University. The presence of General Lafayette, then on his tour throughout the United States, gave great interest to the occasion. This was the first of a long series of occasional addresses delivered by Mr. EVERETT. It established his fame as an orator. About this time a vacancy occurred in the representation of the congressional district to which Cambridge belongs. The most influential politician in the district was put in nomination as the regular candidate. A few young men met at Lexington, and made a volunteer nomination of EDWARD EVERETT. It was cordially responded to by the people of Middlesex, and he was chosen by a very large majority.

The old party lines were at this time obliterated. Nearly the whole of

EDWARD EVERETT.

New England had united in the election of John Quincy Adams. Mr. EVERETT, in common with nineteen-twentieths of the people of Massachusetts, was a supporter of his administration. In December, 1825, he took his seat in congress, to which he was reëlected for the four following terms, by great majorities. He was from the first one of the most laborious members of the house. For the whole period of ten years he was a member of the committee of foreign affairs, and for a part of the time its chairman. Even when not chairman he drew many of its reports; among others that on the Panama Mission, the principal subject of debate at the first session of the nineteenth congress. After having made two or three reports on the subject of the claims of American citizens on foreign powers for spoliations committed upon our commerce during the French continental system, he continued to discuss the subject in the North American Review. He finally collected all the facts and arguments on the subject in reference to each foreign power, and published them in a separate volume. Much of the credit of having finally procured the adjustment of those claims is due to him, for the manner in which the subject was thus kept before the public mind.

He was chairman of the select committee, during Mr. Adams's presidency, on the Georgia controversy; and always took a leading part, while in congress, in the efforts that were made to protect the Indians from injustice. In the spring of 1827 he addressed a series of letters to Mr. Canning on the subject of the colonial trade, which were extensively re-published. He always served on the library committee and generally on that for the public buildings. Together with the late Hon. John Sergeant, he constituted the minority on the famous retrenchment committee. He drew the report for the committee in favor of the heirs of Fulton. Together with Governor Ellsworth of Connecticut, he constituted the minority of the bank investigating committee, which was despatched to Philadelphia, and wrote the minority report. He wrote the minority report of the committee of foreign relations in reference to the controversy with France, in the spring of 1835; distinguished himself by the high ground he took on the subject in debate; and supplied the words of the resolution unanimously passed in reference to it, by the house of representatives. He also, at the same session, prepared a statement on French spoliations prior to 1800, which was printed by order of the house.

Such were some of his congressional labors. He was emphatically there, as everywhere, a working man. He made himself perfectly acquainted with every subject that came before the house. His speeches and reports exhaust all the facts and arguments that belong to their topics. His manner of speaking was simple, elegant, and persuasive; and always secured attention. He was firm and steadfast in his political course; but urbane, respectful, and just toward his opponents. He disarmed his enemies, and was faithful to his friends; and his whole deportment was consistent with the history of his life, and will be readily acknowledged by his associates, of every party, to have been every way becoming the gentleman, the scholar and the patriot.

In the interim of congress, during the summer of 1829, he made an extensive tour through the south-western and western states, and was everywhere received with marked attentions, having been honored by public dinners in Tennessee, Kentucky and Ohio, without distinction of party.

On the election of Governor Davis to the senate of the United States, Mr. EVERETT was nominated as his successor in the chief-magistracy of Massachusetts and chosen by a large majority in the autumn of 1835. He was afterward three times reëlected. Among the measures introduced and matured during his administration were the subscription of the State to the stock of the Western Rail Road, which insured the execution of that great work; the organization of the Board of Education and the foundation of Normal schools, both measures of very great importance and utility in reference not merely to the schools of Massachusetts but of the United States generally; the scientific and agricultural surveys of the commonwealth, by which much light was thrown upon its productive resources; and the establishment of a commission for the revision of the criminal law. These measures were all suggested by Governor EVERETT, and materially promoted by his concurrence and support.

In the autumn of 1839, after four years of successful and highly popular administration, local questions connected with the license laws and the militia defeated his reëlection. Judge Morton, who for a long course of years had been an unsuccessful candidate for the office of governor of Massachusetts, succeeded by one vote out of more than one hundred thousand.

Thus relieved from public duty, Mr. EVERETT was led by domestic reasons to visit Europe a second time. He sailed with his family in June 1840. They passed the summer in France, and the following year in Italy, principally in Florence and its vicinity. It was their intention to remain in Italy another winter. The presidental election in November, 1840, having resulted in the election of General Harrison and the appointment of Mr. Webster as secretary of state, Mr. EVERETT was in the course of the summer sent as minister of the United States to the court of St. James. Our relations with England at that time were in a most critical condition. The controversy relative to the north-eastern boundary had reached a point of extreme irritation on both sides, and one at which further amicable discussion seemed almost hopeless. The more recent affairs of the burning of the "Caroline" and the arrest of M'Leod had, both in the United States and in England, greatly excited the public mind. A correspondence of a very uncompromising character had passed between the British minister and Mr. EVERETT's predecessor on the seizure and detention of American vessels on the coast of Africa by British cruisers. It is a striking proof of the confidence placed in his discretion, that, as we learn from his late speech on the affairs of Central America, he was sent to London to discuss all these questions, without any specific instructions from the government of the United States, every thing being left to his own judgment and knowledge of the various subjects.

Many other questions of great magnitude and interest were also pending between the two governments, some of a private nature relating to the claims of individuals, others of a public character. The most important of the last class was the question relative to the construction of the first article of the convention between the two countries on the subject of the fisheries. After an elaborate correspondence of a year or two, Mr. EVERETT obtained from the British government the concession of the right of American fishermen to fish in the bay of Fundy. This concession has been pronounced by competent authority the only one ever obtained by the United States from Great Britain on the subject of the fisheries. It is scarcely necessary to say that what was yielded by Great Britain as a concession was claimed by Mr. EVERETT, on the most conclusive grounds, as the right of the United States under the convention of 1818.

In the spring of 1843, when it was determined by the United States to send a minister to China to open the intercourse with that country on the new basis, Mr. EVERETT was selected by the president and senate for this important trust, which appointment he declined. He also received full powers from the president for the final adjustment of the Oregon question. The English government had, however, in the meantime, sent Sir Richard Pakenham to Washington with a view to the transfer of the negotiations to this country.

On the return of Mr. EVERETT to the United States in the autumn of 1845, he was immediately appointed president of Harvard university, and after much hesitation accepted the office. Having kept up his literary pursuits and tastes, and always taken a practical interest in education, even during the most active period of his life, there was much that was congenial to him in this new sphere of duty. He had scarce ever ceased to be in some way connected with the college since he entered it as a boy in 1807. His administration lasted three years and was of the highest value to the institution. He devoted to its service all the enthusiasm inspired by his earliest associations; all the ardor of his character; his habits of severe application to business; and the mature fruit of the studies and experience of his life. It was a matter of deep regret to his friends, and the friends of the institution, that the trivial and burdensome details of official duty and of the discipline of the college so wore upon his health, as to compel him at the end of three years to tender his resignation.

Mr. EVERETT devoted a portion of his leisure time after resigning the presidency to the preparation of the edition of his orations and speeches, which appeared in two volumes octavo, in 1850. This collection contains a series of addresses on almost every variety of public occasion, scattered over a period of more than a quarter of a century. Among them are several speeches delivered at public meetings in England, and received with great favor by the most enlightened audiences in that country.

When it was proposed to issue a new edition of the selected works of Mr. Webster, the superintendence of the publication was, at Mr. Webster's request, undertaken by Mr. EVERETT. The first volume of the collection contains a detailed memoir of the public life of the great American statesman. This work was, in all respects, a labor of love. They had been from an early period the most intimate personal friends, and at a later period confidential associates in political life. In the speech in Fanueil Hall, to which we have already alluded, Mr. EVERETT quoted a sentence to the following effect, from the last letter but one ever received by him from Mr. Webster: "We now and then see, stretching across the heavens, a clear, blue, cerulean sky, without cloud or mist or haze. And such appears to me our acquaintance, from the time when I heard you for a week write your lessons in the little school-house in Short street, to the date hereof, 21st July, 1852." By Mr. Webster's will, Mr. EVERETT was appointed chairman of his literary executors.

A few months only elapsed after the publication of his works when the lamented death of the great statesman took place. At the time when his resignation had been contemplated, a year before, he had recommended Mr. EVERETT as his successor. On Mr. Webster's decease, his place at the head of Mr. Fillmore's cabinet was immediately tendered to Mr. EVERETT. He has himself alluded to the circumstances under which he took charge of the department of state, in the following terms:

"Called as I was in the month of November, without a day's preparation, and after a retirement of seven years from all active participation in political life, to occupy—but, alas! how far from filling—the place of one of the foremost statesmen of the age; called upon within three or four weeks, the greater part of which was passed in the bustle of a public house, without a book to refer to, without a leisure moment for research or inquiry, to take up and dispose of such difficult questions as the Lobos Islands, the Crescent City affair, the difficulty about the Fisheries, and then this last great subject of the tripartite convention,—called upon to take up all these questions under the daily pressure of the routine of the department, (enough of itself to put to the test the stoutest capacity of labor and endurance,) I did feel that this was a task of no ordinary magnitude, and one that should entitle a person to some charitable consideration for any imperfection or defect in the performance of the duty."

The arduous duties of the department of state, thus referred to here, in the concurrent opinion of the public, were discharged in a manner not merely satisfactory, but highly honorable to Mr. EVERETT and creditable to the country. His letter to the French and English ministers, on the subject of the proposed Cuban convention, was welcomed with a unanimity of public favor rarely enjoyed by public documents on questions which divide the public mind.

Mr. EVERETT was always distinguished for the readiness with which he responded to the calls made upon him to address public meetings on occasions of almost every description. His speech before the American Colonization Society during the winter of 1853, has attracted much notice, and may be fairly classed among the most successful discussions of the great objects of that important institution.

On the 4th of March, 1853, Mr. EVERETT took his seat in the Senate of the United States as successor to Mr. John Davis. While this special term was passing, the newspapers contained a report of his first speech in this new position, being an exposition of our relations with Central America. It may be proper to say, that while Mr. EVERETT was Secretary of State, he made a report to the President on this subject, and recommended an important change in our diplomatic arrangements in that quarter. This recommendation was adopted and the requisite appropriation made by congress. His speech is thus characterized by a leading New York journal:

"Mr. EVERETT's speech will be read with universal interest The sentiment and principles of the speech, as well as its language and temper, will commend themselves to the warm approbation of the great mass of the American people. Taken in connection with the letter on the tripartite treaty, and Mr. Webster's letter to Mr. Hülsemann, it completes the best and most authoritative exposition ever made of the true relations of the American Republic to the rest of the world—of the duties which those relations involve, and of the policy we ought to pursue in our intercourse with other nations. It is saturated with the true spirit of American progress—remote alike from the conservatism which ignores liberty, dignity, and the inevitable changes of time in its timid apprehensions of danger, and from the rash radicalism which scoffs at experience and prudence, and takes counsel only of its courage, its conceit, and its ambition."

Mr. EVERETT was the special and the applauded orator on several occasions during the summer. At the assembling of the thirty-third Congress he found his health greatly impaired, but he applied himself with his usual industry to the duties of his position in the Senate. Had not the term been one of high excitement, and had not the questions agitated been of such importance, as to demand the most arduous labor and deep research on the part of all statesmen, he might have reserved his strength and continued a longer time in the national councils. But the bill for the repeal of the Missouri Compromise was producing intense agitation throughout the country. Everywhere the Nebraska-Kansas bill was discussed. In the Senate the opposing parties were brought into violent and protracted antagonism. The speeches were vehement and impassioned. Mr. EVERETT could not prove recreant to the trusts and demands of his constituents. He felt that he must not resign, nor, if he remained, must he be silent. He thoroughly prepared himself, and in February, 1854, he delivered a speech against the bill. He was moderate and conservative in his views, and his language was marked by his elegant taste and his calm temper. Official toil and excitement preyed upon his health; it grew worse and worse; his physician imperatively advised him to retire, and in the following May he resigned his seat.

A new sphere of loyal, national duty was opening for him as soon as rest and medical remedies should prepare him for it. Several months before, Miss Ann Pamela Cunningham had started the pro ject of purchasing Mount Vernon by private subscriptions, to be taken throughout the whole country. It was everywhere felt that the Home of Washington should belong to the nation. In several of the States the ladies formed Mount Vernon Associations for collecting funds. The great want was an orator, to whose heart the object would be sacred, and whose tongue would make effective the appeal to the people.

The Mercantile Library Association, of Boston, invited Mr. EVERETT to deliver one of the lectures of their course, during the winter of 1855-6. He proposed that the association should celebrate the next anniversary of Washington's birth-day, and offered to deliver, at the time, an oration upon the character of the Father of his Country, the proceeds to be applied to some commemorative purpose. The offer was accepted, and, on February 22, he pronounced, for the first time, to an immense audience, the eloquent oration on Washington, which will ever associate the names of the brilliant orator and the immortal patriot. It was soon repeated in other Eastern cities, and the rich proceeds were applied to various objects.

Here was the man, and here the oration to make successful the patriotic scheme of purchasing Mount Vernon. Why not secure them? Mr. EVERETT only waited for a popular request. It soon came from Richmond, Va., and in the following March he stood in that city, and gave his eloquence to the cause which enlisted his enthusiasm. Thenceforth he went through the towns and cities of the land, speaking hundreds of times to thousands of people, reviving the memories of Washington, and contributing the large proceeds to the Mount Vernon fund. It was a labor of love gratuitously rendered, and he, doubtless, hoped that one result of his efforts would be to make stronger the bonds of union between the people and the States. By his pen also he raised thousands of dollars for the patriotic object. This will ever be regarded as one of the most interesting periods of Mr. EVERETT's life. It illustrates the genius of the American people, and the relations which the general community sustains to those men, who, from their abilities, attainments and accomplishments, are the natural leaders of public sentiment.

Mr. EVERETT's delight and power were in his oratory. In an affectionate tribute to his memory, the historian, George Bancroft, says, "There was no voice which his countrymen so loved to hear on questions of public interest, the culture of science, the advancement of learning. Others live only for themselves and within themselves; EVERETT lived for others, and was never so happy as when he played upon the great instrument of the national mind, and found that his touch brought out tones in harmony with the movements of his own soul. This mode of life was attended with something of trial; for the sensitiveness which was a requisite to his success in keeping up a sympathy with the mind of the people left him more than ever acutely susceptible of pain from public censure, and even from the idle cavils of triflers, or the sneers of the envious and malign. But the current of public opinion was so strong in his favor, he called out so much affectionate approval of his singularly disinterested devotion to the public good, that his last years were among the happiest of his three-score and ten — happier than the years of impatient, aspiring youth; happier than the years of political conflict. . . .

"He touched the chord of public feeling with instinctive accuracy and power; at seventy he could hold a vast audience enchained, as he spoke without notes, with a clear, melodious, and unbroken voice for two hours together; and when he prepared himself for a public speech, all learning and all science seemed to come at his bidding, and furnish him with arguments, analogies and illustrations. What he has spoken with his golden mouth was always in behalf of good letters, of patriotism, of the advancement of his country in science and art; of union; of the perpetuation of republican institutions. From the Charles River to the Missouri the air still rings with his eloquence."

The same eminent writer thus speaks of Mr. EVERETT's personal connection with the political affairs of the country:

"To promote the great end of maintaining the Union, EVERETT was not an advocate for concession, but for conservatism. He had in his manhood resisted nullification with all his might; he now resisted everything that tended to secession. To keep the Constitution as it was and thus to avoid all conflict with the South, was the key-note of his policy; and when men sought to avert the storm which threatened ruin, one party looked to him, in connection with another name, to bear, in the Presidential contest, the standard on which was inscribed 'the Constitution and the Union.' . . . Without attempting to solve the question whether he was right in the attitude which he assumed, it is certain that he was honest, and that the place as candidate which he consented to occupy, fitted the conduct and opinions of his life. It is, perhaps, less known, that in the threefold division which prevailed at the Presidential election in 1860, it had been the intention of Mr. Douglas, as he avowed to one or two at least of his friends, in case the decision had gone to Congress, to have given his influence to secure the election of the ticket which bore the name of EVERETT.

"When the storm burst he could not remain quiet, and there was but one direction in which he could move. Like Douglas, to whom in so many respects he formed a contrast, he rallied to the support of the Government, as the only mode in which he could rally in support of his country. Those who had before charged him with want of firmness, had not kept in mind that his delay grew out of his desires and his convictions; when events left no hope of a peaceful issue, he was instant in season and out of season, abroad and at his fireside, with friends and before the people, in giving to the contest unity of action and definiteness of purpose; and while he at the last spoke bravely for universal emancipation, that gentleness which made him so slow to acquiesce in the stern and terrible necessity of civil war, inspired him in the last public act of his life to send consolation to those who had been subdued."

His youth seemed to be renewed as he gave his time, his strength, his means, his tongue and pen to the service of his country. He refused to go abroad on a confidential mission to all the leading courts of Europe, in the cause of the Government; but, wherever his presence among his fellow-citizens could aid the Union he was always ready at the call. Among his many patriotic orations, there is one that has a permanent historical value. The occasion was the dedication of the Soldiers' National Cemetery, at Gettysburg, Pennsylvania, where thousands had fallen in making the Fourth of July, 1863, resplendent with victory. It had been the great battle of the war, fought on Northern soil. The Governors of the loyal States felt that this was the field for a National Cemetery. They unanimously concurred in requesting Mr. EVERETT to deliver the oration on the Nineteenth of the following November. The day came. Everything was propitious. The President, Abraham Lincoln, was present with a heart as tenderly interested in the consecration of that soil to so hallowed a purpose, as if he had a son to be buried there. The Cabinet was represented; so, too, were the loyal States by their Governors and eminent men. Never was more expected of the distinguished orator, who had been called "Our Statesman and our Scholar." He was equal to the pathetic occasion. He summoned to his aid the literature of the past, the history of the present, the hopes of the future. He carefully sketched the invasion into the State, and the fearful conflict of three days on the field where he stood. He argued the unconstitutionality of the rebellion, and eloquently predicted its overthrow. He proved, what Bancroft says of him, that he might have been "one of the first of historians." His description of the great battle will descend to posterity as a document of permanent historical value.

Space forbids us to record his activity in promoting art, science, agriculture, education, and philanthropy. He labored to the last for the welfare of his fellow men. The telegraph announced to the nation his sudden death, January 15, 1865, in the 71st year of his age. The grief was universal. By order of President Lincoln, unusual and appropriate honors were rendered to his memory, at home and abroad, wherever the national name and authority were acknowledged. From the pulpit, at the bar, in public assemblies, his eulogies were pronounced. Lips of eloquence proclaimed his worth, and, in his own words, it may be said that he lived "to reconcile the progressive spirit and tendency of the country and the age with the preservation of the public faith, with the sanctity of the public honor, and with the dictates of an enlightened and liberal conservatism."

L.D. F R S

Nathl Bowditch

NATHANIEL BOWDITCH,
LL. D. F. R. S.

OF all the various branches of intellectual pursuit, that science which explains the system of the universe, and reveals the mechanism of the heavens, must always take the lead as the most sublime and marvellous; and the foremost and most successful cultivators of this science will always be classed among the greatest of men. What, indeed, can be more astonishing than that a being like one of us, endowed, apparently, with no higher or different powers, should be able to obtain so minute and accurate knowledge of those distant planets, and be as well acquainted with their constitution, elements, and laws, as the geologist, the chemist, the botanist, with the appropriate objects of their sciences? Nothing gives so exalted an idea of the power of man, and the extent and reach of his capacities, as his ability to calculate with unerring precision the distances of those twinkling orbs; to determine their figures, magnitudes, and velocities; to measure their weight, estimate their relative attractions and disturbing forces; delineate their orbits, register their laws of motion, fix the times of their revolution, and predict the periods of their return. To a common mind, uninstructed in the science, there is nothing that appears so much like divine wisdom. A Galileo, a Kepler, a Newton, seem to him to belong to another race, a higher order of beings. They appear to possess some additional faculties.

Nothing can be more certain than the doctrines of Astronomy. They rest on impregnable foundations, on the demonstrations of mathematical evidence, than which nothing, except the evidence of consciousness, can be more satisfactory and conclusive. It was a science that early engaged the notice of men, and it has always exercised a purifying and elevating influence on its votaries. Indeed, how could it be otherwise? Who can look upon those brilliant points, and not fancy them the spangled pavement of a divine abode? There is virtue, as well as poetry and philosophy in them. They shed down a healing and restorative influence upon their worshippers. They are the symbols of endurance and perpetuity.

In the removal of NATHANIEL BOWDITCH, death deprived the scientific world of one of its noblest ornaments—one, who occupied the most prominent place among the scientific men of this country. His position as a public man, the various offices he filled, and especially the value of his works to the advancement of science, the improvement of navigation, and the security of commercial enterprizes, justify the notice which we now propose to take of his life and character. There was much of that life instructive and encouraging, particularly to the young, the friendless, and the poor: there was much in that character worthy of eulogy and imitation.

NATHANIEL BOWDITCH was born at Salem, Massachusetts, on the 26th day of March, 1773. He was the fourth child of Habakkuk and Mary Ingersoll Bowditch. His ancestors, for three generations, had been shipmasters; and his father, after retiring from that employment, carried on the trade of a cooper, by which he gained a scanty and precarious subsistence for a family of seven children. He enjoyed no other advantages of early instruction than such as could be obtained at the common public schools of his native town, which were at that time very inferior to what they have since become, being wholly inadequate to furnish even the ground-work of a respectable education. It was highly honorable to him that, although he had not himself the benefits of a liberal education, he felt the importance and acknowledged the value of it; and accordingly gave to his children the best which the country afforded, and took a deep interest, and, for many years, an efficient agency in the University at Cambridge. The advantages of school, such as they were, he was obliged to forego at the early age of ten years, that he might go into his father's shop and help to support the family. He was, however, soon transferred as an apprentice to a ship-chandler, in whose shop he continued until he went to sea, first as clerk, afterwards as supercargo, and finally as master and supercargo jointly. It was whilst he was in the ship-chandler's shop that his characteristic attachment to mathematical pursuits first developed itself. Every moment of leisure was given to the slate.

From his earliest years he was a diligent reader; and he has been heard to say that, when quite young, he read through a whole Encyclopedia without omitting a single article.

He sailed on his first voyage on the 11th of January, 1795, at the age of twenty-two, as clerk to Captain Henry Prince on board the

NATHANIEL BOWDITCH.

ship Henry, of Salem. The ship sailed for the Isle of Bourbon, and returned home after an absence of exactly a year.

His second voyage was made as supercargo on board the ship Astræa, of Salem. The vessel sailed to Lisbon, touched at Madeira, and then proceeded to Manilla, and arrived at Salem in May, 1797. He made his third voyage the following year, to Cadiz and the Mediterranean. He continued in the same ship, and sailed on his fourth voyage in 1799, to Batavia and Manilla, and returned in 1800. He continued in the East India trade until 1804, when he quitted the sea, and became President of a Marine Insurance Company in Salem.

In the course of these voyages Mr. BOWDITCH took great interest in the instruction of the sailors, who could read and write, in the principles of navigation; and he never appeared so happy as when he could inspire a sailor with a proper sense of his individual importance, and of the talents he possessed, and might call into action. In this he was remarkably successful; and at Salem it was considered a high recommendation of a seaman that he had sailed with Mr. BOWDITCH, and it was often sufficient to procure for him an officer's berth.

His attention was directed, at an early age, to the *Principia* of Newton; but as that work was published in Latin, a language which he had not learned, he was obliged to obtain assistance in translating it; but he soon discovered that his own knowledge of the subject, with the aid of the mathematical processes and diagrams on the pages of the work, enabled him to comprehend the reasoning of the author; and by dint of perseverance he acquired a sufficient knowledge of Latin to enable him to read any work of science in it. He afterwards learned French, for the purpose of having access to the treasures of mathematical science in that language; and to indulge his taste for general literature, he studied Spanish, German, and Italian.

It has been stated, in relation to the origin of one of Mr. BOWDITCH's principal works, that on the day previous to his sailing on his last voyage he was called on by Mr. Edmund M. Blunt, then a noted publisher of charts and nautical books at Newburyport, and requested to continue the corrections which he had previously commenced on John Hamilton Moore's book on navigation, then in common use on board our vessels. This he consented to do; and in performance of his promise he detected such a multitude of errors, that it led to the construction of his "New American Practical Navigator," the first edition of which was published in 1800, and has been of immense service to the nautical and commercial interests of this country. It is a work abounding with the actual results of his own experience, and containing simple and expeditious formulas for working nautical problems. Had he never done any thing else, he would, by this single act, have conferred a lasting obligation to his native land. Every vessel that sails from the ports of the United States, from Eastport to New Orleans, is navigated by the rules and tables of his book. It is also extensively used in the British and French navies.

In 1802, at the age of twenty-nine, his ship lying wind-bound at Boston, he went out to Cambridge to attend the exercises on commencement day; and whilst standing in one of the aisles of the church, the President announced his name amongst those on whom had been conferred the degree of Master of Arts. The annunciation came upon him wholly by surprise. It was the proudest day of his life; and of all the distinctions which he subsequently received from numerous learned and scientific bodies at home and abroad, there was not one which afforded him half the pleasure, or which he prized so highly, as this degree from Harvard.

In 1806 Mr. BOWDITCH published his admirable chart of the harbors of Salem, Beverly, Marblehead, and Manchester, the survey of which had occupied him during three summers. This was a work of great exactness and beauty.

On the establishment of the Massachusetts Hospital Life Insurance Company, at Boston, in 1823, he was invited to take charge of it, with the title of Actuary. He accepted of the appointment, and accordingly removed to that city, where he continued to reside till the time of his decease. He discharged the duties of his trust with skill and fidelity, and to the entire satisfaction of the company.

While he resided at Salem, he undertook his translation and commentary on the great work of the French astronomer, La Place, entitled *Mécanique Céleste*. This was the great work of his life. The illustrious author of that work undertakes to explain the whole mechanism of our solar system, to account for all its phenomena, and to reduce all the anomalies in the apparent motions and figures of the planetary bodies to certain definite laws. It is a work of great genius and immense depth, and exceedingly difficult to be comprehended. This arises not merely from the intrinsic difficulty of the subject, and the medium of proof being the higher branches of the mathematics, but chiefly from the circumstance that the author, taking it for granted that the subject would be as plain and easy to others as to himself, very often omits the intermediate steps and connecting links in his

NATHANIEL BOWDITCH.

demonstrations. He grasps the conclusion without showing the process. Dr. BOWDITCH used to say, "I never come across one of La Place's '*Thus it plainly appears*,' without feeling sure that I have got hours of hard study before me to fill up the chasm, and find out and show *how* it plainly appears." This gigantic task was begun in the year 1815, and was the regular occupation of his leisure hours to the time of his death. His elucidation and commentaries, while they show him to have been as thoroughly master of the mighty subject as La Place himself, will make that great work—the most profound of modern times—accessible to innumerable students, who, without such aid, would be compelled to forego the use of it. Let it not be said, in disparagement of the labors of Dr. BOWDITCH, that this was not an original work, but merely a translation. Suppose it had been so. What then? Was it not still a benefaction to those who are acquainted only with the English language to bring this great work within their reach? But he did more. It is more than half an original commentary and exposition, simplifying and elucidating what was before complex and obscure; supplying omissions and deficiencies, fortifying the positions with new proofs, and giving additional weight and efficacy to the old ones; and, above all, recording the subsequent discoveries, and bringing down the science to the present time. It has been asserted that La Place, to whom Dr. BOWDITCH sent a list of errors, (which, however, he never had the grace to acknowledge in any way,) once remarked, "I am sure that Dr. BOWDITCH comprehends my work, for he has not only detected my errors, but has shown me how I came to fall into them."

The first volume of the work was published in the year 1829, the second in 1832, and the third in 1834; each volume containing about a thousand quarto pages. The fourth and last volume was nearly completed at the time of his decease. He persevered to the last in his labors upon it; preparing the copy, and reading the proof-sheets in the intervals when he was free from pain. Though the work, on its appearance, met with more purchasers than he expected, yet its cost was a heavy draft on his income, and an encroachment on his little property. Yet it was cheerfully paid; and besides that, he gladly devoted his time, his talents, his health, and his life, to the cause of science and the honor of his native land. *That work is his monument.* He needs no other.

The progress of Dr. BOWDITCH's last illness was so unremitting, that he was not able to complete the final revision of the whole of his great work. The fifth and only remaining volume is, comparatively, of little importance, and it probably would have had but little revision if he had survived.

Dr. BowDITCH was eminently a self-taught and a self-made man. Whatever knowledge he possessed,—and it was great,—was of his own acquiring, the fruit of his solitary studies, with but little assistance from abroad. From his youth up, he was a pattern of industry, enterprise, and perseverance; suffering no difficulties to discourage, no disappointments to dishearten him. He combined qualities and habits which are usually considered incompatible. He was a contemplative, recluse student; and at the same time an active public man. He lived habitually among the stars, and yet he was a shrewd, practical man, and one of the most skilful of financiers. Judging from his published works, it might be supposed he had neither taste nor time for business, or the ordinary affairs of life; and judging from the large concerns which he managed, and the vast funds of which he had the supervision, it would seem impossible he could have had any time for study. He accomplished all by an economy of time, and the regularity of his habits. He was a remarkably domestic man. His affections clustered around his own fireside. His attachment to the calm and simple pleasures of his home was one of the most beautiful traits of his character. His time was divided between his office and his house; he was seldom drawn into company. When at home, he spent his time in his library, which he loved to have considered the family parlor. By very early rising, in winter two hours before light, he was enabled to accomplish much before others were stirring. After taking his evening walk he was again always to be found in the library, pursuing the same attractive studies, but ready and glad, at the entrance of a visiter, to throw aside his book, unbend his mind, and indulge in all the gaieties of a light-hearted conversation. There was nothing that he seemed to enjoy more than the free interchange of thought on all subjects of common interest. At such times the mathematician, the astronomer, the man of science disappeared; and he presented himself as the frank, easy, familiar friend. It was hardly credible that the agreeable, fascinating companion, who talked so affably and pleasantly on all the topics of the day, and joined so heartily in the quiet mirth or the loud laugh, could really be the great mathematician who had expounded the mechanism of the heavens, and taken his place with Newton, and Leibnitz, and La Place, amongst the great proficients in exact science.

Although mathematics was his chief and favorite pursuit, Dr. Bow-DITCH still had a taste for general literature. He was fond of Shakspeare, and Burns, and Bryant, and Sprague; and remembered and could repeat whole passages from their works.

He was a man of unsullied purity and most rigid integrity; and was always true to his moral as well as intellectual convictions.

From his boyhood, his mind had been religiously impressed. He had read the Bible under the eye of a pious mother, and he loved to repeat the sublime and touching language of Holy Writ.

His last days were marked by the same cheerfulness and serenity of mind that we naturally look for on the death-bed of the pure and good. The disease of which he died was a schirrus in the stomach. For four weeks previous to his death, he could take no solid food, and hardly swallowed any liquid. He suffered, however, but little from hunger, but constantly from thirst; and the only relief and refreshment he could find was, in frequently moistening his lips and mouth with cold water. His frame was consequently exceedingly attenuated, and his flesh wasted away. At intervals his sufferings were intense, and the body at times triumphed over the spirit; but it was only for a moment, and the spirit again resumed its legitimate sovereignty. On the morning of his death, when his sight was dim and his voice almost gone, he called his children around his bed-side, and, like the patriarch Jacob, addressed each by name. "You see," said he, "I can distinguish you all, and I now give you my parting blessing. The time is come; Lord, now lettest thou thy servant depart in peace according to thy word." These were his last words. He died on Friday, the 16th day of March, 1838; and was buried privately, on the morning of the following Sabbath, under Trinity Church, in Summer Street, Boston.

Dr. BOWDITCH twice held a seat in the Executive Council of Massachusetts, under the administration of Governors Strong and Brooks; but he had no taste for public life, no ambition for political honors.

He was admitted a member of the American Academy of Arts and Sciences in 1799, and was its President from 1829 to the time of his decease. He received his degree of LL. D. from Harvard University in 1816, and was elected a member of the Royal Society of London in 1818. He contributed a great number of valuable papers to the Memoirs of the American Academy, and was the author of the article on Modern Astronomy, in Vol. XX. of the North American Review. There is also a brief account of the comet of 1806 furnished by him, and published in the Monthly Anthology, Vol. IV. He was an active and efficient member of the Boston Athenæum, the

East India Marine Society of Salem, and of several other societies of a literary or benevolent character.

Dr. BOWDITCH was held in very high estimation as a man of science by the whole learned world; and in social life he was regarded with the strongest feelings of attachment. By not a few he was spoken of as "*The Great Pilot*," and by all was emphatically characterised as "a *live* man." Quickness and activity marked all his faculties, affections, and habits. Though devotedly attached to science, he could not cherish the idea of selling his works for his own advantage to those who might not be able readily to profit by them. Indeed he carried his feelings of independence so far, as to refuse to have his great translation of *La Place* published by subscription or at the expense of others, but chose to wait till he could afford to sustain the expense himself; saying, that he would rather expend a thousand dollars a year in this way, than by keeping a carriage. Friendship will long refuse to bury his name; science shall very long appreciate the services he rendered to the world; and benevolence will yet be found weeping at his tomb.

THOMAS SAY.

SCIENCE, and particularly Natural Science, has fewer holds upon the popular attention than the achievements of war or policy. Laboring to render some small service to the whole human race, and occupied in preparing the workmanship of their minds for the scrutiny of men in foreign countries and future ages, the votaries of philosophy may perhaps feel their task even more dignified; as its field is more extensive and permanent than the changes of empires. They lean, perhaps, habitually less to the applause of the age and country in which they live, than to that gradually accumulating sanction of mankind which begins in obscurity, and gradually diffuses itself—a scattered and posthumous fame.

> "Not all at once, as thunder breaks the cloud:
> The notes at first, were rather sweet than loud;
> By just degrees they ev'ry moment rise,
> Fill the wide earth and gain upon the skies!"

Yet as our countrymen have never shown themselves deaf to the praise of honorable actions, though achieved in a field in which the great mass takes but little interest, and as they pride themselves in the reputation of the men who have done honor to America in the closet, we do not fear to entrust the fame of a naturalist to those who cherish with a just delight the memories of Godfrey and Rittenhouse, or the scientific renown of a Franklin. The political institutions of America, and the abstract researches of the intellect, have at least this quality in common—that they are applicable to a wider field than a single age or nation, and that the lessons they teach, however desirable for those who are engaged in them, derive their principal value from their adaptation to the general service of mankind.

The family of THOMAS SAY was settled in Pennsylvania from the time of its first colonization. His ancestors by the father's side are understood to have been Huguenots, who migrated to England in pursuit of religious liberty: and his lineal predecessor, in the fourth degree of proximity, came to America with William Penn, accompanied by others of his family. The integrity and activity of these high principled and determined men were rewarded by a liberal share of the Divine blessings upon the external circumstances which surrounded them. They and their descendants generally lived to an extreme age, surrounded by peace and abundance, and enjoying the confidence and respect of their fellow-citizens within the colony. His grandfather, Thomas Say, a very patriarchal man, was united, early in the eighteenth century, to the religious society of Friends. Dr. Benjamin Say was long known in Philadelphia as a skilful and benevolent practitioner of medicine, and enjoyed in that capacity a large share of public confidence and patronage. Having been connected with military proceedings during the war of Independence, he joined that seceding portion of the society of which he had been a member, known by the name of Free Quakers.

The immediate subject of our memoir was born July 27th, 1787; and was the eldest son of Dr. Benjamin Say, and Anna, his first wife, a daughter of Benjamin Bonsall, Esq., of Kingsessing. In his early youth he was brought up in rigid compliance with many of the peculiar observances of his religious connexion. He received a considerable part of his education at their school at Westtown in Pennsylvania, and the remainder of it generally at their other institutions. He manifested at this period a remarkable docility of temper, a profound and confiding respect for his parents and teachers, and a great fondness for study. He pursued, in independence of any one's advice or suggestion, a very extended course of reading among the writers of his own language; a pursuit, however, soon destined to give way to the accumulation of fact or natural truth.

At an early period of his life, a near family connexion with the celebrated naturalist, William Bartram, of Kingsessing, induced the young SAY, together with several of his acquaintance, to devote a considerable amount of time to collecting objects for their venerable friend's museum. This occurrence seems to have fixed his destiny. The student, young as he was, felt himself at once in his proper sphere. He immediately commenced the study of natural history; a pursuit which, though occasionally suffering a temporary interruption, was never wholly laid aside for the remainder of his life. The natural gaiety of youth, the attractions of fashion, the multiform allurements which surround a young man of easy fortune, and even the serious claims of a commercial establishment, were all capable of occupying his mind but for a short season, to be super-

THOMAS SAY.

seded by those boundless cravings for knowledge which an Almighty power had placed within his breast. When, in compliance with the earnest wishes of his father, he entered into commercial engagements, the future naturalist was found by his friends occupied with those pursuits for which nature had designed him, and leaving the details of business to others. The commercial efforts proved unsuccessful; and Mr. SAY, deprived of his patrimony, instead of endeavoring to repair the loss, resolved to devote himself exclusively to Natural History. From this may be dated the commencement of his purely scientific career; he now began to consider science as a profession, and the loss of worldly property seemed the road to higher intellectual distinction and more enlarged usefulness.

The studies of the youthful naturalist, about this period, underwent a temporary interruption from his service as a volunteer in the last war between our country and England. In common with several of his friends and relations, he became a member of the first troop of city cavalry; and in that capacity proceeded to Mount Bull, where he remained for some time during the years 1812 and 1813.

On the breaking up of this military post at the conclusion of peace, he had already devoted considerable labor to the study of natural history and the collection of the natural productions of our country, when he found the arena of his usefulness suddenly extended by the formation of the Philadelphia Academy of Natural Sciences. When, on the 25th of January, 1812, a little association, which had previously met in a more private manner, resolved to assume this style and character, it was considered of importance that THOMAS SAY, though absent from the meeting, should be assumed as an original member.

The compliment thus paid to a modest and retiring man, shows, as was intended, the value which was then set upon his adhesion by the six others who thus associated him to their number. How amply his subsequent course justified their selection, the Academy has gladly testified. Such was the effect of private study, that his subsequent acquaintance had no opportunity of witnessing the infancy of his scientific powers. His elementary knowledge was complete, his acquaintance with classification adequate, and his power of observing and discriminating, accurate and ready. He was at once prepared for the difficult and laborious task of describing and cataloguing American productions in natural history. From this period, and for a considerable interval, his labors are almost exclusively directed in co-operation with the institution which he had assisted in founding.

NATIONAL PORTRAITS.

In the tasks undertaken by Mr. SAY, almost every thing was to be done. The examination of the invertebral animals was to be introduced to the notice of our citizens; the myriads of minute objects of this class which attract the eye in our country, were to be investigated and described; the study was to be created, and the students induced to prosecute it.

For these purposes his efforts were truly unremitting. He was attentive and regular in his presence at the meetings of the Academy; and during the intervals, may be said to have been always at his post. Those who were in the habit of visiting the building will abundantly recollect the uniformity with which he was to be found there. The value of such assiduous attendance, by such a man, may be easily imagined. Those who were disposed to visit the establishment were at all times certain of agreeable society; for Mr. SAY was ever attentive to all reasonable calls for conversation, so much as even to surprise his friends. The effect of his liberality of disposition, with his amenity of manner, was peculiarly fascinating; and tended forcibly to produce in the same individuals a combined feeling of love for the science, and for the naturalist who had thus gained their affections.

This indefatigable and eminent man was at all times ready to bestow the fruits of his own researches upon those of his friends who felt an interest in similar pursuits. In this manner he was incalculably serviceable to young students in natural history by his advice and assistance; feeling far more anxious to extend the sphere of science in his country than to increase his own fame. This generosity in bestowing upon others the results of his own industry, so highly characteristic of true genius and real love for science, might be referred, in part, to a sense of his own strength. He had reputation to spare, and could hardly avoid feeling aware that the inquirer who grew in science must inevitably form a higher estimation of the teacher of whose merits he thus became a better judge.

In May, 1817, the Journal of the Academy was commenced; and Mr. SAY continued, during the next ten years, to be one of its steadiest and most laborious contributors.

In the autumn of that year an expedition to Florida was organized, for the purpose of procuring objects of natural history. The party consisted of Messrs. Maclure, Ord, SAY, and Peale, who spent the winter in that country, and collected a large number of specimens, with descriptions of many of which they afterwards enriched the Journal. In 1819 and 1820 the celebrated expedition to the Rocky

Mountains took place, in which Mr. SAY took a part. His learning, his patient industry, and the confidence reposed in him by the officers of the detachment, are visible in every page of the narrative; and the very large portion which he contributed to the work is acknowledged by the editor. This embraces the whole of his favorite department, the invertebral animals, together with a great variety of additional subjects, to which, from circumstances of various kinds, it was convenient that Mr. SAY should direct his attention. In the expedition to the sources of St. Peter's River, &c., performed in 1823, at least equal labor, in proportion to the time employed, was bestowed by him upon the collection of materials, although a portion of the preparation for the press was saved him by his friend, W. H. Keating, Esq., the editor.

During the period of our narrative, compliments from abroad came thick upon him; on these, however, he set but a limited value, except where they were the means of extending or increasing a knowledge of natural history. His correspondence with distinguished foreign naturalists occupied a large portion of his time, although constantly confined to matters of science.

In the year 1825, on the foundation of the well-known settlement made by the suggestion of Mr. Robert Owen at New Harmony, Indiana, Mr. SAY removed to that place, at the request of his friend, William Maclure, Esq., for the purpose of assisting with others in the erection of a school of natural science. By the munificence of the distinguished individual last named, he enjoyed, in the wilds of the far west, all the advantages of a splendid library, abundant facilities for making collections, and a ready printing press. The scientific world is in possession of two volumes, the second and third of his splendid American Entomology, and six numbers of his Conchology; all which were among the fruits of his industry while at New Harmony. The volumes of the Entomology were published in Philadelphia, the others in Indiana.

It was while at New Harmony that Mr. SAY's domestic happiness was enhanced by his union with Miss Lucy W. Sistare, of New-York, a lady in every way qualified to add to the felicity of such a man. In addition to many elegant accomplishments, Miss Sistare possessed the advantage of a fondness for the same pursuits, and great readiness and neatness with the pencil—a talent which was employed to the advantage of the beautiful works of which we have just spoken.

Besides the elaborate description of a number of natural objects collected at New Harmony, and also in Mexico during the tours in that country made by Mr. Maclure, Mr. Say found himself, at this late period of life, again involved in the cares of business and the superintendence of property. Amid the chaos of mind which the settlement presented, Mr. Maclure felt the value and necessity of old and tried friendship, tested honor, and untiring industry, in the care of his vast estates. In none could he confide with more unhesitating promptitude than in the subject of our memoir; and he who in early youth had sacrificed his own property to the pursuit of science, was willing, in maturer age, to devote his talents to the care of that of his friend; thus proving, like the Ionian philosopher, that his neglect of pecuniary affairs had not arisen from want of ability, but from disinclination.

Amid these accumulating tasks and this honorable charge, the termination of his labors was now gradually approaching. The season was one of unusual mortality, and the ordinary and general causes of disease could only coöperate with the severe and devoted application of the naturalist. Mr. Say's habits of steady and protracted application, excessive abstinence and loss of sleep, had long before this period exerted an injurious influence upon his health, exhibiting their effects in repeated attacks of fever and dysentery; and when, in 1833, he paid a short visit to his friends in Philadelphia, for the conjoined objects of health and science, the ravages of disease were but too visible. Still, those who knew him were not conscious that it was then for the last time that he visited his native city or the walls of his beloved academy. After several renewals of disease, the same maladies returned with a highly nervous character; and finally, the 10th of October 1834, he sunk into the arms of death by an easy dissolution.

Thus perished, while yet in the vigor of his years, an individual on whom creative wisdom appeared to have stamped in the strongest manner the characters of a master mind in the study of the works of God.

The character of Mr. Say was in every way singularly fitted for the task which he thus made the business of his life. He was gifted with a strong intellect, accurate powers of observation, vast assiduity, a freedom from those unsettled wanderings of the mind which are so frequently the bane of genius, and an enthusiastic attachment to the subject of his studies. In philosophy, he was an advocate for that doctrine which attached exclusive importance to the evidence of the senses. Fact alone was the object which he thought worthy of his researches. Such was the ardor of his perseverance, that for a long period he actually lived at the Academy, sleeping within the walls, and only leaving the institution when necessary to obtain his meals. The hours of refreshment were forgotten, and sleep unhesitatingly sacrificed, not as an occasional exertion, but as a permanent and persevering habit. His extraordinary power of concentrating his industry had an effect in producing the peculiar style of his pieces. The manner of writing in which he most delighted, was that of the utmost abridgment of which the subject was capable, cutting off every unnecessary word. It was not that he was incapable of a fluent style, for various parts of his writings demonstrate the contrary, such as some of his contributions to the narrative of the Expedition to the Rocky Mountains; but he seemed to think it an injustice to the reader and to science to detain them from knowledge with the smallest redundancy of language. At the same time this severe judge was far from criticising others with the same rigor which he exercised towards himself, and readily forgave the luxuriance of style in their works. His own manner, when he indulged in his beloved brevity, was certainly liable to the objection of difficulty to untutored readers; but still more, perhaps, to the risk of alarming students by its apparent obscurity, than to the reality, as the knowledge which was requisite was always actually present, though comprised in few words. It is unnecessary to add, that the naturalists are not a few to whom this abridged style is a recommendation.

The communications of Mr. Say to natural science are numerous and of considerable bulk; and their number has probably surprised even some of his acquaintance. They are scattered through a variety of publications, not all devoted to natural history, and one of these even a newspaper; the student finds it impossible, without considerable exertion, to avoid overlooking some of them, and it is too much to be feared that individual memoirs are irrecoverably lost. No estimate of their value, and the labor necessary to produce them, can, however, be founded on their simple bulk; nor can they be compared to others upon such a principle. If we take into view the extreme labor which he uniformly bestowed upon his productions, first to insure their accuracy, and then to compress them within the smallest possible space, the amount of work executed by this indefatigable writer will appear very greatly augmented.

But it is not by the rules of arithmetic that the labors of Mr. Say are to be judged in any respect. To form a just idea of the space in public utility occupied by him, it would be desirable, if possible, to make an estimate of the vacuities which existed in American science, of the judgment which he formed of them, and of the success of his endeavors to fill them. This task we shall not attempt to execute. It was in the immense range of the invertebrals that Mr. SAY exhausted his labor.

And among these it may be said, as of a former writer, that he left scarce any department untouched, and none that he touched unimproved. His descriptions of species are most numerous among the annulose and the molluscous animals, although he also made investigations among the radiated, as appears from the list of his publications, and among the entozoary. It is not to be supposed that he exhausted any of these departments: the stores of nature within our country are too extensive, and much, doubtless, remains for future observers. Yet he described the large and laborious numbers which serve for the general materials of classification; he outlined the extended and accurate map, to which the task of making local additions is easy, but which forms the necessary and only guide to those who would make further admeasurements. It is not that there is no more gold in the mine; but in raising his own ore, Mr. SAY has constructed the shafts and galleries, pointed out the veins, and indicated by his example the best manner of working them. He laid down the broad masses of coloring, which, however they may be augmented and retouched by the persevering pencil of the future artist, must still form the basis, and in very numerous cases, the perfection of the picture. Every familiar object in these departments, that frequently met the eye, but produced a feeling of dissatisfaction because no description or place for it was to be found in the writers on natural history, received its character from his hands. His task was that of Adam, to name the animals as they passed before him.

His modesty at first induced him to attempt few and isolated species, and departments of small extent; and as time gave him experience of his powers, he ventured farther. A few scattered insects and shells, ascertained to be undescribed, with great labor and precaution first received their characters and names from him. Next he undertook the crustacea of the United States, which he described and classified. He then extended his labor to a larger number of shells, selecting those of the land and of the fresh waters. Next, after despatching several detached and limited groups, he entered among the vast masses of the Insect Kingdom. In this immense field he described a very large number of species, belonging to nearly all its departments. Perhaps, even here we may discover a new illustration of the character of the man; and a dislike of show may not improbably have been among the reasons which induced him to postpone his attention to the brilliant and popular department of butterflies and moths. Our naturalist had now achieved so much of his task that he could afford to be desultory; and his pieces from this period assume a more diversified character. His share in the two expeditions by Major Long, is truly multifarious. Besides the departments which he considered peculiarly his own, it embraces, as we have already had occasion to observe, a very large amount of matter foreign to his ordinary habits of study, and requiring a different manner of composition. Some of the most interesting portions are those which describe the manners of the Indians. He is the historian of all the facts that were collected in those districts which he traversed with a small detachment of troops under his separate command; he obtained, although not professing philology, the vocabulary of the Killisteno language; and on the expedition to the sources of St. Peter's River, he made the whole of the botanical collections, which afterwards formed the basis of a memoir appended to the published narrative by the late Mr. De Schweinitz. In fossil zoology, his description of new species of the Crinoidea is considered highly valuable. Several other memoirs in this department, in which America until lately presented such a mass of unknown objects, will be found in the catalogue of his papers. Several of Mr. Say's papers appear, however elaborate, to have been at first but little known to naturalists; it appearing to have been his first object in many instances to procure a public record of his papers in print, so as to establish his claims to the date of his discoveries, while at the same time he obtained duplicates to transmit to his learned correspondents; leaving it to subsequent times to republish them, and thus secure their wider diffusion and more easy access.

His natural temper was one of the most amiable ever met with. The phrase was frequent in the mouths of his friends, that, "it was impossible to quarrel with him." His great respect for his parents, and his compliance with their wishes, have been already mentioned. He was repaid, notwithstanding his retired life and exclusive devotion to science, by a singular strength of attachment on the part of his friends; and we have already spoken of the confidence of Mr. Maclure. His modesty was so retiring, and the wish which he frequently expressed "to save trouble" to others so great, that to men in the habit of living much in the world they might perhaps appear incredible. The contrast of these with surrounding manners, was occasionally so remarkable as almost to amount to eccentricity and a satire on the times.

It may be interesting to add, that he was tall and spare, but muscular, and apparently endowed, before his health was injured by repeated illness, with considerable strength. This enabled him better to struggle with the fatigues of toilsome journeys and the wasting inactivity of study. His complexion was dark, with black hair.

Mr. SAY will always be remembered by those who pursue the study of Zoology as one of the greatest American naturalists; while at the same time, his fame will be cherished in his native city as one of the most efficient founders and supporters of his favorite academy, and one of the individuals who have contributed most to diffuse a taste for these sciences among the American youth. Few men who have died at forty-seven years of age ever accomplished so much, especially on ground heretofore untrodden. The American "*Journal of Science and the Arts,*" bore true witness when it said, "It is no exaggeration to assert, that he has done more to make known the Zoology of his country than any other man. All his contributions to scientific and other works evince the most sagacious discrimination and the most laborious industry. Philadelphia, the place of his birth, and Indiana, the State which witnessed his death, yet contain many who are ever ready to shed a tear to his honored memory."

John W. Francis.

JOHN W. FRANCIS, M. D., LL. D.

PROFESSIONAL life, especially in young republican America, is often diversified; but the physician's is, perhaps, less frequently so than that of any of the members of the three liberal pursuits to which academic honors are awarded. Medical men, from the very nature of their studies, and the active cares in which they are involved in the subsequent discharge of their responsible trusts, necessarily pass their existence rather within the secluded chambers of the sick and afflicted, than before the gaze and immediate observation of the multitude. But, in defiance of this restriction, the cultivators of the venerable art of healing have been justly accounted among that class of individuals whose daily vocations lead to a substantial acquaintance with human nature, and the principles of human action; while their peculiar energies are ever directed to investigations, embracing a multitudinous variety of circumstances by which sound science is increased, and the lasting interests of society better secured. Knowledge, therefore, in the medical profession, serves not only to dignify its rank, but in the exercise of its powers becomes the agent of innumerable blessings to society; and is elevated equally by the importance of its ultimate object, and by those qualifying attainments which render their possessor the efficient instrument of its philanthropic designs.

There is, besides, in the history of physic, abundant evidence to show how much the advancement of man has been furthered by the professors of the healing art; how greatly the interests of humanity have been promoted by their efforts; how largely the charities of life, an elevated literature and exalted science have been aided by the broad foundations of public institutions, in which physicians have borne a prominent part. The annals of Continental and of British medicine demonstrate this truth; nor are examples wanting in our own country of similar establishments, generously cherished by this order of men. Hence, though the transactions of one day in the physician's career seldom differ from those of another, the lives of eminent professors in the medical faculty become worthy of notice; they are the guardians of the public health, and they deserve to rank among public characters; and he, who possesses a deep and enthusiastic veneration for the art, and while, in the daily exercise of its salutary precepts fosters, the cause of learning and the general welfare of his species, merits, at our hands, some recorded testimonial of his actions.

Among the many living examples in the United States of those in that profession, who by their acquisitions adorn the science of physic; who, by the faithful and conscientious performance of its arduous duties, have conferred benefits of acknowledged importance upon humanity; and by the publication of the results of experience have added to the medical literature of their country, the respectable individual, whose name is at the head of this biographical sketch, occupies a conspicuous place.

Dr. John W. Francis, was born in the city of New-York on the 17th of November, 1789. His father, Melchior Francis, who came to this country shortly after the peace of 1783, was a German from Nuremberg, well known in New-York as an enterprizing, upright grocer, of an enthusiastic temperament, and of a liberal and charitable spirit, whose career of usefulness was suddenly arrested by death from yellow fever in 1795, in the 35th year of his age. His mother was a native of Pennsylvania; her family, of the name of Somer, were originally from Bern, in Switzerland from whom there are numerous descendants in this country, now residing in the above-named State. Her children were mere infants when her husband died; but she was left in circumstances sufficiently easy to give them a good education. John, the eldest, after receiving the common early instruction, was sent to a school of no little reputation under the charge of the Reverend George Strebeck, with whom he commenced the study of mathematics and the Latin language, and afterward continued his classical pursuits under the direction of the Reverend John Conroy, a profound scholar, and a distinguished graduate of Trinity College, Dublin. By the aid of this excellent teacher he was enabled to enter an advanced class in Columbia College, where, in 1809, he received the degree of Bachelor, and in 1812 that of Master of Arts.

While an under-graduate, the subject of this memoir, having resolved to adopt the medical profession, devoted a portion of his time to its studies; he was enabled to accomplish this by a strong natural capacity, and by an ardor and perseverance which have marked his whole course of life; he had not only mental energy, but a vigorous constitution, which sustained his intense application in the acquisition of knowledge.

In 1807, then still an under-graduate as above-mentioned, he commenced his professional studies with the late Dr. David Hosack, the able and eloquent teacher, at that time professor of Materia Medica and Botany in Columbia College, and among those most entensively engaged in the practice of physic in New-York. Under this eminent preceptor Mr. FRANCIS had ample opportunities of witnessing the principles of the art illustrated by their practical application. During the period of his professional studies for four collegiate years, he never absented himself from a single lecture, nor attended one without making notes or abstracts on the subject taught by the lecturer. His clinical knowledge was also much increased by a constant attendance at the New-York Hospital, then enjoying the rich experience of Drs. Post, Kissam, Stringham, and others; and at the City Almshouse, an extensive charity, the medical department of which was under the management of Drs. Hosack and Macneven, the clinical instructors.

Several laws for the greater improvement of medical science were enacted about this period by the Legislature of the State of New-York. County Medical Societies had been formed the year before, and promised much advantage to the cause of professional learning. The College of Physicians and Surgeons, under the authority of the Regents of the University, was organized in 1807. From this institution, in 1811, Mr. FRANCIS received the degree of M. D. This was at the first commencement of that school under the Presidency of Dr. Samuel Bard, and the subject of this memoir was the first graduate who recorded his name in the College Album. Dr. FRANCIS's inaugural thesis was a dissertation on mercury, embracing its medical history, curative action, and abuse in disease. His researches were extensive, while many of his views were novel and profound, and have since been confirmed by the philosophical inquiries of British and other foreign practitioners. This production acquired for him great credit at once among his fellow graduates and the faculty generally; it has been repeatedly noticed by different writers in various languages, and maintains its reputation at the present day.

Dr. FRANCIS had been in practice a few months only, when his late preceptor proposed to him a co-partnership in business. This proposition, from the high standing of Dr. Hosack, was too flattering to be declined. This connection lasted till 1820, since which time Dr. FRANCIS has continued in practice by himself.

From the first organization of the College of Physicians and Surgeons, the professorial chairs were filled by men of acknowledged learning and ability most of whom were much distinguised as teachers.

In the spring of 1813 Dr. Francis received from the trustees of the institution the appointment of lecturer on the Institutes of Medicine and Materia Medica. Shortly after this period, an union being effected between the rival institutions, the medical faculty of Columbia College and the College of Physicians and Surgeons, he received from the regents the professorship of Materia Medica. He delivered his first public course of instruction to a class of one hundred and twenty students, declining all compensation for his services, that the consolidation of two schools of medicine, which had brought together so numerous a body of professors, might not too much enhance the price of education to those who wished to attend a full course of lectures. About this time he published a historical account of the College, with a syllabus or outline of the several courses of lectures. The students of this new school, upon its chartered establishment, had formed themselves into a medical society, similar to that at the University of Edinburgh, to improve their minds by weekly discussions on medical and surgical subjects. The President of the Society, which was termed the Medico-Chirurgical Society, was chosen from the professors of the College; and for many years Dr. Francis was elected to preside over it, succeeding in this appointment the learned Dr. Mitchill.

Strongly impressed with the conviction that the city of New-York possessed all the requisites for a great medical school, alive to the importance of an extended system of medical education, and cheered by the rising prospects of the institution to which he was attached, Dr. Francis resolved to visit Europe, having in view, as well to profit by the lessons of instruction afforded by the old world, as to transfer, as far as lay within his power, what was valuable and practicable to the new. While in London he became a pupil of the illustrious Abernethy, and witnessed the practice of St. Bartholomew's hospital; attended the lectures of Brande at the Royal Institution, those of Pearson at St. George's hospital, &c. Between Abernethy and Francis there sprung up so strong an attachment, that the former offered the latter a share of his business, which at that time was oppressively extensive.

According to a memoir to which this biographical sketch is much indebted,* besides England, Dr. Francis visited Scotland, Ireland, Holland, and France.

With eager curiosity he examined most that was rare and promi-

---

* New England Magazine, vol. 7th.

nent in these countries. His letters gave him access to scholars and men of science wherever he travelled. In Edinburgh he shared the hospitality of the great professors, and visited their schools so renowned for practical wisdom. Here he listened to the eloquent and classical lectures on medicine of Dr. James Gregory, and the able expositions of Professor Jamieson on the Wernerian formations; and witnessed the early experiments of the philosophic Brewster, in his private study, on the polarization of light. In Dublin he was received with true Irish cordiality; and found in the anatomical preparations of McCartney, specimens which rival even those of John Hunter. Regarding his professional object as the most important one of his mission, he was obliged to resist the strong impulse which prompted him to pass beyond the Rhine; and most reluctantly turned his back upon the country, toward which, as the land of his fathers, he felt the dutiful yearnings of a son; and for which, as the birth-place of Herder, Schiller, and Goethe, he entertained the reverence of a scholar. In Holland, the anatomical theatre where Ruysch once taught, and the garden where Boerhaave once displayed the harmonies of the vegetable kingdom, awakened to recollection the glories which have long since departed. In France, with Denon, he viewed in his cabinet, and in those institutions under his care, all that was magnificent in the arts. Gall displayed to him the rich materials of his collections, on which he founded his system of craniology; while the " Jardin des Plantes," under the direction of M. Thouin, gave him new ardor for a knowledge of the wonders of creation. With Cuvier he examined the objects more intimately connected with his own profession.

We are not wanting in proofs of the enthusiasm and success with which the subject of this article prosecuted his European tour. It was such as to excite the notice of many of his most enlightened foreign acquaintances. One thus speaks : " I feel much gratified by the opportunity you afforded me of making the acquaintance of Dr. Francis. A mind more ardent in the pursuit of useful knowledge perhaps never existed ; and I have no doubt he will, in a few years, stand at the head of his profession. I introduced him to my son-in-law, Dr Yeates, who is an able and learned physician; he entertains a high opinion of your friend's talents, and I am sure will at all times be happy in the opportunity of being useful to him."* Dr. Francis is warm in his admiration of those lights of knowledge he everywhere encountered in his travels; but though enamoured with the learned

* Letter of the late Patrick Colquhoun, author of the Police of London, &c. Life of Eddy, by S. L. Knapp.

men he met in different countries, his political affections were wedded to his own; and in the midst of his European attachments, he was still a republican in his principles.

On his return to New-York he found that some changes had been made in the disposition of the professorships in the College; the duties of the chair of Materia Medica had been added to that of Chemistry. He was at once appointed by the Regents of the University professor of the Institutes of Medicine. On the death of Dr. Stringham, in 1817, the department of Medical Jurisprudence, heretofore taught with applause by that gentleman, was assigned to Dr. Francis. Another change took place in 1819, by resignation, by which Dr. Francis became Professor of Obstetrics and Medical Jurisprudence. This appointment he held until 1826, when he resigned, at the same time with his colleagues, Drs. Hosack, Mott, Mcneven, and Mitchill; Dr. Post had given up the professorship of Anatomy a short time previously. The board of regents accepted the resignation of the faculty, and presented them their thanks " for the faithful and able manner in which they had filled their respective chairs as instructors and lecturers in said College."

During the same year in which the resignation of the professors of the College of Physicians and Surgeons occurred, a majority of them founded and organized a new institution at their individual expense, under the name of Rutgers' Medical College. In the place of Professor Post, Anatomy and Physiology was assigned to the late distinguished Dr. Godman, who, at the instance of Professor Francis, left Philadelphia for a larger sphere of usefulness and profit. The success of this new school for four terms was triumphant, at the end of which period the legislative wisdom of the State thought proper to close the doors of the College. It is believed that every friend and patron of sound practical medicine now admits that the interests of medical learning sustained a severe loss by this measure.

In the Rutgers' Medical College Dr. Francis was chosen Professor of Obstetrics and Forensic Medicine. In the number of pupils, his classes were second only to those of Anatomy, which are always most fully attended in every well-arranged medical institution. The close relationship between many parts of the physiological portion of a course of instruction on Obstetrics, with numerous topics discussed in legal medicine, justified, on the part of the professor, repeated disquisitions of the most interesting nature; and these, by an ample museum, were made the more clear and satisfactory. In his third edition of the work of Dr. Denman, a large amount of medico-legal facts and opinions is introduced; and in the same volume is embraced his history of the Obstetric art, from the time of the ancients to that of the latest writers on the subject, which has received the approbation both of the erudite and the practical. The number of students under his care while he was connected with the institutions above-named, was probably greater than that of any other professor in the city. He devoted from four to six hours a day to public and private instruction in the several departments of the science; other portions of time were devoted to the labor of practice. With the termination of all collegiate duties, he resolved to confine his attention to the practice of physic exclusively. In his parting address to his public class, he stated the causes which would thereafter dissolve the relationship of pupil and preceptor, paid the tribute of grateful respect to the magnanimous patrons by whom the College had been countenanced, and held up to admiration and example that guardian genius of all establishments for the diffusion of useful knowledge,—Dewitt Clinton.

DR. FRANCIS's early introduction to practice and teaching, however laborious and anxious the task, led not to the neglect of those intervals of leisure which occur in the lives of all. Convinced that the charms of medical reading, and the diffusion of medical and scientific knowledge, would both be promoted by the establishment of a new periodical journal in New-York, he, while a student, united with his preceptor, Dr. Hosack, and issued, in 1810, a prospectus for the American Medical and Philosophical Register. This work was published quarterly, and continued for four years. It was filled almost entirely with original materials. After the completion of the fourth volume, the editors assumed the responsibility of the work, and announced their names. In conjunction with the late Dr. Dyckman and Dr. Beck, he was for some time editor of the New-York Medical and Physical Journal, which was projected in 1822. He continued as one of the editors until the termination of the third volume. This work contains a number of his medical observations and records.

DR. FRANCIS has written papers, in many different medical and scientific journals in the United States, on subjects connected with his profession: among the most prominent of these, and of a practical nature, are his observations on the use of vitriolic emetics in croup, with details of cases in which this remedy was effective after the formation of the adventitious membrane lining the trachea. This novel method of cure has since often proved successful in other hands in this country, and has since been adopted abroad: remarks on the goitre as it prevails in the western parts of New-York and Canada:

cases of ovarian disease; on the medicinal properties of the sanguinaria Canadensis: history of a remarkable case of a diverticulum of the ilium: cases in morbid anatomy: facts and inferences in medical jurisprudence: on phlegmasia dolens occurring in the male subject; on caries of the lower jaw in children: on elaterium and croton oil: cases of icthyosis: observations on the mineral waters of Avon in Livingston County, New-York, deduced from chemical experiments and medicinal trials. His letter on febrile contagion, dated in London, 1816, and addressed to Dr. Hosack, contains an exposition of certain British writers, on the insusceptibility of the human constitution to a second attack of the yellow fever. This curious fact concerning the nature of this disease in certain latitudes, which was strongly maintained by various authors of Great Britain and the West Indies, received additional support, in many striking cases, from the observations which this letter brought to light, that had been made by many American physicians upon the pestilence in different seaports of the United States. Other papers might be referred to containing his clinical opinions; his reflections upon the nature and treatment of scarlet fever and other disorders may be found in the improved edition of Good's Study of Medicine edited by Dr. Doane.

State medicine, or that division of science which comprehends the principles of evidence afforded by the different branches of medicine, in elucidating and determining questions in courts of law, had been long and advantageously taught in German and other continental universities, when, in 1807, the chair of Medical Jurisprudence was founded at the University of Edinburgh, and Dr. Duncan, Jun., appointed Professor. The following year Dr. Stringham, who had graduated at that school, gave a course of lectures, the first delivered in the United States, on the same subject, in the college at New-York. As his successor, Dr. Francis was among the earliest teachers in the United States of this important and now generally cultivated department of knowledge. But it was not merely as a teacher that he exhibited the extent of his inquiries and practical researches in forensic medicine, and enlisted the enthusiasm of the student. During the greater part of his professional career, in almost every case of criminal prosecution in our judicial courts, his opinions have been solicited, and have seldom or ever been the subject of doubt or controversy. Dr. Francis invariably availed himself of the deductions which anatomy and pathology afford.

Nor have either his studies or his writings been confined to subjects strictly professional. Several of his biographical notices are valuable

JOHN W. FRANCIS.

contributions to the stock of elegant and general literature: these sketches are drawn with a free and manly hand, with faithfulness and discrimination. Among the most valuable of them may be mentioned his account of Cadwallader Colden, one of the earliest practitioners of physic in New York; those of Edward Miller, Benjamin Rush, Archibald Bruce, James S. Stringham, Thomas Eddy. His record of Dr Samuel L. Mitchill, is an honorable testimony to the memory of that remarkable man, whose genius and character will be more highly valued the longer his merits are contemplated. The occasional addresses of Dr. FRANCIS are written with taste and spirit united with candor and good feeling. His address to the New York Horticultural Society, in elegant language, portrays the beauties of nature adorned by art. The oration before the literary societies of Columbia College, in May, 1831, exhibits an important outline of the life and services of that distinguished patriot, the late Chancellor Livingston. The venerable President Madison transmitted a letter of approbation to the author, for the service he had rendered to American Biography, by his interesting account of the revolutionary patriot, which will be found in this volume. His discourse at the opening of the new hall of the Lyceum of Natural History, as yet but partially in print, is perhaps his most extensive production. It was delivered in December, 1836: its object is to recommend the cultivation of the natural sciences, and to bring together the most striking and important facts yet made known, concerning the natural history and physical resources of the new world.

The humane physician is perhaps more exposed than any other member of society to taxes on his time and benevolence: in seasons of pestilence and calamity, the claims of charity are not to be slighted or avoided. The later visitations of the yellow fever, and of the malignant cholera, bear witness to the sensibility of Dr. FRANCIS to the cause of humanity, and to his intrepid discharge of his duties. His clinical views of the new Asiatic plague, as it prevailed in New York in 1832, in which city it entombed upwards of four thousand inhabitants, were published in a letter to Dr. Reed of Savannah. This letter was so favorably received at that anxious period, that more than one hundred thousand copies, in various forms, were circulated in different sections of the Union. In France it excited the attention of professional men; d the authorities at Havana, when the cholera appeared there, had the pamphlet translated into the Spanish language, and widely diffused through the island of Cuba.

DR. FRANCIS was honored with membership in many humane,

literary, and scientific societies at home and abroad, and held correspondence with several of their associates. In 1850, Trinity College conferred on Professor FRANCIS the degree of LL. D.

The sketch here given of Dr. FRANCIS exhibits a life more active than eventful, but evidently one that would have been far more eventful had it been less active. Engaged in the duties of a laborious profession, in a great city, at the early age of twenty, and soon after called upon to apply all his unexpended energies to sustain and advance the reputation of a newly-established medical school, and to assist in editing a medical journal, he could have found but little leisure for unbroken study, or the preparation of elaborate treatises on the art to which he was devoted. Untiring activity in his proper vocation, and scrupulous devotion to its claims, characterized his whole professional career. The hope of being able to relieve his suffering fellow-beings was ever sufficient to call forth every exertion, and every sacrifice in his power to make. The call of poverty was always quite as loud in his ear, and was answered with as much alacrity, as that of wealth. It is well known that his services and his contributions to the relief of distress, would together amount to sums surpassing the charities of many men of the largest means. There are many extraordinary traits in the character of the subject of this memoir, which have scarcely been touched upon from its necessary brevity; among them none more remarkable than the facility and fidelity with which he went through his duties; the every-day demands constantly developed in him an energy, a power of endurance, and a disregard to personal comfort, that are called forth in others only by great emergencies and trying occasions. The amount of labor performed by him is almost unexampled; he accomplished more of every thing, and besides had more of social enjoyment, than most others. It was the same with his mind as with his body: no drafts upon it exhausted its power; its stock was always at command. The possessor of such a mind must naturally sigh for a release from the thraldom of professional toil, and the liberty to expatiate freely and widely in the regions of thought. If such a boon was ever earned by years of faithful service, and benevolent exertion in the cause of humanity, Dr. FRANCIS did not fail of obtaining it; and we know that he asked for himself no higher reward, nor would we ask for him greater glory, or for science more honor, than he conferred upon her, and he was allowed to enjoy it.

This outline of a remarkably active professional career gives but an inadequate view of the character of its subject. There is a great similarity in the outward experience of the successful practitioner of medicine in a large metropolis; but the endowments of each individual, and the circumstances of life, essentially modify his influence and usefulness. In the case of Dr. FRANCIS, a strong natural bias for literary pursuits, and an uncommon degree of public spirit, as well as sympathy with artists, authors, and men of science, induced the exertion of his talents, and the devotion of his leisure in other spheres, than that of his special vocation. He presented one of the rare instances where this has been accomplished, without the slightest interference with regular duty. Blest with a vigorous constitution, great powers of endurance, and a singular facility both of thought and action, he was well enabled to achieve a wide range of reading in all the departments of learning and taste, and at the same time to cultivate the intimacy of those whose lives are devoted to literature, science, and art. The effect of this twofold culture is apparent, not only in the essential aid rendered by Dr. FRANCIS to the cause of social progress, by means of his cordial support, cheering sympathy, and intelligent coöperation, — but also by many eloquent contributions to American letters. These consist, besides his medical writings, to which allusion has already been made, of addresses, biographical memoirs of distinguished characters, and personal reminiscences. In the latter department, Dr. FRANCIS was a proficient. His anecdotes of interesting personages have a remarkable significance: gleaned during many years of familiar acquaintance, caught up by quick and accurate observation, and preserved by a memory wonderfully retentive, they rendered his conversation admirable, suggestive, and memorable. In some few instances, as those of the old physicians of New York; Cooke and Kean, the celebrated actors; some of the original editors, naturalists, and artists, such as Freneau, Wilson, Jarvis, Fenimore Cooper; and distinguished Knickerbockers, like Pintard, Livingston, Fulton, and others. These attractive memorials appeared in the journals of the day, or the occasional discourses of the author. One of the most characteristic and valuable of the latter was delivered on the anniversary of the New York Academy of Medicine, of which Dr. FRANCIS was the first president. No more able vindication of medicine as a science, or more powerful appeal to its votaries for its advancement and elevation, has ever appeared. It is rich, too, in historical illustration and local anecdote, and has a rhetorical finish which amply sustains the literary reputation of its author. All this was admirably illustrated, too, in the profoundly interesting address he delivered at the New York

Typographical Society Banquet, January 16, 1852, — an occasion which his hearers never forgot. In his social character, Dr. FRANCIS represented an almost obsolete class. He was emphatically a New-Yorker in his feelings and associations. The frank hospitality of the early colonists was combined around his fireside with the discursive intercourse of the *savan*, and the patriotic sentiment of the citizen. In American history and biography he was an oracle, and he was an efficient member of all the institutions originated to advance the interests of literature and science in his native city. With enlarged benevolence, a mind unwearied in inquiry, constant association with men and books, and an ardent love of knowledge, as well as friendship for its promoters, Dr. FRANCIS found time, even amidst the unceasing claims of an extensive practice, thus to identify his name with the progress of the age and the literature of his country. His labors ceased with his death, in February, 1861. His name is so inwrought with the literary and scientific progress of the country, that it will long prove a light to those who struggle with difficulties in their zeal to serve the cause of humanity and liberty.

NATHANAEL GREENE.

THE important influence of the example of the American Revolution on the rights of man and the liberties of nations, is, as yet, but partially estimated. It is not, however, too much to say, that the working of our political institutions, for far more than half a century; the happy operation of religious freedom; the liberty of the press; the general diffusion of education; the skill and bravery of our chivalry on the field, and on the ocean; but above all, perhaps, the prosperity and happiness of our country, are now winning the admiration of the world. On the continent of Europe we have always been regarded with respect; but the unhappy consequences of the French revolutions have retarded the onward march of liberty, which must eventually triumph. Time, and that not far distant, will there unfold a series of revolutions, "a war of opinions," based on that which was fought and won for us at Bunker Hill, Yorktown, and the Eutaw Springs. A love of liberty is implanted in the bosom of man, and it will be seen, that, with feeble means, the will to attain it will prevail. For us it has been attained; and we shall now address ourselves to the task of sketching out the character and services of one of those, by whom the glorious work was accomplished. In the midst of prosperity, nations, like individuals, are apt to forget their benefactors; and republics have been proverbially ungrateful. It is incumbent on us to remove the stain.

NATHANAEL GREENE, the fourth in descent from one of the early English settlers of New England, was born on the 27th of May, 1742, in Warwick, Rhode Island. His family were very respectable members of the society of Friends, among whom his father was a preacher. In the peaceful principles of that sect, NATHANAEL was instructed. His early years were passed in the attainment of the mere rudiments of an English education, and succeeded by variations of labor in the field, the mill, or at the anvil, as his age and strength increased. In his youth, he excelled most of his companions in strength and agility; and it is evident from what has been written of him, that he enjoyed, with great delight, the amusements and pleasures of his companions. At the age of fourteen, he became acquainted with a lad from the university of Rhode Island, who opened to his view new objects of attention. From that time, books were eagerly sought for, and their contents devoured in the intervals of his work. The desire to obtain books stimulated him to extraordinary exertions at the forge, where the work was so heavy, as to produce a permanent lameness in one of his feet; but his object could be accomplished in no other way. Geography, travels, and history, were his delight; he made himself master of Euclid, and acquired a knowledge of Latin. When about seventeen, he attracted the notice of President Styles, of Yale college, at that time a resident of Newport, and formed an intimate acquaintance with Lindley Murray, who was also there on a visit. From those gentlemen he derived much valuable information, as to the choice of books and a proper course of study. When twenty years of age, he commenced the study of the law; not with an intention, like young Murray, of making it a profession, but to acquire a knowledge of the principles of jurisprudence. When the celebrated stamp act began to agitate the country, the ardent mind of GREENE was immediately interested in the subject; and, after deliberate reflection on the principle involved, he came to the firm resolution of supporting the cause of his country, if necessary, by an open resistance.

In the year 1770, he was elected a member of the legislature of his native state, to which, from that time, until he was called to the command of the southern army, he was uniformly reëlected. There, the mass of information which he had accumulated by many years of study, gave him an influence, and he became a leading and popular member. When the states, in 1773, began to organize their militia, his attention was, as in former instances, turned to the subject, and he began a new and corresponding course of studies. Military books now engrossed his attention, until he had studied the histories of all the ancient and modern wars within his reach. For this, he was dismissed from the society of Friends; yet, he ever after regarded the sect with deep respect. In July, 1774, he married Catharine Littlefield, an intelligent and engaging lady; but his public duties left him little time for the enjoyment of domestic bliss. He had now laid aside the plain dress of his early associates, and had become a member of the "Kentish Guards," a military company, composed of the most respectable young men of the county. In the ranks of this corps he continued, until after the battle of Lexington; when the

NATHANAEL GREENE.

state of Rhode Island embodied three regiments of militia, and placed them under the command of Brigadier General NATHANAEL GREENE, who conducted them to Cambridge. Here he gained the confidence and friendship of Washington, which he retained through life. He was commissioned as a brigadier general in the continental army on the 22d June, 1775, and, as a major general, on the 9th August, 1776. He accompanied the army to New York, and had command of the troops on Long Island; but when the disastrous battle was fought at Flatbush, the army was deprived of his services, by a sickness, which reduced him nearly to the grave. When the commander-in-chief found himself obliged to retreat across New Jersey, General GREENE was his constant and firm supporter. At that period of the war, a train of misfortunes had spread despondency and gloom over the country; yet the confidence and cheerfulness of General GREENE never forsook him, and the spirits of the troops were cheered by his example, though in want of almost every necessary.

On the night of the 25th December, 1776, General GREENE crossed the Delaware, in command of the left wing of the army, which, in the surprise of Trenton, seized the artillery of the enemy, and cut off their retreat to Princeton. He was constantly with the army, during that trying winter, and shared its hardships and its glories. He was present at the battles of Brandywine, in August, and of Germantown, in October, 1777. Such was the distressed situation of the American army through the winter of that year, that Washington was doubtful of his ability to take the field the ensuing season. Every exertion was made to put the army in a condition for the campaign, and General GREENE was pressed to accept the appointment of quartermaster-general. The office was accepted with great reluctance, for his inclination was, to serve in the line; and the charge and distribution of the public money was of all things disagreeable. The necessities of the army, however, and the strong expression of Washington, that "some one must make the sacrifice," at last induced him to consent; but not until the condition was acceded, that, he should not lose his right to command in action. Of this he availed himself at the battle of Monmouth, and on the retreat from Rhode Island.

The duties of his new station were arduous and embarrassing, but were rendered more so, by the unhappy factions which divided the councils of the country. Notwithstanding the distress and poverty which threatened ruin to the cause, intrigue and slander were in active operation, to undermine the reputation and character of the men, who were devoting themselves to accomplish the almost hopeless work. Washington himself was assailed; and GREENE, who was supposed to have been his favorite officer and confidential adviser, was made an object of suspicion. It appears strange to us, at this time, that calumny could have had the effect of injuring the reputation of such a man, under the circumstances in which he was placed. Constantly with the army, and under the eye of the commander-in-chief; often without a dollar at command, and made desperate by witnessing the distresses of the brave men who had been his companions in arms through years of toil and suffering. "Hard is the lot of a man in public life, where the expenditure of money constitutes a part of his duty." The purity and integrity of General GREENE's character bore him above the storm, congress did him justice, and his personal friends never faltered in the discharge of their duty towards him. In August, 1780, he resigned the office, a poorer man than when he entered upon it.

After the fall of Charleston and the captivity of General Lincoln, the war in that quarter required the presence of a commander, on whose talents the army and the inhabitants might rely. The high reputation which General Gates had acquired by the capture of Burgoyne's army, obtained for him the command of the southern department. His arrival in North Carolina revived the hopes of the patriots, and he very soon collected an army of about four thousand men. He at once prepared to drive the British force from their line of posts across the state of South Carolina, and to carry the war to the gates of Charleston. But near Camden he was met by an army under Lord Cornwallis, and suffered an overwhelming defeat. The consequences were awful. Lord Cornwallis considered himself a conqueror in full possession, and adopted a course of proscriptive measures, which finally recoiled upon himself. He hung several respectable men at Camden, and he seized a number of the most influential and patriotic of the prisoners on parole, whom he transported to St. Augustine: he then prepared to overrun that part of Carolina which had not been devastated; and his progress was marked by rapine, conflagrations, and blood. The lion-hearted patriots of Carolina were again roused to the defence of their lives, their families, and their homes. From that time, there was no neutrality; and the horrors of a regular warfare were heightened, by all the ruthless accompaniments of party fury, malignity, and revenge. General GREENE was appointed to supersede Gates, on the 14th of October, 1780; and four days after, he sat out from West Point for his command.

On arriving at Charlotte, on the second of December, he found the southern army a mere skeleton, without artillery, baggage, or stores. In a letter to La Fayette, he says, "Were you to arrive, you would find a few ragged, half starved troops in the wilderness, destitute of every thing necessary for the comfort or convenience o soldiers." In his front was an enemy, flushed with victory and well provided; around him, an exhausted country; and the inhabitants divided into hostile parties, "plundering each other with little less than savage fury." Money, he had none; for he had been furnished with only sufficient to defray the expenses of his journey. But he had around him a number of active, spirited, and devoted officers, on whose exertions he could depend, and the *promise* of reinforcements from the states through which he had passed on his route.

Cautiously he adapted his operations to his means. The prudent policy of Washington, and the precipitate imprudence of Gates, were both before him. His first care was to remove to a place, where subsistence and the means of transportation could be obtained. Cornwallis was at Winnsborough, and Leslie was advancing with a powerful reinforcement towards Camden. The only mode of carrying on the war was, to cut up these forces in detail, by sudden assaults on their detachments; by enticing them into the interior; and by striking at the posts, and keeping up an alarm on every side, until the American commander should find himself in sufficient force to face his antagonist. General GREENE, with the main body, marched to the Cheraw hills on the Pee Dee; and detached General Morgan to the west of the Catawba, to act on the left of Cornwallis, to collect provisions and forage, and annoy the enemy as circumstances would permit. This movement alarmed the British commander for some of his posts, and he despatched Colonel Tarleton, with a force, to destroy him, which was, itself, annihilated at the Cowpens. Galled at this unexpected result, Cornwallis hastened to cut off Morgan's retreat with his prisoners, and to prevent him uniting with the main body. Foiled in the attempt, he vigorously pursued GREENE, who was moving in a direction to unite with Morgan.

This is the commencement of the celebrated retreat from South Carolina, across the state of North Carolina, into Virginia, which has won for the American commander a high rank, in the estimation of military men. With the force of Morgan united to his own, he was unable to meet the foe. Cornwallis sought to force him to an action, and he was as resolutely determined to avoid one. Having taken the precaution to secure the passage of the Dan, the American army crossed that river in safety, and were secure. Here General GREENE had expected to find reinforcements, and to have been able to turn on his pursuers; but not a man was there.

Cornwallis saw the dangers of his situation; so sure had he been of crushing the Americans, that he had destroyed his baggage to accelerate his movements; his force was diminishing by death and desertion, while that of his wary adversary he knew must increase, for the states of North Carolina and Virginia were collecting recruits, and the cry "to arms" was universal. He accordingly retired to Hillsborough, to collect the royalists in that vicinity, by liberal offers of gold and land; in this he succeeded for some time, but suddenly they began to diminish. The partisan whigs were hovering around in force, cutting off the advancing parties; and the rapid concentration of volunteers, had enabled GREENE to resume offensive operations, and throw himself between Cornwallis and the upper country. The noble earl now found himself surrounded by timid friends and inveterate enemies; his stores decreasing, and the country wasted by the loyal followers of his army; and it was evident, that whenever his adversary pleased, there must be a trial at arms. The activity and vigilance of GREENE's light troops kept him constantly informed of every movement of the British forces, and enabled him to rest and refresh his troops against the day of action, which he determined to draw on whenever his reinforcements should arrive, being confident, that if he could not ruin his adversary, he could at least cripple him severely. According to this determination, the battle of Guilford Court-house was fought on the 15th March, 1781. The result of that engagement was, that the British remained masters of the field, but with the loss of six hundred men. Victory at such a price was defeat to Cornwallis, who retreated, and left his wounded to the benevolence of his enemy. In a few days, General GREENE found himself in a condition to pursue; he left the wounded of both armies behind, in the care of a congregation of Friends, and followed with great vigor, until finding it impossible to overtake the foe, he halted at Ramsay's Mill to refresh his troops, and Cornwallis pushed forward towards Wilmington. When GREENE was satisfied of the onward course of the British army, he took the resolution to march directly into South Carolina, to revive the spirit of the people, to destroy the line of posts between Charleston and Camden, to live on the spoils of the enemy, and, if possible, induce Lord Cornwallis to return for their protection. But that commander, after a fruitless endeavor to divert GREENE's attention, took a contrary course to Petersburg; Colonel Lee, with his legion, and a small corps of infantry, were detached to form a junction with Marion, on the Santee; while GREENE, with the main body, moved off to Camden, and, on the 20th of April, took post at Hobkirk's Hill, about a mile and a half from the British redoubts. On the morning of the 25th, whilst the American soldiers were preparing their breakfast, Lord Rawdon attempted a surprise, by passing through a swamp to the left of the encampment. But in this he was disappointed. The pickets received him promptly, and retired deliberately and in good order, disputing the ground bravely. In the mean time, the American army was formed in order of battle, and every disposition was made before the enemy appeared. The battle commenced with vigor, and a sanguinary conflict ensued. But the Americans were obliged to abandon the field, and Rawdon immediately returned to Camden, which he soon after evacuated, and retired to Charleston. Orangeburgh, Fort Motte, Granby, and several other posts, were captured by American detachments; whilst the commander carried on the siege of Ninety-Six, a strongly fortified post. But before it could be reduced, Rawdon had received reinforcements, which enabled him to raise the siege, and GREENE was compelled to fall back on North Carolina, with the enemy in full pursuit. It was discouraging to be thus made the sport of fortune, but the firmness and decision of the general's character sustained him through the trial; for being at this time advised to abandon South Carolina, he replied, "I will recover the country, or perish in the attempt." Lord Rawdon soon perceived that pursuit was vain; that while he was removing from all support, GREENE was falling back on his magazines and reinforcements, and leading him towards the very route, over which he had before led Cornwallis; and, being already short of provisions, he returned to Ninety-Six, and from thence to Charleston, taking with him all the loyalist families in that district of country. General GREENE then retired to the high hills of Santee, to indulge his army in a short repose during the heat of the summer.

Near the end of August, he again sought the enemy, and met him in battle, at the Eutaw Springs, on the 8th of September. This battle was described by the American commander, as the most obstinate and bloody he had ever seen. The militia, with a firmness "which would have graced the veterans of the great king of Prussia," advanced with shouts into the hottest of the enemy's fire; but one part of the line faltering for a moment, the British, elated at the prospect, sprang forward to improve that moment, but at the same time deranged their own line. General Greene, who was watching for such an incident, "ordered the second line to advance, and sweep the field with their bayonets." The order was promptly obeyed, and the enemy were driven from the ground, through their camp in the rear. But their pursuers were diverted by the spoils of the tents, and became irretrievably confused; in the mean time, the enemy rallied, and under cover of the fire from a large party who had taken possession of a brick house, recovered their camp. Had it not been for the temptation, so unexpectedly thrown open, the British forces must have surrendered; as it was, their power in South Carolina was prostrated, for in this action they lost upwards of one thousand men. This was the last of General Greene's battles. The enemy abandoned the whole of South Carolina, except Charleston and its vicinity, and the American army retired to their former encampment, until after the capture of Cornwallis at Yorktown. The soldiers, left for a time to repose, the mind of the commander was meditating on the future. He had been induced to expect, that the French fleet, with a part of the land forces on board, would pass from the Chesapeake to Charleston, to coöperate with him in the recovery of the three most southern states. Disappointed in that aid, he still was bent on the expulsion of the foe from North Carolina and Georgia, if not from their strong hold in Charleston. Although the spirit of enterprise was high in the American army, there were presented few opportunities for adventure. We cannot recount the minor affairs, but will pass to events of another character, and view the conduct of General Greene under other circumstances. It was discovered, that a part of his army had entered into correspondence with the British, and had agreed to deliver him up; but the ringleader was detected, convicted, and shot, and twelve of his associates deserted. Had their plan succeeded, the southern army would have been dissolved; for it was the commander's personal influence alone which held it together: he was the idol and pride of his soldiers; and it is to their honor, that amongst the conspirators, not one native American was implicated. Much as the army had suffered, their commander had felt no less; and the only instance of impatience we have found in all his correspondence, is about this time, when he had to witness the sufferings of his soldiers, without the power to relieve them. While engaged in the duties of the field, the southern army had endured privations and hardships almost beyond belief; but we have it from undoubted authority, that a large proportion of that army, at times, were literally, "as naked as they were born;" that the loins of

NATHANAEL GREENE.

many of the brave men who carried death into the enemy's ranks at the Eutaw, were galled by their cartouch boxes; and that their shoulders were protected from chaffing, only by a piece of rag or a tuft of moss. Can we be surprised then, that, when left to repose, they should think over their sufferings, and expect, at least, to be noticed by the country they had saved? Yet, so it was, they for a time appeared to be forgotten, and they murmured; and the mind of the commander was burdened by the most painful anxieties. Symptoms of mutiny made their appearance in the Maryland line, but they were preceded by a pathetic address to their general. They asked his attention to their thinned ranks, reduced from a brigade to the number of two hundred; but he had not the means to relieve them. *His army at this time had received no pay in two years; was nearly naked; often short of meat and bread; and the sick and wounded perishing for want of medicines and proper food.*

When discontent existed among the officers of the legion, on the appointment of Colonel Laurens, and they all tendered their resignations, complaining of partiality and injustice, he reminded them of their right to appeal to congress, but their reply was petulant and haughty; and the general, after giving them a private hint of his intention, accepted their commissions. This was unexpected; they found that their attachment to him was such, that they could not leave him in the face of the enemy; and they availed themselves of his suggestion, to refer their complaint to congress, and returned quietly to their posts. Thus the general had not only conquered the enemy, but had overcome the demon of discord in his own army.

Except for the purpose of procuring provisions from the surrounding country, the enemy lay inactive in Charleston. With all their force, they had been unable to keep possession of the country; and with their diminished means it would have been folly to renew the strife. They therefore prepared to evacuate the city, having agreed with the American commander to leave it uninjured, and to be permitted to depart unmolested. Accordingly, on the 14th December, 1782, the American army entered the city as the British rear departed from it. To the citizens of Charleston, it was a day of joy and congratulation. Upwards of two years, they had been under the arbitrary restrictions of an enemy's garrison; cut off from all intercourse with their friends, and ignorant of their fate; now they beheld them returning, the liberators of their country. Solemn thanks were offered to THE ALMIGHTY in places of public worship, and the whole city presented a scene of festivity. The object of regard to every eye, and of praise from every tongue, from the governor of the state to the humblest citizen, GREENE alone appeared to be unconscious of having himself merited distinction, while he deeply felt the attentions, which were liberally bestowed on his gallant army.

The difficulty of supplying rations for the army after this period, for a time, threatened serious consequences, but by the commander becoming responsible himself, as an endorser for the contractor, the evil was removed; but the transaction was the cause of much subsequent embarrassment to himself, and to his family after his decease.

Peace was at length restored,—the army was disbanded, and General GREENE returned to his native state.

In every place, through which he passed on his journey home, he was received with enthusiasm and expressions of gratitude and admiration. On his arrival at Princeton, where the congress was then in session, that body resolved to present him with two pieces of ordnance, taken from the British army, "as a public testimony of the wisdom, fortitude, and military skill, which distinguished his command in the southern department." They had previously voted him a British standard and a gold medal, commemorative of the battle of Eutaw. The state of Georgia presented him with a beautiful and highly improved plantation, a few miles from Savannah; and South Carolina conveyed to him a valuable body of land. This he was obliged to part with, to free himself from the pecuniary obligations before referred to; and to the former he removed with his family in the fall of 1785, when he commenced the cultivation of his land, and the education of his children. But this period of repose and domestic pleasure was brief; for being attacked by inflammation of the brain on the 12th, his mortal career was closed on the 19th of June, 1786.

Thus have we sketched the life of one of the most conspicuous men of the American revolution; and whether we view it, as illustrative of what may be accomplished by the native energy of genius, or as an example of deep, pure, devoted, patriotism, it is equally entitled to our regard. Through it, we can trace the same invincible spirit, in the humble, industrious, youthful Quaker, as in the heroic firmness of the illustrious warrior. In the former, it was incited by a thirst for knowledge, which never abated; and in the latter, by a determination to deliver his country when overrun by hostile armies. The influence of his early moral discipline should not be overlooked, for it gave a peculiar hue of modesty and virtue, patience and benevolence, to his subsequent actions; which, like the pearly tints of a picture, at once harmonize and beautify the whole.

Edmund Pendleton Gaines

EDMUND PENDLETON GAINES.

EDMUND PENDLETON GAINES, the third son of James Gaines, was born on the 20th of March, 1777, near the eastern base of the blue ridge, in the county of Culpepper, Virginia. His father was married while very young to Miss White, who died a year after the marriage, leaving one daughter. He afterwards married Elizabeth Strother, by whom he had four daughters and two sons elder, and three daughters and one son younger than EDMUND. His father served in the latter part of the revolutionary war at the head of a company of volunteers; and was soon after chosen a member of the legislature of North Carolina, to the northwest border of which state he had moved with his family at the close of the war. He was afterwards elected a member of the convention of that state to which the federal constitution was submitted, and by which it was rejected. If upon the final vote of rejection the name of James Gaines stands recorded in favor of that measure, his objections were entirely removed by the adoption of the "*Bill of Rights;*" and he lived to see its excellence demonstrated by a trial of forty-two years duration. He witnessed the progress and issue of this trial with a steadfast belief that the federal constitution, so amended, and taken in connexion with the constitution of the several states of the union, embraced the most perfect, as well as the most powerful, system of government known to man. James Gaines was the nephew of Edmund Pendleton, a profound lawyer, and for many years the presiding judge of the court of appeals of the state of Virginia, and a statesman whose services were most prominent in the cause which produced a Washington, and has enrolled the names of Henry, Jefferson, Madison, Randolph, Lee, and Mason, among the most distinguished in the annals of American history.

To an early association with such an individual, and to the affectionate solicitude and guardian care of a highly gifted mother, are to be imputed the stern integrity and devoted sense of duty which always distinguished the subject of this memoir. Upon the memory of his mother his heart always rested with an abiding love, and to her care and prudence he delighted to acknowledge himself mainly indebted for the principles which sustained and strengthened him amid the trying and perilous scenes of his eventful life.

Born in a frontier settlement, and during a state of civil war, hi earliest recollections were painfully connected with deeds of blood and rapine. A main object of maternal care was manifested in an anxious zeal to merge the baleful influences in a recital of the triumphs of her countrymen in the great cause of civil liberty, and of the brilliant consequences that were to flow to her children and posterity from such pressing and impending calamities. It is not, therefore, to be wondered at that the subsequent career of her favorite son should be devoted to the profession of arms; and less, that that career should be distinguished not more on the field of battle, than by a loyal devotion to the constitution and the laws of his country, both as a soldier and a private citizen.

At the close of the war of independence, his father's estate consisted of a plantation of a few hundred acres, and that but indifferently stocked: of money, like the rest of his neighbors, he had none, except in the form of the old valueless continental bills.

Under these circumstances of poverty, in which all classes were at the time more or less involved, it will not be matter of surprise that the early education of our hero should be limited to the acquirement of such attainments as he could occasionally find time to receive at the neighboring county school.

The greater portion of his youth was necessarily devoted to labor. His daily toils were, however, amply compensated by the reflection that the burden of the farm was lessened to the advancing years of his father, and that the declining days of his mother were comforted and consoled by every act of filial duty.

In the subsequent toils of his professional career, he more than once had reason to congratulate himself on the habits acquired in following the plough and in wielding the axe. His heart was early imbued with the pleasures which result from the performance of duties, and his body hardened by healthful and vigorous exercise. To an early friend, whom he often delighted to name, one Ralph Mitchell, he was indebted for the attainment of so much of the elements of the mathematics as to become an accurate surveyor.

the country prepared for war, determined to appoint a military collector of the customs for the district of Mobile. For this office, GAINES, who had in 1802 been promoted to a first lieutenancy, was selected. He accepted the office in the confident expectation that his position at Fort Stoddert, thirty-six miles north of the town of Mobile, where he was stationed, would insure to him, sooner or later, the honor of taking possession of the disputed territory.

In the year 1806, our military collector of the customs, in addition to the duties hitherto assigned to him, was honored with the appointment of postmaster, and that of agent to the postmaster-general, with authority to suspend certain postmasters and mail contractors, whose delinquencies were in anywise attributable to the influence of persons then known to be engaged in what was termed the *Burr war*. As commandant of Fort Stoddert, GAINES was authorized to employ such of the United States troops as he should deem necessary and proper to afford protection to the persons employed as inspectors of the revenue, as well as those employed in carrying the mail between the city of New Orleans and Athens, Georgia; the principal part of the intervening country, near six hundred miles, being at that time a wilderness.

While in the discharge of the various and complicated duties of the civil and military trusts confided to him, it became his duty, in obedience to the proclamation of the president, to arrest Colonel Burr, and to send him under a mounted guard, in charge of Major Nicholas Perkins, who volunteered his services for that purpose, to Virginia for trial. Of the propriety of this act Captain GAINES never for a moment entertained a doubt.

It is a fact, however, not to be concealed, that, notwithstanding the arrest and confinement of Colonel Burr was a duty, and a duty performed in a spirit of as great delicacy and forbearance as was consistent with the perfect security of his person; and notwithstanding he was confided to the care of Major Perkins, than whom a more humane, honorable man could not have been found; yet from the time of his arrival in Richmond, Captain GAINES found arrayed against him an influence which he always in vain endeavored to account for.

The president, on being advised through the department of war that Burr had been arrested by Captain GAINES, authorized the appointment of marshal to be added to his various other civil appointments, with authority to notify his veteran commander, General

Wilkinson, with such other public officers and others at New Orleans acquainted with the projects of Burr, to attend his trial. With these officers the acting marshal embarked in a United States vessel of war in May, 1807, at New Orleans, and arrived at Old Point Comfort early in June, a few days previous to the attack on the frigate Chesapeake.

In the course of this trial, which immediately followed, Captain GAINES had reason to put in practice the principles of forbearance which he had early prescribed to himself. The counsel of Burr deemed it expedient to animadvert with much harshness, not only on the arrest of his client, but likewise on the conduct of the officer who made the arrest. The captain, satisfied with the good and faithful service he had rendered his country, was neither moved by these animadversions, nor for a moment thrown off the manly propriety of his deportment.

History will not hesitate to say, that whatever may have been the designs of Colonel Burr, they were at once frustrated by his prompt arrest and speedy conveyance to a proper place of trial. To Captain GAINES she will award the full merit of this act.

Our hero had now attained the thirtieth year of his age; he had thus far laboured through what may be considered the apprenticeship of his profession; he had acquired full confidence in his capability to serve his country in either a civil or a military capacity, and believed himself equal to any command in the army the government might see fit to confide to him.

Shortly after the trial of Colonel Burr, he determined to retire from the army, and engage in the profession of the law. The execution of this resolution was, however, for a while suspended, in consequence of the increased probability of a war with England. The chances of this event were soon, however, rendered nearly hopeless by the turn of public affairs. In this state of suspense, GAINES at length decided upon asking for a leave of absence.

This was promptly granted to him by his commanding general, Wade Hampton, with the understanding that if the prospect of war should subside within a year, he should be permitted to resign; otherwise, that he would remain in service. In this interval he commenced the practice of the law in the counties of Washington and Baldwin, Mississippi territory.

Scarcely had he completed his second circuit, under auspices of the most flattering character, when the alternative under which he

NATIONAL PORTRAITS.

stood pledged to his general, occurred. The nation determined to maintain her rights. War was declared against Great Britain, and Captain GAINES joyfully resumed his sword, with a firm determination never again to abandon it so long as his country should need his services.

In the war which followed, he soon became distinguished among the most steadfast in the faithful performance of every arduous duty. The post of greatest danger was to him the post of honor. There he was always to be found, distinguished alike by the fertility of his resources, the imperturbable coolness of his courage, and the amiable simplicity of his manners. The details of his services are too voluminous for the limited space allowed in this memoir.

It must suffice to state, that after being on duty in the north-western division of the army, he was, subsequently to the battle of the Thames in Upper Canada, engaged in the operations on the northern frontier; where on various occasion his conduct as an officer received the highest commendation. In the action at Chrystler's Field, he was particularly distinguished; and at the memorable and brilliant defence of Fort Erie, in August, 1814, (at which post he commanded in chief, and was severely wounded by the bursting of a shell,) his bravery and skill were most conspicuous; nor was he ever wanting in magnanimity or humanity.

In the midst of the sanguinary conflicts in which he was then engaged, his conduct as a soldier won the admiration even of the enemy to whom he was opposed, and against whom he was then in arms on the field of battle. The credit acquired by General GAINES and his regiment was unsurpassed by that of any others of our corps or commanders in that engagement.

In the course of the war, GAINES received the several successive, rapid promotions, of lieutenant-colonel, colonel, adjutant-general, brigadier-general, and major-general; the last being the highest rank authorized by law, and conferred in a form the most acceptable to the soldier, inasmuch as it was "*a war brevet,*" expressly stating the fact that *it was conferred on him in consequence of his gallant and meritorious conduct in battle.* The federal government also honored him and the officers and men of his command, with a unanimous vote of thanks, and authorized the president to provide and present to him a gold medal, five States of the Union also offered him their thanks, whilst the three great and patriotic states of New York, Virginia, and Tennessee, awarded to him unanimous resolutions of thanks, with a fine gold-hilted sword which he received from each of these states.

EDMUND PENDLETON GAINES.

From this period General GAINES continued to serve his country with skill and assiduity, giving full proof that his honors had not led him to indulge in inglorious repose. He was engaged in the Creek war, and afterwards commanded in the southern military district until the reduction of the army in 1821, when he was retained as a Brigadier, and the western division assigned to him. During the Sauk (Indian) and Seminole wars, the General was engaged, endured great personal danger and hardships, but manifested the bravery and skill which usually distinguished his career.

Perhaps little more need be said of the active life of the General. Although he repeatedly applied for employment in the field of the Mexican war, we believe he was never actively engaged in it. It is said that the reason given at head quarters was, that he was, "too old for field service;" but in the opinion of some of his friends another reason might be found in the fact, that he did not conceal his disapprobation of the system adopted by government in carrying on that war—a system which, in common with many other military men, he regarded as weak and dilatory, though ultimately rendered successful by the imbecility of our adversaries.

To a plan of defence projected in 1839, by General GAINES, for this country, his friends point with pride. It was his opinion that the recent application of steam to the propulsion of ships of war, had in a great measure destroyed the utility of the old system of fortification for the defence of harbors; inasmuch as it would in most cases enable the attacking party to pass in a few minutes beyond the guns of any ordinary fortress. He therefore earnestly recommended the substitution of movable floating batteries for the forts now in use, and strenuously advocated the immediate construction of railroads, as a means of concentrating force indispensable to the national defence. The correctness of these views has not yet been tested by experience; but as it is generally admitted that the discovery referred to, has wrought a great improvement in the means of attack, it seems reasonable to suppose that the modes of defence must undergo a corresponding revolution. We leave the question to those to whom it belongs, merely calling attention to this matter, as illustrative of General GAINES' earnest thought as to the exigences of his profession, and of his ardent desire to apply the results of his observation for the public benefit. Certainly the system seems to bind the States together in almost indissoluble bonds, with its great arteries of communication equally applicable and valuable for purposes of war and peace, putting the whole country in a perfect state of defence.

NATIONAL PORTRAITS.

The last office sustained by General GAINES was that of commander of the eastern division, with his head quarters at New York, which city he left for the south only during the winter preceding his death. That event occurred at New Orleans, June 6, 1849, at the age of 72 years. He was a man of extreme simplicity and transparency of character, of the most unquestionable integrity, and of unwearied zeal in the welfare of his country. His history presents a fine example of the gradation of an American soldier maturing his mind and character for the position of a DIVISION commander. We refer to it as exhibiting a capacity, morally and mentally, that can be excelled by few. While the history of our wars proves that no one has exhibited more valor upon the field of battle, or more unceasing efforts for the safety of the country, than EDMUND PENDLETON GAINES,—the records of peace show that no citizen soldier has manifested a greater degree of ardor in the cause of the nation's defence.

WILLIAM C. C. CLAIBORNE.

On the 20th December, 1803, the beautiful, rich, and extensive region of Louisiana, having been ceded to the United States by France, was formally surrendered to the republic. The American commissioner on this occasion was invested with the title and powers of intendant and governor-general of the province, as exercised under the former French and Spanish dominion. To him was conferred almost unbounded authority; upon him rested the delicate task of reconciling to a new dominion, and organizing into a new government, a people long inured to forms and usages entirely different. Though yet but in the spring of life, no man could have exercised the former with greater mildness and moderation, none could have performed the latter with more judgment and ability. When he came, followed by a gallant band of Americans, to unfurl the banner of his country over its new territories, all were pleased with the blandness of his manners and the beauty of his person; all were astonished to see so young a man invested with so high a trust: but the subsequent virtue and wisdom of his measures during a long and tempestuous administration of thirteen years, excited the love and admiration of all, and have left in the memory of his countrymen of Louisiana a monument more lasting than the marble which they have consecrated to his virtues. The American who in this high station thus did honor to himself, and to the judgment of the distinguished statesman who appointed him, was WILLIAM CHARLES COLE CLAIBORNE, the subject of the present memoir.

Governor CLAIBORNE was born in Virginia, of a family who had been settled in that state for nearly two hundred years. When the revolution broke out, it is believed that without an exception his family took the side of the people against arbitrary government, and continued their efforts, in common with their countrymen, until the glorious result of the contest. The subject of our sketch was at the close of the revolution a mere child, and hence could not have been an actor in it; but he soon learned to appreciate the magnitude of the task our fathers had accomplished, and the perils through which it was achieved. His own father had shared its toils, and it was the custom of the old gentleman, in his retreat, to recount to his children the exploits of the American soldiers, the hardships they had encountered, the battles they had fought, and the victories won. All was painted in glowing colors, even to the horrors of the prison-ships, and the brutality of the British soldiery, who were often guilty of horrible atrocities. Endowed with some learning, a fine imagination, and an eloquence bold and expressive, he thus early impressed on the minds of his sons an invincible attachment to free government; a determination, when necessary, to lift their arms in its defence; and an abhorrence for whoever would raise a parricidal hand upon the fair fabric of American liberty. Mr. Claiborne, however, could leave no inheritance to his children, but education and this warm patriotism which he so early inspired; youthful indiscretions in part, but principally an honorable zeal in the service of his country, had dispersed the wealth which he had inherited from his fathers. Thus the principles of WILLIAM, the second of his four sons, may be said to have been fixed when he was yet only eight years of age; they were then, what they remained through life, eminently republican. At that early age he excited the admiration of Mr. Eldridge Harris, the worthy president of the Richmond academy, when he saw this motto which his scholar WILLIAM had written in his Latin grammar, "Cara patria, carior libertas; ubi est libertas, ibi est mea patria."

Young CLAIBORNE having spent a short time at the college of William and Mary, which he left on account of improper conduct of one of the ushers towards him, returned to the Richmond academy, and there acquired a thorough knowledge of his own, with the Latin and Greek languages, and the most important branches of the mathematics. While at school, he learned with great facility, and was universally esteemed and beloved by his professors and fellow students. At the age of fifteen, he was apprized that for his future establishment in life he had to depend entirely upon his own exertions; he determined, therefore, on his course, and carried it into immediate execution. He told his father he knew very well he could do nothing more for his children than educate them; that he had resolved on his course, and with his permission would enter upon it forthwith. "I," said he, "have some acquaintance with Mr. Beckley, clerk to congress; I will go to New York, and endeavor to get employment in his office: if I succeed,

WILLIAM C. C. CLAIBORNE.

my fortune is secured; if I fail with him, my education will recommend me elsewhere, and in as thriving a place as New York, I can surely do something to support me. All I ask is a small addition to my stock of clothes, and my passage paid to New York." The manly firmness with which he addressed these words to his father, the confidence which they implied in his abilities, virtue, and energy, excited the old man's admiration; he gazed with rapture on his enterprising son, and the plan was acceded to. Being now fixed in his resolution, Mr. CLAIBORNE left school, having first delivered a valedictory address to the professors and students. Previous to the delivery of this address, he had submitted it to the inspection of a learned judge, whose corrections he solicited; the next day it was returned with one or two immaterial alterations, and a note from the judge, which told his young friend " to continue moral and industrious, and he would become useful and celebrated; his path, with the blessings of Providence, would be strewed with roses, and lighted by the sun of true glory."

Thus encouraged, and fortified by a moral and solid education, with a mind embellished with stores of Grecian and Roman literature, with manners urbane, a tall and manly form, and a face uncommonly beautiful, Mr. CLAIBORNE, not yet sixteen years of age, bade farewell to his family, and took his departure from Richmond in a sloop bound to New York. He was kindly received by Mr. Beckley, who gave him immediate employment in his office. The business which devolved on him, consisted in copying bills and resolutions of congress, and drawing original bills for members and committees of that body. These duties giving occupation to only half of his time, a portion of each day was devoted to reading political works of merit, attending to the debates of congress, and learning the French language. His evenings were almost invariably consecrated to the ladies, to whose society he was devoted through life. To Mr. Beckley he gave entire satisfaction, and subsequently repaid all the favors he had received at his hands. Congress soon removed to Philadelphia, and hither Mr. CLAIBORNE went. Soon after his arrival in that city, he became acquainted with Vice President Adams, and Mr. Jefferson, then secretary of state. By both these gentlemen, he was treated with great kindness: he afterwards proved his gratitude to both. Hitherto, Mr. CLAIBORNE had not fixed on any profession on which to depend for his future establishment in life; he had thought of the navy, the army: his dreams were sometimes golden, and he had even hoped to rise in the ranks of diplomacy. The bar had not yet presented itself to his mind in a tempting light; inconsiderable circumstances, however, have sometimes a decisive influence on the destiny of man; Mr. C. had for some time been a member of a polemic society, at which were discussed such questions as from time to time agitated the public mind. At last a question was proposed for discussion which Mr. C. had deeply reflected on; he determined, therefore, to enter the lists, and try himself at a public speech. He had now entered his eighteenth year; we have told the reader that his person was fine, his pronunciation was also distinct, accurate, and well-disciplined, and his tones of voice admirably adapted to public disputation: to these advantages he superadded, without being himself conscious of it, that grace of gesture which generally belongs to youth, beauty, and innocence. The success of the effort he made on this occasion was surprising; it elicited from a crowded audience reiterated bursts of approbation, and an enlightened member of congress who was present, declared "it shivered to atoms the arguments of his opponents, and bore off the uncontested prize of superior eloquence." The success of this effort gave an additional stimulus to his rising hopes, and he determined to enter on the practice of the law.

It should have been mentioned that Mr. CLAIBORNE had become intimately acquainted with General John Sevier, then a delegate in congress from the territory, and afterwards governor of the state of Tennessee. A friendship grew up between them which continued unimpaired during their lives, and of all the benefactors Mr. CLAIBORNE met with in the beginning of his career, there was none like this distinguished man, in the number and greatness of his favors. General Sevier had frequently advised Mr. C. to settle in the territory south-west of the Ohio; he stated the opening then was there for a lawyer, augured that his success would be great, and tendered his assistance and friendship. These flattering assurances determined his young friend. He accordingly gave Mr. Beckley notice that he intended to leave him as soon as another clerk could be procured, and in a short time took an affectionate leave of this good friend to repair to Richmond, where he remained three months. "During this stay in Richmond," says his brother, the Hon. Nathaniel Claiborne, "he was devoted almost entirely to the society of the ladies, and I have heard him repeatedly say, he had in that time been enabled to read only through the revised code, and a few chapters in the first volume of Blackstone's Commentaries. With this *dispreparation*, as he humorously called it, he was an applicant for a license, and, strange as it may seem, he passed with great credit, as I have been assured by a gentleman who was examined and licensed at the same time. This my brother attributed to the polemic society in Philadelphia, which he considered at the time one of the best law schools in the union. Here he had acquired that general and enlarged view of natural, national, and municipal law, without labor and without expense, which years of study could not have afforded."

The object in getting a license in Virginia, was to enable him the more readily to obtain admittance to the territorial bar; without license in another state, a probationary residence was required. And now bidding adieu to the scenes of his youth, and the charms of large cities, he directed his steps to Sullivan county in the now state of Tennessee, and entered on the practice of the law. He continued at the bar, however, only two years, and his success in this short period was equal to that of any lawyer who ever went before him. No cause of moment and expectation occurred in a court where he practised, in which he was not employed. He was frequently sent for to the neighboring court in Virginia; and he commenced his career by receiving a fee of five hundred dollars, with his expenses paid, for coming to Virginia to defend a man on a charge of murder. At another time, he went two hundred miles to argue a case, in the decision of which was involved property to an immense amount, on the promise of a fee so large, that Mr. C. refused to receive it, although the cause was gained, and took only an elegant horse in lieu thereof. Instead of devoting, as heretofore, much of his time to gay amusements, he was now occupied with his books, and had already raised himself to the first rank in his profession; as an advocate in a criminal case, it is said he stood unrivalled. Juries have been often dissolved in tears, and enlightened tribunals have been deeply moved by his touching eloquence. He now determined to move back to Richmond, and enter on the practice of the law there. "My brother," says Mr. Nathaniel Claiborne, "had a quickness of comprehension, a goodness of heart, and a laudable ambition to be distinguished, in a degree we rarely meet with; but unfortunately he was constitutionally lazy, and when we see him marching with giant strides to eminence in his profession, we are constrained to acknowledge that he was urged on by the joint influence of virtuous ambition and hard necessity. He was attached to Virginia, and had left it with regret. The very trees that had shaded him from the summer heat were to him objects of veneration; these, were the beautiful seats of his early ancestors: they have long since passed into other hands, but the everlasting marble records the names of the first proprietors. There he had received his earliest instruction, and enjoyed the society of friends who loved him. The determination of my brother to return was heard by the family with enthusiastic pleasure, and as the pressure on him for exertion would be greater, those who knew the powers of his mind were convinced that he must succeed."

An occurrence now took place which caused the resolution to remove to Richmond to be abandoned. The population of the territory having been ascertained to amount to seventy-five thousand, they demanded admission into the union, and a convention was called to form a state constitution. Mr. CLAIBORNE was proposed and elected one of the five members for Sullivan county.

In the convention which soon after assembled, he appeared to great advantage. It was an enlightened body, and the constitution that issued from their hands is based upon the truest principles of liberty; in the formation of this constitution, WILLIAM C. C. CLAIBORNE had a principal agency. The education he had received, the books he had read, the political circles he had frequented, all conspired to give him an imposing stand. He now stood for the first time before a whole state, and the goodness of his heart and the magnitude of the object, united to bring into action all the powers of his mind. His merit was universally acknowledged. Governor Blount declared, that making the necessary allowance for his youth, he was the most extraordinary man he had met with, and that if he lived to attain the age of fifty, nothing but prejudice could prevent his becoming one of the most distinguished political characters in America. In the convention of Tennessee, he began his political career, and without intermission he was thereafter in public life. General Sevier was elected governor of the new state of Tennessee, and among his first acts was the appointment of Mr. CLAIBORNE as a judge of the supreme court of law and equity of the state. Mr. CLAIBORNE was urged by his friends not to accept; but in vain. "My motto," said he, "is honor and not money; Governor Sevier is my friend, and if I can, I am bound to aid his administration." At the time of his appointment to a judgeship, and that too in the highest tribunal in the state, he was not *twenty-two* years of age. He continued but a short time in this office, when a vacancy occurring in the house of representatives of the United States, at the solicitation of several gentlemen who had served with him in the convention, he resigned his seat on the bench and became a candidate for congress. He was elected by an immense majority over his opponent, who was a man of talent, of great wealth, and extensive connections. A few days after his election to congress, Mr. CLAIBORNE entered his twenty-third year. This astonishing and rapid promotion becomes still more surprising, when we consider that he had but recently come into the district, that he was poor, and had not the advantage of any kindred blood, even in the most remote degree, in the state of Tennessee. During the first congress that Mr. CLAIBORNE sat in, he participated little in debate, but enough to show that he was an acquisition to the republican party. On the bill providing for the military establishment, however, the talents of the house were brought out, and the strength of parties put to trial. On this occasion, Mr. CLAIBORNE delivered his sentiments; his speech was adorned with the choicest flowers of ancient and modern literature; it showed a heart deeply convinced, and earnestly engaged in convincing others; and if it discovered on its face less labor than other speeches bespoke, it was exempt from the venom which conflicting political prejudices had on this occasion developed: and the spirit of benevolence which it breathed, with the classic purity of the style, recommended it to general attention. A listener thus described it: "It seemed to be a spontaneous effort, the object was to persuade and convince, not to surprise; it had passion and feeling in every sentence, but it was the passion of the heart; satisfied he was right, he was bent on the conviction of others. So earnest was Mr. C., that he forced himself on the affection of the most indifferent, and excited the enthusiastic admiration of his friends: though he was zealous, it was without bustle; he was ardent, but not acrimonious; and if he fell short of some of the veterans who preceded him, you were loath to make the admission, while you reflected that he was the youngest man who had ever appeared on the floor of congress."

The constitution had not required that the electors should designate on their tickets the person they voted for as president, and the one voted for as vice president, but simply that they should give their votes for two persons; that the one having the highest number of votes should be president, and the one having the next highest should be vice president. Now it so happened, that Mr. Jefferson and Mr. Burr had an equal number of votes, and it devolved on the house of representatives to decide which of them should be president, the choice to be made by ballot, and each state in the union to have but one vote. The contest was extremely animated, for on this occasion the great federal and republican parties came into violent conflict. It was clear that Jefferson had been voted for as president, and Burr, vice president; they had been so nominated before the election, and in every vote given for the two, Jefferson was first named; when, therefore, it was understood that they were returned with an equal number of votes to the house of representatives, it was supposed of course that the public voice would be obeyed, and Jefferson made president. The federal party, however, determined to support Colonel Burr; they knew very well the political sentiments of every member of the house of representatives, and they early ascertained that the election depended on the vote of Mr. CLAIBORNE, the sole representative from the state of Tennessee. Mr. C., who, on this occasion had been reëlected to congress, was young and aspiring; the federal party knew, too, that he was poor. They flattered themselves that his vote might be secured, and indirectly proffered various temptations to obtain it. But Mr. CLAIBORNE was too firm to be brought over: he knew the public voice, and thought it honorable and proper to obey it. The day at last arrived, when this great question of the presidency was to be decided, and the states were equally divided on the first ballot; several other ballots took place, and the result was the same, when the house adjourned. The news spread through the union like fire, and everywhere produced the liveliest sensation. The importance of Mr. CLAIBORNE's vote was so well understood, that he went armed to the house; for what might occur from the extraordinary excitement that prevailed, no one could foresee: rumors were even afloat that the parties in the country were beginning to arm.

For several days, congress, and the country around, were a scene of terrible confusion: thirty-six ballots had been had, and the result was the same; an equality of votes for Mr. Jefferson and Mr. Burr. On every ballot, Mr. CLAIBORNE had voted for Jefferson, and declared that as he felt satisfied that that gentleman was the choice of the people, he was determined to adhere to him, let the consequences be what they would. On the thirty-seventh ballot, the state of Vermont, that had hitherto voted for Colonel Burr, threw in a blank ballot, and Jefferson was elected. Mr. C. did what he considered his duty with a determined mind, and to his vote was owing, in a great measure, the result of this important contest.

Mr. CLAIBORNE remained but a short time after this in congress. A serious misunderstanding having arisen between the people of the Mississippi territory and their then governor, many distinguished individuals of that country signified a wish for the appointment of Mr. C. as their governor, and, in conformity therewith, he received and accepted an appointment to that office in 1801, from President Jefferson.

Mr. CLAIBORNE proceeded to his new government with all possible despatch. He reached the beautiful hills of Natchez on the 23d of November, where he was received with enthusiasm, and he immediately entered with zeal upon the duties of his charge.

WILLIAM C. C. CLAIBORNE.

On his arrival, he had found the infant community over which he was to preside torn by local dissensions and personal animosities; by these different factions he was hailed with gladness, each hoping to make him the instrument of separate views or private vengeance; but he repelled all such attempts with firmness, though mildly, and taking sides with none, he made it his duty to hear all parties: to sooth and conciliate all, but to act for himself, with independence, impartiality, and justice.

Mr. CLAIBORNE had lately married Miss Eliza Lewis, of Nashville. She was tall and graceful, with perfect symmetry of feature, and her wealthy and indulgent parents had early procured for her those advantages of education that add new charms to the female character. Thus blessed with the affections of an amiable wife, in possession of an independent fortune, and without an enemy on earth, Mr. C. spent two years most happily as governor of the Mississippi territory; and how far he enjoyed the love and confidence of the people during this period, may be seen by the following address, which he received after he had repaired to New Orleans, on a mission of still higher importance.

"*To His Excellency* WILLIAM C. C. CLAIBORNE, *governor of the Mississippi territory, exercising the powers of governor-general and intendant of the province of Louisiana:*

"The exertions of a public officer to confer happiness on the community by dispensing equal and impartial justice, and preserving unimpaired the constitutional liberties of the people, deserve the return of grateful acknowledgments. The citizens of Washington and its vicinity, therefore, pray your excellency to accept their undivided approbation of the firm and dignified measures of your late administration in this territory. If integrity of conduct, united to an enlightened mind filled with benevolence and universal philanthropy, are worthy of eulogium, *all* that those virtues merit we offer you as a just tribute.

"We congratulate your excellency on the unanimity and harmony with which the American government is received by our new fellow-citizens of Louisiana; this great and interesting event cannot fail to exhibit ' the fairest page in the volume of faithful history;' and the high characters who so ably managed the negotiation, from its commencement to the ever memorable surrender on the 20th day of December last, will share the warmest affection of the American people.

"On this auspicious occasion, we reflect with honest pride and exultation, that in discharging the highest trust and confidence reposed in your excellency by the president of the United States, nothing has appeared repugnant to the principles of inflexible justice, mingled with humanity. We earnestly desire the return of your excellency to the Mississippi territory. We anticipate no change by which we can gain either a better friend, or a more patriotic governor; but should the general government require your aid in another quarter, we tender you this pledge of undissembled friendship, and a sincere wish that you may ever continue to merit and obtain the confidence of your country."

In this conspicuous station, the highest in the gift of the general government, and to discharge which required judgment, prudence, and ability, far beyond the lot of ordinary men, Mr. CLAIBORNE had a diffi cult and perplexing task to perform. He had found the province of Louisiana in some parts almost fallen into anarchy, and throughout the administration every thing to reform or reorganize. Government had scarcely a nerve not wounded by corruption, and the business in every department was wrapped in mystery and intrigue, and had been left in confusion often inexplicable. Under the last Spanish governor, not only many posts of honor and profit in his gift were sold, but even when exercising the sacred character of a judge, he often vended his decisions to the highest bidder. Such being the character of the head, it is not surprising that the same depravities pervaded every branch of the system. The Louisianians, however, were a well-disposed and generous people; the greater part gave a cheerful and sincere welcome to the American government and its new institutions; but generally their defect of education, which had been the policy of their former rulers, their ignorance of the English language, and especially of political affairs, rendered them credulous, and often liable to become dupes to the machinations of individuals, who for their own ends are ever busy in exciting discontent in the public mind.

Thus Governor CLAIBORNE soon had to contend against the most unprincipled intrigues and factions, directed principally by some of his own ambitious countrymen, who had emigrated to the new territory, and who, envious of his authority and high station, used every means to thwart his administration, and to destroy him in the eyes of the people and of his government. So violent were these attacks, that the governor was brought to the field, to defend his character against the calumnies of a Mr. Daniel Clarke, who, by his wealth, his ambition, and his talent for intrigue, had acquired some influence in the country. He was severely wounded on this occasion, and confined a long time to his bed; but he sustained himself in his station, and persisted in his honorable course. He made it his especial care to protect and encourage the people he had been sent to govern; he used every means in his power to conciliate them to their American countrymen, and to spread among them the blessings of education, and of that political information, which alone could enable them to govern themselves, and to use and appreciate properly the great privileges of freemen, which they were to enjoy. He became sincerely attached to these his adopted countrymen; and from the purity of his character, the mildness of his official and private conduct, and the benevolence that beamed from his noble countenance, no man was better calculated to have reconciled and attached this new and foreign people to the government he represented. The Louisianians often proved their attachment to him, and when they were admitted into the union as an independent state in 1812, they sanctioned the choice of the general government, by electing him governor, by their own free, and almost unanimous voice.

Mr. CLAIBORNE, however, during this period had met with many private misfortunes. During the first summer in which he had been exposed to that climate so baneful to strangers, he had nearly succumbed himself to an attack of the yellow fever; his lady fell a victim to that fatal disease, his infant daughter accompanied her mother, and his brother-in-law young Lewis, who had followed him to Louisiana, fell in a duel. All three had expired on the same day, and were consigned to the same tomb. When time had allayed the grief of this great calamity, Mr. C. subsequently married Miss Clarissa Duralde, a young creole lady of great beauty and mental qualities, whom he had the misfortune to lose also, two years after marriage. His situation rendering the position of a single life in some measure unbecoming, he again married, in 1812, Miss Bosque, an accomplished lady of Spanish extraction, who survived him.

In 1814 and '15, during the memorable invasion of that state by the English, Mr. CLAIBORNE was still in the executive chair of Louisiana, and had been active and highly instrumental in preparing the military defence of the country, and giving to General Jackson, previous to his arrival on that station, all the necessary information relative thereto He, however, voluntarily surrendered to the general, when he arrived, the command of the militia of his state, and consented himself to receive his orders; a measure which he thought a just tribute to the military experience of General Jackson, and which he adopted, also, to avoid to his state all the expenses of the equipment and movements of her militia, which would have fallen upon her alone had he kept the command. Thus, to his great regret, it was not the fortune of Governor CLAIBORNE to have participated personally in the glorious contest of the 8th of January. He was marching rapidly, to join in the action of the 23d of December, at the head of a select corps of Louisiana militia, eager to meet the enemy, when he received orders from General Jackson to turn back immediately, and repair with his troops to Gentilly, to occupy the important pass of Chef-Menteur, where it was feared that the English had made a diversion; he obeyed, and reluctantly directed his march to that station, which he fortified, and remained in that command during the whole contest, which terminated in the memorable battle of New Orleans. Previous to this, an occurrence had taken place, which may be worthy here of insertion. All have heard of the adventurer Lafitte, whose piratical character was some

NATIONAL PORTRAITS.

what extenuated by many traits of valor and generosity, and against whose depredations in our southern seas, the efforts of Governor CLAIBORNE and of the general government had been long directed, with but little success. The British commander of the naval expedition against Louisiana, aware of the intrepidity of this buccaneer, and of his perfect topographical knowledge of this region, when he approached the waters of the Mississippi, addressed a letter to Lafitte, offering a large sum of money, and a captaincy in the British navy, for his aid and counsel to the invading expedition. Lafitte rejected with contempt these offers; to prove his sincerity, he immediately sent the letter of the British commander to Governor CLAIBORNE, by a confidential agent, and tendered his services with those of his band to the American government, provided all criminal prosecutions against them by the United States should be suspended. The governor immediately accepted the proposal, upon consultation with the proper authorities. Lafitte and his determined band were admitted into our ranks, and subsequently rendered the most efficient services at the head of our artillery; we need not say that they obtained the pardon which their conduct merited.

In 1817, on the expiration of his term as governor of the state, Mr. CLAIBORNE was elected to represent Louisiana in the senate of the United States; but fate had here decreed a premature end to his career: he died in New Orleans, of a liver complaint, on the 23d of November, 1817, and in the forty-second year of his age. All ranks attended his remains to the grave with undissembled grief. The municipal authorities on the same day decreed a public mourning, and appropriated a sum of money to erect a marble monument to his memory.

Thus guided by the firm integrity, the virtue, and the sincere and warm devotion to his country, which particularly distinguished him, Governor CLAIBORNE had sustained his character throughout his eventful administration, as a pure and devoted, an able, dignified, and virtuous chief magistrate. It was his lot to have been at the helm of the important post of Louisiana during all the critical periods of our early collisions with Spain upon our southern frontiers, of the Burr conspiracy, and of the invasion of Louisiana by a British army. In all these circumstances, he remained the able agent, and the faithful sentinel of his country upon the outskirts of the union. No man had ever enjoyed greater honors at so early an age: seldom has virtue been rewarded by a more rapid and brilliant career.

JOHN RANDOLPH.

THE interest excited by the first appearance in public life of JOHN RANDOLPH continued until he had passed away from among the living, and did not die with him. His aboriginal descent, extraordinary eloquence, and independent but eccentric course through life, seemed to unite in securing to every thing he said or did, an attention on the part of his countrymen, which has been given to but few of the great American family. He was born on the 2d of June, 1773, at Matoax, the seat of his father, three miles above Petersburg, in the state of Virginia. His English ancestors were from Yorkshire, and he was descended, through his paternal grandmother Jane Bolling, in a direct line from the celebrated Pocahontas. Like Sir Walter Scott, and other celebrated men, he appears, from his own account, prepared in 1813 for a nephew who was desirous to "know something of his life," to have received a very irregular education. He was sent to a country school at an early age, where he learned the rudiments of the Latin language, and had mastered the Greek grammar *perfectly*, when the state of his health induced his mother to send him to Bermuda, where he remained more than a year, losing all his Greek, but reading with great avidity many of the best English authors. After his return to the United States, he was sent, with his brother Theodorick, to Princeton college, where they entered the grammar school in March, 1787. He there attracted the attention of Dr. Samuel Stanhope Smith, the president of the college, who thought that he found, in the Indian descent of his pupil, some support to a theory, which he gave to the world in an Essay more remarkable for its ingenuity than its accurate statement of facts. In the year 1788, after the death of his mother, he was sent to college in New York, but returned to Virginia in the summer of 1790; and in the autumn of that year came to Philadelphia, with the view of studying law under the direction of Edmund Randolph, then recently appointed attorney-general of the United States. Beyond *almost* the first book of Blackstone, he seems to have done nothing towards being admitted to the bar; and from that time till June, 1794, when he became of age, he appears to have led an irregular, desultory life, with scarcely a fixed residence, and no decided object of pursuit.

His reading, according to his own account given to a relative at a later period of his life, is so indicative of the man that any attempt to portray him would be defective without it. "I think you have never read Chaucer. Indeed, I have sometimes blamed myself for not cultivating your imagination when you were young. It is a dangerous quality, however, for the possessor. But if from my life were to be taken the pleasure derived from that faculty, very little would remain. Shakspeare and Milton, and Chaucer and Spencer, and Plutarch, and the Arabian Nights' Entertainments, and Don Quixote, and Gil Blas, and Tom Jones, and Gulliver, and Robinson Crusoe, 'and the tale of Troy divine,' have made up more than half my worldly enjoyment. To these ought to be added Ovid's Metamorphoses, Ariosto, Dryden, Beaumont and Fletcher, Southern, Otway, Pope's Rape and Eloisa, Addison, Young, Thomson, Gay, Goldsmith, Gray, Collins, Sheridan, Cowper, Byron, Æsop, La Fontaine, Voltaire's Charles XII, Mahomet and Zaire, Rousseau's Julie, Schiller, Madame de Stael—but above all, Burke. One of the first books I ever read was Voltaire's Charles XII; about the same time, 1780—1, I read the Spectator, and used to steal away to the closet containing them. The letters from his correspondents were my favorites. I read Humphry Clinker also, that is Win's and Tabby's letters, with great delight; for I could spell at that age pretty correctly. Reynard the Fox, came next, I think; then Tales of the Genii and Arabian Nights. This last, and Shakspeare, were my idols. I had read them, with Don Quixote, Gil Blas, Quintus Curtius, Plutarch, Pope's Homer, Robinson Crusoe, Gulliver, Tom Jones, Orlando Furioso, and Thomson's Seasons, before I was eleven years of age; also Goldsmith's Roman History, 2 vols. 8vo., and an old history of Braddock's War. At about eleven, (1784—5,) Percy's Reliques and Chaucer became great favorites, and Chatterton and Rowley. I then read Young and Gay, &c. Goldsmith I never saw till 1787."*

In 1799, he made his first appearance in public life as a candidate for a seat in congress, and was elected. He owed his success

---

* Letters to Dudley, p. 190.

to his eloquence alone; for he possessed neither family influence nor connexion in the district, and was a mere boy in appearance. The all-absorbing political questions arising out of Mr Madison's celebrated Virginia Resolutions of 1798, of which Mr RANDOLPH was a strenuous supporter, were then deeply agitating the country. Patrick Henry, accused of having abandoned his early principles, appeared at the same time, and for the last time in his life, as a candidate for the assembly, avowedly in opposition to the resolutions; for he approved of the alien and sedition laws as good measures. This state of affairs brought these two remarkable men before the people in mutual opposition; and tradition has handed down to us an anecdote characteristic of both. Mr. RANDOLPH was addressing the people in answer to Colonel Henry, when a countryman said to the latter, "Come, colonel, let us go—it is not worth while to listen to *that boy*." "Stay, my friend," replied the veteran statesman, "there is an old man's head on that boy's shoulders."

Mr. RANDOLPH found the party whose measures he supported in the minority when he entered congress. His fearless course, ready, sarcastic wit, and general power as a public speaker, soon placed him among the most distinguished of the opponents of the administration then in power, and attracted the attention and admiration of the party against which they were exerted, as well as of that of which he soon became the leader. The records of his exertions are widely spread and scanty, and he pronounced most of the sketches of his speeches to be inaccurate.* No collection of American speeches, however, has been deemed complete without some of them; and, imperfectly as they have come to us, the impress of genius is upon them all.

With the party which supported the administration of Mr. Jefferson, Mr. RANDOLPH, after a time, found himself in the majority, and he was for several sessions chairman of the committee of ways and means. It has been suggested, that *with* the majority his efforts were less propitious to his reputation than those which arose from the excitement of opposition; that business habits and discipline of mind were wanting; and that the position of assailant best suited his peculiar disposition, and was his true element. In 1806, he

---

* "The least inaccurate sketches of my speeches will be found in the 'Spirit of '76,' but they are extremely imperfect."—*Letters to Dudley*, p. 116.

joined the opposition, and is said to have declared that his own opposition to the then administration would be "perpetual." The journals indeed, of the house, from the period we have mentioned, exhibit him in the character of its industrious assailant; and the warfare which he carried on against it, in the shape of calls for information, in relation to the well known allegations against General Wilkinson, will be long remembered.

About this period of his life a change came over him, the cause of which even his friends could not understand; he became moody, morose, capricious, suspicious of his friends, sarcastic and bitter towards those he loved best, and a riddle to all around him. This state of things was explained at last, in 1811, by a paroxysm of insanity, attributable to the ill health to which he had been subject almost from the time he arrived at manhood, and of which he seems to have had some lurking consciousness himself.* Of this malady he had frequent returns during his lifetime;† but upon political subjects his mind was clear; and many of his constituents seemed to think of him as the Mohammedans do of madmen, that on such subjects, at least, he was inspired, and they might commit their interests to his charge with safety. It will not be difficult to account, after what has been just stated, for the numerous instances of eccentricity which were made known to the world through every medium, and were used as materials for every sort of attack upon his principles and person.

On the 27th of February, 1808, Mr. RANDOLPH united with his friend Joseph Clay, and fifteen other members of congress, in a protest against the nomination of Mr. Madison for the presidency. This proceeding, which may be considered as a declaration of war upon the administration which was to follow the nomination, gave an earnest of what his course would be; and he was true to the declaration. His speech on the 10th of December, 1811, was directed against the raising of an addition to the army, and against the war against Great Britain, which he saw approaching; and was strongly marked by the *Anglo-mania* which seems afterwards to have attended him to his last hour. He followed up his speech of the 10th of December, 1811, by moving a resolution, "that the

---

* Speech of the 10th of December, 1811, in the house of representatives, on the second resolution of the committee of foreign relations, "that an additional force of ten thousand men ought to be raised," &c.

† Letters to Dudley, p. 203, August, 1818.

president of the United States be authorized to employ the regular army of the United States when not engaged in actual service, and when in his judgment the public interest will not be thereby injured, in the construction of roads, canals, or other works of public utility." This resolution he supported in a few but very pungent remarks, which, however, brought to his aid but fourteen votes; the resolution, on the question being taken on its passage, being negatived by one hundred and two members voting against, and fifteen for it.

To the declaration of war itself he opposed all possible resistance. On the 29th of May, 1812, he offered a resolution, "That under existing circumstances it is inexpedient to resort to war against Great Britain." The remarks with which Mr. RANDOLPH prefaced the introduction of this resolution led to an angry debate, principally upon the various questions of order which arose out of the subject matter of the remarks, produced difficulty between him and the speaker, Mr. Clay, whose decision against him on the points of order was sustained by the house. The prefatory remarks to which we have alluded, involved the then existing state of the public relations of the United States with France and Great Britain, exhibiting a strong leaning against the former, and which, after he had spoken about an hour and a half, were decided to be out of order, because a member was bound to submit his motion to the house previously to debating so much at large. Mr. RANDOLPH chose to consider the decision as an "invention for stifling debate;" and he addressed, on the 30th of May 1812, an appeal to his constituents, the freeholders of Charlotte, Prince Edward, Buckingham, and Cumberland, which we give as affording the best specimen of his peculiar views and mode of reasoning, at the period of its publication.

To the Freeholders of Charlotte, Prince Edward, Buckingham, and Cumberland.

FELLOW CITIZENS.—I dedicate to you the following fragment. That it appears in its present mutilated shape, is to be ascribed to the successful usurpation which has reduced the freedom of speech, in one branch of the American congress, to an empty name. It is now established *for the first time, and in the person of your representative*, that the house may, and will refuse to hear a member in his place, or even to receive a motion from him upon the most momentous subject that can be presented for legislative decision. A similar motion was brought forward by the republican minority in the year 1798,* before these modern inventions for stifling freedom of debate were discovered. It was discussed as a matter of *right*, until it was abandoned by the mover in consequence of additional informa-

---

* This motion was drawn, it is believed, by Mr. Gallatin, but moved by Mr. Sprigg, declaring it to be inexpedient at that time to resort to war against the French republic.

tion (the correspondence of our envoy at Paris) laid before congress by the president. In the "reign of terror," the father of the sedition law had not the hardihood to proscribe the liberty of speech, much less the right of free debate on the floor of congress. This invasion of the public liberties was reserved for self-styled republicans, who hold your understandings in such contempt, as to flatter themselves that you will overlook their every outrage upon the great first principles of free government, in consideration of their professions of tender regard for the privileges of the people.

It is for you to decide whether they have formed a just estimate of your character. You do not require to be told that the violation of the rights of him whom you have deputed to represent you is an invasion of the rights of every man of you, of every individual in society If this abuse be suffered to pass unredressed—and the people alone are competent to apply the remedy—we must bid adieu to a free form of government for ever!

Having learned from various sources that a declaration of war would be attempted on Monday next, *with closed doors*, I deemed it my duty to endeavor, by an exercise of my constitutional functions, to arrest this heaviest of all possible calamities and avert it from our happy country. I accordingly made the effort of which I now give you the result, and of the success of which you will already have been informed before these pages can reach you. I pretend only to give you the substance of my unfinished argument.

The glowing words—the language of the heart—have passed away with the occasion that called them forth. They are no longer under my control. My design is simply to submit to you the views which have induced me to consider a war with England, under existing circumstances, as comporting neither with the INTEREST nor the HONOR of the American people, but as an *idolatrous sacrifice of both*, on the altar of FRENCH RAPACITY, PERFIDY, AND AMBITION!

France has for years past offered us terms of undefined commercial arrangement, as the price of a war with England, which hitherto we have not wanted firmness and virtue to reject. That price is now to be paid. We are tired of holding out, and following the example of the nations of continental Europe; entangled in the artifices, or awed by the power of the destroyer of mankind, we are prepared to become instrumental in his projects of universal dominion. *Before these pages meet your eye, the last republic of the earth will have enlisted under the banners of the tyrant, and become a party to his cause.* The blood of the American freemen must flow to cement his power, to aid in stifling the last struggles of afflicted and persecuted man; to deliver up into his hands the patriots of Spain and Portugal, to establish his empire over the ocean and over the land that gave our forefathers birth; to forge our own chains! And yet, my friends, we are told, as we were told in the days of Mr. Adams, "*the finger of Heaven points to war.*" Yes the finger of Heaven DOES point to war. It points to war, as it points to the mansions of eternal misery and torture; as a flaming beacon warning us of that vortex which we may not approach but with certain destruction. It points to desolated Europe, and warns us of the chastisement of those nations who have offended against the justice and almost beyond the mercy of Heaven. It announces the wrath to come upon those, who, ungrateful for the bounty of Providence, not satisfied with the peace, liberty, security, and plenty at home, fly, as it were, into the face of the Most High, and tempt his forbearance.

To you, *in this place*, I can speak with freedom, and it becomes me to do so: nor shall I be deterred by the cavils and the sneers of those who hold as "foolishness" all that savors not of worldly wisdom, from expressing fully and freely those sentiments which it has pleased God, in his mercy, to engrave upon my heart.

These are no ordinary times. The state of the world is unexampled; the war of the present day is not like that of our Revolution, or any which preceded it, at least in modern times. It is a war against the liberty and happiness of mankind. It is a war in which the

JOHN RANDOLPH.

whole human race are the victims, to gratify the pride and lust of power of a single individual. I beseech you, put it to your own bosoms, how far it becomes you as freemen, as Christians, to give your aid and sanction to this impious and bloody warfare against your brethren of the human family. To such among you, if any such there be, who are insensible to motives not more dignified and manly than they are intrinsically wise, I would make a different appeal. I adjure you by the regard you have for your own security and property, for the liberty and inheritance of your children, by all that you hold dear and sacred, to interpose your constitutional powers to save your country and yourselves from the calamity, the issue of which it is not given to human foresight to divine.

Ask yourselves if you are willing to become the virtual allies of Bonaparte? Are you willing for the sake of annexing Canada to the northern states, to submit to that overgrowing system of taxation, which sends the European labourer supperless to bed? To maintain by the sweat of your brow, armies at whose hands you are to receive a future master? Suppose Canada ours; is there any one among you who would ever be, in any respect, the better for it? the richer—the freer—the happier—the more secure? And is it for a boon like this, that you would join in the warfare against the liberties of man in the other hemisphere, and put your own in jeopardy? Or is it for the *nominal* privilege of a licensed trade with France, that you would abandon your lucrative commerce with Great Britain, Spain, and Portugal, and their Asiatic, African, and American dependencies? In a word, with every region of those vast continents. That commerce which gives vent to your tobacco, grain, flour, cotton, in short, to all your native products, which are denied a market in France!

There are not wanting men so weak as to suppose that their approbation of warlike measures is a proof of personal gallantry, and that opposition to them indicates a want of that spirit which becomes a friend to his country; as if it required more courage and patriotism to join in the acclamation of the day, than steadily to oppose one's self to the mad infatuation to which every people and all governments have, at some time or other, given way. Let the history of Phocion, of Agis, and of the De Witts, answer this question. My friends, do you expect to find those who are *now* loudest in the clamor for war, foremost in the ranks of battle? Or is the honor of this nation indissolubly connected with the political reputation of a few individuals who tell you *they* have gone too far to recede, and that you must pay, with *your ruin*, the price of *their consistency?* My friends, I have discharged my duty towards you; lamely and inadequate I know, but to the best of my poor ability. The destiny of the American people is in their own hands. The net is spread for their destruction. You are enveloped in the toils of French duplicity; and if, which may Heaven in its mercy forbid, you and your posterity are to become hewers of wood and drawers of water, to the modern Pharaoh, it shall not be for the want of my best exertions to rescue you from the cruel and abject bondage. This sin, at least, shall not rest upon my soul.

JOHN RANDOLPH *of Roanoke.*

May 30*th*, 1812.

This appeal drew, on the 17th of June, 1812, from Mr. Clay, then speaker of the house of representatives, an answer addressed to the editor of the National Intelligencer,* the insertion of which is not

---

* Niles' Weekly Register, vol. ii, p. 266.

within the views or limits of this sketch, but which, though nearly twenty years have diminished the interest of the occurrence to which it relates, may still be read with pleasure and advantage.

The health of Mr. RANDOLPH was seriously affected in the year 1811; and he seems never to have recovered entirely from the effects of the attack which he then experienced; his life, subsequently, seems to have been "one long disease."* The idea of a restoration from change of air and scene, induced him to visit England in 1822. Of England, Ireland, and Scotland, he possessed, previously to having been there, the most minute and accurate local knowledge, derived, as he himself asserted, from books and conversation aided by a very retentive memory, and he sometimes amused himself not a little at the surprise it created. The attention he attracted upon his first appearance in London was very great, and many characteristic anecdotes of him reached this country. He went again to England in the spring of 1824, with the same hope of improving his health which led to his former voyage, and returned to the United States in the autumn of the same year. Disease, however, had taken such firm hold of him, that his subsequent public life received constant interruptions from its visitations.

In June, 1830, Mr. RANDOLPH was appointed, by president Jackson, minister to Russia upon the recall of Mr. Middleton. He sailed shortly after his appointment, and arrived in London in July, from whence he reached St. Petersburg in September following. His stay in Russia was very short; the severity of the climate was ill adapted to the state of extreme infirmity under which he was suffering, and he returned to London, where, on the 26th of December, 1830, he delivered a speech at the lord mayor's dinner. Many rumors of the extraordinary conduct and behavior of the minister of the United States at the court of St. Petersburg reached this country soon after Mr. RANDOLPH's arrival in Russia, were made public, and were seized upon with that avidity which affords such stringent proof of the predominance in human nature to enjoy whatever renders our neighbor less in general estimation. Mr. John Randolph Clay, the son of his old friend, who accompanied him as secretary of legation, deemed it right to repel the attacks which were made upon the strength of these rumors, by the publication of a letter, dated at St. Petersburg on the 17th of January, 1831, in

---

* Letters to Dudley, *passim.*

which he asserted, distinctly, that the statements which had been given to the public on the subject of Mr. RANDOLPH's behavior and conduct, had no foundation in truth. The appointment of Mr. RANDOLPH called forth innumerable attacks upon the president, and upon himself; the most vehement of which were founded upon the allegation that he received the outfit, when he knew he could not discharge the duty of a minister; and an imposing parade of figures was made* upon the subject of the cost to the country of his mission. He returned to America in October, 1831, in a state of extreme exhaustion and weakness.

The tariff or "American system," as it has been sometimes termed, met with the most distinct opposition from Mr. RANDOLPH. He seems to have held the doctrine, that the manufacturing interests were never, in any country, satisfied with the extent of the legislative protection granted to them; and he insisted that the tariff system was one which must end in the utter subversion of the rights of the states generally, and that it would be impossible for the slave-holding states to submit long to its oppression. His views are set forth in a letter dated November 22d, 1832, which he addressed to a writer in the Richmond Enquirer under the signature of a " Friend to Truth."

On the 20th of May, 1833, Mr. RANDOLPH arrived in Philadelphia, on his way to New York, where he intended to embark for Europe, again to try the effect of a voyage. He was in the last stage of a pulmonary disease; and, after lingering three days, he died at the City Hotel in Third street.

Few individuals of modern times have attracted more notice in their own country than JOHN RANDOLPH; but it may be long before his true history and character will be portrayed; before the division of his life into periods shall furnish the materials even for a proper estimate of his views, feelings, and powers. It is conceded that among the orators of his own land, he was a star of the first magnitude, but that his aberrations rendered his lustre worse than useless. He drew an attentive audience together in congress more certainly than any other speaker; his sayings, in which the manner and occasion was often more than the matter, were in every man's mouth, and his fame extended throughout the union. But it has been said,

---

* Niles' Weekly Register, September 24th, 1831, p. 69, where the amount is stated at 107,000 dollars.

that, while this was the case, he was brilliant, and nothing more; that he wanted sound, efficient sense, and useful knowledge, and was thus deficient in the most essential qualifications for the station he held in the councils of his country; that, like Cassandra, he was listened to, but never heeded; and was a living example that talent without wisdom leads to nothing. That with all the fame acquired by his eloquence, he was without any real influence, and that while assemblages were gathered together whenever he delivered one of his brilliant harangues, no man set the smallest value upon his opinion. It has been peremptorily denied that he was a statesman; though his career has exhibited him always in the front rank of whatever party he chose to ally himself to, his efforts have been deemed as injurious to his political friends as to their adversaries; and that his whole life was an exhibition of the futility of a mere man of genius, whose career was signalized by words, but left no deeds or great public acts to perpetuate his memory. Let us hope, however, that one day some one from among those who knew him best, may give us the truth in regard to one of the most remarkable of men, whose race was run, and whose voice was loudest in the council of the nation during some of the most difficult periods of existence; it seems almost impossible that such great and general interest and curiosity should have been excited by a mere talker, and that after a long and active life devoted almost exclusively to public affairs, he should have been gathered to his fathers having achieved nothing.

John McLean

JOHN McLEAN.

The subject of this notice is one of those remarkable men, who, by the force of their own independent exertions, have risen from obscurity into great reputation, and into the highest offices in the nation. History has been said to be philosophy teaching by example; and this is more eminently true with regard to Biography, where every lineament of the character is marked with more distinctness, and is seen under a clearer light.

John McLean was born 11th March, 1785, in Morris County, New Jersey. When he was about four years of age his father removed to the western country. He remained a year at Morgantown in Virginia, and then removed to that part of the State which has since been erected into the State of Kentucky. He first settled on Jessamine, near where the town of Nicholasville is now situated; but in 1793 he removed to the neighborhood of Mayslick, where he continued to reside until the year 1797, when he emigrated to the then northwestern territory (now Ohio), and settled on the farm on which the son now lives. At an ealy age John was sent to school, and made unusual proficiency for one whose general opportunities were so limited.

The old gentleman being in narrow circumstances, and having a pretty large family, was unable to send John from home to be educated. He continued, therefore, to labor on the farm until he was about sixteen years of age, when his father consented to his placing himself successively under the instruction of the Reverend Matthew G. Wallace and of Mr. Stubbs, by whose assistance he made great advance in the study of the languages. During this period, his expenses, both for board and tuition, were defrayed by himself; for so limited were the circumstances of his father, that he generously refused any assistance from him.

When about eighteen years of age young McLean went to write

in the clerk's office of Hamilton County. This employment, at the same time that it would enable him to support himself, would also initiate him into the practical part of the law, the profession on which he had already fixed his ardent and aspiring mind. The arrangement was, that he should write in the office for three years, but reserving a certain portion of each day for study; and at the same time he was to prosecute the study of law under the direction of Arthur St. Clair, an eminent counsellor, the son of the illustrious General of that name. It is in this way that a mind animated by a genuine ambition, and firm and determined in its purposes, is frequently able to overcome the greatest difficulties, and to show with how much ease industry and virtue can triumph over all the disadvantages of obscurity and poverty.

During his continuance in the office, young McLEAN was indefatigable in the prosecution of his double duties. He also became a member of a debating society, the first which was formed in Cincinnati; and it is a fact entitled to notice, that most of the young men who contributed to its formation have since distinguished themselves in the public service of their country. Young McLEAN took an active part in the discussions which were held in this society. The notice which his efforts attracted still further confirmed him in the determination which he had already taken not to aim at any ordinary mark, but to make the highest intellectual distinction the prize of his ambition.

In the spring of 1807, Mr. McLEAN was married to Miss Rebecca Edwards, daughter of Dr. Edwards, formerly of South Carolina; a lady who, to the most amiable manners, united the utmost benovolence of character, and presided over the cares of a large family with the greatest judgment and discretion. She died in December, 1840.

In the autumn of the year 1807, Mr. McLEAN was admitted to the practice of the law, and settled at Lebanon. Here he immediately attracted notice, and soon rose into a lucrative practice at the bar. In October, 1812, he was elected to congress in the district in which he resided, by a very large majority over both his competitors.

From his first entrance upon public life Mr. McLEAN was identified with the democratic party. He was an ardent supporter of the war and of the administration of Mr. Madison; not that he was the blind and undistinguishing advocate of every measure which was proposed by his party; for he who will take the trouble to turn over the public journals of that period, will find that his votes were mainly given in reference to principle, and that the idea of supporting a dominant party, merely because it was dominant, did not influence his judgment, or withdraw him from the high path of duty which he had marked out for himself. He was well aware that the association of individuals into parties was sometimes absolutely necessary to the prosecution and accomplishment of any great public measure. This he supposed was sufficient to induce the members composing them, on any little difference with the majority, to sacrifice their own judgment to that of the greater number, and to distrust their own opinions when they were in contradiction to the general views of the party. But as party was thus to be regarded as itself only an instrument for the attainment of some great public good, the instrument should not be raised into greater importance than the end, nor any clear and undoubted principle of morality be violated for the sake of adhering to party. Mr. McLean often voted against his political friends; and so highly were both his integrity and judgment estimated, that no one of the democratic party separated himself from him on that account, nor did this independent course in the smallest degree diminish the weight which he had acquired among his own constituents.

The first session which he attended was the extra session in the summer after the declaration of war. At this session, the tax bills were passed to sustain the war. The law which was passed to indemnify individuals for property lost in the public service was originated by Mr. McLean, and very naturally contributed to add to the reputation with which he had set out in public life. At the ensuing session he introduced a resolution, instructing the proper committee to inquire into the expediency of giving pensions to the widows of the officers and soldiers who had fallen in the military service, which was afterwards sanctioned by law. At this session he also delivered a very able and effective speech in defence of the administration in the prosecution of the war. This was published in the leading journals of that day, and gave an earnest of the future eminence which our subject was destined to attain.

Mr. McLean was a member of the committees of foreign relations and on the public lands.

In the fall of 1815 he was re-elected to Congress with the same unanimity as before. During the same year he was solicited to become a candidate for the senate, which he declined, inasmuch as the House seemed at that time to present the widest arena for the display of talents and for the acquisition of public fame. Mr. McLean was at this period barely eligible to a seat in the senate, having just attained his thirtieth year.

NATIONAL PORTRAITS.

Finding that the expenses of a family were greater than the compensation he received as a member of Congress, and having no other resources than were derived from his personal exertions, he consented to become a candidate for the bench of the Supreme Court of Ohio, and was elected to that office in 1816, unanimously. The duties of this station he discharged with great ability. His mind seemed to combine all the leading qualities which are requisite in a Judge, and his advancement to the office was felt to be a public advantage to the whole State. Meanwhile his reputation abroad was increasing in proportion; and in the summer of 1822 Mr. Monroe appointed him Commissioner of the General Land Office. The emoluments of this office were larger than the salary of Judge. This was a consideration which was entitled to great weight. Judge McLean had a growing family, whom he was anxious to educate; and at the same time that he would now be better able to accomplish this darling object, the schools in the district would present a better opportunity for attaining the higher branches of education. He remained in this station, however, only until the first of July, 1823, when he was appointed Postmaster-General.

Many of his friends endeavored to dissuade him from accepting this office. They urged that the former incumbents had found its duties exceedingly arduous, while at the same time they were not exempted from a large share of that abuse and calumny which is so often wantonly and indiscriminately heaped upon the public servants. It was argued by many that no one could acquire reputation in the office. But Judge McLean determined to repose upon the virtue and intelligence of the people, and he went into the office with the determination of devoting his days and nights to the discharge of its duties.

The finances of the department were in a low condition, and it did not possess the public confidence. But immediately order was restored, and the public confidence revived. And it soon became evident how easy it is to manage the most complicated business when the requisite ability and industry are put in requisition for the task. In a short time the finances of the department were in a most flourishing condition; despatch and regularity were given to the mails, and the commercial intercourse of the whole country was prosecuted with the utmost celerity and ease.

Inefficient contractors were dismissed, and the same course was adopted with regard to the postmasters and other agents of the department. Judge McLean controlled the entire action of the department. The whole correspondence was superintended and directed by him

He gave his undivided and personal attention to every contract which was made or altered. All appointments, all charges against postmasters, were acted on by him. In short, there was nothing done, involving the efficiency or character of the department, which was not done under his immediate sanction.

When he accepted the office, the salary of the Postmaster-General was four thousand dollars. A proposition was made to increase it to six thousand, and was sanctioned by the House of Representatives, by an almost unanimous vote, in 1827. There were, indeed, very few votes against it; and some of the members who were opposed to it, regretted that they were compelled to pursue that course. In the senate, the bill passed also, almost unanimously. Mr. Randolph voted against it, and said the salary was for the officer and not for the office; and he proposed to vote for the bill if the law should be made to expire when Judge McLean left the department.

During the whole period that the affairs of the department were administered by Judge McLean, he had, necessarily, a most difficult part to act. The country was divided into two great parties, animated by the most determined spirit of rivalry, and each bent upon advancing itself to the lead of public affairs. A question of great import was now started, whether it was proper to make political opinions the test of qualification for office. Such a principle had been occasionally acted upon during preceding periods of our history, but so rarely, as to constitute the exception rather than the rule. It had never become the settled and systematic course of conduct of any public officer. Doubtless every one is bound to concede something to the temper and opinions of the party to which he belongs, otherwise party would be an association without any connecting bond of alliance: but no man is permitted to infringe any one of the great rules of morality and justice for the sake of subserving the interests of his party. It cannot be too often repeated, nor too strongly impressed upon the public men of America, that nothing is easier than to reconcile these two apparently conflicting views. The meaning of party is that it is an association of men for the purpose of advancing the public interests. Men flung together, indiscriminately, without any common bond of alliance, would be able to achieve nothing great and valuable; while, united together, to lend each other mutual support and assistance, they are able to surmount the greatest obstacles, and to accomplish the most important ends. This is the true notion of party. It imports combined action, but does not imply any departure from the great principles of truth and morality. So long as the structure of the human mind is so different in different individuals, there will always be a wide scope for diversity of opinion as to public measures; but no foundation is yet laid in the human mind for any material difference of opinion as to what constitutes the great rule of justice.

The course which was pursued by Judge McLean was marked by the greatest wisdom and moderation. Believing that every public officer held his office in trust for the people, he determined to be influenced by no other principles, in the discharge of his public duties, than a faithful performance of the trust committed to him. No individual was removed from office by him on account of his political opinions. In making appointments, where the claims and qualifications of individuals were equal, and at the same time one was known to be friendly to the administration, he felt himself bound to appoint the one who was friendly. But when persons were recommended for office, it was not the practice to name, as a recommendation, that they were friendly to the administration. In all such cases the man who was believed to be the best qualified was selected by the department.

On the arrival of General Jackson at Washington, after his election, and when he was about selecting the members of his cabinet, Judge McLean was sent for to ascertain whether he was willing to remain at Washington. Gen. Jackson having stated the object he had in view in requesting an interview, the Judge remarked to him, before he submitted any proposition on the subject, that he was desirous to explain to him the line of conduct which he had hitherto pursued. He observed, that the General might have received the impression from some of the public prints that the Postmaster-General had wielded the patronage of his office for the purpose of advancing the General's election to the Presidency: that he wished it distinctly to be understood that he had done no such thing, and that if he had pursued such a course, he would deem himself unworthy of the confidence of the President elect, or of any honorable man. The General replied with warm expressions of regard and confidence, that he approved of his course, and wished him to remain in the post-office department. He at the same time expressed regret that circumstances did not enable him to offer the Judge the Treasury department. The War and the Navy departments were subsequently tendered to him, but he declined them both. Afterwards Gen. Jackson sent for him, expressed great regret at his leaving Washington, and made unbounded professions of friendship if he would consent to remain. But the Judge's resolution had been taken, and he was determined to adhere to it. The spirit of party had become unusually bitter and acrimonious, and threatened to overleap all the fences with which it had been hitherto confined. He believed that it would be difficult, if not impossible, for him to pursue the even and measured course which he had hitherto followed with so much credit to himself and advantage to the nation. Retirement from political life seemed, under such circumstances, most desirable. The President, however, wishing to avail himself of abilities which had been exerted so long in behalf of the public welfare, offered him the place of Judge of the Supreme Court, the highest judicial station in the country; and on his signifying that he would accept, he was immediately nominated, and the nomination ratified by the senate.

Soon after this appointment many of the public journals in the northern, middle, and western states introduced his name to the public as a candidate for the presidency at the succeeding election. Many of the opposition papers adhered to Mr. Clay, and the name of Mr. Calhoun was brought out in some parts of the South. The Anti-Masonic party showed a strong disposition to rally upon Judge McLean, and it was clear that that party could not elect, unless the other elements of opposition should unite with them.

The Anti-Masons met in convention in the fall of the year 1831, and Judge McLean addressed a letter to the members of the convention, declining a nomination. In this letter he declared, that "If by a multiplicity of candidates, an election by the people should be prevented, he should consider it a national misfortune. In the present agitated state of the public mind, an individual who should be elected to the chief magistracy by less than a majority of the votes of the people, could scarcely hope to conduct successfully the business of the nation. He should possess in advance the public confidence, and a majority of the suffrages of the people is the only satisfactory evidence of that confidence."

Shortly after the re-election of Gen. Jackson, his name was again brought forward, in the first instance by a nomination of the people in Baltimore, which was followed by similar nominations in Pennsylvania, Ohio, New Jersey, and several other States. A majority of the members of the Ohio legislature also nominated him for the same place. At length, in August, 1835, he addressed a letter to the chairman of one of the principal committees, in which he expressed the same sentiments he had declared on the preceding occasion. He was aware that this course would discourage his friends, but he was not desirous to attain the office, except on such terms as would enable him to carry out those principles which would elevate and tranquillize the political action of the country.

For several years Judge McLean was the only survivor of the members of the Supreme Court on the bench, at the time he was appointed: Judge Washington was the first stricken down, after that period, from that elevated tribunal. His place was filled by Judge Baldwin, who has also fallen. Johnson next followed the demise of Washington. His place was filled by the appointment of Mr. Justice Wayne. The shaft of death then brought to the dust Chief Justice Marshall, who had long been the chief ornament of the bench. Judge Barbour was appointed to fill his vacancy; and he too has fallen; and Mr. Justice Daniel became his successor. Judge Duval resigned under the pressure and infirmity of age, and shortly after died; he was succeeded by Chief Justice Taney. Judge Thompson was the next victim of the fell destroyer, and Mr. Justice Nelson succeeded him. Mr. Justice Grier succeeded Judge Baldwin. Judge Story, whose learning and ability gave renown to that tribunal, was the last of the old bench who fell, leaving Judge McLean the survivor of the court as it was in 1829. Judge Woodbury succeeded Judge Story, and he too fell after a short career; and Judge Curtis became his successor.

In 1837, two Judges were added, making the number nine. Judges Catron and McKinley were appointed to the seats thus created.

The labors of the Judges of the Supreme Court, in their extent and importance, are not appreciated except by those of the legal profession, who occasionally argue causes in that court. On an average fifteen hours in every twenty-four, Sundays excepted, the Judges are laboriously engaged in the performance of their duties. Every part of these require research and intense thought. In hearing arguments in court, the mind must be engaged to the exclusion of other subjects; and in weighing the arguments and looking into the records in each case, and in discussing the legal questions in consultation, as well as writing opinions, the mind is constantly on the stretch. No duties performed by public officers of the government are as exhausting, mentally and physically. Yet it is a singular fact that Judge McLean was never absent except one or two days, at the session of the Supreme Court, after he took his seat in January, 1830. This cannot be said of any other Judge.

The powers of that court are more extensive than those which have ever been committed to any other tribunal. It takes cognizance of controversies between states; and where an act of the legislative power, state or federal is in conflict with the constitution of the Union, it has the power to declare the act void. No questions can arise under the laws of nations, the commercial, or the maritime law, the civil, or the laws of real property, but what may be considered and decided by the Supreme Court. In its hands are deposited the balance power of the nation, and on a faithful discharge of its duties, depend in no inconsiderable degree, the prosperity and permanancy of the government. These great duties have at all times, and under all circumstances, been discharged by that high tribunal in such manner as to receive in a very large degree the public confidence. Whilst the political and executive branches of the government, have been subjected to many changes, which have endangered the great interests of the nation, and sometimes seriously involved the integrity of the Union, no party or body of men have undertaken to deride the powers of the Supreme Court of the Union; and in the most perilous party times, the parties of every hue have looked to that tribunal as the hope of the nation.

Causes involving local rights and feelings may produce much excitement, but resistance to a judgment or decree of the Supreme Court has been rarely threatened, and never carried into effect. Such an attempt has always been frowned upon by the friends of order and good government. And when the day shall come that an organized power, under the auspices of state sovereignty, or otherwise, shall successfully oppose the solemn decisions of that court, it will be followed by the disorganization of the government.

Judge McLEAN took a prominent part in all the leading questions, constitutional or otherwise, which were decided after he took a seat on the bench. In some of them he delivered the opinion of the court, in others he gave his individual opinion, coinciding in the result with the majority of his brethren, and in some cases he dissented and assigned his reasons for doing so.

From the nature of the duties of the supreme bench, and the durable manner in which the acts of each of its members are spread out before the community, a judgment will be made up by the public, as to his ability and fitness for the place, which no effort, friendly or hostile, can materially change. His monuments in the reports of that tribunal, for good or for evil, are written in undying words, and must sustain or depress his public character in all time to come. But few comparatively are called to pass this awful ordeal. Some have passed it, who no longer have an interest in human concerns, but who shed so clear and steady a light upon their path, that throughout the annals of civilization and the common law, it will be regarded. A Judge of the Supreme Court must rest upon his personal qualifications for his public character, and no man had more reason to rejoice in this arrangement than Judge McLean. It will not be forgotten that, in the celebrated Dred Scott case, he dissented from the decision of the court as given by Judge Taney.

As evidences of the high esteem in which Judge McLean was held by those most competent to judge of his intellectual and moral excellencies, we may state that the honorary degree of Doctor of Laws was conferred upon him by Harvard University, at Cambridge, the Wesleyan University, and by one or two other colleges in the United States. He was for several years also the President of the American Sunday School Union, the seat of whose operations is in Philadelphia.

We have already said that in 1840, the Judge suffered the severest affliction which such a man can endure, in the loss of the companion of his youth and the mother of his children. She died as she had lived, an example of virtue, and the triumphs of religion. In 1843, he married Mrs. Sarah Bella Garrard, daughter of Israel Ludlow, Esq., one of the founders of Cincinnati, a lady extensively known and admired for the graces of her person, the amiable charm of her manners, and the accomplishments of her refined and cultivated intellect.

Judge McLean was long identified with the party opposed to the extension of slavery, and his name was prominently before three several conventions, in 1852, 1856, and 1860, for nominating a candidate for the Presidency. He died in 1861, a few weeks after the inauguration of his compatriot in the cause of human liberty, Abraham Lincoln. He saw the coming of the great crisis, when the principles he had long advocated were to be tried; but he lived not to see the triumph which he anticipated for them.

Judge McLean was tall and commanding in person, well-proportioned, with an appearance indicating great physical vigor and intellectual energy. His general habits of life were always very simple, and free from ostentation. His temper was highly cheerful, his manners were frank and pleasing, his conversation instructive and eloquent; so that he possessed in a very rare degree the faculty of inspiring confidence and warm attachment towards him in all who came within his influence, especially the younger members of the bar, towards whom he always especially extended his kindness and courtesy. For many years past he was a communicant with the Methodist church, and his public and private life was in perfect harmony with his profession. Diligence, justice, and benevolence guided him in his whole career as a citizen, a lawyer, and a judge.

Lydia Huntley Sigourney

LYDIA HUNTLEY SIGOURNEY.

WERE we called upon to point out the woman, of America, most worthy to be held up as the pattern and glory of her sex, without a second thought, we should turn, heart and mind, to Mrs. LYDIA HUNTLEY SIGOURNEY.

She was the only child of Mr. Ezekiel Huntley, and a native of Norwich, Connecticut. Her mother, whose maiden name was Wentworth, had a nature enriched with the old pilgrim strength, which gave such distinctive lineaments to the women of her time, and possessed also a wealth of that pure unwritten poetry which found expression in her child. LYDIA HUNTLEY was born a true woman, and a true poet. To speak of her birth as being high or low, would be affectation; for, the seat of nobility in our republic, is the soul which comes from God. Though LYDIA HUNTLEY must have had a laudable pride in the staunch New England character of her parents, in their probity, natural intelligence, and high respectability, yet the birthright which gives her fame and features a place in this gallery, is from Heaven.

Some day—when the hearths and tombs of our great spirits shall become shrines,—Norwich, Connecticut, will be haunted by those who render homage to genius, for it was her birthplace—and Hartford also, for it was long her home; where henceforth her tomb shall be pointed out to all who honor her name.

Mr. Huntley was a landholder, and had also charge of an estate belonging to Madam Lathrop, the widow of Dr. Daniel Lathrop, and daughter of Joseph Talcott, Governor of Connecticut in 1735 and 1741. In this lady's mansion, his family resided, a separate establishment, but with all the social links of existence drawn close by the hourly intercourse thus enjoyed. Madam Lathrop was a widow and childless, when the little LYDIA brought the charm of infant genius to her dwelling. She had nearly reached the limits of fourscore, when the bloom of childhood, and the ripe wisdom of green old age blended their holy contrasts at one fireside. You can see traces of this early association in her amiable life. Her meekness was that of one early impressed with hallowed reverence for the great and good. The subdued manner—the thoughtful care of everything around her—the sweet self-forgetfulness, which half concealed the under current of affection swelling strong and deep beneath this womanly gentleness—all these beautiful traits must have received their most vivid impulses from her infant intercourse with venerable and saintly age.

It is said that the child was precocious, and this is not wonderful, with her own fine nature gathering up the moral strength and golden experience of her aged friend. How could it well be otherwise? But, unlike the generality of precocious children, her after life has been a bright progression. Perhaps this precocity originated in the heart, and excited by love, the brain sprang forward in fervent and healthful sympathy.

Madam Lathrop was a highly gifted lady, with all her strong powers of mind and warm affections unimpaired, and possessed of that personal dignity which insured universal respect. Her memory ranged back through almost the entire eighteenth century, and her friendships had been among the most powerful intellects of her time. Her actual life embraced the most thrilling portion of our national history, and her mind was enriched with that pure old English literature, which had not then been diluted by the froth of desultory authorship. The venerable lady, with all this rich store of intelligence fresh in her memory, still felt the infirmities of advanced years, and but for this gentle child, must have spent many lonely hours while her mind was still athirst for the mental aliment which impaired sight denied. Was not this enough to arouse the soul of a child full of affection and bright with genius? At three years of age, she could read the Bible, and we soon find her in that "low browed and ample room; the wood fire gleaming upon crimson moreen curtains; the gilded clock,—ebony framed mirrors, and polished wainscot, giving back the light from two stately antique candlesticks, reading Milton, and Young, and Sherlock, to her loved friend who sits knitting in the cushioned easy chair." Thus it would seem that through her affections, LYDIA HUNTLEY became precocious. It was no feverish excitement of the brain, but the early and wholesome growth of noble qualities that have strengthened to her present vigorous maturity.

Madam Lathrop's library was rich with chaste English authors, and amid these ancient books her little friend first began to dream those bright imaginings that softly as the dew falls, took to themselves melodies, and at length swelled into poems that will live among the first and best that have enriched our national literature.

LYDIA HUNTLEY SIGOURNEY.

The early inspirations of her genius met the most encouraging sympathy from her revered benefactress, and at eight years of age the child had secured two rare blessings, a judicious loving friend, and the power to express the thoughts that tranquilly, like unfolded blossoms lay in her heart.

Seldom has it fallen to the lot of a being so gifted, to be thus favored, and fostered. A fond, vigorous minded, and truly religious father; a mother possessed of rare practical sense, with that delicate fancy which must unconsciously have imbued the child with its own unwrought romance; a friend such as few persons were privileged ever to possess; surrounded by all that refines in wealth, without the selfishness and pampered appetites that too often follow in its train, or attend its expectations. We cannot imagine a state of things more favorable to the development of a mind like hers!

Thus, for fourteen years, LYDIA HUNTLEY lived in the sweetest and purest of life's enjoyments: but at that period, her noble friend having reached the age of 88—died. Like the fruit of a tropical climate, she had drunk the sunshine and dew of heaven upon the same bough with the blossom, and now fell away, fully ripe, leaving the delicate flower but half unfolded. To the child of genius this was the first great sorrow.

Among the coevals of the subject of this sketch, there was no one to whom she was so tenderly attached as to Ann Maria Hyde, a young lady whose moral and fine mental powers were graced and rendered winning by sweetness of disposition, unaffected modesty, and varied acquirements. The friendship of these two young persons was intimate and endearing. They were companions in long rural walks, they sat side by side at their studies, visited at each other's dwellings, read together, wrought the same embroidery, or, with paint and pencil, shaded the same flower. Youthful friendships are usually so transient, that this might scarcely demand notice, save for the strength of its foundation. It appeared to be based upon a mutual desire to do good; a fixed purpose to employ the talents which God had given them, for the benefit of the world upon which they had entered. In pursuance of this object, they not only assiduously cultivated their mental powers, but engaged with alacrity in domestic affairs and household duties; finding time, also to make garments for the poor, to instruct indigent children, to visit the old and infirm, and to watch with the sick and dying.

Among the plans for future usefulness, which these young friends revolved, none seemed so feasible, or so congenial to their tastes, as that of devoting themselves to the work of education. This, therefore, they adopted as their chosen sphere of action, and resolutely kept this object in view through the course of their own intellectual culture. The books they read, the studies they pursued, the accomplishments they sought, all had reference to this practical design. After qualifying themselves to teach those English sciences which were considered necessary to the education of young females, together with the elements of the Latin and French, they spent some time in schools at Hartford, principally to acquire those ornamental branches, which were then deemed essential. On their return, they entered, at the age of nineteen, upon the business of instruction. A class of young ladies in their native town gathered around them, and into this circle they cast not only the affluence of well stored minds, and the cheering inspiration of youthful zeal, but all the strength of their best and holiest principles. Animated, blooming, happy, linked affectionately, arm in arm, they daily came in among their pupils, diffusing love and cheerfulness with knowledge, and commanding the most grateful affection and respect. After a pleasing association of two years, the young teachers parted, each to pursue the same line of occupation in a different sphere. But another separation, fatal and afflictive, was appointed. Miss Hyde became the victim of a fever, at the age of twenty-four, in the midst of usefulness and promise. Of this beloved companion, Miss HUNTLEY published an interesting memoir, soon after her decease; and again recurs to her with gushing tenderness, in the piece entitled "Home of an Early Friend," written nearly thirty years after the stroke of bereavement. In flowing verse, and prose almost as harmonious as music, she has twined a lasting memorial of the virtues of the departed, and of that tender friendship which was a marked incident in her own young life.

Before the death of her friend, she had entered with fresh enthusiasm, at Hartford, upon the task of instruction. In this path she was still happy and successful. It was regarded a privilege to be received into her circle, and many of her pupils became life-long friends. She there resided as a welcome and cherished inmate of the family of Madam Wadsworth, relict of Col. Jeremiah Wadsworth, whose mother was a Talcott, and nearly connected with the revered Madam Lathrop. The mansion-house in which Madam Wadsworth and the aged sisters of her husband dwelt, stood upon the spot now occupied by the Wadsworth Atheneum. It was a spacious structure, unadorned, but deeply interesting in its historic associations. The poem "On the Removal of an Ancient Mansion," is a graphic delineation of the impressions made upon Mrs. SIGOURNEY's mind, by her acquaintance with the threshold and hearth-stone of this fine old house, and her communion with its excellent inmates.

Another member of the same family, Daniel Wadsworth, Esq., a man of great taste and erudition, manifested a lively interest in her mental cultivation. He had known her from infancy, under the roof of Madam Lathrop, and had there seen some of her early effusions, both in prose and verse.

At his earnest solicitation, she consented that some of these should be arranged for the press. The selection, which was principally from her journals, with some fugitive poems prompted by passing occurrences, was made by himself; and with his influence and liberality, cast round her as a shield, she first ventured to appear before the public. Seldom has it been the lot of a young author to find a patron so wise, and a friend so true. His kind regard, and that of his amiable lady for her, suffered no diminution until their death, which took place in the years 1845 and 1848, when each had attained the age of seventy-seven. Full of years, and full of honors, they passed away; and her grateful affection for them has been often expressed in her writings, while the memory of their munificence and piety, is held dear among the people where they dwelt. "Moral Pieces in Prose and Verse," the book just alluded to, was followed by the "Memoir of Ann Maria Hyde;" and being urgently solicited by the various periodicals of the day, she became as frequent a contributor to their pages, as the absorbing duties of a teacher would permit. "Traits of the Aborigines," a poem in five cantos, and the longest of her poetical works, was also composed during this period, though not published until after her marriage.

We have now glanced at the principal circumstances that would seem to have had an influence in forming the intellectual and moral character of Miss HUNTLEY. Among these, doubtless, the discipline of her life as a teacher, was strong and salutary. The later emanations of her genius, are enriched with deeper trains of thought, and melodies of higher and more varied power, the outpourings of fresh affections, and the ripened fruits of a meridian sun.

Her marriage with Charles Sigourney, Esq., of Hartford, took place in the summer of 1819. This gentleman was a native of Boston, a merchant of high standing, and a prominent member of the Episcopal Church. His early education had been conducted in one of the thorough and excellent schools of the mother-land, where the foundations are laid deep and strong, by a more energetic discipline than would be tolerated

NATIONAL PORTRAITS.

in our republic. A more convincing proof of the perfection of their system, can scarcely be adduced, than the fact that though the period of his scholastic culture terminated at the age of fourteen, when he returned to his native clime, and devoted himself to the mercantile profession, his critical knowledge of the Latin classics, as well as of the French language, remains unimpaired, though more than three score and ten years have passed over him. To these attainments, he added after the age of fifty, during the brief intervals of business, so much knowledge of Greek, as enabled him to read the Scriptures in that language. Such were his intellectual tastes and habits of application, and so critical the style of whatever has proceeded from his pen, that had he entered the department of either literature or science, there is no doubt that he might there have won a distinguished reputation.

Mrs. SIGOURNEY, as far as attention to new and important duties would admit, continued her literary pursuits, and was sustained by an increasing fame, both at home and abroad.

A few years after her marriage, a volume of poems appeared from the Boston press, which of itself was enough to secure the position which she still maintains, as first among the female poets of America. But previously to this, a collection of her poetical writings, so far as they could be collected from the periodicals in which they first appeared, had been published in London, under the title of "Lays from the West." As a writer of prose, she has been received with marked favor. "Letters to Young Ladies," and "Letters to Mothers," rank with the most beautiful and useful of her productions. Not less than *five* editions of the former work, have been issued by two publishing houses in London. Quite a number of juvenile books have proceeded from her pen, some of which were prepared as assistants in the instruction of her own little ones. Her works, of different sizes and pretensions, amount to between forty and fifty, more than twenty of which are now in active circulation. Some have passed through numerous editions, others are entirely out of print. Several of them have been published in England and Scotland, with high appreciation. Her latest volume of poems was an illustrated octavo, from the Philadelphia press, issued in a uniform series with Bryant, Willis, Longfellow, and Mrs. Osgood.

Among her poems, the longest ones, "Traits of the Aborigines," "Zinzendorff," and "Pocahontas," have not been the most popular, though the last named, is a highly wrought piece of sterling value. Her most beautiful effusions, those which are favorites now, and destined to lasting fame and favor, are short productions—tender, lyrical, impassioned, descriptive, simple in thought and complete in finish. Such are "The Coral Insect," "Death of an Infant," "Western Emigrant," "Connecticut River," "Niagara," "Return of Napoleon," "The Last Supper," "Indian Names," "Berkshire Jubilee," and countless others, all of the same unrivalled grace; and though each be but a single bud or flower, yet, woven together, they form a wreath of undying bloom, verdure, and fragrance, which would adorn the brow of any poet of any age.

Her works have been ever held in subservience to the duties of the domestic sphere, and written amid interruptions, which only an early and fixed attention to system in the division of time could have overcome. Of her poems, she herself says, "the greater part were suggested by passing events, and partake of the nature of extemporaneous productions. Like wild flowers amid the dells or clefts of the rock, they have sprung up wherever the path of life has chanced to lead."

More freely than any of our authors, she has been invoked for anniversary odes, hymns for benevolent societies, and elegiac verses to solace mourning strangers; services which must from their nature be promptly rendered, and were seldom refused, though their payment could not be in fame, but in the pleasure of obliging. Miss Edgeworth, in her critique upon the writings of Mrs. SIGOURNEY, thus alludes to this species of extemporaneous composition.

"Mrs. SIGOURNEY appears to have the power of writing extempore on passing events, at the moment they are called for. But few persons of genius, especially of poetic genius, have ever possessed this power. She must have great command over her own mind, and what a celebrated physician used to call *voluntary attention,* in which most people are lamentably deficient, so that they can never write anything well, when the subject is suggested, and the effort bespoken. Those powers are twice valuable, that can well accomplish their purpose on demand. Certainly, as it regards poetic gifts, they who give promptly, give twice.

"Yet how few, even of professed and eminent writers, have been able to produce any effusions worthy of their reputation, or even worth reading, on what the French call 'de sujets de command,' and what we English designate, as on the spur of the moment. Addison could not. Gray could not. Mrs. SIGOURNEY's friends will be ready to bear testimony that she can."

During her whole life, Mrs. SIGOURNEY had been a devoted daughter, venerating and honoring her parents, almost like a child, even in her maternity. Her love soothed her pious mother upon her death bed, and when her venerable father, who five years survived his life's companion, had no one to rest upon, but that noble daughter, she became all the world to him. By that deep love, with which genius like hers brightens life, she cheered him with more than a child's devotion, along his widowed path, and when the good old Christian, in his eighty-eighth year, went gently down to the grave, his memory became to her a holy thing. Those who visited her pretty cottage home in Hartford, found the portrait of this venerable father over the parlor mantel-piece, the face pleasant and tranquil, the hair untouched by a thread of silver, for so it was, even to the last—and a smile lingering not upon the lips alone, but diffused in a gentle glow of benevolence all over the features. In its old place, by the chimney-piece of his own small apartment, stood the staff that supported his last footsteps; and in the daughter's face, as she pointed out those objects, you would read that undying love, which was only turned more reverently heavenward, by the death of its object.

In 1840, Mrs. Sigourney having had a voyage recommended by her physician, spent a year in England, Scotland, and France. No American ever visited Europe, who, either as a lady or a poetess, was more generally respected. With Samuel Rogers, Joanna Bailey, Maria Edgeworth, Mrs. S. C. Hall, and some of the best families among the nobility, she became an honored friend and guest. Among the different classes of Christians in Europe, Mrs. Sigourney moved as a lady, not only of high moral worth, but as distinguished by a spirit, the very opposite of bigotry. She did much to recommend piety in connection with dignified and easy manners, especially among young ladies, some of whom will ever cherish the recollections of her visit among the richest gems of memory. From the Queen of the French, she received after her return, the gift of a superb diamond bracelet, which is now endowed with a touching historical interest.

This year abroad, gave origin to "Pleasant Memories of Pleasant Lands," one of the most exquisite books of travel ever issued from the American press, and which has ministered to the gratification of many thousands in Europe, as well as in this country.

Up to the present time, Mrs. Sigourney's are among the purest gems of our magazine literature, and her position as first in purity and talent among the lady writers of America, has never been disputed by a person worthy the name of critic.

Two children, a son and daughter, have rewarded Mrs. Sigourney for the affection bestowed on her own parents. The daughter was long by her side. All the pure taste and sweet feminine qualities of the mother brightened again in the young life of her daughter. But her son, a youth of noble promise, joined his grandfather in Heaven, in the bloom of nineteen. How the bereaved mother suffered, how her woman's heart wrestled with its grief, those who know how deeply and tenderly she has sympathized with the sorrows not only of friends, but of strangers, can well imagine. It is impossible for those who know and loved her, to think of this bereavement, without a thrill of sympathy for the sublime submission of that weeping mourner, enabled to exclaim in the depth of her anguish—"God's time and will are beautiful, and through blinding tears I would fain give him praise."

It was in the summer of 1850, that she was called to resign to the tomb, this only son, with whose peculiarly susceptible nature, her own had an intense indwelling, and who early evinced uncommon maturity of mind, extent of intelligence, refinement of spirit, and thoughtful piety. This sorrow has called forth the most tender and impressive of all her works, "The Faded Hope," which was published in England and Scotland, immediately after its appearance in this country. We venture to say, that this touching, simple portraiture, cannot be read without tears. Should the system of intellectual and moral culture, which it unfolds, suggest some important improvements in home-education, which we trust it will, there may yet be reason to rejoice in the happy results of the removal of one, so deeply beloved.

It has already been mentioned that the writings of Mrs. SIGOURNEY have been kindly received, and warmly appreciated in the mother land. Two volumes of her poems, which appeared from the English press during her visit in Europe, the London Atheneum describes as "Reprints of the sweet and graceful compositions which have raised the name of Mrs. SIGOURNEY to the highest rank among the female ornaments of American literature and poetry;" and adds, "So many specimens of her muse, however, have found place in almost every sort of English publication, reviews, magazines, selections, &c., that we will not quote any further examples of their well known beauties, but commend them heartily to the favor of our reading community."

After all, we conceive that Mrs. SIGOURNEY had never fully reached the point, to which her intellectual endowments entitled her to aspire. She had labored in too many fields, and been too strenuous, that no womanly duty should be left undischarged, to have allowed unobstructed scope to her genius. The most striking feature in her habitudes was intense and systematic industry. In the laborious work of an educator, in the sphere of a New England housekeeper, which is expected to comprise care, active effort, and economy, and in the various departments of benevolence, which our age continually multiplies, she has performed almost as much as though she had not been a writer. Whatever employment was pressed on her, by her position, and by what pity or piety seemed to ask of her sex, she considered as a duty to be discharged first; and the pen, as partaking more of the nature of a solace, has been held secondary. Had literary fame been her paramount object, this classification would not have been adopted. Yet we doubt not she preferred it thus to be, not having "loved the praise of men, more than the praise of God."

On a review, we find the history of Mrs. SIGOURNEY, like herself, unpretending, and full of beautiful quietude. It is marked with no strong passages—no overweening ambition—no unwomanly aspirations. Timid, shrinking, gentle as a child—one is almost startled to find her the pioneer of female literature in America, and to learn that she became an author when authorship required courage, when its reward was more than doubtful, and when it was yet undecided, whether fame or reproach would be the result of literary exertion, in a woman. With all her domestic habits, and sweet feminine qualities unimpaired, her genius became triumphant. She had established a noble reputation for herself, a beautiful precedent for her sister women, and yet remained true to her sex, true to her nationality, and true to her God; she had witnessed the rise, the eminence, and the death of many literary personages; and she died in 1865, contented that she had employed her pen and her purse to some good purpose in her own humble way. Well does a Hartford poet write over her grave.

"What noble theme has she not sung?
 Her fame to other lands has flown;
Wherever sounds our mother-tongue
 They hold her memory like our own.

"And here where our broad river sweeps
 By tower and spire and swelling dome,
Here by the grave where Genius sleeps,
 From distant lands shall pilgrims come—

"And here recount her varied lore,
 Tell of the wonders she has done,
And spread her fame from shore to shore,
 The Good, the Pure, the Gifted one.

ISAAC SHELBY.

GENERAL Evan Shelby, the father of the late Governor SHELBY, when a small lad, emigrated from Wales with his father, and settled in the then province of Maryland, near the North mountain, about 120 years ago. He possessed a strong mind and an iron constitution of body, with great perseverance and unshaken courage. His skill as a hunter and woodsman led to his appointment as captain of a company of rangers, in the French and Indian war, which commenced in 1754; during which year he made several successful expeditions into the Alleghany mountains. He was afterwards appointed a captain in the provincial army destined for the reduction of Fort Du Quesne, now Pittsburg. He fought many severe battles in what is called Braddock's war. He laid out the old Pennsylvania road across the Alleghany mountain, and led the advance of the army under General Forbes, which took possession of Fort Du Quesne in 1758. His gallantry was particularly noticed in the battle fought at Loyal Hanning, now Bedford, Pennsylvania. In 1772 he removed to the Western Waters, and commanded a company in 1774 in the campaign, under Lewis and Dunmore, against the Indians on the Scioto river. He was in the sanguinary battle of 10th October, 1774, at the mouth of the Kenhawa, and near the close of the action was the commanding officer, Colonels Lewis, Fleming, and Field, being killed or disabled. The result gave peace to the frontier at the critical period of the colonies venturing into the eventful contest of the revolution, and deterred the Indians from uniting with the British until 1776—in that year he was appointed by Governor Henry, of Virginia, a major in the army commanded by Colonel Christian against the Cherokees, which destroyed their towns and crops. In 1777 he was appointed colonel of sundry garrisons posted on the frontier of Virginia, and a commissioner with Colonels Preston and Christian, to hold a treaty with this tribe at the Long Island of the Holston. In 1779 he led a strong expedition against the Chicamauga Indians, on the Tennessee river which resulted in the destruction of their towns and provisions; and which, occurring at the precise period when General George Rogers Clark captured Governor Hamilton at Vincennes, secured a temporary peace to Tennessee and Kentucky, afforded time for the introduction of population and the opening of land offices, and gave a permanence to the settlements of Kentucky and Cumberland, that never could be broken up by British influence, aided by savage intrigue. By the extension of the boundary line between Virginia and North Carolina in 1779, he was included in the latter state, and was appointed by the governor a brigadier general, the first officer of that grade on the Western Waters.

ISAAC SHELBY, the subject of this memoir, was born on the eleventh day of December, 1750, near to the North mountain, in the province of Maryland, where his father and grandfather settled after their arrival in America from Wales. In that early settlement of the country, which was annoyed during the period of his youth by Indian wars, he obtained only the elements of a plain English education; but, like his father, born with a strong constitution, capable of bearing great privations and fatigue, he was brought up to the use of arms and the pursuit of game.

At the age of twenty-one, he took up his residence in Western Virginia, beyond the Alleghany mountains, and was engaged in the business of feeding and attending to herds of cattle in the extensive natural range which distinguished that section of country. He was a lieutenant in the company of his father in the memorable battle fought 10th October, 1774, at the mouth of the Kenhawa, already mentioned, and, at the close of that campaign, was appointed by Lord Dunmore to be second in command of a garrison, ordered to be erected on the ground where this battle was fought. This was, probably, the most severely contested conflict ever maintained with the north-western Indians; the action continued from sunrise to sunsetting, and the ground, for half a mile along the bank of the Ohio, was alternately occupied by each of the parties in the course of the day. So sanguinary was the contest, that blood was found on each of the trees behind which the parties were posted. The Indians, under the celebrated chief, Cornstalk, abandoned the ground under cover of the night.

Lieutenant SHELBY continued in this garrison until it was disbanded, in July, 1775, by order of Governor Dunmore, who was apprehensive it might be held for the benefit of the rebel authorities. He proceeded immediately to Kentucky, and was employed as a surveyor under Henderson & Co., who styled themselves proprietors of the country, and who had established a regular land office under their purchase from the Cherokees. He resided in the then wilderness of Kentucky for nearly twelve months, when, from continued exposure to the inclemency of the weather, and being without bread or salt, his health was impaired, and he returned home.

In July, 1776, during his absence from home, he was appointed captain of a minute company by the committee of safety in Virginia. In the year 1777, he was appointed, by Governor Henry, a commissary of supplies for an extensive body of militia, posted at different garrisons to guard the frontier settlements, and for a treaty to be held at the Long Island of Holston river, with the Cherokee tribe of Indians. These supplies could not have been obtained nearer than Staunton, Va., a distance of three hundred miles; but by the most indefatigable perseverance, (one of the most conspicuous traits of his character,) he accomplished it to the satisfaction of his country.

In 1778, he was engaged in the commissary department, providing supplies for the continental army, and for an expedition, by the way of Pittsburg, against the north-western Indians. In the early part of 1779, he was appointed by Governor Henry to furnish supplies for the campaign against the Chicamauga Indians, which he effected upon *his own individual credit*. In the spring of that year, he was elected a member of the Virginia legislature from Washington county, and in the fall of that year, was commissioned a major, by Governor Jefferson, in the escort of guards to the commissioners for extending the boundary line between that state and the state of North Carolina. By the extension of that line, his residence was found to be within the limits of the latter state, and shortly afterwards, he was appointed by Governor Caswell a colonel of the new county of Sullivan, established in consequence of the additional territory acquired by the running of that line.

In the summer of 1780, Colonel SHELBY was in Kentucky, locating and securing those lands which he had five years previously marked out and improved for himself, when the intelligence of the surrender of Charleston, and the loss of the army, reached that country. He returned home in July of that year, determined to enter the service of his country, and remain in it until her independence should be secured. He could not continue to be a cool spectator of a contest in which the dearest rights and interests of his country were involved. On his arrival in Sullivan, he found a requisition from General

NATIONAL PORTRAITS.

Charles M'Dowell, requesting him to furnish all the aid in his power to check the enemy, who had overrun the two Southern states, and were on the borders of North Carolina. Colonel SHELBY assembled the militia of his county, called upon them to volunteer their services for a short time on that interesting occasion, and marched, in a few days, with three hundred mounted riflemen, across the Alleghany mountains.

In a short time after his arrival at M'Dowell's camp, near the Cherokee ford of Broad river, Colonel SHELBY, Lieutenant-colonels Sevier and Clarke, the latter a refugee officer from Georgia, were detached with six hundred men to surprise a post of the enemy in front, on the waters of the Pacolet river. It was a strong fort, surrounded by abattis, built in the Cherokee war, and commanded by that distinguished loyalist, 'Captain Patrick Moore. On the second summons to surrender, after the Americans had surrounded the post within musket shot, Captain Moore surrendered the garrison with one British sergeant major, ninety-three loyalists, and two hundred and fifty stand of arms, loaded with ball and buck-shot, and so arranged at the port-holes as to have repulsed double the number of the American detachment. Shortly after this affair, Colonels SHELBY and Clarke were detached, with six hundred mounted men, to watch the movements of the enemy, and, if possible, cut up his foraging parties. Ferguson, who commanded the enemy, about twenty-five hundred strong, composed of British and tories, with a small squadron of British horse, was an officer of great enterprise, and although only a major in the British line, was a brigadier general in the royal militia establishment, made by the enemy after he had overrun South Carolina, and was esteemed the most distinguished partisan officer in the British army. He made several attempts to surprise Colonel SHELBY, but his designs were baffled. On the first of August, however, his advance, about six or seven hundred strong, came up with the American commander at a place he had chosen for battle, called Cedar Spring, where a sharp conflict ensued for half an hour, when Ferguson approached with his whole force. The Americans then retreated, carrying off the field fifty prisoners, mostly British, including two officers. The enemy made great efforts, for five miles, to regain the prisoners; but the American commander, by forming frequently on the most advantageous ground to give battle, so retarded the pursuit, that the prisoners were placed beyond their reach. The American loss was ten or twelve killed and wounded. It was in the severest part of this action, that Colonel SHELBY's

ISAAC SHELBY.

attention was arrested by the heroic conduct of Colonel Clarke. He often mentioned the circumstance of his ceasing in the midst of the battle, to look with astonishment and admiration at Clarke fighting.

General M'Dowell having received information that five or six hundred tories were encamped at Musgrove's Mill, on the south side of the Enoree, about forty miles distant, again detached Colonels SHELBY, Clarke, and Williams of South Carolina, with about seven hundred horsemen, to surprise and disperse them. Major Ferguson, with his whole force, occupied a position immediately on the route. The American commanders took up their line of march from Smith's ford of Broad river, just before sundown, on the evening of the 18th of August, 1780, continued through the woods until dark, and then pursued a road, leaving Ferguson's camp about three miles to the left. They rode very hard all night, frequently on a gallop, and just at the dawn of day, about half a mile from the enemy's camp, met a strong patrol party. A short skirmish ensued, and several of them were killed. At that juncture, a countryman, living just at hand, came up and told them that the enemy had been reinforced the evening before with six hundred regular troops, (the Queen's American regiment, from New York,) under Colonel Innes, destined to reinforce Ferguson's army. The circumstances attending the information were so minute, that no doubt was entertained of its truth. To march on and attack the enemy then seemed to be improper; fatigued and exhausted as were the Americans and their horses, to attempt an escape was impossible. They instantly determined to form a breastwork of old logs and brush, and make the best defence in their power. Captain Inman was sent out with twenty-five men to meet the enemy, and skirmish with them as soon as they crossed the Enoree river. The sound of their drums and bugle horns soon announced their movements. Captain Inman was ordered to fire upon them and retreat, according to his own discretion. This stratagem (which was the suggestion of the captain himself) drew the enemy out in disorder, supposing they had forced the whole party; and when they came up within seventy yards, a most destructive fire commenced from the American riflemen, who were concealed behind the breastwork of logs. It was an hour before the enemy could force the riflemen from their slender breastwork; and just as they began to give way in some parts, Colonel Innes was wounded, and all the British officers, except a subaltern, being previously killed or wounded, and Captain Hawsey, a noted leader among the tories, being shot down, the whole of the enemy's line commenced a retreat.

The Americans pursued them closely, and beat them across the river. In this pursuit, Captain Inman was killed, bravely fighting the enemy hand to hand. Colonel SHELBY commanded the right wing, Colonel Clarke the left, and Colonel Williams the centre. According to M'Call's History of Georgia, the only work in which this battle is noticed, the British loss is stated to be sixty-three killed and one hundred and sixty wounded and taken—the American loss to be four killed and nine wounded. Amongst the former Captain Inman, and amongst the latter, Colonel Clarke and Captain Clarke.

The Americans returned to their horses, and mounted with a determination to be before night at Ninety-Six, at that time a weak British post, distant only thirty miles. At that moment, an express from General M'Dowell came up in great haste, with a short letter in his hand from Governor Caswell, dated on the battle ground, apprizing M'Dowell of the defeat of the American grand army under General Gates, on the 16th, near Camden, and advising him to get out of the way, as the enemy would, no doubt, endeavor to improve their victory to the greatest advantage, by destroying all the small corps of the American army. It was a fortunate circumstance that Colonel SHELBY knew Governor Caswell's handwriting, and what reliance to place upon it; but it was a difficult task to avoid the enemy in his rear, his troops and their horses being fatigued, and encumbered with a large number of British prisoners. These, however, were immediately distributed amongst the companies, so as to make one to every three men, who carried them alternately on horseback, directly towards the mountains. The Americans continued their march all that day and night, and the next day until late in the evening, without even halting to refresh. This long and rapid march saved them; as they were pursued, until late in the afternoon of the second day after the action, by a strong detachment from Ferguson's army. Colonel SHELBY, after seeing the party and prisoners out of danger, retreated to the Western Waters with his followers, and left the prisoners in charge of Colonels Clarke and Williams, to convey them to some point of security in Virginia; for at that moment there was not the appearance of a corps of Americans south of that state. The panic which followed the defeat of Gates and of Sumter, induced the corps of M'Dowell's army to disperse, some to the west and some to the north. The brilliancy of this affair was obscured, as indeed were all the minor incidents of the previous war, by the deep gloom which overspread the public mind after the disastrous defeat of General Gates.

ISAAC SHELBY.

Ferguson was so solicitous to recapture the prisoners, and to check these daring adventures of the mountaineers, that he made a strenuous effort with his main body to intercept them; but failing of his object, he took post at a place called Gilbert town, from whence he sent the most threatening messages by paroled prisoners to the officers west of the mountains, proclaiming devastation to their country if they did not cease their opposition to the British government.

This was the most disastrous and critical period of the revolutionary war, to the South—no one could see whence a force could be raised to check the enemy in their progress to subjugate this portion of the continent. Cornwallis, with the main army, was posted at Charlotte town, in North Carolina, and Ferguson, with three thousand, at Gilbert town, while many of the best friends of the American government, despairing of the freedom and independence of America, took protection under the British standard. At this gloomy moment, Colonel SHELBY proposed to Colonels Sevier and Campbell, to raise a force from their several counties, march hastily through the mountains, and attack and surprise Ferguson in the night. Accordingly, they collected with their followers, about one thousand strong, on Doe Run, in the spurs of the Alleghany, on the 25th of September, 1780, and the next day commenced their march, when it was discovered that three of Colonel Sevier's men had deserted to the enemy. This disconcerted their first design; and induced them to turn to the left, gain his front, and act as events might suggest. They travelled through mountains almost inaccessible to horsemen. As soon as they entered the level country, they met with Colonel Cleveland with three hundred men, and with Colonels Williams, Lacy, and other refugee officers, who had heard of Cleveland's advance, by which three hundred more were added to the force of the mountaineers. They now considered themselves to be sufficiently strong to encounter Ferguson; but being rather a confused mass, without any head, it was proposed by Colonel SHELBY, in a council of officers, and agreed to, that Colonel Campbell, of the Virginia regiment, an officer of enterprise, patriotism, and good sense, should be appointed to the command; and having determined to pursue Ferguson with all practicable dispatch, two nights before the action they selected the best horses and rifles, and at the dawn of day commenced their march with nine hundred and ten expert marksmen. As Ferguson was their object, they would not be diverted from the main point by any collection of tories in the vicinity of their route. They pursued him for the last thirty-six hours without alighting from their horses to refresh but once, at the Cowpens for an hour, although the day of the action was so extremely wet, that the men could only keep their guns dry by wrapping their bags, blankets, and hunting shirts around the locks, which exposed their bodies to a heavy and incessant rain during the pursuit.

By the order of march and of battle, Colonel Campbell's regiment formed the right, and Colonel SHELBY's regiment the left column in the centre: the right wing was composed of Sevier's regiment, Major Winston's and M'Dowell's battalions, commanded by Sevier himself—the left wing was composed of Colonel Cleveland's regiment, the followers of Colonels Williams, Lacy, Hawthorn, and Hill, headed by Colonel Cleveland in person. In this order the mountaineers pursued until they found Ferguson, securely encamped on King's mountain, which was about half a mile long, and from which he declared the evening before, that "GOD ALMIGHTY could not drive him." On approaching the mountain, the two centre columns displayed to the right and left, formed a front, and attacked the enemy, while the right and left wings were marching to surround him. In a few minutes the action became general and severe; continuing furiously for three fourths of an hour, when the enemy being driven from the east to the west end of the mountain, surrendered at discretion. Ferguson was killed, with three hundred and seventy-five of his officers and men, and seven hundred and thirty captured. The Americans had sixty killed and wounded; of the former, Colonel Williams.

This glorious achievement occurred at the most gloomy period of the revolution, and was the first link in the great chain of events to the South, which established the independence of the United States. History has heretofore, though improperly, ascribed this merit to the battle of the Cowpens, in January, 1781; but it belongs, justly, to the victory on King's mountain, which turned the tide of war to the South, as the victory of Trenton, under Washington, and of Bennington, under Stark, did to the North. It was achieved by raw, undisciplined riflemen, without any authority from the government under which they lived, without pay, rations, ammunition, or even the expectance of reward, other than that which results from the noble ambition of advancing the liberty and welfare of their beloved country. It completely dispirited the tories, and so alarmed Cornwallis, who then lay only thirty miles north of King's mountain with the main British army, that on receiving information of Ferguson's total defeat and overthrow by the riflemen from the West, under

Colonels Campbell, SHELBY, Cleveland, and Sevier, and that they were bearing down upon him, he ordered an immediate retreat, marched all night in the utmost confusion, and retrogaded as far back as Winnsborough, sixty or eighty miles, whence he did not attempt to advance until reinforced three months after by General Leslie, with two thousand men from the Chesapeake. In the mean time, the militia of North Carolina assembled in considerable force at New Providence, on the border of South Carolina, under General Davidson — General Smallwood, with Morgan's light corps, and the Maryland line, advanced to the same point. General Gates, with the shattered remains of his army, collected at Hillsborough, also came up, as well as the new levies from Virginia, of one thousand men, under General Stevens; — this force enabled General Greene, who assumed the command early in December, to hold Cornwallis in check.

The legislature of North Carolina passed a vote of thanks to Colonel SHELBY and several other officers, and directed each to be presented with an elegant sword, for his patriotic conduct in the attack and defeat of the enemy on King's mountain, on the memorable 7th October, 1780. This resolution was carried into effect, as to Colonel SHELBY, in the summer of 1813, just at the moment when, in the language of Secretary Monroe, "disclaiming all metaphysical distinctions tending to enfeeble the government," he was about to lead his troops far beyond the limits of the state of which he was governor. The presentation at that particular time afforded a presage of the new glory he was to acquire for himself and country in that eventful campaign.

If any were entitled to special commendation in this band of heroic spirits on King's mountain, the claim of Colonel SHELBY would be well founded. He originated the expedition, and his valor and unshaken resolution contributed to rally the right wing when driven down the mountain by a tremendous charge from the enemy, at the onset of the battle. Nor have the histories of the war at the South done justice to the sagacity and judgment of Colonel SHELBY upon another interesting occasion, just following the affair on King's mountain. As soon as he had placed the prisoners beyond the reach of the enemy, he repaired to the head quarters of General Gates, and suggested to him the plan of detaching General Morgan towards the mountains. The details of this arrangement were submitted by him and approved by Gates, and Greene had the good sense to adopt them, after he assumed the command. The result of his advice was exhibited in the splendid affair at the Cowpens, which added fresh laurels to the veteran brows of *Morgan, Howard,* and *Washington.*

In the campaign of the fall of 1781, Colonel SHELBY served under General Marion, a distinguished partisan officer, of the boldest enterprise. He was called down by General Greene to that lower country, with five hundred mounted riflemen from the Western Waters, in September, 1781, to aid the General in intercepting Cornwallis, at that time blockaded by the French fleet in the Chesapeake, and who, it was suspected, would endeavor to make good his retreat through North Carolina to Charleston; but upon his lordship's surrender in Virginia, Colonel SHELBY was attached to General Marion's command below, on the Santee, and was second in command of a strong detachment of dragoons, under Colonel Mayhem, ordered to carry a British post at Fairlawn, near Monk's Corner, eight or ten miles below the enemy's main army, under General Stuart. Information had been received by General Marion, that five hundred Hessians at that post were in a state of mutiny, and would surrender to any considerable force that might appear before it. But the officer commanding the post having some apprehensions of their fidelity, had marched them off to Charleston, the day before Colonel Mayhem appeared before it. The post, however, was surrendered, with one hundred and fifty British prisoners. The British general at Ferguson's Swamp, nine miles in the rear, made great, though unavailing efforts to intercept Mayhem's party on their return with the prisoners to General Marion's encampment. Immediately after this excursion, the British commander retreated with his whole force to Charleston.

As the period for which the mounted volunteers had engaged to serve was about to expire, and no farther active operations being contemplated, after the retreat of the enemy towards Charleston, Colonel SHELBY obtained leave of absence from General Marion, to attend the assembly of North Carolina, of which he was a member, which would sit two hundred miles distant, about the first of December. Marion addressed a letter on the subject to General Greene, which Colonel SHELBY was permitted to see, speaking in high terms of the conduct of the mountaineers, and assigning particular credit to Colonel SHELBY for his conduct in the capture of the British post, as it surrendered to him after an ineffectual attempt by an officer of dragoons.

In 1782, Colonel SHELBY was elected a member of the North Carolina assembly, and was appointed one of the commissioners to settle the preëmption claims upon the Cumberland river, and to lay off the lands allotted to the officers and soldiers of the North Carolina line, south of where Nashville now stands. He performed this service in the winter of 1782–3, and returned to Boonsborough, Kentucky, in April following, where he married Susanna, second daughter of Captain Nathaniel Hart, one of the first settlers of Kentucky, and one of the proprietors styled Henderson & Co., by their purchase of the country from the Cherokees. He established himself on the first settlement and preëmption granted in Kentucky, for the purpose of pursuing his favorite occupation, the cultivation of the soil; and it is a remarkable fact, pregnant with many curious reflections, that at the period of his death, forty-three years after, he was the only individual in the state residing upon his own settlement and preëmption.

He was a member of the early conventions held at Danville for the purpose of obtaining a separation from the state of Virginia; and was a member of that convention which formed the first constitution of Kentucky, in April, 1792. In May, following, he was elected the first chief magistrate, and discharged its arduous duties with signal advantage to the state. The history of his administration of an infant republic in the remote wilderness would fill a volume with deeply interesting incidents, exhibiting him advantageously in the character of a soldier, of a lawgiver, and of a diplomatist; but the limits prescribed to this sketch will not permit a detail of them. At the expiration of four years he retired to private life, being the first period of a general peace with the savages he had ever experienced from his childhood.

He was occasionally chosen as an elector of president; and when another war with Great Britain was expected in 1812, he was again elected to fill the highest executive office. His second administration commenced, also, at an interesting period. The whole western frontier was menaced by a savage foe, aided and supported by British intrigue; our first army captured, and the Michigan territory in possession of the enemy. It was a crisis requiring a display of all the energies of his character, and, at the request of the legislature, he organized a body of four thousand volunteers, which he led in person, at the age of sixty-three, under General Harrison, into Canada, in the fall of 1813. He was the rallying point of patriotism in the state, and but for the unauthorized though judicious step, which he assumed upon his own responsibility, of calling out *mounted* volunteers, the favorable moment for operation at the crisis of the campaign would have been lost, and the nation deprived of the important results of the memorable victory on the Thames. His gallantry and patriotism on that interesting occasion were acknowledged by the commanding general. and by President Madison ; and in resolutions by the legislature of Kentucky, which recognised "his plans and the execution of them as splendid realities, which exact our gratitude and that of his country, and justly entitle him to the applause of posterity." His conduct was approved, also, by a vote of thanks from the congress of the United States, awarding a gold medal as a testimony of its sense of his illustrious services.

In March, 1817, he was selected by President Monroe to fill the department of war ; but his advanced age, the details of the office, and his desire, in a period of peace, to remain in private life, induced him to decline an acceptance of it. In 1818, he was commissioned by the president to act in conjunction with General Jackson in holding a treaty with the Chickasaw tribe of Indians, for the purchase of their lands west of the Tennessee river, within the limits of Kentucky and Tennessee, and they obtained a cession of the territory to the United States, which unites the western population, and adds greatly to the defence of the country, in the event of future wars with the savages, or with any European power. This was his last public act.

In February, 1820, he was attacked with a paralytic affection, which disabled his right arm, and which was the occasion of his walking lame on the right leg. His mind continued unimpaired until his death, by apoplexy, on the 18th July, 1826, in the seventy-sixth year of his age. It was a consolation to his afflicted family, to cherish the hope that he was prepared for this event. In the vigor of life, he professed it to be his duty to dedicate himself to God, and to seek an interest in the merits of the Redeemer. He had been for many years a member of the Presbyterian Church, and in his latter days, he was the chief person in erecting a house of worship upon his own land.

The vigor of his constitution fitted him to endure active and severe bodily exercise, and the energetic symmetry of his person, united with a peculiar suavity of manner, rendered his deportment impressively dignified; his strong natural sense was aided by close observation on men and things ; and the valuable qualities of method and perseverance, imparted success to all his efforts.

EDWARD LIVINGSTON.

NOTHING is more becoming to a country, or affords better proof of the excellent spirit of its people, than to find the reward of popular praise and popular honors bestowed upon those, whose labors have been guided by a wise philanthropy, and whose objects have been the welfare and improvement of mankind. It is, therefore, a matter of just pride, that the subject of the present notice should have his memory cherished by his grateful countrymen, as one who rendered important services in his day to the country which gave him birth.

EDWARD LIVINGSTON was born in the year 1764, at Clermont, (Livingston's manor,) Columbia county, New York. His education was commenced at Albany, and continued afterwards at a grammar school at Esopus, in Ulster county, which, on the destruction of that village in the year 1777, was removed to the neighboring village of Hurley. At this school he was prepared for the junior class of Princeton college, which he entered in 1779, and took his degree two years afterwards. The period was the most unfortunate for the attainment of a classical or scientific education. Frequent incursions of the enemy drove the professors from their chairs. The spirit-stirring incidents of the time made the students more anxious to join the bands hastily summoned for defence, than to seek for the more modest honors of literature; and when, as happened on more than one occasion, they were permitted by their teachers to embody themselves in a little company, and march to meet the enemy, they returned with feelings little suited to the calm pursuits of a college. Their number rapidly became very small; the library was scattered; the philosophical apparatus was destroyed; and the college building itself was shared with a detachment of troops quartered in the town. Yet under all these disadvantages, some, at that period, laid the foundation of future celebrity. The class which graduated in the year 1781, consisted but of four young men, yet of these, three met twelve or thirteen years after, as members of the house of representatives of the United States; they were Mr. LIVINGSTON, William B. Giles, a late governor of Virginia, and Abraham Venables, who perished in the dreadful conflagration at Richmond. The former on leaving college, commenced the study of the law at Albany, under the direction of the late Chancellor Lansing, and was admitted to the bar in the year 1785.

From this period until 1794, Mr. LIVINGSTON was employed assiduously in the practice of the law. When, however, the constitution framed by the national convention was submitted to the people, he took a warm part in the question of its establishment, which was more zealously opposed in New York than in any other state. This circumstance, joined with his success at the bar, led to his election, in the year last mentioned, to represent the city of New York, and the counties of Queens and Richmond, in the fourth congress. The whole representation of the state consisted at that time of ten members.

The public career of Mr. LIVINGSTON during the succeeding six years, is embraced in the political history of his country. He was a distinguished and leading member of the republican party, maintaining an elevated position in congress, not less from his talents than from the liberal and candid spirit, the industry, zeal, and philanthropy which he displayed. A few days after he had taken his seat, he called the attention of the house to the existing provisions of the criminal code of the United States, and endeavored, though at that time without effect, to reform their sanguinary character, and adapt them more justly to the nature and quality of offences. He introduced, and after repeated efforts, carried, several laws for the protection and relief of American seamen left by accident or misfortune on foreign shores. He ardently promoted the establishment and gradual increase of the navy, and he supported the existing government, though opposed to its general policy, in every measure which was necessary to sustain the honor, or protect the rights of the country.

It was at the commencement of one of the sessions, during which Mr. LIVINGSTON sat in the house of representatives, that General Washington, in a speech to congress, referred to the occasion as the last on which he should meet them, and the address which it was proposed to make him in reply, contained some remarks, in allusion to this circumstance, which led to an animated debate. The vote of Mr. LIVINGSTON, on that occasion, was afterwards represented as evidence of hostility to General Washington; but he fortunately survived to refute the unworthy charge on the floor of the senate of the United States, with an eloquence worthy of the occasion, and with a feeling natural to one who had grown up in admiration of that great man, and who had seen him in his hours of peril and triumph, with a heart filled with sentiments of sincere veneration. It was indeed shortly after this, while his votes, speeches, and conduct, were fresh in the recollection of his constituents, that his term of service expired, and he was reëlected by an increased majority. A man, entertaining the sentiments towards Washington, that were ascribed to him, would not have received the votes of a city, where his name was adored. If further evidence were necessary, it is found in what occurred some years after. Mr. LIVINGSTON was selected, by the veteran relics of the revolutionary war, the chosen companions in arms of their venerated commander, the New-York Society of Cincinnati, as one of the very few honorary members on whom the distinction has been bestowed. The venerable remnant of the friends and companions of Washington, associated under his auspices for the purpose of cherishing the friendships contracted during the contest he so gloriously conducted, and watching over his fame, so inseparably connected with their own, would not have conferred that distinction on one, who had, at any period of his life, shown himself his enemy or detractor.

After the close of the session of Congress, in the spring of 1801, Mr. LIVINGSTON declined a reëlection, determined to devote himself exclusively to the practice of his profession, in the city of New York. He had not, however, long retired from public life, when he was appointed by the president to the honorable post of attorney of the United States for New York, and he was elected about the same time mayor of the city. This office, which he held upwards of two years, then required high judicial as well as executive talents. He devoted himself to its duties with the industry and zeal which at all times marked his character, and he was called upon to add to these, the active exercise of those benevolent feelings by which he was always equally distinguished. In 1803, the city was afflicted by a desolating pestilence; many of the inhabitants fled in dismay, and death frightfully extended its ravages among those who remained. Mr. LIVINGSTON never for a moment deserted his post, but he sacrificed his own comforts, and fearlessly endangered his own life, in his unremitted cares to lessen the calamity that had befallen his fellow-citizens. He was at last attacked himself by the pestilence, and reduced to the point of death. On recovering from his illness, and resuming, as soon as he was able, that attention to his private concerns which he had been obliged to neglect, he found them greatly deranged; he had been unable, particularly, to give the strict attention necessary to a proper scrutiny into the conduct of persons whom he had intrusted with the collection of debts, due to the United States, and he found himself suddenly and unjustly subjected to heavy responsibilities. Under these circumstances, he did not hesitate as to the course he was to pursue. He immediately resigned the offices which he held. He determined to remove to Louisiana, and there, succeeding in the great object for which he did so, he was, as he expected, enabled, by the arduous pursuit of his profession, to discharge the debt in which he had been involved, with interest to the last farthing. As soon as his difficulties and embarrassments became known to his fellow-citizens, and his intention to leave New York was declared, he received renewed testimonials of public respect. The venerable George Clinton, then governor of the state, addressed him a complimentary letter, expressing his regret; and the common council of New York unanimously presented him an address, which describes, in the most warm and affectionate language, their sense of his services and devotion, their high estimate of his abilities and integrity, their deep regret at his departure from among them, and their prayers for his prosperity and happiness.

In February, 1804, Mr. LIVINGSTON arrived at New Orleans, Louisiana, having then been lately transferred to the United States, pursuant to the treaty negotiated by his brother, Chancellor Livingston. Soon after his arrival, he was called on by some of the principal inhabitants to prepare a memorial to congress, stating their dissatisfaction at being kept in what they considered a state of vassalage, under the first degree of territorial government, instead of being admitted into the union, as the treaty provided they should be, on the footing of an independent state. This paper attracted much attention at the time, though it did not produce the effect which was desired. After Mr. LIVINGSTON had resided some years at New Orleans, his fortune was injured by a controversy, which has become well known, from the important principles it involved, and the ability with which they were discussed. Mr. Jefferson, then president of the United States, deceived by misrepresentations of fact, and entertaining a most erroneous opinion of his official powers, committed a violent invasion on the private property of Mr. LIVINGSTON, which produced the Batture question, the controversy alluded to. This deprived him of an immense property, the result of his professional labors, and involved him for many years in most expensive litigation. The merits of the subject have been long before the public, in a pamphlet of Mr. Jefferson, and the answer of Mr. LIVINGSTON, which last was truly termed an answer to which no reply could be made. None was made. The legal decision was in his favor, and the controversy ended honorably to both parties;—to Mr. LIVINGSTON, in his forgiveness of the injury; to his distinguished adversary, in the more difficult, and more meritorious task, if the maxim be true, of forgiving the man he had injured.

Mr. LIVINGSTON pursued his professional duties without interruption, until the invasion of Louisiana by the British. As soon as he learned that General Jackson was appointed to the military command of the district, he wrote to him and offered his services as an aid, or in any other capacity in which they might be considered useful. His offer was accepted, and as soon as the general arrived at New Orleans, he joined his family, and continued with him during the short but glorious campaign. During this eventful period, he was employed on several important missions, and enjoyed the confidence of the general. At the close of the war he received from him the most flattering testimonials of that regard which has since been more signally evinced. When, shortly afterwards, the well known arrest of General Jackson occurred, and he appeared before the court to account, or atone for breaches of the municipal laws, which, necessity had obliged him to commit, for the preservation of the country; his written defence, remarkable for the eloquence and simplicity of its style, and for the clear and vigorous view of the circumstances and the law which it presents, was prepared and submitted by Mr. LIVINGSTON, who acted as his counsel on the occasion.

But the services of Mr. LIVINGSTON to his adopted state were destined to be of a character even more important and enduring, than a participation in the gallant military exploits by which she was defended and saved. When he first arrived there, he had found the jurisprudence of the province in a state of extreme confusion. Judges from the United States, were appointed to administer laws written in a language they did not understand, and according to forms of which they were entirely ignorant. The legislative power was incompetent to provide a remedy, and even had it been, it was entrusted to men, who, though highly respectable, were unused to such duties. It soon became essential, therefore, that, although the body of laws could not be at once changed, a mode of procedure under them should be established. Mr. LIVINGSTON, and Mr. James Brown, since well known as a senator from Louisiana, and an able representative of the United States to France, were requested to perform this duty.

NATIONAL PORTRAITS.

Discarding alike the fictions and technicalities of the common law and the prolixity of the Spanish code, they prepared a simple, cheap, expeditious, and intelligible mode of conducting suits. An attempt was made to defeat it, which was chiefly sustained by those members of the bar, who had become accustomed to the modes of legal practice in other states. They endeavored, by taking advantage of an equivocal expression in the ordinance, organizing the government of the new territory, to establish the system prescribed by the English common law. Their attempt was successfully resisted by Mr. LIVINGSTON and Mr. Brown, though manifestly against their own interest. They saw that the tranquillity of the country would have been endangered, by imposing on the people, a law at once so complex and so different from that under which they had lived. The legislative council adopted their views, their system of procedure was introduced, and it has ever since stood the test of experience.

The system of municipal law which had continued in use, since the cession of the province, consisted for the most part, of a digest chiefly compiled from the Napoleon code, but it was found to want so much amendment, that in the year 1820 the legislature determined on its complete revision, and appointed Mr. LIVINGSTON, and Mr. Derbigny, and Mr. Moreau, a commission to execute it. This was a laborious task, and too little time was allowed for its execution. It was, however, completed in 1823, and submitted to the legislature, by whom it was adopted, with the exception of the commercial code, to some of the provisions of which, opposition was made. In this arduous duty, the well known industry of Mr. LIVINGSTON gives assurance that he took his full share, and the whole title of "obligations" is said to be exclusively his. He was, however, at the same period, engaged in a work of at least equal importance, with which he was solely charged. Having, a few years before, introduced into the state legislature, of which he was a member, a bill for preparing a system of penal law for the state, he was himself elected by that body, in 1821, to perform this arduous and responsible duty. The following year he presented a report, containing a plan of a penal code, and specimens of its execution. These were unanimously approved, and he was earnestly requested to finish it. Thus encouraged, he devoted himself to the task, and as early as the autumn of 1824, notwithstanding his very extensive professional engagements, and the share he took in the labor of preparing the civil code, he had ready for the press, the whole system of penal law. It consisted of a code of crimes and punishments, a code of criminal procedure, a code of evidence, a code of reform and prison discipline, and a book of definitions, together with introductory reports to each, pointing out the changes made in existing laws, the new enactments proposed, and the principles and reasons on which they were founded. Having received authority to print it, for submission to the legislature, he had caused a fair copy to be made. Before it was delivered to the printer, anxious that no errors might remain in it, he passed a great part of the night, in comparing it himself with the original draught. He went to bed at a late hour, with the pleasing reflection of having finished a most laborious task. Not long afterwards he was awakened by a cry of fire, which was found to proceed from the room where his papers had been left. They were all consumed. Not a note or memorandum was saved. Though stunned at first by the sudden misfortune, his equanimity and industry soon led him to repair it. Before the close of the same day, he quietly commenced the task of re-composition; and, in two years afterwards, he presented his work to the legislature of Louisiana, in a shape more perfect than that in which it originally was. It displays its author's extraordinary talent, and the philanthropist and the jurist must look with equal anxiety and interest to its adoption. The beauty of its arrangement, the wisdom of its provisions, the simplicity of its forms, and the clearness of its language, equal, but do not surpass, the philanthropy, the wise views of human character, the knowledge of social intercourse, and the insight into the sources of happiness and misery, by all of which it is distinguished, far beyond any similar system of criminal law, that has emanated from the jurists of any age or country. To those who have made penal jurisprudence their study, and who have examined and reflected on, not merely the codes, but the admirable introductory reports by which they are preceded, this praise will not appear exaggerated. Whatever may be the fame of Mr. LIVINGSTON, as a statesman or an advocate, whatever reputation his patriotic and his professional exertions have gained for him, among his own countrymen, this great work will secure to him enduring honor, wherever the cause of philanthropy is cherished, and wherever men exist who love and admire just and simple laws.

More than twenty years had now elapsed since Mr. LIVINGSTON had deserted the scenes of political life. He had arrived at an age when most men are desirous to leave it altogether; but being chosen by the people of Louisiana to represent them in congress, he again took his seat in that body in the month of December, 1823. He no longer desired to assume the active position he had formerly held.

He was a less frequent speaker; but he nevertheless originated several important measures, and engaged in the debates on many that were brought forward by others.

In 1829, he was elected by the legislature of Louisiana to represent the state in the senate of the United States, and he there introduced and carried several measures of extensive and permanent benefit to his country. On all questions of general policy; on all such as related to the exercise of constitutional powers, or to the development of great principles of legislation, he was listened to with the confidence and respect which were yielded, not less to his well established abilities and extensive knowledge, than to the simplicity, the dignity, and the patriotism that marked his character and actions. His speech on the celebrated resolution of Mr. Foote, relative to the public lands, is certainly among the most eloquent and able that were delivered on that occasion; and it is peculiarly interesting, from the view it presents of the principles on which the great party distinctions of the people of the United States were originally founded; of the comparative powers and duties of the different branches of the government; and especially of the relations, which, by the constitution, ought to exist between the government and the states. The views he adopted were shown to be those, which, from the earliest periods of the government, had been acted upon and supported by his political friends.

In the spring of 1831, Mr. LIVINGSTON was called by the president to fill the honorable post of secretary of state. His course there is of too recent a date, and his duties were necessarily of a character too confidential, to be perfectly known, or to be publicly discussed if they were known. We believe, however, that it may be said, with propriety and truth, that the offer of the first place in his cabinet, when made by General Jackson to Mr. LIVINGSTON, was as unexpected as it was unsolicited; and that he hesitated for some time before he accepted it. With the modesty and unaffected diffidence which are striking traits of his character, he distrusted his ability to perform the duties of the office, and in comparing his own talents with those of some of the distinguished men who had preceded him, in the same station, he was for a while inclined to doubt the wisdom of embarking in the same career. Such, however, was not the sentiment of his fellow-citizens. Their anticipations of his course were the reverse of his own, and they proved to be more just. No act of the president was hailed with more satisfaction by the country, nor was any attended with more advantage to its prosperity, its interests, and its fame. All the public documents from the pen of Mr. LIVINGSTON, having reference to the foreign relations of the United States, present a clear view of those interesting concerns. The instructions under which the treaty with Naples was formed, were soon after published by order of congress, and in their energetic tenor and unanswerable reasoning were found prominent causes for the success of the negotiations with that government, and for the conclusion of the treaty by which the claims of our merchants were so amply recognized. While he remained in the department of state, instructions were given to our ministers at London, Paris, St. Petersburg, Lisbon, the Hague, Mexico, and the South American states, on all the important points of discussion between those governments and our own; and when these documents shall be made public, it will no doubt be found, that in clear language, in political wisdom, and in enlightened spirit, they will redound as much to the honor of the administration to which they belong, as any of the various state papers of which the American people are so justly proud. Just before Mr. LIVINGSTON left the department, he negotiated and signed a treaty with the minister of Belgium, and he exchanged with the minister of Russia, the ratification of another previously made, under his instructions, at St. Petersburg. In all these negotiations, he is understood to have been particularly anxious to introduce stipulations which will ameliorate the intercourse between nations, in a degree corresponding with the improvement of the times; to extend, advantageously, our commerce with remote nations; and to obtain new fields for American enterprise, the results of which have been found highly beneficial as they have been more fully developed. In the same spirit which governed him in these negotiations, were his reports made to congress on our diplomatic establishments, and on the regulation of our consulates abroad; all containing recommendations eminently deserving attentive consideration, and calculated to contribute not less to our interests, than our national honor. In those measures of the government, which belonged less to a particular department, than to the general policy of the administration, the abilities and experience of Mr. LIVINGSTON could not fail to render him an able counsellor, and secure for him unlimited respect and confidence. When the president adopted the resolute and patriotic course of issuing his proclamation relative to the proceeding of South Carolina, it was well understood that he met with the undivided assent of his cabinet; if, therefore, public opinion has assigned to Mr. LIVINGSTON, more than his share in that measure, it has probably been guided by the similarity of the views, taken on this occasion, with those declared by him in his remarks in the senate, on the resolution of Mr. Foote, to which we have already referred; or perhaps to the well known fact, that his sentiments coincide entirely with the doctrines so admirably expressed in that celebrated instrument.

On the reëlection of General Jackson, in 1833, Mr. LIVINGSTON retired from the department of state, and accepted the honorable but less laborious office, which was tendered to him by the president, of minister to France—an office in which his brother, Chancellor Livingston, had previously acquired a distinguished reputation; and which he probably accepted with more gratification from this circumstance, as well as from having unexpectedly received about the same time, the highest testimonials of respect and honor, from the most distinguished literary and scientific institutions of that country.

His continuance in France was not very long; his health failed, as well it might when he had laboriously served his country till he had attained the full age of man. In his mission to the French court, as in every other engagement, he more than satisfied his countrymen. He returned to New York, and at Rhinebeck, in that state, he peacefully yielded his spirit to God, May 23, 1837, in the seventy-second year of his age.

As in public life Mr. LIVINGSTON showed whatever excellencies the man always standing before the world, should manifest, so in his private character he was always distinguished for benevolence and modesty; he was remarkable for transparent simplicity, elegant taste, and earnest desire for the happiness of mankind.

BENJAMIN LINCOLN.

THIS distinguished individual, who truly deserves, in the language of one of his biographers, "a high rank in the fraternity of American heroes," was a native of the pleasant little town of Hingham, situated on a small bay which sets up south from Boston, at the distance of about thirteen miles from the city, and within a few years become one of the principal summer resorts of such of its residents as grow weary at that season of the dust and din of its "populous streets." He was born January 23d, (O. S.,) 1733, in the same house which he died in, and which is still pointed out to the stranger by the members of the large and highly respectable family of his own name, who are among the inhabitants of the place to this day.

The parentage and early situation and education of LINCOLN, although far enough from being remarkably imposing, were well calculated, like those of many others of the greatest men of the revolutionary period, to prepare him for the trying contest in which he was destined to act a conspicuous, as well as a laborious part. His father, Benjamin Lincoln, was a maltster and farmer, in good circumstances, and a man much respected by his fellow-citizens, who repeatedly elected him, during times of no little political interest, the representative of Hingham in the general court, as the legislature was then usually termed. The young man enjoyed also, during the entire period of his early life, the eminent advantages implied in a good Massachusetts common school education; an opportunity of access to a considerable variety of books, and frequent leisure to read them; and especially, so far as his moral character was concerned, and upon that very much depended during his after life—in the exemplary, religious, orderly, and cheerful habits of his father's household.

Previous to the revolution, though his regular vocation was farming, and his robust constitution enabled him to pursue it with an industrious perseverance, he was several times called on to interest himself in the civil and military affairs of the county and province. At the age of twenty-two, he was appointed an adjutant in the regiment of militia then commanded by his father, and not long afterwards major, under Colonel Josiah Quincy—Bernard being at that time governor. In 1772, Governor Hutchinson made him lieutenant-colonel of the regiment. He also sustained several of the town offices, and was elected its representative in the legislature.

When the disputes between the colonies and the mother country grew warm, he espoused the cause of the former, and supported it with energy and effect. This course brought him necessarily into political life, and in 1775, he was chosen a member of the provincial congress, which assembled at Cambridge and Watertown: that respectable body made him one of their secretaries, and a member of the important committee of correspondence who were instructed to communicate with the towns throughout the province, and with the other colonies, in relation to the critical circumstances of the times.

During this year he was not called into actual military service. On the memorable 19th of April, when blood was shed upon the plains of Lexington and Concord, he summoned the troops under his command to march to the scene of contest; but the rapid return of the British to the capital that same night, prevented the movement. The celerity with which the intelligence of this affair, we may here remark, travelled in all directions over the commonwealth and the continent, was perhaps till that time unexampled in colonial history. The writer has frequently conversed with a venerable citizen of Concord,* since deceased, then an artisan in the village, who, having at the first news of the approach of the enemy some time before day-break, commenced the voluntary labor of alarming the neighboring country, actually rode on horseback more than one hundred miles during the next twenty-four hours, in the performance of that duty—a task which, considering the condition of some of the roads he traversed, may be regarded as a feat worthy to be mentioned. This gentleman's wife and her young children had, meanwhile, deserted his house, and gone off to find security in the neighboring woods, with a large number of inhabitants situated like themselves.

Having been appointed by the council of Massachusetts a brigadier in February, 1776, and a major-general by the same authority,

---

* Mr. Reuben Brown.

in May of that same year, he employed himself industriously during the summer, in the exercise of the militia under his command. In August the council appointed him, by virtue of the supreme executive power reposed in their hands, to the control of all the troops of the state, doing duty at and about Boston; and the high opinion generally entertained of his ability and fidelity is still farther manifested by the selection which the general court, in the following months, made of him as commander of the regiments to be raised by the state to reinforce the army of Washington in New York and New Jersey, which had now become the chief theatre of the war. Previous to leaving the environs of Boston, he had the honor of heading an expedition of provincial troops and volunteers, who succeeded in clearing the harbor of the last remnants of the enemy. Until the 13th of June, they remained about Nantasket, with a fifty gun-ship, and several other vessels. The general embarked at Long Wharf, with the view of dislodging this force; and having landed upon Long Island, made arrangements for a vigorous cannonade; but a few shots soon convinced the British commodore of his danger, and he hastily abandoned the Boston waters, never more to infest them. "Thus," in the language of the Journal of Dr. Thatcher, who was himself one of the party—"is the port again opened by our own authority, after being closed during two years by virtue of an act of the British parliament."

The acquaintance which the illustrious commander-in-chief of the American army had formed with LINCOLN, while at Cambridge, induced him to recommend the latter to the continental congress as an officer whose services it was desirable to secure in the federal line, and accordingly, in February, 1777, he was appointed by that honorable body a major-general of their forces. During the spring and summer of this year, he was intrusted by Washington with the command of divisions or detachments of the main army, and was frequently in situations which required the exercise of a high degree of military skill, though by no means fruitful in the means of brilliant distinction. The inferiority of the American force to that of the enemy, and the uncertainty of the operations of the latter, rendered the campaign a continual trial of vigilance and perseverance, much rather than of more imposing qualifications, on the part of the American generals.

On one occasion, notwithstanding all his caution, he was very near being surprised. He was at Bound Brook, on the Rariton, near the enemy, with a detachment of a few hundred men, appointed to guard a line of some five or six miles. About day-break of the morning of April 13th, owing to the negligence of his patrols, he was suddenly assaulted by a large British party under Cornwallis and Grant. They had arrived within two hundred yards of his own quarters when discovered, and the general, with one of his aids, had hardly time to mount and leave the house before it was surrounded. The other aid, with the baggage and papers of the party, fell into the enemy's hands, as did also a few small pieces of artillery, while the general led off his troops between two columns of the British, who had nearly closed, and made good his retreat to the pass of the mountains near his encampment, with the loss of sixty killed and wounded.

The commander-in-chief on all occasions manifested great confidence in the talents and patriotism of LINCOLN, and with the view of turning these to the best account, he directed him, in July, to join the northern army under Schuyler, (afterwards Gates,) which was to oppose Burgoyne. "My principal view," said his letter to the general, "in sending you there, is to take command of the eastern militia, over whom, I am informed, you have influence, and who place confidence in you. I have this day received two letters from General Schuyler, *in such a style as convinces me that it is absolutely necessary to send a determined officer.*" This, for Washington, who was not a man of many compliments—was saying a good deal.

Having made his first station at Manchester, in Vermont, to form the militia as they came in from the northern sections of New England, and to operate in the rear of the enemy, LINCOLN soon distinguished his energy and good judgment advantageously by an expedition which he sent out on the 13th of September, under Colonel Brown, with five hundred men, to the landing at Lake George. The object was to release the American prisoners, and destroy the British stores, and this was effected completely by the capture of the fort and two hundred batteaux, with two hundred and ninety-three of the enemy's soldiers, and by the liberation of about one hundred American prisoners, while the loss of our party was only three killed and five wounded; an incident which contributed not a little to raise the spirits of the northern militia at this critical period.

After some other operations, LINCOLN joined the army of Gates, to whom he was second in command, and arrived in camp on the 29th September. Here he distinguished himself by his usual acti-

BENJAMIN LINCOLN.

vity until after the warm engagement of the 7th October. The day succeeding that action, he had occasion to ride from one part of his line to another about a mile distant, and before his return the same route was taken by a party of the enemy. The general knowing that a number of the captured German uniforms had been placed on his own troops, mistook these soldiers for Americans, and came within reach of their fire before the mistake was discovered. They discharged a volley, and wounded him in the lower part of the leg so severely, that he apprehended for some weeks the loss of the limb. This disabled him, and he was removed, first to Albany, and thence to Hingham. He joined the army again in August of 1778, but suffered for several years from the effects of the wound.

In the course of this season, the reputation of LINCOLN induced the delegates in congress from South Carolina to request that body to appoint him to the command of the southern army, which he accordingly assumed, and reached Charleston in December. Here he was soon engaged in the bustle of an active campaign; for on the 25th of the month, he learned the arrival of the enemy's fleet at Tybee, and on the 29th, that they had effected a landing, routed the Americans under Howe, and gained Savannah. He immediately put his own forces in motion, while the enemy extended himself into Georgia; but was unable to commence offensive operations until the last of February. On the 2d of March, General Ashe was defeated at Brier Creek, and thus LINCOLN lost nearly a fourth part of his army. From this time until June, a variety of movements took place; but of an inconclusive character. On the 20th of that month he attacked the enemy at their works near Stono Ferry, and a very warm action ensued, in which nearly two hundred were killed and wounded on each side. The battle was bravely fought, but did not effect a decisive result. The general was on this occasion, after being without sleep the previous night, ten hours on horseback at one sitting. Both armies rested in their summer quarters till September, the enemy being at Savannah.

In the beginning of that month, Count D'Estaing arrived off the place just mentioned, with a considerable French force, and LINCOLN joined soon afterwards with one thousand men, though not in time to prevent the garrison being largely reinforced. A siege and bombardment ensued, which proving too slow an operation for D'Estaing's temperament, he determined on an assault. This occurred on the 9th of October, and was one of the bloodiest engagements of the whole southern war, but less successful than glorious. The count reëmbarked his troops for the West Indies, and LINCOLN recrossed the Savannah, and made his head-quarters at Charleston.

At this time he stated to congress his conviction, that the British would soon commence a more serious campaign in the southern department, with a view to its permanent acquisition, than either of the preceding had been; and he made an urgent call upon them for a supply of troops adequate to the approaching contest. He was accordingly reinforced, but not to a sufficient extent, and his little army was soon engaged in the defence of Charleston, where, on the 30th of March, General Clinton encamped in great strength, in front of the American lines. The works of the enemy were carried on industriously, so that on the 10th of April, the first parallel was completed, and the garrison summoned to surrender. The second parallel was finished in ten days more, and another summons given and rejected on the 20th. A vigorous cannonade was kept up on either side for several days more. On the 23d, the third parallel was begun, from eighty to one hundred and fifty yards from our lines. Batteries were erected upon it, and a new summons issued on the 8th of May. On the 11th it was found necessary to capitulate, and the negotiation was concluded on the following day.

"Having received," says the general on this occasion, "an address from the principal inhabitants, and from a number of the country militia, desiring that I would accept the terms—and a request from the lieutenant-governor and council that the negotiations might be renewed,—our provisions, saving a little rice, being exhausted, the troops on the line being worn down by fatigue, having for a number of days been obliged to lie upon the banquette,—our harbor closely blocked up,—completely invested by land by *nine thousand men at least*, the flower of the British army in America; besides the large force they could always draw from their marine, and aided by a great number of blacks in their laborious employments;—the garrison at this time (exclusive of sailors) but little exceeding two thousand five hundred men, part of whom had thrown down their arms,—the citizens in general discontented, the enemy being within twenty yards of our lines, and preparing to make a general assault by sea and land,—many of our cannon dismounted, and others silenced for want of shot,—a retreat being judged impracticable, and every hope of timely success cut off, we were induced to offer and accede to the terms executed on the 12th."

On the whole, it is generally conceded, that situated as General LINCOLN was during this campaign, with a force inadequate, not only to any brilliant achievement, but to any effective defence, he "deserves great praise," in the language of Ramsey, "for his judicious and spirited conduct in baffling, for three months, the greatly superior force of Sir Henry Clinton and Admiral Arbuthnot. Though Charleston and the southern army were lost, yet, by their long protracted defence, the British plans were not only retarded, but deranged, and North Carolina was saved for the remainder of the year 1780." Lee, in his memoirs, correctly remarks, that "so established was the spotless reputation of the vanquished general, that he continued to enjoy the undiminished respect and confidence of the congress, the army, and the commander-in-chief." His exertions and fatigue during this laborious campaign, were such as few constitutions would have been able to endure. He was on the lines night and day, and for the last fortnight never undressed to sleep.*

Being admitted to his parole, he returned in the summer to his residence in Hingham. In November following he was, to his great joy, exchanged for Major-General Phillips, and in the spring of 1781, he again joined the army of Washington, then occupying the high grounds bordering on the North River. The operations of the troops in this quarter, though important, are not sufficiently interesting to be detailed here. The crisis of the war, however, was approaching. All eyes began to be turned towards Virginia, and the armies of Lafayette and Cornwallis. The brilliant campaign which ensued in that state is familiar to the memory of all readers. General LINCOLN commanded a central division, during the siege of Yorktown, and had his full share in the honors of the splendid consummation in which it closed. He had the duty appointed him on this occasion, of conducting the conquered army to the field where their arms were deposited, and of receiving the customary submission. These were of course among the last of his revolutionary services.

On the last day of October, 1781, he was chosen by congress secretary of war, with power still to retain his military rank. He immediately entered on the duties of his new office, and continued in it for two years, when he resigned. Congress accepted his resignation with the following emphatic expression of regard:—

"Resolved, That the resignation of Major-General LINCOLN, as secretary at war for the United States, be accepted, in consideration of the earnest desire which he expresses, the objects of the war being

---

* Memoir in Massachusetts Historical Collection, Vol. III., Second Series.

so happily accomplished, to retire to private life; and that he be informed, that the United States, in congress assembled, entertain a high sense of his perseverance, fortitude, activity, and meritorious services in the field, as well as of his diligence, fidelity, and capacity in the execution of the office of secretary at war, which important trust he has discharged to their entire approbation."

For some years subsequent to this abandonment of the honors of public life, the general, in the true spirit of republican simplicity, not only *contented* but *indulged* himself in the favorite employments of his early life. Most of his time was spent on his native estate, but the government of the state still called him occasionally from his "dignified ease." He busied himself in treating with the Penobscot Indians once or twice, and was also induced to take command of the first division of the Massachusetts militia. At another period he busied himself in settling a tract of land in the district of Maine, one of the towns and counties in which state were honored with his own name.

The famous insurrection of Shays' breaking out in the beginning of 1787, summoned the veteran once more to the field. The rebels having gone so far as to obstruct the sessions of the court of justice with bodies of armed men, the governor and council appointed him to the command of the militia of the state, who were ordered out in a force of between four and five thousand. He began his march from Boston on the 20th of January, for Worcester, where, having protected the court in their session, he hastened to the relief of General Shepherd, at Springfield, where he had already engaged with Shays once, and routed him, though not with any conclusive success. The latter was now at Wilbraham, and his chief ally, Day, with another detachment of rebels at West Springfield. LINCOLN pursued and attacked the latter and put them to rout. Shays moved off to Amherst, and LINCOLN followed him; Shays fortified himself at Pelham, and LINCOLN sent an address to him, calling on him to disband his force, and submit to the government—agreeably to instructions he had received from the state. A correspondence ensued, but without effect; and Shays beginning to draw off again, LINCOLN still pursued him. During the night of February 2d, he marched in remarkably severe weather, to Petersham, the present encampment of the rebels, and there came upon them in the centre of the town, without giving them time to call in even their guards. About one hundred and fifty of them were taken, and the rest fled. Some other parties of rebels were broken up in other places, and the insurrection thus terminated, the general himself, with two distinguished civilians, was appointed under a state commission to determine who should have the benefit of certain acts passed by the legislature for the exemption of some of the insurgents from trial; and having executed this delicate duty, early in the spring he returned again to his farm.

Here he was not permitted to remain long, for in April he was elected lieutenant-governor by the legislature; an office in which he was succeeded, however, the next year, by Samuel Adams, the candidate of the anti-federal party, which at this time had gained the ascendency.

The general was a member of the convention which ratified the new constitution. After that event, in the summer of 1789, he was made collector of Boston; and that office he continued to hold till within two years of his death, when his earnest request to resign it was complied with, by Mr. Jefferson. In 1789 also, he was appointed a commissioner to treat with the Creek Indians; and in 1793, a commissioner with Timothy Pickering, and Beverly Randolph of Virginia, to treat with the western tribes. In the latter years of his life, he interested himself occasionally in literary and scientific pursuits; and several essays, the result of this leisure, are to be found among the collections of the Massachusetts Historical Society, and in other works. As early as 1780, Harvard University had given him a degree of master of arts. He was subsequently one of the first members of the American Academy of Arts and Sciences, and belonged to several other similar associations. His decease occurred after a short illness, on the 9th of May, 1810, at the age of seventy-seven years.

The bravery, energy, and indefatigable industry of General LINCOLN, as a military officer, have never been denied, even by those who, at critical periods, doubted the policy of some of his movements during that unfortunate southern campaign, where he was left to contend single-handed against such fearful odds as have already been described. His courage, too, was unalloyed by rashness. It has been said that his perfect calmness in danger seemed like unconcern; but it was one of his own remarks, that he never was exposed without feeling deeply interested, as he was free to acknowledge, as well for his own life, as for that of the soldiers around him. He was humane as he was brave.

In private life few men have been more respected. He was a practical and rational Christian from his childhood up, and to his practice joined also the profession of his principles, being during most of his life a communicant, and for many years a deacon in the church with which he worshipped. Amidst all the licentiousness of the army, no stain came upon his character, and no impurity fell from his lips. The warmth of his disposition was plainly perceptible in all his habits, in his liberal charity, his hospitality, his fondness for the company of the young, his constancy in friendship, and the pleasure which he communicated, through the medium of agreeable manners and lively conversation, in the intercourse of domestic and social life. With the wife of his youth he lived in great conjugal happiness more than fifty-five years, and had by her a number of sons and daughters, among whom it gave him pleasure to distribute a considerable part of his handsome property on two occasions previous to his decease.

General LINCOLN was of middle height, remarkably broad-chested, muscular, in his latter years corpulent, with open intelligent features, and a countenance distinguished by its benignant aspect. The author of "Familiar Letters on Public Characters and Events," years ago published at Boston, says "his hair was combed back from his forehead unpowdered, and gathered in a long queue. He was usually dressed in a blue coat and light under clothes, and wore a cocked hat. He always appeared in boots, in consequence of the deformity of his left leg, occasioned by his wound at Saratoga." This writer remarks upon a peculiarity of the general's constitution, which is well recollected by many other individuals now living; his remarkable *somnolency;* this overcame him to such an extent, that he would fall into a sound sleep at table, and when driving himself in a chaise; and it is related, that when he commanded the militia against the insurgents, he dictated despatches, and slept between the sentences; for his sleep rarely appeared to disturb his perceptions of the circumstances passing around him. "This he considered an infirmity, and his friends never ventured to speak to him of it."

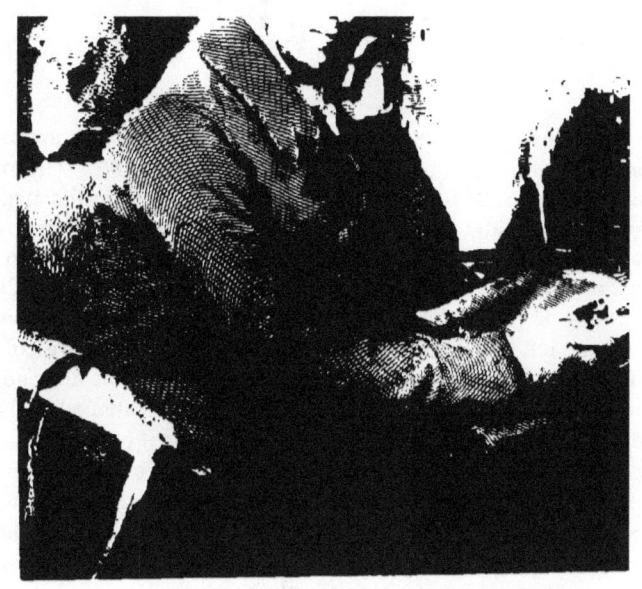

Benjamin Rush

BENJAMIN RUSH, M. D.

BENJAMIN RUSH was born on his father's farm, in Byberry township, Philadelphia county, on the 24th day of December, 1745. His great-grandfather, John Rush, commanded a troop of horse in the army of Oliver Cromwell, and on the restoration of the monarchy, emigrated to Pennsylvania, in 1683. He had been personally known to the Protector. One day, seeing his horse come into the camp without him, Cromwell supposed he had been killed, and lamented him, by saying "he had not left a better officer behind him." The Bible, watch, and sword, which he owned, are still in the possession of his descendants in Pennsylvania. He settled on the farm already mentioned, and died at the age of about eighty. No lengthened account of the parentage of Dr. Rush, is deemed necessary to a brief narrative like the present. His ancestors were plain and peaceful farmers, known in their neighborhood for their integrity and industry. Having lost his father, John Rush, in his early childhood, the care of his education devolved upon his mother, whose strength of mind and good principles proved fully adequate to the trust. His veneration for this parent knew no intermission during her long life. She died under his roof at the age of eighty; and of the illustrious individuals whom she lived to see that roof often shelter, none received from its owner more constant kindness and scrupulous attention than herself. To the judicious care she bestowed on him in his youth, he always attributed the useful aims and the many blessings of his life. Having been taught by her the rudiments of the English language, she sent him, at the age of nine years, to a grammar-school at Nottingham, in Maryland, at that time under the direction of her sister's husband, the Rev. Dr. Finley, afterwards president of the college at Princeton, in New Jersey. Here he rapidly advanced in the studies prescribed to him; and from the pious precepts and example of his instructer, and, perhaps, the primitive innocence of the secluded country in which he lived, he imbibed in childhood that veneration for religion which he cherished to the end of his days.

NATIONAL PORTRAITS.

Having finished his preparatory course of the Latin and Greek languages, he was sent in the fourteenth year of his age to Princeton college, then under the presidency of the Rev. Mr. Davies, a man distinguished for his piety and uncommon eloquence. He received at this institution the degree of Bachelor of Arts, in 1760, before he had completed his fifteenth year. He next commenced the study of medicine in Philadelphia, under the direction of Dr. John Redman, an eminent physician, who was a kind and useful instructer to him, and whose attention he requited by faithful and untiring service. He relates, himself, that during the whole of the six years of his pupilage under Dr. Redman, he could enumerate not more than two days of interruption from business. This was an earnest of that regularity and indefatigable application which characterized his whole life. During the period of his apprenticeship, he studied with eager attention the writings of Hippocrates, Sydenham, and Boerhave, and translated the aphorisms of the former, from Greek into English. He also began to keep a note-book of remarkable occurrences, the plan of which he afterwards improved and continued through life. From a part of this record, written in the seventeenth year of his age, is derived the only account of the yellow fever, as it appeared in Philadelphia, in 1762, which has descended to posterity.

In 1766, having passed through the elementary studies in medicine, and being intent on acquiring further advantages for his destined profession, he went to Edinburgh, at that time the most esteemed medical school of Europe, where, after attending for two years the public lectures and hospitals in that capital, he received the degree of Doctor of Medicine. His thesis, by the custom of the school, was written in the Latin language, and its title was " *De concoctione ciborum in ventriculo.*" He adventured, in his own person, several experiments in support of his arguments, both revolting and perilous. These arguments displayed abilities rare even among the distinguished pupils and rivals by whom he was surrounded. The style was correct and elegant; Dr. Ramsay,* who was among the best classical scholars of our country, and who knew Dr. Rush well, says, of this thesis, that "it was written in classical Latin," and adds, " I

---

* In the present sketch of the life of Dr. Rush, we are indebted to Dr. Ramsay's Eulogium upon him, as well as to the memoir of him in the Biography of the signers to the Declaration of Independence, for various details which those excellent productions have made familiar to the public; in several instances, the phraseology of their recitals has been necessarily and willingly adopted.

BENJAMIN RUSH.

have reason to believe without the help of a *grinder*, (teachers of Latin, then frequently employed for such purposes,) for it bears the characteristic marks of the peculiar style of its author." We are somewhat minute on this point, because it is connected with another, often referred to in Dr. Rush's history—his alleged disparagement of the learned languages. He ranked them among the general accomplishments of a liberal education; and having, according to his ingenious and forcible essay upon the subject, spent too many years in their acquisition, he continued in after life his familiarity with them, perhaps from the desire, by which he happily says in the same essay men are sometimes influenced, of reviving, by reading the classics, the agreeable ideas of the early and innocent part of their lives. Dr. Rush's objections to the engrossing instruction of youth in the Latin and Greek languages, have been often and elaborately questioned; but whilst his arguments upon the subject continue to be read, their vigor, and fertility in illustration, will always be impressive to the candid, if they convince not the opposing reader.

Whilst a student at Edinburgh, Dr. Rush was commissioned by the trustees of Princeton college, to negotiate with Dr. Witherspoon, of Paisley, in Scotland, his acceptance of the presidency of their institution. His efforts and address in the fulfilment of this trust, were successful; he gained in Dr. Witherspoon a constant friend, and for the college, the advantage of a principal eminent in science and literature. He was, whilst in Scotland, ardent in his pursuit of knowledge; and was careful and fortunate in making friends, who improved his mind, and strengthened his virtues. An accidental acquaintance, formed whilst attending the same medical class with the eldest son of the earl of Leven, made him an approved intimate in the family of that pious and respected peer. The letters written in after years by this individual and the different members of his family to Dr. Rush, prove the uncommon and affectionate impression he made upon them. We allude to this intimacy, because, though anticipating a little the order of our narrative, it is connected with an interesting incident in the life of Dr. Rush. It happened to him a few years after, and during the war of the American revolution, to recognise among the British officers slain on the battle-field at Princeton, the dead body of one of the sons of this earl of Leven, the Honorable Captain William Leslie, who, in common with his elder brother, had shared Dr. Rush's fond regard whilst at Edinburgh. On the person of the deceased officer was found a letter to Dr. Rush, who, being then in the medical staff of General Washington, was the first to discover his deceased friend among the slaughtered of the vanquished enemy. Dr. RUSH had Captain Leslie's remains conveyed to Pluckamin, in New Jersey, where he gave them an honorable grave and a recording tomb. A few years ago, a friend of the family of this officer came to this country, on purpose to erect a befitting monument to his memory; "but when he reached his grave, he saw," says a modern British publication, wherein further interesting details of the occurrence are given, that "the work was *already done.* Believing that no monument he could erect, no honors he could pay, would be equal to those rendered by the spontaneous act of a generous foe — nothing remained but to drop a tear to the memory of the unfortunate Leslie, and another of gratitude to his generous eulogist."

From Edinburgh, Dr. RUSH went to London, where he passed the winter of 1768, attending the hospitals and medical lectures of that metropolis. Dr. Letsome of Great Britain, in his "Recollections of Dr. RUSH," relates an anecdote of him whilst in London, which is creditable to his fervor of patriotism and vigor of speech; it is in the following words: "At that time there was generating great commotion in the American colonies, and a disposition to revolt from the mother country was very generally manifested. In London, several disputing societies were formed for the discussion of the question of the propriety of American resistance. A political orator warmly inveighed against the spirit of what was deemed rebellion, and observed, that "if the Americans possessed cannon, they had not even a ball to fire." These reflections called up Dr. RUSH, (then a student of medicine in London,) who said in his reply, that "if the Americans possessed no cannon balls, they could supply the deficiency by digging up the *skulls* of those ancestors who had courted expatriation from the old hemisphere, under the vivid hope of enjoying more ample freedom in the new."

The succeeding summer he devoted to his improvement in Paris, and returned, in the autumn of the same year, to his native country. He fixed his residence at Philadelphia, and at once began the practice of his profession, where he was soon established in business as a physician.

In 1769, he was elected professor of chemistry in the college of Philadelphia. In 1789, he succeeded in the same institution to the chair of the theory and practice of medicine, vacated by the death of Dr. John Morgan. In 1791, the college having been elevated to the University of Pennsylvania, he was elected in this latter establishment professor of the institutes and practice of medicine and of clinical practice. In 1796, he received, on the resignation of Dr. Kuhn, the additional professorship of the practice of physic, which he held with the two preceding branches, though they required much laborious application, until the end of his life.

As a lecturer, Dr. RUSH's manner was most agreeable and impressive. His talent for public speaking enabled him, by frequent extemporaneous elucidation, to relieve and enliven the details of the science which he taught. His lectures were nightly retouched and enhanced from the full stores of his observation and retentive memory. The zealous student hung on his accents whilst he spoke; and the loiterer was accustomed to watch for his varieties, his fervor, and his persuasiveness. When Dr. RUSH began to lecture in the University of Pennsylvania, his medical class in that institution consisted of about twenty students: in the winter of 1812-13, at the last course he delivered, they amounted to four hundred and thirty. It is estimated that during his life he had given instruction to more than two thousand pupils, who propagated his principles and improvements in the science of medicine throughout the United States, and, in a few instances, to South America, the West Indies, and Europe. He was for many years one of the physicians of the Pennsylvania hospital, and contributed much to the usefulness of that institution, by his wise suggestions and ardent exertions in its behalf.

The medical career of Dr. RUSH was like that of other successful practitioners, until the appearance of the yellow fever in Philadelphia, in 1793. This event exhibits the most busy scene of his professional life; by its trials, he acquired his most valuable reputation. This disease, as we have already remarked, appeared in Philadelphia, in 1762, and returned after a lapse of thirty-one years with frightful violence and fatality. It commenced the first week in August, and ended towards the close of October. The city was deserted by nearly all those whom wealth or health enabled to flee. The rank grass sprung up from the untrodden pavements; and the dying crawled from their sick-beds, and breathed their last in vain implorations after their abandoning kindred and friends. Dr. RUSH was among those who staid to witness and to help in this awful calamity; and in one of the volumes of his lectures, has given a deeply interesting account of it. At one time, when not less than six thousand persons were prostrated with the disease, three practitioners only remained to administer to their necessities. From the 8th to the 15th of September, he visited and prescribed for about one hundred and twenty patients daily. His house was thronged by multitudes imploring his assistance. He was constrained by more pressing duty to fly himself from many of these, and even to drive through the streets with such speed as might secure him from interruption, or place him beyond the cries of his wretched petitioners. His sense of duty, his charity, and the force of that precept which he often used to inculcate in his lectures, "to dispute every inch of ground with death," were the incentives to his fearless conduct during that memorable pestilence. Had the love of pecuniary gain actuated him, the wealth he might have amassed from known instances of its offers, is almost incalculable. An opulent citizen tendered him a deed for one of his best houses in Market street, if he would attend his son who was lying ill. A captain of a vessel once took from his purse twenty pounds, offering them to him if he would pay his wife a single visit. A patient whom he had cured, directed, in his first feelings of gratitude, his desk to be opened, in which large sums were heaped, requesting that he would take a part or, if he pleased, the whole as his compensation. It need scarcely be added, that where it was in his power to attend the patient, he would only receive his regular professional charge. When the illustrious Zimmerman heard of the services of Dr. Rush during the yellow fever of '93, he wrote to a friend this enthusiastic praise: "*Sa conduite a mérité que non seulement la ville de Philadelphie, mais l'humanité entière, lui élève une statue.*" But Dr. Rush, himself, artlessly gave the best encomium on his services at this period, *in a dream*. Its moral makes it worthy of record, and calls to mind the classic authority of the divine origin of such visions. He was attacked with this same epidemic, and his life was despaired of; he providentially recovered, and whilst convalescent, told a friend who was watching at his bed-side, that he thought in the sleep from which he had just awoke, a vast crowd of persons assembled before his front door, and besought him to come and visit their respective sick friends. True to his impressions from previous and trying days, he dreamed that he resisted their intreaties, and somewhat impatiently was about to turn from them and hurry into his carriage, when a poor woman ran forward to him, and, with outstretched hands, said, "O doctor! don't turn away from the poor! You were doomed to die of the yellow fever; but the prayers of the poor were heard by heaven, and have saved your life!" This dream may have increased his fondness for Boerhave's immortal sentiment, that "the poor were his best patients, for God was their paymaster."

The services of Dr. Rush, before and during the war of the revolution, were conspicuous and valuable. He wrote indefatigably in favor of American independence; and, along with John Adams, he persuaded Thomas Paine to undertake with his pen the defence of the colonies. He suggested to Paine the words "Common Sense," as the title of his first political paper. In June, 1776, he was a member of the provincial conference which met in Philadelphia, and on the 23d of that month moved the appointment of a committee to draft an address expressive of the sense of the conference respecting the independence of the American colonies. Dr. Rush, who, with James Smith and Thomas M'Kean, had been appointed for this purpose, the next day reported a declaration, which was adopted in the conference, and presented to the American congress the day after. This declaration, similar even in its phraseology, anticipated almost the whole of the Declaration of Independence. It may be found, together with the preceding facts, in the first volume of the Journal of the house of representatives of Pennsylvania. Immediately after this, he was chosen a member of the American congress of '76, and on the 4th day of July, in that year, signed the memorable charter of his country's freedom.

In 1777, he was appointed for the middle department, physician-general of the military hospitals; and, as such, attended his wounded countrymen at the battles of Princeton and Brandywine. In 1787, he was a member of the convention of Pennsylvania for the adoption of the federal constitution. In a letter to a friend in a distant state, dated in October of the same year, he says, "The new federal government will be adopted by our state. It is a masterpiece of human wisdom, and happily accommodated to the present state of society. I now look forward to a golden age. The new constitution realizes every hope of the patriot, and rewards every toil of the hero. My fellow-citizens insist on putting me in the state convention, which will meet on the last Tuesday in next month. Will my mind bear such numerous, complicated, and opposite studies and occupations? I love my country ardently, and have not been idle in promoting her interests during the session of the convention. Every thing published in all our papers, except 'The Foreign Spectator,' during the whole summer, was the effusion of my federal principles. Since the convention has risen, I have been followed by many writers who have great merit. I enclose you some of my paragraphs from Hall and Seller's paper, to be republished in your state." When this convention adjourned, and the plan of the federal constitution was published, he was actively engaged at frequent meetings with the members of the legislature, in fixing the outlines of a new form of state government.

NATIONAL PORTRAITS.

After the establishment of the federal government, he withdrew altogether from public life and political occupations; devoting himself exclusively to the duties of his profession, its cheerful studies, and its social services. Although the history of his country, and the brief allusion we have made to it, enrol Dr. Rush amongst its pure and efficient patriots, it is as a skilful, humane, and accomplished healer of diseases, that he is to this day most vividly remembered; it is as a medical and moral writer, who so often "adorned" what he "touched," that his memory comes frequently and gratefully to an after age.

Dr. Rush was a public writer for forty-nine years, from the nineteenth to the sixty-eighth year of his age and a public teacher of medicine, from the age of twenty-four, to the end of his life. The brief limit of his present biography, allows but a general notice of the system of medicine which he taught. It differed materially from those of Hoffman, Cullen, and Brown. His chief medical principle was to attend to the state of the system, under every circumstance of age, idiosyncrasy, epidemic, and climate, and prescribe accordingly. He rejected the nosological classification of diseases, upon the ground that they comprehended under their nomenclature an aggregate of variable phenomena, for which remedies varying according to the symptoms of the patient, rather than uniform rules of practice, were to be preferred. He was assured of the efficacy of this system, by an experience, which, in extensive and successful contention with disease, could not have been surpassed. Time, with its proverbial discernment, has adopted his improvements in medicine as familiar truths, and rewards him who taught them with its lasting honor. He also first believed in and promulgated the domestic origin of the yellow fever, a doctrine greatly opposed by his medical contemporaries, and the community in which he lived. Time, in this instance also, has affixed to his opinion the seal of its practical truth. Dr. Chirvin, who, by the direction of the French government, lately collected the opinions of the medical profession in America as to the contagion of the yellow fever, ascertained the ratio of non-contagionists to be five hundred and sixty-seven, to twenty-eight contagionists.

The space allotted to the present biographical notice of Dr. Rush, will not allow a full enumeration of his printed works. The principal of these are, Medical Inquiries and Observations, in four volumes; a volume of Essays, literary, moral, and philosophical; a volume of Lectures, introductory, for the most part, to his course of lectures on the institutes and practice of medicine. He wrote an Inquiry into the effect of public punishments upon criminals and upon society; and soon afterwards, an Essay on the consistency of capital punishments with reason and revelation. His "Inquiry into the effects of ardent spirits upon the body and mind," is written with all the force of his genius and knowledge. It was published in the form of a pamphlet, and distributed gratuitously among the poor. "Except," says one of his biographers, "Dr. Franklin's Way to Wealth, no small publication ever had a more extensive circulation, or did more good." His Essay on the influence of physical causes on the moral faculty, "has been," says the same authority, "universally admired as one of the most profound productions of modern times." The last work of Dr. RUSH was "Medical Inquiries and Observations upon the Diseases of the Mind," "which," it has been said, "were all his other writings lost, would keep alive the memory of his usefulness." It has been pronounced "at once a metaphysical treatise on human understanding; a physiological theory of organic and thinking life; a book of the best maxims to promote wisdom and happiness; in fine, a collection of classical, polite, poetical, and sound literature." He received, during his life, various testimonials of his meritorious services. The board of health of Philadelphia, gave him a massive piece of plate for his gratuitous attendance on the poor, during the epidemic of 1793. In 1805, he received from the king of Prussia a gold medal for his replies to queries on the yellow fever. In 1807, the queen of Etruria presented him with a similar medal for a paper upon the same subject, written at her request. In 1811, he received a diamond ring of great value from the emperor of Russia, as a proof of that monarch's estimation of his medical character and writings. Through the cordiality of a friend, the latter gift was noticed with approbation in the newspapers of the day, and it is remembered that its notoriety gave positive annoyance to the honored and modest subject of it. He was a member of many foreign literary and scientific societies; and for the last sixteen years of his life, was treasurer of the mint of the United States.

Dr. RUSH's social qualities were founded in the kindness of his heart, and brightened by the polish that his intellect was constantly receiving. The sick found in him their friend and enlivener, as well as their physician. Superior minds sought him for pleasure and for profit. And at the mind of his inferiors, he hesitated not to knock for admission; for all of these, he believed, had something within, however small, that was worth his surveying. He was prompt to discern and assist the efforts of struggling merit, and was emphatically *the friend of young men.* His religious principles were practical and fervent, they were fostered by the purity and humility of his heart, in deeds of kindness and "good will to men," and in unabating reverence to the word and the ministers of God. To a friend who once asked him if he was not almost tired of promoting new societies he replied, "there is *one more*, I wish to see established, and that is a *Bible Society*." The term was practically unknown in this country, when he thus used it.

In January, 1776, he was married to Julia, the eldest daughter of Richard Stockton, of New Jersey, a member of the American congress of that year. The father and son-in-law were soon doubly united by the enduring national instrument to which they both set their names. Of this marriage, a widow and large family survived him.

Dr. Rush, in person, was above the middle size, slender, and well proportioned. His forehead was prominent and finely shaped, his eyes blue and very expressive; the rest of his features were regular and comely. All his biographers have described his appearance as dignified and pleasing.

In the undiminished vigor of his mental faculties,—in the fullest season of his activity, prosperity, and value,—he was seized with an epidemic, termed typhus fever, then prevalent in Philadelphia, and died in that city, after a few days' illness, on the 19th of April, 1813, in the sixty-ninth year of his age. The community regretted his death as a public and serious loss; and the poor—they who had always been his care, and whom he remembered in his dying words—pressed into his house to touch his coffin ere it was laid in the earth. He was buried in the Christ Church graveyard, where a plain tomb marks the place of sepulture of the man who said, in one of his lectures, "Medicine without principles, is an humble art, and a degrading profession. It reduces the physician to a level with the cook and the nurse, who administer to the appetites and the weakness of sick people. But directed by principles, it imparts the highest elevation to the intellectual and moral condition of man. In spite, therefore, of the obloquy with which they have been treated, let us resolve to cultivate them as long as we live. This, gentlemen, is my determination as long as I am able to totter to this chair; and if a tombstone be afforded after my death to rescue my humble name for a few years from oblivion, I ask no further addition to it, than that 'I was an advocate for principles in medicine.' "

JOHN TYLER.

JOHN TYLER was the tenth president of the United States, and the sixth occupant of that high office born in the Old Dominion.

The father of the subject of our present biography (and bearing the same name) distinguished himself in the period of the Revolution as an ardent patriot, and was intimately associated with Henry, Jefferson, Edmund Randolph, and other eminent men of that day. He was from an early day of the war of Independence a member of the house of delegates of Virginia, bearing at all times a prominent part in its deliberations, and in 1781 was elected the speaker of the house, which place he continued to fill by repeated reëlections until the close of the war. After having filled other important stations, among which was a seat in the highest judicial tribunal of the state, he was in the year 1808 elected governor of the commonwealth, to which office he was twice reëlected. A vacancy having occurred on the bench of the United States district court, he was appointed to the seat by President Madison, which he occupied until his death in 1813. The legislature being in session at the time, and regarding his death as a public calamity, passed resolutions expressive of its sorrow, and clothed itself in mourning.

JOHN TYLER was born in Charles City, in the county of that name, Virginia, May 29, 1790. He was the second of three sons who survived their father. His school-boy days were remarkable for nothing but an extraordinary love of books, especially those of history. At the early age of twelve years he entered the college of William and Mary, where he attracted the attention of Bishop Madison, the venerable president of that institution, whose warmest friendship he enjoyed till death effected a separation between them. Nor was he less the object of the friendship and esteem of his fellow-collegians. At seventeen he took his degree, and on that occasion delivered an address on "Female Education," which the faculty pronounced the best commencement oration delivered there within their recollection.

On leaving college, JOHN TYLER devoted himself to the study of law, on which indeed he had entered during his collegiate course. He passed two years in reading, partly with his father, and partly with Edmund Randolph, formerly governor of Virginia, and one of the most eminent lawyers of the state. His progress in the law, as in all his other studies, was rapid, and his acquisitions solid. He soon obtained a very extensive practice.

Scarcely had he reached the age of twenty-one, when he was almost unanimously elected by the people of his native county to represent them in the state legislature. He took his seat in that body in December, 1811, and soon showed himself zealous in advancing the interests of his constituents, and of that ancient commonwealth. The breaking out of the war with Great Britain soon after, gave full scope for his oratorical powers, which he often employed with a view to their improvement. Here he showed himself an ardent lover of his country, zealously opposed to the conduct of Great Britain, and a firm advocate of the principles which had elevated Mr. Madison to the presidency.

During the five successive years which Mr. TYLER served his county in the legislature, he often manifested great powers of eloquence. The last year of his membership of the house of delegates, he was elected a member of the executive council. He continued to act in that capacity until November, 1816, when, by the death of the Hon. John Clopton, a vacancy occurred in the representation in congress from the Richmond district. The contest, which was a very severe one, was between Mr. Stevenson, afterwards minister to England, and then speaker of the house of delegates, and Mr. TYLER. It was merely a trial of personal popularity, as the candidates concurred in political principle; and when Mr. TYLER retired from congress, he warmly advocated the election of Mr. Stevenson to that responsible station. At the period of his taking his seat in the house of representatives, Mr. TYLER had but reached his twenty-sixth year—an age at which it has been the lot of very few to be elevated to a station of as high trust and importance as a representative in the congress of the United States. But habits which, from boyhood, had led to the development of his talents—the lessons of a patriot father—constant employment in public office, and a character for ability, energy, and honesty of purpose—gave ample earnest of the manner in which his duties would be fulfilled. His diffidence in the outset of his congressional career was great, but by degrees he took a part in all the prominent questions of that day, and more than satisfied his constituents, who, by an increased majority, in 1819 again sent him to Wash-

JOHN TYLER.

ington, where he remained till 1821, when increasing ill health compelled him to leave his seat, and for a time seriously threatened his life.

Mr. TYLER left the house of representatives, carrying with him the respect of all who knew him. After five years of faithful service as a representative of one of the most respectable districts of Virginia, he could look back with satisfaction on his course, discovering not one act in his political career which he had reason to regret. On nearly all the great subjects which had agitated congress during that period he had occupied a prominent position. Against the Bank of the United States, which, in some shape or other, had come before the house at nearly every session, he waged unceasing war, as an institution most dangerous to the best interests of the community, and certain, one day, to use its tremendous power with a deleterious effect upon the elections of the country, and declaring at every suitable opportunity his unalterable convictions of the unconstitutionality of its creation. He was firm in his opposition to every wild scheme of innovation upon established principles, and watchful against all attempts to turn the current of public expenditure from its legitimate course; and the unflinching advocate of national economy, though always liberal when public justice would sanction such a course.

With broken health and shattered constitution Mr. TYLER returned to his farm, in Charles City county, happy that nothing but physical inability had compelled him to leave the public service. He soon rejoiced in improved health, and in the spring of 1823 was requested again to become a candidate for the legislature, and with very little opposition he was returned to the scene of his former usefulness. But he was not allowed long to remain there, for in December, 1825, the office of governor of Virginia was conferred upon him without solicitation. In this station he devoted himself to the development of the resources of the state, to the maintenance of her laws and constitution, and to those political principles with which her renown is identified.

The year 1826 was marked by an event which threw the whole nation into mourning—the deaths of Thomas Jefferson and John Adams. That two of the three only survivors of the signers of the Declaration of Independence should breathe their last on the same day, and that day the anniversary of the promulgation of that great paper, was a remarkable coincidence, to which history has no parallel. Mr. Jefferson died at Monticello, just fifty years after the declaration, on the very day, and, it is said, the very hour, at which that immortal work of his hands was read in the congress of the United States. Governor

NATIONAL PORTRAITS.

TYLER was requested to deliver at Richmond a funeral oration, with which request he complied, one week after the death of that illustrious man.

Such was the satisfactory manner in which Governor TYLER discharged the first term of his office, that he was reëlected by an unanimous vote. He was not long destined to occupy this position, for a few days after his reëlection the expiration of the term for which Mr. John Randolph had been elected senator in congress arrived, and against his strongly expressed wish to the contrary, Mr. TYLER was elected his successor. To such a choice on the part of the legislature he deemed it his duty to accede, and took his seat in the senate December 3, 1827, where he at once arrayed himself with the opposition. In 1833 he was again elected, and in the following year was elected president *pro tempore* of the senate. During the session of 1835–36, as he conscientiously objected to some instructions he received from the legislature of Virginia, and could not vote according to their wishes, he resigned, thus surrendering three unexpired years of his term. Such an act of devotion to the great principle of representative responsibility deserves to be recorded both for its rarity and its magnanimity.

The different course of conduct pursued by Mr. Leigh, the colleague of Mr. TYLER, was the subject of much comment throughout the United States. Mr. Leigh, in reply to the call upon him, wrote a very long and ingenious letter, in which he took the distinction between the obligation of a representative to obey instruction in all cases where no constitutional point was involved, and that which he contended existed where well-founded doubt arose as to the constitutionality of particular measures; in which latter cases he insisted, that the representative was not bound to obey, and to do an act which would be a violation of the constitution he was sworn to support. Mr. Leigh, for these reasons, refused to obey the instructions or then to resign his seat, which, however, he did resign in 1836. Mr. TYLER stated to the people of his state, and to the public generally, in his letter of resignation to the legislature of Virginia, the principles by which his conduct as a public man had been governed, and the motives which led to his immediate resignation. He at the same time placed in the hands of Mr. Van Buren, then vice-president of the United States, and president of the senate, a letter informing the senate that he had resigned into the hands of the general assembly of Virginia his seat as a senator from that state.

Relieved from all political anxieties, Mr. TYLER joyfully returned

JOHN TYLER.

to his farm and his profession. By public dinners, and in every other form, he was made acquainted with the satisfaction his conduct had given to his countrymen. His affairs, thrown into disorder by the neglect of his personal interests during the time he had served in congress, required his attention, and he gladly hailed a return to private life, that he might be enabled in some measure to restore them. The anxieties, labors, and fatigues of public employment had no longer any charm. At the age of forty-six he had run a brilliant career in the state and national councils; and, after twenty-five years of service, during which he had devoted himself faithfully and untiringly to advance the public welfare, he looked forward with great delight to a period of repose. No spot or blemish had attached itself to his political fame—no discontent or dissatisfaction had been created by the manner in which he had discharged his political duties; and happy in the consciousness of having served the people who had entrusted him with their confidence with honesty, fidelity, and to the best of his ability, he was well content again to enter on more peaceful walks. In his retirement, however, he was not permitted to remain unsolicited. Shortly after his return to Virginia, he was selected as the vice-presidential candidate, with Hugh Lawson White as president. No election of vice-president having been made by the people on this occasion, the senate elected Richard M. Johnson, of Kentucky.

He was not suffered long to remain inactive; for, in 1838, having removed to Williamsburg for the better education of his children, and the citizens of James City and York counties having elected him to the post, he again consented to serve in the legislature of Virginia; and during the subsequent session he would again have been returned to the senate of the United States, but for the unfortunate dissension which at that time prevailed in the republican party in Virginia. In 1839, he was nominated by the Harrisburg convention as vice-president of the United States, having General W. H. Harrison for his chief.

The speeches, letters, and declarations of Mr. TYLER during the political canvas of the year 1840, seem to have been deemed entirely in accordance with the views of the Whig party, and no doubt was then entertained that he would coöperate with General Harrison, and aid in carrying out their designs and wishes in the event of an election then confidently expected. It is well known that the Whigs were completely successful; and their triumph made General Harrison President of the United States, Mr. TYLER Vice-President, and secured a Whig majority in the house of representatives and senate of the

NATIONAL PORTRAITS.

United States. It has been asserted, however, with great confidence that Mr. TYLER miscalculated his ability to unite himself to, and act with the Whig party, and mistook, therefore, his position in accepting their nomination for one of the highest offices in the nation, the result of which, upon the death of President Harrison, placed him in the presidential chair, invested with all the patronage and power of that high station. The Whigs also, it has been asserted, evidently acted without due caution in his nomination. From these causes arose embarrassment, difficulty, and loss of popularity with both the great parties of the nation, to the President, and to the Whigs, bitter disappointment and chagrin.

The day of the inauguration arrived, and on the 4th of March, 1841, President Harrison delivered his inaugural address, and took the oath of office, in the presence of the largest assemblage which had ever been collected in the federal city. In the senate chamber the vice-president elect appeared, took the prescribed oath, and assumed his place as president of the senate. On the 17th of the same month President Harrison issued his proclamation, calling upon congress to convene on the 31st of May following, for the consideration of "sundry important and weighty matters, principally growing out of the condition of the revenue and finances of the country." An all-wise Providence, however, decreed that before that day arrived he should be laid in the tomb. The president had entered on the duties of his high office with a zeal and earnestness which a frame, exhausted not alone by the cares of a long life spent in various laborious public services, but by the fatigues of a triumphant campaign, was hardly capable of sustaining. His incessant labors, caused chiefly by those who were intent on office, as the reward of their efforts, shattered his health, and on the 4th of April, just one month after his inauguration, he died.

For the first time in the annals of our country, a chief magistrate died while occupying the presidential chair, and the wisdom and stability of our institutions were to be submitted to a new test. The cabinet immediately dispatched a letter, by a special messenger, to Mr. TYLER, at Williamsburg, Virginia, and on the 6th of that month he arrived at the seat of government, and took the oath of office as President of the United States.

The circumstances under which he had been called on to assume the high office which now devolved upon him, without the opportunity for that preparation to execute its duties which is secured to one who succeeds to the presidency by immediate election, subjected him to disadvantages such as no former chief magistrate had ever had to

JOHN TYLER.

encounter. Such a position would try the strength of any man, but Mr. TYLER showed that he was at no loss as to the steps he should pursue. He at once issued an address to the people, asserting principles coincident with those of Mr. Jefferson, and reasserting the purpose expressed by Mr. Madison in his inaugural, "To hold the union of the states as the basis of their peace and happiness; to support the constitution, which is the cement of the Union, as well in its limitations as in its authority; to respect the rights and authorities reserved to the states and the people, as equally incorporated with, and essential to the success of the general system." This, it was seen, was the doctrine, though not the language, and loud were the commendations which the address received throughout the land.

It is no part of the plan of THE NATIONAL PORTRAIT GALLERY to discuss the politics of parties, or to express an opinion as to which of the contending classes was right. Certain it is, that at the time neither one or the other of the two great political schools were satisfied. The president contended that the people had declared against the Bank, and the financial schemes of the two preceding administrations, while those opposed to him asserted the contrary. The dissolution of cabinets, the issuing of vetoes, and the expressions, in various ways, of public opinion, followed each other, till the period of his presidency expired.

Thus have we reported the chief facts connected with the public life of JOHN TYLER; and while abstaining in this, as in all other cases, from any expression of party politics, it must be conceded that connected with his presidency occurred the most anomalous and extraordinary events. On the death of General Harrison, Mr. TYLER was raised by the operation of a fundamental law to the chief magistracy of the Republic, and from that hour was deserted by his professedly warmest friends. Those who shouted hozannas in praise of his political views, threw in the way of his executive acts every legislative obstacle which could be devised, and even the cabinet deserted him at a crisis of great importance. On the other hand, after the negotiation of many years, he obtained a final settlement of our claims on Mexico for her spoliations on our commerce, ended triumphantly the war in Florida, honorably and advantageously arranged our differences with Great Britain, preserved all our foreign relations on the most desirable footing, conducted to completion the negotiations for the annexation of Texas, diminished by millions the annual expenses of the government, and left the country, when he resigned the presidential chair, in a state of full credit and confidence. Time will declare the position in state of full credit and confidence. Time will declare the position in which he shall stand before posterity.

Twice during his presidency afflictions fell heavily upon Mr. TYLER and his family. In 1842 he was bereaved of his excellent wife, after a union of twenty-nine years. With him six children lamented their loss. Nearly two years afterwards he married at New York, Julia, daughter of David Gardiner, Esq., a gentleman who perished, about nine months later, by the explosion on board the United States steamship Princeton.

At the close of his term of office Ex-president TYLER retired to his estate, Sherwood Forest, Charles City County, Virginia. Having reached the age when repose is usually sought, he manifested no disposition to engage in the toils and difficulties of public life. We are told that all who had the pleasure of being numbered in his social circle were attracted by the brilliancy, versatility, and charms of his conversation. His correspondents enjoyed the elegance and intellectual vigor displayed even in his most hasty and familiar letters. Courtly in his address, affable among his acquaintances, frank and open in his communication with strangers, affectionate at home and genial everywhere, his society was regarded as a privilege. His house and table always gave proofs of unbounded hospitality.

He remained in retirement until the early part of 1861, when he appeared as a member of the "Peace Convention," composed of delegates from different States, which met at Washington. He was elected president of the convention. Various schemes were discussed in the attempt to form a compromise between the seceding States of the South and the Federal Government, and to ward off the coming war. But nothing effective resulted from those deliberations. Mr. TYLER afterwards renounced his allegiance to the United States, and gave his earnest support to the Confederate cause. At the time of his death he was a member of the Confederate Congress, then assembled at Richmond. He did not live to see the war ended, the Union triumphant, and peace restored. His death was lamented by all who were engaged in the cause which enlisted his last energies, and in which his youthful vigor seemed to be renewed.

JAMES K. POLK.

NORTH CAROLINA was founded chiefly by Covenanters from Scotland, and Scotch-Irish Presbyterians from the north of Ireland, all of whom left their country for "conscience sake." We cannot, therefore, be surprised that in that state the seeds of independence were early sown; nor do we wonder that its sons claim to be the first who declared their freedom from all obligations to obey the government of Great Britain.

Among the leading men in the Revolution, were the now widely extended family of *Polk*, originally *Pollock*. They are said to have been the first Democratic family of note in the country, and one of them was the prime mover, and a signer of the celebrated "Mecklenburg Declaration" of May 20, 1775. This was the great uncle of the President.

Samuel, the father of JAMES KNOX POLK, was an enterprising farmer. He was throughout life a firm Democrat, and a warm supporter of Mr. Jefferson. Thrown upon his own resources in early life, he became the architect of his own fortune, and in the year 1806, he removed with his family of ten children, from North Carolina to Tennessee, where he was among the pioneers of the fertile valley of the Duck river, now one of the most flourishing and populous portions of the State. He was followed by the Polk family, with the exception of one branch, and they added character to that portion of the great valley of the Mississippi.

JAMES KNOX, who was named after the worthy father of his mother, was the oldest of the ten children of his father. He was born in Mecklenburg County, N. C., November 2, 1795. Removing, as we have seen he did, in very early life to Tennessee, it could be no matter of surprise that his early education was very limited. The opportunities for instruction furnished in an infant settlement were few, besides which he was no stranger to daily labor. He assisted his father in the management of his farm, and was his almost constant companion in his surveying excursions. They were frequently absent for weeks together, treading the dense forests, and traversing the rough canebrakes which then covered the face of the country, and were exposed to all the hardships of a life in the woods. Here JAMES resided till elected to the presidential chair of this great country.

When but a lad, notwithstanding all his disadvantages, the greatest of them a painful disease, from which after years of suffering, he was finally relieved by a surgical operation, he acquired the elements of a good English education. He was even then strongly inclined to study, and often employed himself in mathematical calculations. All the elements of his future character might then have been traced. To obtain a liberal education was his chief desire, and a profession was the great end at which he aimed. His habits, formed by the moulding hand of his exemplary mother, peculiarly fitted him for success in the sphere toward which his thoughts were directed, and on which his hopes were fixed. He was correct, punctual, industrious, persevering, and, in a word,—*ambitious.*

The health of the future President having so greatly failed, his father, fearing the evil effects of confinement to study, determined, though greatly against the will of the son, to place him under the care of a merchant, with a view to commercial life. He remained in this situation, however, but a few weeks, for he found means to change the mind of his father, who in July, 1813, consented that he should study under the tuition of the Rev. Dr. Henderson, and subsequently at the Academy of Murfreesborough, Tenn., then under the direction of Mr. Samuel P. Black, justly celebrated in that region as a classical teacher. The difficulties in the way of his education were now removed; and in the autumn of 1815, after preparatory studies for two years and a half, he entered an advanced class in the University of North Carolina, being then in his twentieth year. Here he was most exemplary in the performance of all his duties, not only as a member of college, but also of the literary society to which he belonged. He was regular and punctual at every exercise, and never absent from recitation, or any of the religious services of the institution. So remarkable was his character in this matter, that one of his classmates, who was something of a wag, was in the habit of averring, when he wished his friends to place confidence in his assertions, that the fact he stated was "just as certain, as that POLK would get up at the first call."

The results of such habits were just what might have been expected. At each semi-annual examination, he bore away the highest honors, and graduated in June, 1818, with the reputation of being the first scholar in both mathematics and classics. Of the former science he was passionately fond, though equally distinguished as a linguist. Of his *Alma Mater*, he was never forgetful; and of the high estimation in which she held him, evidence was given in June, 1847, when the degree of LL. D. was conferred on him within her walls.

From the University, Mr. POLK returned to Tennessee with health greatly impaired by incessant application to study. Happily a few months of relaxation improved his strength, and in the spring of 1819, he commenced the study of law, (the profession which has furnished eleven of the fourteen Presidents of the United States,) in the office of Felix Grundy, of Nashville, then in the zenith of his fame. Mr. POLK was admitted to the full privileges of the profession at the close of 1820, where he at once took a distinguished position. He immediately established himself amidst the companions of his childhood, where he practised for several years with eminent success, and enjoyed a rich harvest of professional emoluments.

In this country, the politician and the lawyer are usually found in the same person; to this general rule, Mr. POLK was not an exception. He was a republican of the strictest sect; his character was popular; and his style and manner as an orator were eminently adapted to win the favor of the masses. In 1823, he was chosen to represent his own county in the State Legislature, and was two successive years a member of that body. Most of the measures of the then President, Mr. Monroe, received his unqualified approbation, and he was desirous that his successor should be one who had no sympathy for the latitudinarian doctrines in reference to the constitution, which appeared to be gaining ground. Hence he approved of the nomination of Andrew Jackson for the Presidency, made by the Tennessee Legislature in 1822; and in the following year, aided by his vote to call that distinguished man from his retirement, by his election to the Senate of the United States. These gentlemen maintained a warm, personal and political friendship for each other, till they were separated by death. While a member of the General Assembly, Mr. POLK obtained the passage of a law to prevent duelling; and opposed the doctrine of internal improvements by the general government.

On New Year's day, 1824, Mr. POLK was married to Miss Sarah Childress, the daughter of Joel Childress, Esq., a wealthy merchant of Tennessee, a lady who has proved herself well fitted to adorn any station. To the charms of a fine person, she united intellectual accomplishments of a high order. An amiable disposition, gracefulness of manner, beauty of mind, and sincere piety of heart, have always been happily blended in her character. A kind mistress, a faithful friend, a devoted wife, an affectionate widow—these are her titles to esteem; and they are gems brighter and more resplendent than usually decorate a queenly brow. Affable, but dignified; intelligent, but unaffected; frank and sincere, yet never losing sight of the respect due to her position, she has won the regard of all who have approached her. May she long be spared to perpetuate the memory of him whose name she bears.

In August, 1825, being then in his thirtieth year, Mr. POLK was elected to represent his district in Congress, and took his seat in December following. He brought with him the principles to which he adhered through all the mutations of party. He was at that time, with one or two exceptions, the junior member of the body, but so conducted himself as to satisfy his constituents, so that he was returned for fourteen years in succession, from 1825 to 1839, when he voluntarily withdrew from another contest, in which his success was not even questionable, to become a candidate for the office of Governor in his adopted State. The same habits of laborious application which had previously characterized him, were now displayed on the floor of the House, and in the committee-room. He was punctual and prompt in the performance of every duty, and firm and zealous in the advocacy of his opinions. He spoke frequently, but was invariably listened to with respect. He was always courteous in debate; his speeches had nothing declamatory about them, were always to the point, and always clear. So exemplary was he in his attendance on Congress, that it is said, he never missed a division while occupying a seat on the floor of the House, and was not absent from the sittings a single day, except on one occasion, on account of indisposition. Such punctuality in a legislator, is rarely witnessed, and therefore it deserves to be remembered.

The first speech which Mr. POLK made in Congress, was in favor of a proposition so to amend the Constitution as to prevent the choice of President, in any event whatever, from devolving on Congress. This address at once attracted the attention of the country, by the force of its reasoning, the fulness of its research, and the spirit of honest indignation with which it was animated. As one of the friends of General Jackson, he entered warmly into the subject, and his speech was characterized by what was with him an unusual degree of animation, in addressing a deliberate body. Henceforth the way was clear before him. Although among his associates in Congress there were many of the ablest men in the nation, an honorable post among them was cheer-

JAMES K. POLK.

fully assigned him, and he became henceforth identified with the most important transactions in the Legislature. During the whole of General Jackson's administration, as long as he retained a seat on the floor, he was one of its leading supporters, and at times, and on certain questions of vast importance, its chief reliance. Throughout the period of his connection with the Legislature, he was on the most important committees, and originated many momentous measures.

In December, 1835, Mr. POLK was elected Speaker of the House of Representatives, and was again chosen to that high office in 1837, at the extra session held in the first year of Mr. Van Buren's administration. During the first session in which he presided, more appeals were taken from his decision than had occurred in the whole period since the origin of the government; but he was uniformly sustained by the House, and frequently by the most prominent members of the opposition. He was courteous and affable toward all who approached him, and in his manner, as the presiding officer, dignity and urbanity were admirably blended. Notwithstanding the violence with which he had been assailed, Congress passed at the close of the session, in March, 1837, an unanimous vote of thanks to its presiding officer, from whom it separated with the kindest feelings; and no man now could enjoy its confidence and friendship in a higher degree. His calmness and good temper had allayed the violence of opposition, in a station for which his sagacity, tact for business, and coolness eminently qualified him. In the twenty-fifth Congress, over which he presided as speaker during three sessions, commencing in September, 1837, and ending in March, 1839, parties were more nearly balanced, and the most exciting questions were agitated during the whole period. At the close of the term, Mr. Elmore, of South Carolina, moved the usual vote of thanks. A long and exciting debate arose, when the resolution was adopted. In adjourning the House, Mr. POLK delivered a farewell address of more than ordinary length, and characterized by deep feeling. Thus ceased his connection with the House, for he declined a reëlection. He had faithfully discharged his legislatorial duties fourteen years.

Thus freed from engagements of this kind, he was taken up by the friends of the administration in Tennessee, as a candidate for Governor. After an animated canvass, during which Mr. POLK visited the different counties of that extensive state, and addressed the people on the political topics of the day, the election took place in August, 1839, and resulted in a majority for Mr. POLK, of more than two thousand five hundred votes over General Cannon, and on the 14th of October following, he entered on the discharge of the executive duties. This station, however, he filled but two years. As he was not reëlected, he returned with cheerfulness in 1841 to the duties and enjoyments of private life; where, blessed with a competency which enabled him to be liberal in his charities, and to dispense a generous hospitality to his friends, and favored with a wife whose virtues and graces made his home a paradise, little was left for him to desire.

But can a politician stand still? Mr. POLK was not without ambition, and the expectations of his friends were early fixed on the presidential chair. At the session of the Tennessee Legislature, in 1839, he was nominated by that body for the Vice-presidency, to be placed on the ticket with Mr. Van Buren, and with the expectation that he might succeed that gentleman in the higher office; and he was afterwards nominated in other states for that station, but the design failed.

From the time of the defeat of Mr. Van Buren, in 1840, till within a few weeks of the assembling of the national democratic convention, at Baltimore, in May, 1844, public opinion in the republican party seemed to have been firmly fixed upon him as their candidate for reëlection to the station which he had once filled. But in April, 1844, a treaty was concluded by President Tyler, between the United States and the republic of Texas, for the annexation of the latter to the American confederacy. This measure was fruitful in contention, and destroyed the general expectation that Messrs. Van Buren and Clay would be the rival candidates for the presidency. In the midst of this commotion the democratic convention assembled, and after much discussion and many trials of strength in behalf of various parties, the name of Mr. POLK was mentioned, and it operated like magic; harmony was instantly restored, and in the end the vote was unanimous. The honor to Mr. POLK was entirely unexpected, but who could expect him to decline it? On the 28th of November, the result of the election being then known, Mr. POLK visited Nashville, and was honored with a public reception by his democratic friends, together with a number of their opponents in the late contest, who cheerfully united with them in paying due honors to the President elect of the people's choice. A grand procession, and an imposing illumination testified the hilarity and joy of the people.

Mr. POLK left his home in Tennessee, on his way to Washington, the latter end of January, 1845. · He was accompanied by Mrs. Polk, and several personal friends. On the 31st of that month he had a long private interview at the Hermitage, with his venerable friend, Andrew Jackson. The leave-taking was affectionate and impressive,

JAMES K. POLK.

for each felt conscious, that, in all probability, it was a farewell forever. It was the son, in the pride of manhood, going forth to fulfill his high destiny, from the threshold of his political father, whose trembling lips, palsied with the touch of age, could scarcely invoke the benediction which his heart would prompt. Before another harvest moon shed its light upon the spot hallowed by so many memories and associations, the "Hero of New Orleans," and the "Defender of the Constitution" slept that sleep which, till the morning of the resurrection, knows no waking.

Various pleasant anecdotes, illustrative alike of the character of Mr. POLK and of the manners of the country, are told of his "progress" to the Capital, far more attractive than the movements of monarchs. When the steamboat, on which he proceeded up the Ohio river, stopped at Jeffersonville, Indiana, "a plain-looking man came on board," says a passenger on the steamer, "who from the soiled and coarse condition of his dress, seemed just to have left the plough handles or spade, in the field. He pressed forward through the saloon of the boat, to the place where the President was standing in conversation with a circle of gentlemen, through which he thrust himself, making directly for the President, and offered his hand, which was received with cordial good will. Said the farmer, 'how do you do, Colonel? I am glad to see you. I am a strong democrat, and did all I could for you. I am the father of twenty-six children, who are all for *Polk, Dallas, and Texas!*' Colonel POLK responded with a smile, saying, he was happy to make his acquaintance, feeling assured that he deserved well of his country, if for no other reason than because he was the father of so large a republican family."

On March 4, 1845, Mr. POLK was duly inaugurated President of the United States. An immense concourse of people assembled at Washington to witness the imposing ceremony, every quarter of the Union being well represented. The morning was wet and lowering; but the spirits of the spectators were proof against the unfavorable influences of the weather. All parties joined in the appropriate observance of the day, and the national standard floated proudly from the flag-staffs of both democrats and whigs.

Mr. POLK entered upon the duties of his administration under somewhat unfavorable auspices. He belonged to a younger race of statesmen than the prominent candidates whose names were originally presented to the Baltimore convention, and it was but natural that he should be fearful of incurring the dislike of some one or more of them, which might tend seriously to embarrass his administration. But his

NATIONAL PORTRAITS.

position personally, was all that could be desired. He had no pledges to redeem,—no promises to fulfill; and he was not a candidate for reëlection. He was indifferent, too, as to which of the leading men of his party should be his successor. It was his desire, therefore, to harmonize and conciliate, but, at the same time, to surrender no principle, to maintain his character for independence, and to observe the dignity of his official position. For these reasons, his cabinet was selected from among the most distinguished members of the democratic party, and in it each section of the confederacy was represented.

It will be remembered by our readers, that the treaty for the annexation of Texas, concluded by President Tyler, had been rejected by the Senate of the United States, on June 8, 1844. At the ensuing session of Congress, the subject was again discussed, and joint resolutions providing for the annexation, were adopted on March 1, 1845. The people of Texas, represented in convention, signified their assent to the terms of the resolutions on the 4th of July following, and formed a state constitution, which was forwarded to Washington to be laid before the Congress of the United States by the President. This difficulty was thus settled; as was also the Oregon question, so long an apple of discord between Great Britain and the United States; and the war with Mexico, arising out of the annexation of Texas, soon after ended. All these great events elicited the statesmanlike talents of Mr. POLK and his official advisers, and furnished ground of satisfaction to every lover of his country. Much additional labor had been thrown on the President, but it was all ably and promptly performed.

Other great and grave questions had to be now discussed and acted on, such as the independent treasury system, the tariff of 1846, the course in regard to official appointments, the river and harbor veto, and the territorial bill for Oregon, but our limited space affords no room for discussions, besides which the reader can have no difficulty in obtaining whatever information relative to them he may desire. Congress assembled for the last time during the administration of Mr. Polk, on December 4, 1848. The most important subject then agitating the public mind, was that growing out of the Wilmot Proviso, as to which his opinions had been made known in his last annual message. His vetoes, too, had been attacked, in some of the Northern and Western states, with great asperity, and an effort to amend the constitution, so as to deprive the executive of this power, was said to be in contemplation. He therefore availed himself in his last annual message to vindicate his course, and to express his opinions.

March 5, 1849, the 4th happening on Sunday, General Taylor was

JAMES K. POLK.

duly inaugurated as the successor of Mr. Polk. The latter gentleman took part in the ceremonies, and rode at the side of General Taylor in the carriage which conveyed them to the Capitol. He was also one of the first to congratulate him at the close of his inaugural address, at the same time rejoicing that he was himself relieved from the anxieties of public life. On that afternoon, he and Mrs. Polk took leave of their friends,—many words of mingled regret and endearment being uttered on both sides,—and in the evening commenced their return to their home in Tennessee. Thus ended the most important administration since that of Mr. Madison. As Mr. Jenkins, one of Mr. Polk's ablest biographers, has remarked, "The settlement of the Oregon question, the war with Mexico, and the acquisition of California, will cause it to be long remembered. Ages hence, if the God of nations shall continue to smile on our favored land, the dweller on the banks of the Mississippi, as he gazes on the mighty current that laves his feet, and beholds it reaching forth, like a giant, its hundred arms, and gathering the produce of that noble valley into its bosom, will bless the name of Thomas Jefferson. So, too, the citizen of California or Oregon, when he sees their harbors filled with stately argosies, richly freighted with golden sands, or with silks and spices of the Old World, will offer his tribute, dictated by a grateful heart, to the memory of JAMES K. POLK. At home, his administration was well conducted. Though the war with Mexico was actively prosecuted for nearly two years, the national debt was not largely or oppressively increased, and the pecuniary credit of the government was at all times maintained; more than double the premiums realized in the war of 1812 being procured for stock and treasury notes. Commerce, agriculture, and every art and occupation of industry, flourished during this period; happiness and prosperity dwelt in every habitation. In the management of our foreign relations, ability, skill and prudence, were displayed. Our rights were respected; our honor defended; and our national character elevated still higher in the estimation of foreign governments and their people."

If Mr. Polk was gratified with the enthusiastic demonstrations of regard which attended him on his journey to Washington, to enter on the duties of his administration, he was far more sincerely pleased with the kindly greetings that everywhere welcomed him as he returned to his home in Tennessee. The one might have been selfish, for he had then office and patronage to bestow; but the other was the genuine homage of the heart. At Richmond, he was complimented with a public reception by the citizens, and the Legislature of Virginia, then in session; at Charleston, Savannah, and New Orleans—at every place he passed on his route,—congratulations, prayers, and blessings attended him, like ministering angels, to the home from which he had gone forth in early manhood to carve out his destiny, and to which he now returned with the harvest of fame he had gathered. Perhaps, however, the most gratifying reception he met with on his whole journey, was at Wilmington, N. C., where the people of his native State, came together in crowds to welcome him. Extensive preparations had been made for his reception, and in replying to the orator who addressed him, he said:—"You remark truly, sir, that I still cherish affection for my native State. I receive its welcome as the blessing of an honored parent. North Carolina can boast of glorious reminiscences, and is entitled to rank with, or far above, many who make greater pretensions. It was from her—her counties of Mecklenburg, New Hanover, and Bladen, that the news of treason in the colonies first went to the ears of the British monarch, and here was the spirit of independence first aroused."

The exhausted health and strength of Mr. POLK now demanded rest. He had been eminently devoted to the duties of his great office; friends and enemies acknowledged that his labors had been too great for his comparatively delicate frame to sustain with safety. He had been for a long time subject to frequent attacks of chronic diarrhœa, one of which greatly prostrated him on his journey up the Mississippi. Previously to this period, he had purchased the beautiful house and grounds of his friend and preceptor, Mr. Grundy, situated in the centre of the city of Nashville. Here, surrounded by the conveniences which an ample fortune enabled him to procure, in the constant companionship of his wife and books, and in the frequent society of the friends he esteemed, he had determined to pass the remainder of his life in ease and retirement, fulfilling his duty to himself and the world, but not entering again into public life. On arriving at Nashville, after a few days' rest, he took possession of this elegant mansion, and seemed to be rapidly gaining strength; he devoted himself to the improvement of his grounds, and all now seemed to promise long life and enjoyment.

But, alas, how often are the brightest expectations of man doomed to the darkest disappointment! Even those highest in rank and excellence, are compelled to meet the common lot. Some of the friends of Mr. POLK were observing the rapid improvement of his health, and were struck with his erect and healthful bearing; and the active energy of his manner, which gave promise of long life. His flowing gray

JAMES K. POLK.

locks alone made him appear beyond the middle stage of life. About the first of June, being detained within doors by a rainy day, he began to arrange his extensive library, and the fatigue of reaching his books from the floor to the shelves, brought on a slight fever, which the next day assumed the form of his old disease. The best medical aid was obtained, and for some days no alarm was cherished. But, in defiance of the most eminent skill, he continued gradually to sink, so that when the disease left him four days before his death, there did not remain energy enough for healthy reaction, and on the evening of Friday, June 15, 1849, he expired, in the fifty-fourth year of his age.

The close of life now rapidly approaching was contemplated by Mr. POLK with all the solemnity which its vast importance demanded; and all his conversations on the subject were worthy of his character. He evinced a very thorough knowledge of the Scriptures, which he said he had read a great deal, and deeply reverenced as divine truth; in a word, he had been throughout his life theoretically a Christian; and now, more than ever felt the importance of genuine piety. He said that when in office he had several times seriously intended to be baptised; but the cares and perplexities of public life scarcely allowed time for the requisite solemn preparation; and so procrastination had ripened into inaction, till it was now almost too late to act. About a week before his decease, he received the sacraments of baptism and of the Lord's Supper from the Rev. Mr. M'Ferrin, of the Methodist Episcopal Church, with whom he had long been personally intimate, and then calmly awaited the change which should remove him to another state of existence. About half an hour preceding his death, his venerable mother entered the room, and kneeling by his bedside, in the presence of Major Polk, brother of the ex-president, and the other members of the family, she most solemnly and feelingly commended the departing soul of her son to " the King of kings, and the Lord of lords." Previously to this act, he had taken leave of all he held dear; and could thus say with Lord William Russell, "the bitterness of death is past."

On the day following, the mansion of the lamented ex-president was shrouded in mourning, and the corpse, dressed in a plain suit of black, with a copy of the Constitution of the United States at its feet, lay in one of the drawing rooms, to receive the last look of thousands of friends and neighbors; and the cortege which accompanied his remains to their last resting place, was composed of almost the entire population of the city and adjacent country. The plain silver plate on his coffin, contained merely these words:

"J. K. POLK,
Born November 2, 1795,
Died June 15, 1849."

At Washington, and in every part of the Union, due honors were paid to his memory.

In person, President POLK was of middle stature, with a full angular brow, and a quick penetrating eye. The expression of his countenance was grave, but its serious cast was often relieved by a peculiarly pleasant smile. His private life, which had ever been upright and pure, secured to him the esteem of all who had the advantage of his acquaintance.

The Hon. Mr. Chase, in his "*History of the Polk Administration,*" says very truly, "No one who ever knew Mr. POLK ever considered him a brilliant genius. His mind possessed solidity rather than imagination. His perception was intuitive, and his memory retentive to an extraordinary degree, while his judgment rarely led him into error. His manners were remarkably affable, and always made an impression upon those who knew him. Among his intimate friends, he indulged his wit and humor with perfect freedom, and they always found him a pleasant and instructive companion." The prominent trait of his character was extraordinary energy. In college, at the bar, in his political canvasses, and in the discharge of his executive duties, he was alike distinguished for his untiring industry and indomitable will. This frequently induced him to devote his attention too much to minute details, and had the effect of impairing his constitution. He invariably succeeded in inspiring his friends with his own enthusiasm; no obstacle could deter him from the energetic discharge of his duty. Subsisting upon the plainest food, and perfectly temperate in his habits, he accustomed himself to a rigid system of diet, which alone could have sustained him in his political conflicts. As Mr. Chase has remarked, "Posterity will pronounce his eulogium!"

ZACHARY TAYLOR.

WHILE it is true that our republican principles forbid personal distinctions on account of ancestral rank, it is equally certain, that when men on other accounts rise to eminence, there is a prevalent disposition to add, if it can be done, the honors of their ancestors to their own. Nor ought such a feeling to be censured; for it has its origin, partly at least, in the respect due to our fathers. It cannot be otherwise than honorable to President TAYLOR, that his ancestors left England two centuries ago for Virginia. They were among the most respectable of the men of that day, and gradually became connected with the most distinguished families of the State, such as those of Jefferson, Marshall, Lee, Monroe, Madison, and others of like character; and assuredly ZACHARY TAYLOR has added not a little to the honor of his connexions.

Richard Taylor, the father of our hero, was himself a Virginian, born in 1744, and received a plain education. He was remarkable for a daring and adventurous spirit, and resolved when but a school-boy to distinguish himself for courage as soon as his strength should allow. He joined the army, in due time, was soon raised to the rank of Colonel, and fought by the side of Washington at the battle of Trenton. But his disposition led him to feats of another character. Daniel Boone had already explored the wilds of the west, and Colonel Taylor, not long after, set out and reached "the dark and bloody ground" on which, at that time, the dwelling of a civilized man had not been reared. He penetrated on foot, and without a companion, as far as New Orleans, and then returned with a determination ultimately to make his home in the west. At thirty-five, he married Miss Sarah Strother, a young lady of twenty. Five sons and three daughters were the fruits of this union; of these ZACHARY was the third son, and was born in Orange county, Virginia, November 24, 1784.

Thus was Virginia honored by giving birth to another of the eminent men, of which she has furnished so many to the Union. But he had not breathed her soft and balmy air very long, when his father emigrated with his whole family to Kentucky, in pursuance of his long cherished intention. He had been preceded by his brother Hancock, a brave and intelligent man, who fell a sacrifice in surveying parts of the Ohio valley, and who just previous to his death had selected for a farm on which to locate, the site of the present city of Louisville. Only ten years before the emigration of Richard Taylor, the first habitation of a white man had been erected in the vast region between the western boundary of Virginia and the Mississippi. Within this period a few settlements had been made, insufficient, however, from their isolated positions, to secure to the emigrant adequate protection from the Indians, much less to afford him the most usual comforts of civilized life.

"Under the guidance of such men," as Fry remarks in his Life of Taylor, "and under such circumstances, for the development of his bold spirit and active intellect, ZACHARY TAYLOR passed his infant years. The hardships and dangers of border life were to him as familiar as ease and security to the child of metropolitan luxury." The residence of his father was in Jefferson county, about five miles from Louisville, and ten miles from the Ohio river. Here he acquired a large estate, and was distinguished for his intelligence and patriotism. When Louisville rose into importance, and was made a port of entry, Richard Taylor received from Washington, his personal friend, a commission as collector of the customs.

It will be readily believed that the father of ZACHARY TAYLOR would give his children the best education which the neighborhood would afford; this, however, was comparatively slender. In acts of daring prowess the boy needed no instruction. While his father was from home engaged in contest with the Indians, ZACHARY would be casting bullets for a coming engagement. He was thus familiar from his infancy with the gleam of the tomahawk, and the yell of the savage. An earnest military passion, natural to him, was cherished by the romance of frontier life, and inflamed by household legends of the Revolution. Thoughtfulness, sound judgment, shrewdness, and stability, with a determination which nothing could move, made up his character.

In 1794, it is well known, that the expedition of General Wayne against the western Indians was successful, and in the following year, a peace was concluded; emigration rapidly increased, and civilized labor began to receive its due reward; young TAYLOR engaged in agriculture with his father, and thus laid the foundation of robust health, hardy habits, and persevering industry, which afterwards distinguished his military life for more than thirty years. When Aaron Burr's movements in the west began to excite suspicion, the patriotic young men of Kentucky formed volunteer companies, to oppose his designs by arms, if occasion should demand it. ZACHARY TAYLOR, and one or more of his brothers, were enrolled in a troop raised for this purpose. On the death of his brother, Lieutenant Taylor, ZACHARY, by the influence of his father, James Madison, and his uncle, Major Edmund Taylor, obtained the vacancy, and received a commission from President Jefferson, May 3, 1808, as first Lieutenant in the seventh regiment of United States Infantry. He was then twenty-four years of age, and in possession of a competent fortune, but he chose to relinquish the quiet life of a farmer, to engage in the perilous duties of a soldier. Soon after this, having to report himself to General Wilkinson, then at New Orleans, he was seized by yellow fever, and his life was some time in danger, so that he was compelled to return home in order to recruit his health. Here he diligently studied the duties of his profession, and circumstances soon proved that he had made no small proficiency.

The aggressions of England, at this time, had long been preparing the public mind of the United States for war. The emissaries of Great Britain had excited the Indian tribes north of the Ohio, to new hostilities towards the American settlers on the frontiers, who were kept in constant apprehensions of an attack. Under such circumstances, our government deemed it advisable to make the first demonstration, and General Harrison, then Governor of the North-west Territory, was ordered to march a competent force into the Indian country; for it was not to be endured, that British promises and British gold should bribe the savages to prepare for the extermination of all the whites on the frontiers. To this expedition Lieutenant TAYLOR was attached, and though he had been married but about a year to Miss Margaret Smith, of one of the first families of Maryland, he willingly left his young wife and infant, to engage in his country's service in the camp. At the bloody battle of Tippecanoe, May 7, 1811, his gallant services won the highest esteem of his commander, and soon after, President Madison gave him a captain's commission. He was placed in command of Fort Harrison. The defences of this post were in a miserable condition, and its garrison consisted of only fifty men, of whom thirty were disabled by sickness. With this little band of soldiers, the young commander immediately set about repairing the fortifications, which having done, he was called from a bed of sickness into action, and here he accomplished mighty feats of valor against the Indians, though headed by their great chief Tecumseh. His presence of mind and noble courage, greatly encouraged his men, and the account of the conflict which he sent to General Harrison, indicated alike his modesty, his strong common sense, and the severe style of his composition. The failure of their enterprise against Fort Harrison, greatly disheartened the Indians, and they abandoned for the time, any further attempts against it. The conduct of Captain TAYLOR, gave high satisfaction at head quarters, so that General Hopkins, in a letter to the Governor of Kentucky, said, "The firm and almost unparalleled defence of Fort Harrison, by Captain ZACHARY TAYLOR, has raised for him a fabric of character not to be effaced by eulogy;" and the President, in accordance with the feelings of the whole country, conferred upon him, the rank of Major by brevet—which became before his death the latest instance in the service of this species of promotion. From this time to the close of the war with Great Britain, Major TAYLOR was engaged in the same vicinity, accomplishing the purposes of the government with unremitting vigilance. At length the Indians were reduced to terms of peace, and the white settlers were secured from their incursions.

From this period of 1812 till 1832, the Major was engaged in several important active duties, but our limits will not allow any details respecting them. In 1816, he was ordered to Green Bay, and remained in command of that post two years. Having passed a year with his family, he joined Colonel Russell at New Orleans, where one of his labors was the opening of a military road, and another the erection of Fort Jessup. In 1824, he was engaged in the recruiting service at Louisville, and in the latter part of that year, was ordered to Washington, and appointed one of the Board of Commissioners for erecting Jefferson Barracks. In 1826, he was one of a Board of Officers of the army and militia to consider a system for the organization of the militia of the United States. His duties were subsequently resumed on the north-western frontier, a field on which he afterwards again met an Indian enemy, and sustained the reputation won in his first contest with him. Five years of peace, however, preceded this occasion, years not idly spent, for when unemployed in his duties as a strict disciplinarian, he was studiously engaged in perfecting himself in his profession. A writer in the *Literary World* says, "I have often seen him putting his men through the battalion drill on the northern banks of the Wisconson, in the depth of February. This would seem only characteristic of the man who has since equally proved himself 'Rough and Ready,' under the searching sun of the tropics. But,

ZACHARY TAYLOR.

looking back through long years to many a pleasant hour spent in the well-selected library of the post which Colonel TAYLOR then commanded, we recur now with singular interest to the agreeable conversations held in the room which was the Colonel's favorite resort, amid the intervals of duty."

In 1819, ZACHARY TAYLOR had received the commission of Lieutenant-Colonel, and in 1832, President Jackson appointed him Colonel, and in this capacity, his skill and bravery were distinguished in the Black Hawk war, which, however, unjustly it may have originated, it was assuredly important to terminate by the most vigorous measures. This was accomplished by Black Hawk being surrendered by some of his faithless allies. With his capture, the war ended. The writer in the *Literary World*, already quoted, relates an anecdote, which, as it is strikingly illustrative of Colonel TAYLOR's character, we here give:

"Some time after Stillman's defeat by Black Hawk's band, TAYLOR, marching with a large body of volunteers, and a handful of regulars, in pursuit of the hostile Indian force, found himself approaching Rock river, then asserted by many to be the true north-western boundary of Illinois. The volunteers, as TAYLOR was informed, would refuse to cross the stream; they were militia, they said, called out for the defence of the State, and it was unconstitutional to order them to march beyond its frontier into the Indian country. TAYLOR thereupon halted his command, and encamped within the acknowledged boundaries of Illinois. He would not, as the relator of the story said, budge an inch further without orders. He had already driven Black Hawk out of the State, but the question of crossing Rock river seemed hugely to trouble his ideas of integrity, to the constitution on one side, and military expediency on the other. During the night, however, orders came, either from General Scott or General Anderson, for him to follow up Black Hawk to the last. The quietness of the regular Colonel, meanwhile, had rather encouraged the mutinous militia to bring their proceedings to a head. A sort of town meeting was called upon the prairie, and TAYLOR invited to attend. After listening some time very quietly to the proceedings, it became 'Rough and Ready's' turn to address the chair. 'He had heard,' he said, 'with much pleasure, the views which several speakers had expressed of the independence and dignity of each private American citizen. He felt that all gentlemen here present, were his equals,—in reality, he was persuaded that many of them would in a few years be his superiors, and perhaps, in the capacity of members of congress, arbiters of the fortune and reputation of humble servants of the republic like himself. He expected ther.

NATIONAL PORTRAITS.

to obey them as interpreters of the will of the people; and the best proof he could give that he would obey them, was now to observe the orders of those whom the people had already put in the places of authority, to which many gentlemen around him justly aspired. *In plain English, gentlemen and fellow citizens, the word has been passed on to me from Washington, to follow Black Hawk, and to take you with me as soldiers. I mean to do both. There are the flat boats drawn up on the shore, and here are Uncle Sam's men drawn up behind you on the prairie!*" It is unnecessary to state the effect of this appeal.

Twenty-five years had Colonel TAYLOR been now engaged in the toils of war, with very rare intervals of the tranquillity of home, but when he might have asked for a respite of labor, he was ordered to take command of Fort Crawford, which had been erected under his superintendence, and soon after, in 1836, he was directed to proceed to Florida, to assist in reducing the Seminole Indians to submission. The origin of this war is well known. In 1832, a treaty had been made with this tribe for their removal, and three years was allowed for its fulfillment. This, however, when the time had elapsed, they refused to do, the results of which were truly sad. All friendly conferences with the chiefs having failed, it was determined, in the autumn of 1837, to take more active measures against them. Unlimited power was given to Colonel TAYLOR, to capture or destroy them wherever they might be found. Accordingly on December 20, he left Fort Gardiner with about eleven hundred men, and through dense thickets of palmetto and cypress, and the luxuriant herbage of a wet soil, they made their way towards the everglades, where the foe was concealed. On the 25th of December, with five hundred men, and under the clear range of seven hundred Indian rifles, he gained the victory of OKEE-CHO-BEE. The great satisfaction given alike to the country and the government by Colonel TAYLOR, led to his promotion to the rank of Brigadier-General, by brevet. Soon after this advancement in rank, General TAYLOR was honored with the supreme command of the troops of Florida, General Jessup having been recalled at his own request. Two years longer did General TAYLOR toil amid the morasses and fevers of that region, frequently skirmishing with the Indians, but unable to "conquer a peace." At his own request, he was relieved from the command, and succeeded by General Armistead, in April, 1840.

Relieved as General TAYLOR now was from arduous duty in Florida, it must not be supposed that no further labors were expected from him On the other hand, while hitherto his movements had influenced the fate of districts, now they began to affect the fortunes of empires. His distinguished talents were too well known and appreciated, to allow him to remain idle. He was therefore, immediately appointed to the command of the first department of the United States army in the south-west. This department included the four States at the extreme south-western part of the Union, Alabama, Mississippi, Arkansas, and Louisiana. His head-quarters were at Fort Jessup, in the latter State. In the summer of 1841, being ordered to relieve General Arbuckle, at Fort Gibson, the compliment of a public dinner, while on his way there, was tendered him by his fellow citizens of Little Rock, Arkansas, "as an expression of their esteem for his personal worth and meritorious public services." To the letter of invitation, General TAYLOR made answer, that under ordinary circumstances, it would have afforded him great pleasure to accept the invitation; but having been already detained on his journey to the frontier, an unusual length of time, he did not feel authorized to make on his own account, any delay whatever. He was, therefore, compelled to decline the proffered hospitality. In concluding his reply, he gave assurances of his best exertions to secure the object of his command on the frontier. Time proved to what extent he redeemed the pledge.

A little previously to his removal to Arkansas, General TAYLOR removed his family to Baton Rouge, Louisiana, where he had purchased an estate, but though this added to *their* comforts, they from this period, had for a long season to regret his absence, nor does it appear to have added to their wealth. This was no peculiarity in the case of General TAYLOR, for what servant of our republic, in the honest discharge of his duty, ever became rich?

We feel here a difficulty, arising from the necessarily limited space to which the biographical sketches of the NATIONAL PORTRAIT GALLERY are confined. We have now to do with *the* soldier of the day, the great Captain of the American army, but it is impossible even to sketch the mighty deeds which General TAYLOR now performed. We are, however, relieved by the thought, that already has the historian placed these deeds on record with all needful details, and that they are secured in the archives of our country's history. Our object is rather to glance at *personal history*, and to illustrate individual character. A paragraph or two is all we can give as introductory to larger histories. We may add here, that the Mexican war in its inceptive, had no friend in General TAYLOR; he had, however, been selected to take the field in the outset, before war had been declared, or any act of hostility committed on either side, and he felt it to be his duty to devote himself to the one object of reducing the enemy to terms of peace.

In May, 1845, on the annexation of Texas, General TAYLOR was ordered to place his troops in such a position as to defend that State against a threatened Mexican invasion. In August of that year, he concentrated his troops at Corpus Christi, where he remained till March 11, 1846, when he broke up his encampment, and moved the army of occupation westward; this was composed of only about four thousand regulars. On the 20th of March, he reached and passed without resistance, the Arroya Colorado, and arrived at the Rio Grande, to which point he had been ordered by the authorities at Washington, after considerable suffering, on the 29th of that month. Here he took every means to assure the Mexicans, that his purpose was not war, nor violence in any shape, but solely the occupation of the Texian territory to the Rio Grande, until the boundary should be definitely settled by the two republics.

Encamping opposite Metamoras, General TAYLOR prepared for Mexican aggression by erecting fortifications and planting batteries. Provisions became short, the American army possessed but little ammunition, and were in many other ways discouraged, but the battle of *Palo Alto* was commenced, and gloriously was it won, on May 8, 1846. On the following day, the two opposing armies again met at *Resaca de la Palma,* within three miles of Fort Brown: the battle commenced with great fury; the artillery on both sides did terrible execution, and extraordinary skill was displayed by the opposing Generals; but again conquest declared for the United States army. These victories filled our country with exultation. Government acknowledged the distinguished services of General TAYLOR, by making him Major-General by brevet; Congress passed resolutions of high approval; Louisiana presented him with a sword, and the press every where teemed with his praise.

As soon as means could be procured, General TAYLOR crossed the Rio Grande, took Metamoras without opposition, and made Colonel Twiggs its Governor. The army soon received large volunteer reinforcements, and the American General proceeded to Camargo, thence, through Seralos to *Monterey,* where he arrived the 19th of September. They found the town in a complete state of defence; the walls and parapets were lined with cannons, and the houses barricaded, and planted with artillery; the Mexicans had nearly ten thousand soldiers, and plenty of ammunition; but all were useless against the skill and power of our army. The conflict was terrific, but at length the city capitulated. The terms accorded by the conqueror were liberal, and dictated by a regard to the interests of peace; they crowned a gallant conquest of arms, with a more sublime victory of magnanimity.

To describe the last crowning victory effected by General TAYLOR, is, within our limits, impossible. Its scene was *Buena Vista*, and its time February 22, 1847. Santa Anna commanded the Mexican army of 20,000 men, while TAYLOR had but 4,500. Ten hours did the conflict last, and fearful was the crisis. The character of the General was never more strikingly shown. When Santa Anna summoned him to surrender, he, with Spartan brevity, "declined acceding to the request," and when the demand was repeated, the answer was, "General TAYLOR never surrenders." Nor were his addresses to his army, less sententious and effective. "A little more grape, Captain Bragg," and "'Tis impossible to whip us when we all pull together," are sounds which still live in the ears of those who heard them, and will never be forgotten. History tells not of a battle more bravely contested, or more nobly won; and well did the greatest warrior of the age, on learning it, exclaim, General TAYLOR's a general indeed!" Thus ended the military life of ZACHARY TAYLOR, who returned home carrying with him not only the adoration of his soldiers, but the respect of the people he had vanquished. We need not say he was received in the United States with loud and universal enthusiasm.

As one illustration, among many which might be given, we select an anecdote showing his republican habits, given by a committee appointed by the citizens of New Orleans, to present the General with a sword:—

"We presented ourselves at the opening of one of the tents, before which was standing a dragoon's horse, much used by hard service. Upon a camp-stool at our left sat General ———, in busy conversation with a hearty looking old gentleman, sitting on a box, cushioned with an Arkansas blanket, dressed in Attakapas pantaloons, and a linen roundabout, and remarkable for a bright flashing eye, a high forehead, a farmer look, and 'rough and ready' appearance. It is hardly necessary for us to say, that this personage was General TAYLOR, the commanding hero of two of the most remarkable battles on record, and the man who, by his firmness and decision of character, has shed lustre upon the American arms.

"There was no pomp about his tent; a couple of rough blue chests served for his table, upon which were strewn, in masterly confusion, a variety of official documents. A quiet-looking, citizen-dressed personage, made his appearance upon hearing the significant call of 'Ben,' bearing on a tin salver, a couple of black bottles and shining tumblers, arranged around an earthen pitcher of Rio Grande water. These refreshments were deposited upon a stool, and we 'helped ourselves' by invitation. We bore to the General, a complimentary gift, from some of his fellow citizens of New Orleans, which he declined receiving for the present; giving, at the same time, a short but 'hard sense' lecture on the impropriety of naming children and places after men, before they were dead, or of his receiving a present for his services 'before the campaign, so far as he was concerned, was finished.'

"With the highest possible admiration of the republican simplicity of the manners and character of General TAYLOR, we bade him good day, with a higher appreciation of our native land, for possessing such a man as a citizen, and of its institutions, for moulding such a character."

The people of the United States have in their gift, the office of the Presidency, an honor exceeding that of the greatest throne in the world. Whether it be desirable, to place a soldier in the chair, as is so frequently done, is no question to be discussed in this place; assuredly in the case of General TAYLOR, no small enthusiasm accompanied his selection for the honor by the Whig convention in Philadelphia, June 1, 1848, and scarcely less when the people confirmed the nomination on November 7, following. March 5, 1849, he was introduced to the office, and his inaugural address was considered to be redolent with old-fashioned patriotism, and breathed the very spirit of devotedness to his country. His subsequent administration, though beset by sectional strifes of fearful violence, was conducted with wisdom, firmness, and moderation, on great national principles, and for great national ends. Owing to his profound deference to the coördinate branches of government, and his inability to either dictate or assume, his policy was not, during the short period of his administration, fully proclaimed to congress, and pressed upon its adoption.

History is an illustration of the fact that death loves a shining mark. At the period when the life of a ruler appears most desirable, he is often suddenly removed. One year and five months only, had General TAYLOR become settled in the Presidential chair, and proved his declaration that he was not the President of a party; while occupied in business which demanded all his talents and energies, endeavoring to unite all parties in the prompt and untramelled admission of California into the Union, only five days after he had done homage to Washington, on the birth day of our liberties, and just as he had performed his last official act, in adding a new guaranty to the peace of

ZACHARY TAYLOR.

the world, by signing the convention recently concluded between our country and Great Britain, respecting Central America,—he was cut off in the sixty-sixth year of his age. His illness was only of a few hours' duration, and his love of country was shown to the last hour. Speaking of his own conduct in reference to her interests, his dying declaration was, "*I am prepared—I have endeavored to do my duty.*"

General TAYLOR left behind him a widow, who has since deceased, one son, and two daughters; one married to Dr. Wood, surgeon of the United States army, and the other to Colonel W. W. S. Bliss, of the army. Another daughter, who died some years since, was married to Colonel Jefferson Davis, Senator from Mississippi.

The administration of President TAYLOR is so recent, and therefore so fresh in the minds of our readers, that they may probably consider it improper for the historian at present to describe it. Certainly, however, we may say that his conduct was distinguished by remarkable independence and freedom from party spirit; he was eminently concerned to maintain the union and prosperity of the United States; and as far as consistent with national honor and dignity, desirous of cultivating peace and friendly relations with all foreign powers.

In person, General TAYLOR was about five feet eight inches in height, and like most of our revolutionary generals, was inclined to corpulency. He appeared a much taller man on horseback than on foot, owing to the shortness of his lower extremities. His hair was gray, his brow ample, his eye vivid, and his features plain, but full of firmness and intelligence. Benevolence was a striking feature in his countenance, and in this respect was the true index of his heart. He was kind, forbearing, and humane. His manners were easy and hearty, his tastes, dress, and manners were simple, and his style of living extremely temperate. His speeches, and his official papers, both military and civil, were remarkable for the propriety of their feeling, and their chasteness of diction. All his personal attributes and antecedents made him preëminently the man of the people, and qualified him to sustain his country by uniting all classes. His good temper was remarkable, so that all parties were at home in intercourse with him, even those who were by no means distinguished for courtesy. So that when on the day after his election to the presidency, a man coarsely shook hands with him, and told him that he did not vote for him, for he did not think him fit for the office, the General replied, smiling, "Yesterday I thought as you do, but as the people thought differently, I submit." His mind was of an original and solid cast, admirably balanced and combining the comprehensiveness of reason with the penetration of instinct. Its controlling element was a strong sterling sense, that of itself rendered him a wise counsellor and a safe leader. His martial courage was only equalled by his Spartan simplicity, his unaffected modesty, his ever-wakeful humanity, his inflexible integrity, his uncompromising truthfulness, his lofty magnanimity, his unbounded patriotism, and his unfaltering loyalty to duty. His private life was unblemished, and the loveliness of his disposition made him the idol of his own household, and the favorite of all who knew him. Assuredly no man has ever died among us, whose loss occasioned more intense feeling, or who was more honored in his burial.

WILLIAM H. PRESCOTT, D. C. L.

If it be honorable to a man to have had ancestors eminent for the usefulness they render to society, the subject of our memoir has this honor. His great grandfather was a man of high respectability, and was elected as the agent of the province of Massachusetts to the British Court, but declined the office, which was subsequently filled by Edward Quincy. His grandfather was Colonel William Prescott, who commanded the American forces stationed in the redoubt at the memorable battle of Bunker Hill, June 17, 1775, and with the undisciplined militia of New England twice broke the ranks of the British grenadiers, and drove them in confusion and dismay to their boats. His father, the Hon. William Prescott, LL. D., through a long life of eighty-two years, presented first at the bar, and afterwards in dignified retirement, an eminent example of talent, learning, and moral excellence; enjoying while he lived the character of one of the noblest ornaments of his profession, and mourned over at his death, in 1844, as a vast loss to the community he so long adorned with his presence.

WILLIAM HICKLING PRESCOTT was born in Salem, Massachusetts, May 4, 1796. His early education was undertaken by Dr. Gardiner, a pupil of the distinguished English Grecian, Dr. Samuel Parr, and himself a very eminent classical scholar. Under this gentleman he made great progress in the ancient classics, and passed through a range of studies in the Latin and Greek authors far beyond the limits usually attained at that time in our public seminaries. When WILLIAM had attained twelve years of age, his family removed to the city of Boston, where he afterward mostly resided. At fifteen, he entered Harvard College, at Cambridge, one year in advance; here he gave comparatively little attention to the mathematics and the kindred sciences, but employed his leisure hours, especially in the latter portion of his college life, in the study of his favorite authors. It was then a matter of taste with him, but his subsequent engagements have shown the wisdom of his conduct; as much of the beauty of his style has been the result of the happy union of his genius and learning.

While at college, an accidental blow deprived him of the sight of one of his eyes, and the other became greatly weakened, partly by sympathy, and partly by the increased labor thrown upon it, so that he was threatened with entire darkness. However, he graduated with high honors in 1814, being then but eighteen. He had intended to devote himself to the bar, but was soon compelled to abandon his profession, and even to renounce all reading, for he became for a season entirely blind. In the autumn of 1815, he went to Europe, and spent two years in England, France, and Italy, seeking the aid of the great oculists in London and Paris. He may have been too young to derive a permanent profit from his travels, but he probably enjoyed the novel scenes which opened to him with a higher relish than he would have done at a later period, and thought of the ancients with an enthusiasm which a cooler criticism might have checked. He returned to Boston with greatly renovated health, but not to resume his studies, for, alas, his eye was yet greatly susceptible of inflammation. Still he was not discouraged, but with the natural energy of his character, turned to the studies which yet remained within his reach. In the course of a few years, he married a lady of his own city, a grand-daughter of Captain Linzee, who commanded one of the British vessels at the battle of Bunker Hill; thus presenting another beautiful illustration of the tendency of Christianity and civilization in ameliorating humanity; the grandchildren of some of the opposing parties in the revolution, were now united in the holy bonds of marriage. Dr. Rufus Griswold describes two swords which he saw suspended over one of the book cases in Mr. Prescott's beautiful library, crossed with an Indian calumet, which were worn by the grandfathers at Bunker Hill, one in the people's service, the other in the King's. Cordially do we unite with the Doctor in saying, "Would that the two countries might for ever be united in as firm a bond of peace as that which binds these descendants of their two champions on that memorable day." This marriage has been productive of nothing but happiness, so that Mr. Prescott some years since, wrote to a friend, that "contrary to the assertion of La Bruyère, who somewhere says that 'the most fortunate husband finds reason to regret his condition, at least once in every twenty-four hours,' I may truly say that I have found no such day in the quarter of a century that Providence has spared us to each other."

WILLIAM H. PRESCOTT.

Thus situated, Mr. PRESCOTT resolved to become, in the best sense of the word, an historian. Unlike the majority of intellectual aspirants, he had at his command the means to procure the needful materials, however expensive, for illustrating any subject on which his choice might fix, and to obtain the services of a secretary every way qualified for his office. As he grew older, too, the inflammatory tendency of his system diminished, and his eye became less sensible to the fatigue of study. He gradually recovered his sight, so that he became able to gratify his taste for books to a reasonable extent; he was, however, we are informed, seldom able to use his eyes above an hour a day, but still he cheerfully wrote to a friend, "I am not, and never expect to be, in the category of the blind men." His earliest literary labors were devoted to a series of critical and miscellaneous essays, chiefly in the North American Review; thirteen of which form a volume first published in 1845. They are remarkable for the sustained ease and felicity of expression, the fine enthusiasm and natural brilliancy, which in a still more eminent degree distinguish his later productions. They show that he was always equal to his theme in research, hearty appreciation, and acute critical judgment.

As early as 1819, Mr. PRESCOTT cherished the idea of producing a historical work of a superior character. Ten years did he wisely give himself for preliminary preparations, and ten years more for the preparation of a specific work. The subject he selected was the history of the "*Reign of Ferdinand and Isabella of Spain*," a noble subject for an American, as in their reign the existence of this continent was first revealed to Europe. The plan was a noble one, and nobly has it been carried out; certainly the twenty years devoted to it was time well spent. The years embraced in it presented one of the few important periods in the history of Europe, which seemed to invite the hand of a master. It was the period at which lived Isabella of Castile, the statesman Ximenes, the soldier Cordova, and the navigator Columbus; in which the empire of the Moors was subdued, the Inquisition was established, the Jews were driven from Spain, and a new world was discovered and colonized. Nothing had yet appeared worthy to cover the ground. From Mr. Alexander H. Everett, our minister at the Court of Spain, when Mr. PRESCOTT selected the subject of his work he received much assistance in the transmission of important works from that country, which could not be obtained in the United States. "This History," says Mr. Tuckerman, "is a work which unites the fascination of romantic fiction with the grave interest of authentic events. Its author makes no pretension to analytical power, except in the arrangement of his materials; he is content to describe, and his talents are more artistic than philosophical; neither is any cherished theory or principle obvious; his ambition is apparently limited to skilful narration. Indefatigable in research, sagacious in the choice and comparison of authorities, serene in temper, graceful in style, and pleasing in sentiment, he possesses all the requisites for an agreeable writer; while his subjects have yielded so much of picturesque material and romantic interest, as to atone for the lack of any more original or brilliant qualities in the author."

When Mr. PRESCOTT had written his History of Ferdinand and Isabella, he had resolved against its publication during his life-time, but the remark of his father, that "the man who writes a book which he is afraid to publish is a coward," led him to a different decision, and in 1838, at the age of forty-two, in the freshness, as well as in the maturity of his genius, he appeared before the world, both in Boston and in London, as an author. The reception of his work was every where highly flattering, for all pronounced it a masterpiece, so that his fame became at once firmly established. The Edinburgh and Quarterly Reviews emulated each other in its praise, and it was promptly translated into the Spanish, German, French, and Italian languages. It has passed through very many editions, and the voice of posterity has been anticipated by the unanimous judgment of the learned, who have admitted it into the circle of immortal works.

The biographers of Mr. PRESCOTT have pretty fully detailed the difficulties which he had to contend with in his literary labors, arising from his defective vision. Dr. Griswold tells us, that when his literary treasures reached him from Spain, he "was not able to read even the title pages of the volumes. He had strained the nerve of his eye by careless use of it, and it was several years before it recovered so far as to allow him to use it again. By the sight of his Spanish treasures lying unexplored before him, he was filled with despair. He determined to try whether he could make the ears do the work of the eyes. He taught his reader, unacquainted with any language but his own, to pronounce the Spanish, though not exactly in the accent of the Court of Madrid. He read at a slow and stumbling pace, while the historian listened with painful attention. Practice at length made the work easier for both, though the reader never understood a word of his author. In this way, they ploughed along patiently through seven Spanish quartos. He found at last he could go over about two-thirds as much in an hour as he could when read to in English. The experiment was made, and he became convinced of the practicability

WILLIAM H. PRESCOTT.

of substituting the ear for the eye. He was overjoyed, for his library was no longer to consist of sealed volumes.

"He now obtained the services of a secretary acquainted with the different ancient and modern languages. Still there were many impediments to overcome. His eye, however, gradually improved, and he could use it by daylight, (never again in the evening,) a few hours; though this was not till after some years, and then with repeated intervals of weeks, and sometimes months of debility. Many a chapter, and some of the severest in Ferdinand and Isabella, were written almost wholly with the aid of the eyes of his secretary. His *modus operandi* was necessarily peculiar. He selected, first, all the authorities in the different languages that could bear on the topic to be discussed. He then listened to the reading of them, one after another, dictating very copious notes on each. When the survey was completed, a large pile of notes was amassed, which were read to him over and over again, until the whole had been embraced by his mind, when they were fused down into the consecutive contents of a chapter. When the subject was complex, and not pure narrative, requiring a great variety of reference, and sifting of contradictory authorities, the work must have been very difficult. But it strengthened his memory, kept his faculties wide awake, and taught him to generalize; for the little details slipped through the holes in the memory.

"His labor did not end with this process. He found it as difficult to write as to read, and procured in London a writing case for the blind. This he could use in the dark as well as in the light. The characters, indeed, might pass for hieroglyphics, but they were deciphered by his secretary, and transferred by him to a legible form in a fair copy. Yet I have heard him say his hair sometimes stood on end at the woful blunders and misconceptions of the original, which every now and then, escaping detection, found their way into the first proof of the printer."

When a new author, in addition to a highly flattering reception of his work, is himself conscious of having rendered a benefit to society, he is seldom disposed entirely to lay aside his pen and to indulge in inglorious ease. Especially is a man urged onward when, like Mr. PRESCOTT, he is by nature and principle of energetic habits. Never did Mr. PRESCOTT seek to mingle with the crowd; he never sought the shouts of a multitude, nor even addressed one; but he lived with the historically great, chiefly of the past. He had now tried his literary powers, and satisfied the public even more fully than himself, that he was capable of useful labor; besides which his sight was now gradually improving, and he could work more easily at his books and documents than heretofore. In addition to all which, he had by this time accumulated some valuable manuscript materials, and pictorial works, which aided his imagination and increased his enthusiasm. He sat down, therefore, to his "*Conquest of Mexico,*" which was published in 1843, simultaneously in the United States and in London. It was written with remarkable freedom and spirit, the result both of conscious success, and of the excitement springing from the nature of his romantic and marvellous story; so that the prompt honors it received, were even more brilliant than those awarded to his "*Ferdinand and Isabella.*" Before this, he had been admitted to membership in several of the distinguished academies of Europe, and he was now elected a member of the French Institute. This second historical work attained a higher sale than even the first; the New York publishers sold nearly seven thousand copies of it in one year; in London it very quickly passed to a second edition; it was reprinted in Paris, and translated there, as well as in Berlin, Rome, Madrid, and Mexico. The Mexican translator, Dr. Griswold tells us, a person of some consideration in that country, advertised that he should accommodate the offensive opinions in religion and politics to the more received ideas of the Mexicans! But the version which appeared in Madrid being faithful, the Spanish Americans have perhaps had an opportunity to see the work in an unmutilated form.

We are happy in the opportunity of giving from a critique on this work in the eighty-first volume of the "*Edinburgh Review,*" a few sentences, which will equally apply to every work which our author has written. The Reviewer says:—"Mr. PRESCOTT has a pure, simple and eloquent style—a keen relish for the picturesque—a quick and discerning judgment of character—and a calm, generous, and enlightened spirit of philanthropy. There is no exaggeration in asserting that his '*Conquest of Mexico*' combines—some allowance, where that is necessary, being made for the inferior extent and importance of its subject—most of the valuable qualities which distinguish the most popular historical writers in our own language of the present day. It unites the chivalrous but truthful enthusiasm of Colonel Napier, and the vivacity of the accomplished author of the '*Siege of Granada,*' with the patient and ample research of Mr. Tytler.

"It would be easy to fill our pages with sparkling quotations, with sketches of scenery worthy of Scott, with battle-pieces rivaling those of Napier, with pictures of disaster and desolation scarcely less pathetic than those drawn by Thucydides. But Mr. PRESCOTT has, no doubt, too much taste not to accept it as a compliment, when we say that every reader of intelligence forgets the beauty of his coloring in the grandeur of his outline; and that nothing but a connected sketch of the latter can do justice to the highest charm of his work. Indeed we are by no means certain, that the splendid variety of episode and adventure with which the great enterprises of Cortes are interwoven, does not necessarily withdraw, in some measure, our attention from the naked view of their surpassing audacity; just as, in the wild *Sierras* traversed by his army, the luxuriant vegetation of the tropics serves to render less awful the frowning brow of the precipice and the shadowy depth of the ravine."

Not long after the publication of the work last named, Mr. PRESCOTT was called to sustain the loss of his venerable and excellent father, which for a time interrupted his studies; but the relaxation of his mind only nerved him for new labors, and in 1847 appeared his "*Conquest of Peru*," written, like that of Mexico, in very great part from original materials. It is marked by the same striking merits which distinguished his preceding works, and is quite equal in interest to either of them. Few works of imagination have more power to win the fancy and touch the heart. Facts infinitely more instructive than fiction, are found here—more enchanting and more impressive.

Two of the most touching instances of literary generosity should be noticed in connection with Mr. PRESCOTT. The first was in relation to the "Conquest of Mexico." Washington Irving had prepared himself to enter that golden field, but on learning that his friend had designs upon it, he yielded it to PRESCOTT, saying, "I am happy to have this opportunity of testifying my high esteem for his talents, and my sense of the very courteous manner in which he has spoken of myself and my writings in his 'Ferdinand and Isabella,' though they interfered with a part of the subject of his history." PRESCOTT showed himself worthy of this magnanimity. The other instance was in connection with the last work of Mr. PRESCOTT— "Philip the Second of Spain." Mr. J. L. Motley tells us that he "felt an inevitable impulse to write one particular history," and he had chosen the "Rise of the Dutch Republic." But when he learned what PRESCOTT had projected, he feared a clash, and with sad disappointment thought that he must abandon the subject on which his heart was set. He went to PRESCOTT, and thus describes the visit: "He received me with such a frank and ready and liberal sympathy, and such an open-hearted, guileless expansiveness, that I felt a personal affection for him. from that hour. He assured me that he had not the slightest objection whatever to my plan; that he wished me every success; and that, if there were any books in his library bearing on my subject that I liked to use, they were entirely at my service. Although it seems easy enough for a man of world-wide reputation thus to extend the right hand of fellowship to an unknown and struggling aspirant, yet I fear that the history of literature will show that such instances of disinterested kindness are as rare as they are noble." These two generous men entered upon nearly the same field, and proved, as PRESCOTT said, that "no two books ever injured each other."

Months passed slowly away before Mr. PRESCOTT could enter fully upon his new work. His eyes were in a bad state, and he complained that he could "Philipize" very little. He resolved to dictate history to his secretary. Then for a time he was in fear of a loss of hearing. He went to England, where he was received with distinguished respect and kindness by the most eminent persons in society and letters, their only regret being that his stay among them was not of greater length. While there the ancient University of Oxford conferred on him the degree of Doctor of Civil Law; a dignity to be esteemed the greater, as it was unsolicited, and as that learned body is always very sparing of such honors.

Two years later we find him at home, amid a forest of materials, "still *Philipizing*." His spirited advances were sadly interrupted by the sudden death of his mother. "He wept bitterly. But above every other feeling rose the sense of gratitude for what he had owed to his mother's love and energy." We may know something of his literary persistency when we learn that, besides having attacks of rheumatism, he was compelled to write, "I have been sorely plagued with dyspeptic debility and pains." Yet despite the great difficulties he completed two volumes of "Philip the Second" in 1854.

While their publication was going on, he was occupied with the latter part of the reign and life of Philip's illustrious father. He was unwilling to undertake an entirely new work upon Charles V. of Spain, nor did he wish to compete with Robertson, whose Life of the great Monarch had won him his fadeless laurels. PRESCOTT therefore resolved to employ the new materials concerning the cloister life of Charles V., and make a sup-

WILLIAM H. PRESCOTT.

plement to the work of the Scottish historian. It was published with a new edition of Robertson's history, and PRESCOTT not only won new honors for himself, but also for the transatlantic author.

Early in 1858 Mr. PRESCOTT received his first attack of apoplexy. When, after some time, he could speak, he said to his wife, tenderly leaning over him, "My poor wife! I am sorry for you, that this has come upon you so soon." Never was there a less selfish utterance. It opens to us the heart of the man. In a few weeks he adventured again within the domain of his old and favorite studies. In April the third volume of "Philip the Second" went to the press. It delighted him to think that he was not yet obliged to reduce the amount of his mental exertions. His courage was unfaltering. He did little with his pen toward a fourth volume of his unfinished work, but "amused himself," as he said, "with making a revision of his 'Conquest of Mexico.'"

On a January day in 1859 Mr. Kirk, his ever faithful secretary (lately ushered into fame by his "Charles the Bold"), was reading to him and his family, when he stepped into an adjoining room. Shortly after, Mr. Kirk heard him groan, hurried to him, and found him wholly unconscious from a stroke of apoplexy. His hour had come; remedies availed nothing. He yielded to the death which he would have preferred, had the choice been left to himself. Without apparent suffering his spirit passed away.

On the day of his burial the Representatives of the Commonwealth and the members of the Historical Society paid him their last respects. The whole community was moved. The tears shed at his grave by the poor whom he had befriended were as honorable to his memory as those dropped by men of wealth, men of letters, and men of power. From all parts of the land afterwards came expressions of grief. Europe sent her condolence to America.

The record of such a life affords a powerful stimulus to exertion. What an example of industry, of the power to rise above adverse circumstances, of the courage to undertake labors almost impossible, of the persistency which makes nearly everything possible, of making work a delight and warfare a victory, and of turning the vast difficulties to advantage in the one great purpose of a life! PRESCOTT must sta .d pre-eminer t in literary heroism.

Were this all, his name should go down to the young men of every age, linked with the touching story of his adversities and with the inspiring record of his successes, so that his fire might kindle enthusiasm in others who need such energies, in every department of life. But this is not all. There was a charm in the home-life of Dr. PRESCOTT. He contributed his utmost to the happiness of his family, his friends, his neighbors, and the stranger within his gates. Children knew how condescending he was at a holiday hour or on a Thanksgiving-day. The last words of his private memoranda will long be remembered by the family circle, for he wrote that it had "been brightened by the presence of all the children and grand-children, God bless them!" His domestic affections were almost uppermost in his character. Very charitable was he to the poor. Like his mother, he found happiness in an unseen and free-handed beneficence.

In political opinion he was moderate. He had the truest love for his country, and might be counted in the school of Washington, Hamilton, and Everett. He was in the habit of saying, that he dealt with political discussions only when they related to events and persons, at least two centuries old. This was, perhaps, one reason why he declined to write the Second Conquest of Mexico—that achieved by General Scott. "The theme would be taking," he said, "but I had rather not meddle with heroes who have not been under ground two centuries at least."

He never courted popularity; it followed him. He never sought an office, and his friends did not venture to ask him to come down from his high elevation in order to fill one. He was the model of a retired patriot, whose pen was his sceptre of extended power. In his deep researches he sank Artesian wells into what had been regarded as deserts, but where now are fountains and well-watered plains. He added richly to the standard literature of the age, the literary fame of his country, and the fraternity of nations. If in a past century Spanish chivalry played its last act in the New World, in the present century the historian of the Spanish Conquests affords some proof of the high eminence of America under a more practical, progressive, and Christian civilization. The century-plant has bloomed, never, we trust, to fade nor drop its leaves to the dust

MILLARD FILLMORE.

When a man has honorably discharged duties to which he has been unexpectedly and suddenly called, especially when those duties have been difficult, and their performance has been clearly the result of established principles, our curiosity in reference to his history is great, and to minister to the gratification of such a curiosity in the present case is highly gratifying. Few persons, probably, supposed in the year 1848, when MILLARD FILLMORE was elected vice-president of this vast Republic, that he would soon be called to succeed General Taylor, his popular chief, and that he would so ably perform some of the most difficult duties which ever devolved on the ruler of a great nation. Let us, before we particularly look at this distinguished personage, briefly trace his origin.

John Fillmore, the great-grandfather of MILLARD FILLMORE, and the common ancestor of all of that name in the United States, was the son of English parents, and was born about the year 1702, in Ipswich, Massachusetts; and having a strong propensity towards a sea-faring life, at the age of about nineteen he went on board a fishing vessel which sailed from Boston. The vessel had been but a few days out when it was captured by a noted pirate-ship, commanded by Captain Phillips, and young Fillmore was kept as a prisoner. He remained on board this ship nine months, enduring every hardship which a strong constitution and firm spirits were capable of sustaining; and though frequently threatened with immediate death, unless he would sign the piratical articles of the vessel, he steadily refused until two others had been taken prisoners, who also refusing to join the crew, the three made an attack upon the pirates, and after killing several, took the vessel and brought it safe into Boston harbor. The printed narrative of this adventure details one of the most daring and successful exploits on record. The surviving pirates were tried and executed, and the heroic conduct of the captors was acknowledged by the British government. John Fillmore died in that part of the town of Norwich now called Franklin, in Connecticut.

Nathaniel, the son of John Fillmore, settled at Bennington, in Vermont, then called the Hampshire Grants, where he lived till his death, which took place in 1814. He served in the French war, and was a true whig of the revolution, gallantly fighting as a lieutenant under General Stark, in the battle of Bennington. His son Nathaniel, the father of MILLARD FILLMORE, was born at Bennington, April 19, 1771, and early in life removed to what is now called Summer Hill, Cayuga County, New York, where MILLARD was born, Jan. 7, 1800. Nathaniel was a farmer, and soon after the birth of his son, lost all his property by a bad title to one of the military lots he had purchased. About the year 1802, he removed to the town of Sempronius, (now called Niles,) in the same county, and resided there till 1819, when he removed to Erie county, to cultivate a small farm with his own hands. He was a strong and uniform supporter of Jefferson, Madison, and Tompkins, and is now a firm whig. The mother of MILLARD FILLMORE was Phebe Millard, daughter of Doctor Abiather Millard. She was a native of Pittsfield, Massachusetts, and though of limited education, possessed intellect of a very high order, united with great native beauty, graceful manners, and exquisite sensibility; so that she was eminently distinguished among her connections. She died in 1831, and therefore did not live to enjoy—what only a fond mother can fully appreciate—the national reputation of her son.

The narrow means of his father deprived MILLARD of any advantages of education beyond what were afforded by the imperfect and ill-taught common schools of the county. Books were scarce and dear, and at the age of fourteen, when more favored youths are far advanced in their classical studies, or enjoying in colleges the benefit of well furnished libraries, young FILLMORE had read but little except his common school-books and his Bible. At that age he was sent into the wilds of Livingston county, to learn the trade of a clothier. He remained there about four months, when he was placed with another person to learn the same business and wool-carding in the town where his father lived. A small village library was formed there soon after, which gave him the first opportunity of acquiring general knowledge through books. He nobly improved his privilege, and his intellectual appetite grew by what it fed upon. His thirst for knowledge soon became insatiate, and his every leisure moment was spent in reading. Four years were passed in this way, working at his trade, and storing

MILLARD FILLMORE.

his mind at every hour he could command, from books of history, biography, and travels.

At the age of nineteen, MILLARD FILLMORE fortunately made acquaintance with the late Walter Wood, Esq., one of the most estimable citizens of Cayuga county. Judge Wood was a man of wealth, and of great capacity for business; he had an excellent law library, but had little professional practice. He soon saw that under the rude exterior of the clothier's boy were powers which only required proper development to raise their possessor to high distinction and usefulness, and advised him to quit his trade and to study law. In reply to the objection of a want of education, means, and friends, to aid him in a course of professional studies, Judge Wood kindly offered to give him a place in his office, to advance money to defray his expenses, and wait until success in business should furnish the means of repayment. The offer was accepted. The apprentice boy bought out his time, and entered the office of Judge Wood. We have heard that his former employer protested against the choice which his apprentice made, declaring that he had been intent on the lad's future welfare, but he had been foolish enough to leave a good business to become a lawyer.

For more than two years did MILLARD FILLMORE closely apply himself to business and study, reading law and general literature, and practising as a surveyor. Fearful of incurring too large a debt to his benefactor, he taught school for three months in the year, and thus acquired the means of partly supporting himself. In the autumn of 1821, he removed to the county of Erie, and the following spring entered a law office in Buffalo, where he sustained himself by teaching, and continued his legal studies till 1823, when he was admitted to the court of Common Pleas. Being, however, too diffident of his then untried powers to enter into competition with the older members of the bar in Buffalo, he removed to Aurora, in that county, where he commenced the practice of law. Here, in the year 1826, he married Miss Abigail Powers, the youngest child of the late Rev. Lemuel Powers, by whom he has two children, a son and a daughter, both worthy of their parents. Mrs. Fillmore is descended, on the maternal side, from Henry Leland, one of the earliest settlers of Massachusetts. She is a lady of great moral worth, highly esteemed among those who have the honor of her acquaintance, of exceedingly kind and unobstrusive manners, and is a bright ornament to the high station she has been called to occupy.

In the year 1827 Mr. FILLMORE was admitted as an attorney, and in 1829, as a counseller in the supreme court. Previous to this time his practice had been very limited, but his application to juridical studies had been constant and severe, so that during these few years of comparative seclusion he acquired that general knowledge of the fundamental principles of the law which has mainly contributed to give him an elevated rank among the members of that liberal profession. His legal acquirements and skill as an advocate, soon attracted the attention of his professional brethren in Buffalo, and he was offered a highly advantageous connection with an elder member of the bar in that city, which he accepted, and removed there in 1830. Here he continued to reside till his election as comptroller, and consequent removal to Albany in 1847.

The first entrance of Mr. FILLMORE into public life was in January, 1829, when he took his seat as a member of the House of Assembly, from Erie county, to which office he was reëlected the two following years. The democratic party in those three sessions, as for many years before and after, held triumphant sway in both houses of the legislature, and but little opportunity was afforded a young member of the opposition to distinguish himself. But talent, integrity, and devotion to public business will make a man felt and respected, even amidst a body of opposing partisans; and Mr. FILLMORE, although in a hopeless minority so far as any question of a political or party bearing was involved, on all questions of a general character, soon won the confidence of the house in an unexampled degree. It was a common remark among the members, "If FILLMORE says it is right, we will vote for it."

The most important measure of a general nature which came up during Mr. FILLMORE's service in the state legislature, was the bill to abolish imprisonment for debt. In behalf of that great and philanthropic measure he took an active part, urging with unanswerable arguments its justice and expediency, and, as a member of the committee on the subject, aiding to perfect its details. To MILLARD FILLMORE, with his then coadjutors, are the people of New York indebted for expunging from the statute-book that relic of a barbarous age—imprisonment for debt.

Mr. FILLMORE was first elected to Congress in the autumn of 1832, and took his seat in the stormy session immediately succeeding the removal of the deposites from the United States Bank. In those days, the business of the house, and debates, were led by old and experienced members—new ones, unless they enjoyed a wide-spread and almost national reputation—rarely taking an active and conspicuous part.

MILLARD FILLMORE.

Little chance, therefore, was afforded Mr. Fillmore, a member of the opposition, young and unassuming, of displaying those qualities which so eminently fitted him for legislative usefulness. But the school was one admirably qualified fully to develope and cultivate those powers which, under more favorable circumstances, have enabled him to render such varied and important services to his country.

At the close of his term of service, Mr. Fillmore resumed the practice of his profession, which he pursued with distinguished reputation and success, until, yielding to the public request, he consented again to become a candidate, and was reëlected to Congress in the autumn of 1836. In the twenty-fifth Congress he took a more active part than he did during his first term, and on the assembling of the next Congress, to which he was reëlected by a largely increased majority, he was assigned a prominent place on what, next to that of ways and means, it was justly anticipated would become the most important committee of the house—that on elections. It was in this Congress that the celebrated contested case of New Jersey came before that body, in which he greatly distinguished himself. The prominent part which Mr. Fillmore took in that affair, his patient investigation of all its complicated minute details, the clear, convincing manner in which he set forth the facts, the lofty and indignant eloquence with which he denounced the meditated act, all strongly directed public attention to him as one of the ablest men of that Congress, distinguished as it was by the eminent ability and statesmanship of many of its members. The agitation in Congress of this New Jersey election case, and the currency measures adopted by the administration of Mr. Van Buren, were among the causes which contributed to the overthrow of the democratic party, and the triumph of the whigs in the presidential election of 1840, as well as the majority obtained by them of members elected to both houses in the twenty-seventh Congress.

On the assembling of this twenty-seventh Congress, to which Mr. Fillmore was reëlected by a majority larger than was ever before given in his district, he was placed as chairman of the committee of ways and means. The duties of that station, always arduous and responsible, were at that time peculiarly so. A new administration had come into office, and found public affairs in a state of derangement. The revenue was inadequate to meet the ordinary expenses of government; the already large existing debt was rapidly swelling in magnitude; commerce and manufactures were depressed; the currency was deranged; banks were embarrassed; and general distress pervaded the community. To bring order out of confusion; to replenish the national treasury; to provide means that would enable the government to meet the demands against it, and to pay off the debt; to revive the industry of the country and restore its usual prosperity—these were the tasks devolved on the committee of ways and means. With an energy and devotion to the public weal, worthy of all admiration, Mr. FILLMORE applied himself to the task, and, sustained by a majority in Congress, whose industry and zeal in the public service under peculiar embarrassments, has seldom been equalled, and never surpassed, he succeeded in its accomplishment. The measures he brought forward and advocated with matchless ability, speedily relieved the government from its embarrassment, and have fully justified the most sanguine expectations of their benign influence upon the country at large. A new and more accurate system of keeping accounts, rendering them clear and intelligible, was introduced. The favoritism and other evils in the treasury were checked by the requirement of contracts; the credit of the government was increased; ample means were provided for the exigencies of the public service, and the payment of the national debt was secured. Commerce and manufactures were now revived, and prosperity and hope once more smiled on the land. The labor of devising, explaining and defending measures productive of such happy results, rested chiefly on Mr. FILLMORE. He was ably sustained by his political friends in Congress; but on him, nevertheless, the main responsibility rested.

After his long and severe labors in the committee-room—labors sufficiently arduous to break down any but one of an iron constitution—sustained by a spirit which nothing could conquer, he was required to give his unremitting attention to the business of the house, to make any explanation that might be asked for, and be ready with a complete and triumphant refutation of every objection that the ingenuity of his opponents could devise. All this, too, was required to be done with promptness, clearness, dignity and good temper. For the proper performance of these varied duties, few men are more happily qualified than Mr. FILLMORE. At that fortunate age when the physical and intellectual powers are displayed in the highest perfection, and the hasty impulses of youth, without any loss of its vigor, are brought under control of large experience in public affairs, with a mind capable of descending to minute details, as well as of conceiving a grand system of national policy, calm and deliberate in judgment, self-possessed and fluent in debate, of dignified presence, never unmindful of the courtesies becoming social and public intercourse, and of political integrity unimpeachable, he was admirably qualified for the post of leader of the majority in the twenty-seventh Congress.

Just before the close of the first session of this Congress, Mr. FILLMORE, in a letter addressed to his constituents, signified his intention not to be a candidate for reëlection. He acknowledged with gratitude and pride the cordial and generous support given him by his constituents, but the severe labor devolved upon him by his official duties demanded some relaxation, and private affairs, necessarily neglected in some degree during several years of public service, called for attention. Notwithstanding his declaration to withdraw from the station he filled with so much honor and usefulness, the convention of his district, unanimously, and by acclamation, renominated him, and earnestly pressed upon him a compliance with their wishes. He was deeply affected by this last of many proofs of confidence on the part of those who had known him best; but he firmly adhered to the determination he had expressed, and at the close of the term for which he was elected, he returned to his home more gratified at his relief from the cares of official life, than he had ever been at the prospect of its highest rewards and honors. But though keenly enjoying the freedom from public responsibilities, and the pleasures of social intercourse in which he was now permitted to indulge, the qualities of mind and habits of systematic close attention to business, which so eminently fitted him for a successful congressional career, were soon called into full exercise by the rapidly increasing requirements of professional pursuits, which had never been wholly given up. There is a fascination in the strife of politics, its keen excitements, and its occasional but always tempting, brilliant triumphs, that, when once felt, few men are able to resist so completely as to return with relish to the comparatively tame and dull occupations of private life. But to the calm and equable temperament of Mr. FILLMORE, repose, after the stormy scenes in which he had been compelled to take a leading part, was most grateful. He had ever regarded his profession with affection and pride, and he coveted more the just, fairly-won fame of the jurist than the highest political distinction. He welcomed the toil, therefore, which a large practice in the higher courts imposed upon him, and was as remarkable for the thoroughness with which he prepared his legal arguments, as he was for patient, minute investigation of the dry and difficult subjects it was so often his duty to elucidate and defend in the house of representatives.

In 1844, in accordance with a popular wish too strong to be resisted, Mr. FILLMORE reluctantly accepted the whig nomination for Governor of New York. The issue of that conflict, in which he shared in the signal defeat of his party, has become a matter of history, and he was only pained at what he feared might be the political results. For himself he had no regrets; because he had no desires towards the high and honorable office for which he had been a candidate, and he trusted that with the failure of his election, would end any further demand upon him to serve in public life.

In the year 1847, a popular call, similar to the one just named, was again made upon him, to which he yielded a reluctant assent, and was elected comptroller of the state, by a majority larger than had been given to any state officer at any former election during many years. There were some peculiar causes which contributed to swell his majority at that election, but independently of them, there can be no doubt that the general conviction of his eminent fitness for the office, would, under any circumstances of the opposing party, have given him a great and triumphant vote. That such evidence of the esteem of his fellow citizens was gratifying to his feelings, cannot be doubted, but few can justly appreciate the sacrifices they imposed. The duties of that office could not be discharged without abandoning at once and forever—for who ever regained a professional standing once lost?—a lucrative business which he had been years in acquiring, nor without severing all those social ties, and breaking up all those domestic arrangements, which rendered home happy, and bound him to the city where the best portion of his life had been spent. Yet feeling that the state had a right to command his services, he cheerfully submitted to its exactions, and on the first of January, 1848, removed to Albany, where he displayed, in the performance of the duties of his arduous and responsible office, the high ability and thorough attention which have always characterized the discharge of his public trusts.

We now approach the period in the life of Mr. FILLMORE, when the entire Union evinced its appreciation of his talents and worth, and a new theatre was presented to him for the exercise of his matured judgment, consummate prudence, and an abiding attachment and fidelity to the constitution and Union, not excelled since the days of the Revolution. In the winter of 1844, when the eyes of the whigs were turned to Henry Clay, of Kentucky, as their leader in the contest of that year, by a numerous portion of the party, Mr. FILLMORE was looked to as the candidate for the vice-presidency. The whigs of the state of New York, in general convention, unanimously nominated Henry Clay for president, and MILLARD FILLMORE for vice-president. At the Baltimore convention, in May of that year, the delegates from

MILLARD FILLMORE.

New York, with one exception, supported Mr. FILLMORE, but Mr. Frelinghuysen, a distinguished citizen of New Jersey, received the nomination.

The startling results of the campaign in Mexico, and the admiration and regard everywhere entertained for the bravery, cool judgment and eminent services of the hero of Resaca de la Palma, Palo Alto, Monterey, and Buena Vista, early designated General Taylor as the next president of the United States. While it was well known that General Taylor had but little experience in the civil affairs of the country, the confidence in his integrity, sound common sense, and practical wisdom, was unbounded; and a statesman, ready and willing cordially to coöperate with General Taylor in carrying on the administration, and well versed in the details of the affairs of government, was universally sought for by the whig party, which, at an early day, it was clearly perceived, must be triumphant in the coming contest. In view of all these considerations, the whigs of the Union, in national convention, selected MILLARD FILLMORE for vice-president, and thereafter the names of Taylor and FILLMORE became the rallying cry of that party throughout the Union, and resulted in the triumphant election of the whig candidates.

In February, 1849, Mr. FILLMORE resigned the office of comptroller of the state of New York, to enter upon the discharge of the duties of vice-president; and it is not too much to say, that, distinguished as were his predecessors in the office of comptroller, for integrity of character, financial talents, and a faithful regard to the interests of the state, no one of them left the office with a higher reputation than Mr. FILLMORE, or with a more general conviction on the part of the public, that all the duties of the station had been discharged with ability and fidelity.

On March 4, 1849, Mr. FILLMORE took the oath of office as vice-president of the United States. His address to the senate was commended alike for the combined modesty and dignity of its delivery, and for the sound and patriotic principles which it presented. A new order of talent was now called forth on the part of Mr. FILLMORE, and full evidence was soon afforded that he possessed it.

The session of Congress which commenced in December, 1849, proved more exciting than any previous one, and it soon became apparent to every dispassionate observer, that the strength of our institutions was then to be tested; and that upon the wisdom, firmness, discretion and patriotism of those in power, would depend the continuance of the Union and the constitution. In 1826, the presiding officer of the senate, the late John C. Calhoun, had assumed the position that the vice-president had no power to call a senator to order for words spoken in debate. This decision had been acquiesced in, and was the established usage of the senate. Vice-president FILLMORE resolved to resume what he deemed the proper duties of the presiding officer. In a neat, perspicuous address to the senate, on a fitting occasion, he announced his determination to maintain decorum in debate, and to call senators to order for any offensive words used. The senate evinced its appreciation and sanction of this determination by unanimously ordering the views so expressed to be entered at length on their journal, where they stand as evidence of the firmness of the presiding officer of the senate, and his determination to shrink from no duty. The courtesy, ability, and dignity, exhibited by Mr. FILLMORE, while presiding over the deliberations of the senate, excited universal commendation.

But yet higher honors awaited MILLARD FILLMORE. While he was fully engaged in the discharge of his high and delicate duties as vice-president, the whole country was startled by the announcement of the sudden illness, and almost immediate decease of General Taylor, the President of the United States. At this critical period, the most difficult and exciting questions which had ever agitated the people of this country were pending. The whole Union was aroused; section was arrayed against section; party divisions were broken up; and an universal gloom prevailed. The cabinet at once resigned, but the new president, with dignity and delicacy, declined to consider their resignations until after the obsequies to the lamented dead had been performed.

On the tenth of July, Mr. FILLMORE took the oath, as president, to "preserve, protect, and defend the constitution of the United States"—and all men were assured that solemn pledge would be faithfully kept—that the crisis was passed—and that the Union and the constitution would remain to them and their posterity. Within two weeks the president selected a cabinet, distinguished for its ability, patriotism, and devotion to the Union, and possessing in an eminent degree, the confidence of the nation. With his confidential advisers, the president immediately applied himself to relieve the embarrassments of the country, and to the best means of restoring quiet and confidence to all sections of the Union. His message to Congress on the difficulties with Texas, presented views so calm, just and reasonable, yet firm and decided, that full confidence in the administration was everywhere felt, and this message was regarded as the bow of promise and hope

MILLARD FILLMORE.

The settlement of that vexed question opened the way for the speedy adjustment of others.

The assembling of Congress on the second of December, 1850, was looked forward to with anxiety; as it was well known that then the annual message of the president would be delivered, disclosing the views and principles of the new administration. This document was calm, conciliatory, yet firm, and thoroughly American in all its parts; showing that the president was governed by an earnest desire to conciliate the warring sections and restore harmony to the Union at large.

It is the peculiar boast of our country, that its highest honors and dignities are the legitimate objects of ambition to the humblest persons in the land as well as to those who are most favored by the gifts of birth and fortune. Ours is a government of the people, and from the people, emphatically, have sprung those who, in the army or navy, on the bench of justice, or in the halls of legislation, have shed the brightest lustre on the page of our history. So almost universally is this the case, that when we find an instance to the contrary, of one born to a fortune and enjoying the advantages of influential connections rising to a high place in the councils of the nation, the exception deserves a special note for its rarity. No merit is therefore claimed for MILLARD FILLMORE on account of the fact that from comparatively humble parentage he attained the highest position in the country. His history, however, like many others in our GALLERY, affords a useful lesson, as showing what may be accomplished in the face of adverse circumstances, in a public and private capacity, by intellect, aided and controlled by energy, strict integrity, and resolute perseverance. Mr. FILLMORE is emphatically, one of the people; and for all that he has and is, he is indebted, under God, to his own exertions, the faithful performance of every duty, and steadfast adherence to whatever is right. Born to an inheritance of comparative poverty, he has struggled with difficulties of no ordinary character, and occupies a proud eminence in our land, which attracts the admiration of the world. He retires from the highest honors in the gift of a great and free people with their universal esteem, and his name shall be immortalized in the annals of our history among the choicest of our sons. In every station in which he has been placed, he has shown himself "honest, capable, and faithful to the constitution."

In person, Mr. FILLMORE is about six feet in height, and well proportioned. His complexion is light, and the expression of his face is mild and intelligent, indicating the prominent traits of character by

NATIONAL PORTRAITS.

which he is distinguished; among which are energy, benevolence, firmness, and integrity. His manners are easy and affable, while they indicate great dignity, and show a *royal bearing*. In a word, his deportment has always been that which became his station, and earnestly do we wish him a long life in rendering important services to his countrymen, and enjoying the happiness which ever attends virtue and usefulness. We are content that for a short season he should retire to the enjoyments of social and domestic life, of which he is the pride and ornament, and where he most delights to show the excellencies of his character; but he must be content ere long to return to the duties and toils of public service, for which his talents, his experience, and his enjoyment of public confidence so admirably qualify him.

Franklin Pierce

FRANKLIN PIERCE.

ON the nineteenth of April, 1775, the revolutionary committee of Boston, sent out couriers in every direction to collect recruits for the army. One of these came to the door of a farm house at Chelmsford, in Massachusetts. He there found a young man of eighteen, named Benjamin Pierce, to whom he delivered his message, and passed on. This youth had heard from the messenger the news of the battle of Lexington; he immediately left the plough, shouldered his musket, marched to the army, and took part in the battle of Bunker Hill. This young man became the father of FRANKLIN PIERCE, whom this great country called to the presidential chair. The limit assigned to this memoir, will only allow us to add in reference to the father, that in succession he became Captain in the army, a cultivator of wild lands in Hampshire, Brigade Major, Sheriff of Hillsborough, in his adopted State, Councillor and Governor of the State, and died at Hillsborough, full of days and of honors, in 1839.

FRANKLIN PIERCE, the sixth child of his mother, the second wife of the distinguished man of whom we have just spoken, was born at Hillsborough, in the State of New Hampshire, November 23, 1804. His native county, at the time of his birth, covered a much more extensive territory than at present, and among other men of eminence, gave birth to General Stark, the hero of Bennington, Daniel Webster, Levi Woodbury, Jeremiah Smith, the eminent jurist, and Governor of the State, James Miller, General M'Neil, and Senator Atherton. Benjamin Pierce, the devoted patriot, furnished two sons to the army of 1812, and his eldest daughter became the wife of Major M'Neil, so that few families were more deeply interested in the war, than was that of our hero.

At this period, FRANKLIN was less than eight years of age, but, unlike his noble father, had already commenced his literary studies, and in due time was sent to the academy at Hancock, where he was received into the family of his father's old friend, Peter Woodbury, the father of the Judge. In 1820, at the age of sixteen, he became a student at Bowdoin College, Brunswick, Maine, where he conducted himself, on the whole, in a manner which pleased the professors, and more than met the highest wishes of his fellow students. We have spoken in a somewhat qualified manner of his pursuits, because it must be conceded, that the two first years of his studies he lost much time, which, however, was amply redeemed in the two years which followed, so that he took a highly creditable degree. His frankness of temper, fascination of manner, and benevolence of conduct, then won him hearts which he has never lost. In 1824, he returned home to derive from his father's example and lessons, high and noble feelings of patriotism.

Having chosen the law as a profession, FRANKLIN became a student in the office of Judge Woodbury, at Portsmouth; after which he spent two years at the law school at Northampton, Massachusetts, and in the office of Judge Parker, at Amherst. In 1827, he was admitted to the bar, and began the practice of his profession at Hillsborough. Though by no means eminently successful at first, he rose in the end to a very distinguished position.

In 1829, the town of Hillsborough conferred on FRANKLIN PIERCE his first public honor, by sending him as its representative to the Legislature of the State. His whole service in that body comprised four years, in the two latter of which, he was elected Speaker, by a vote of one hundred and fifty-five, against fifty-eight for other candidates. His merit as a presiding officer was universally acknowledged. He had all the natural gifts which qualified him for the post; courtesy, firmness, quickness and accuracy of judgment, and a clearness of mental perception that brought its own regularity into the scene of confused and entangled debate; and to these qualities he added whatever was to be attained by laborious study of parliamentary rules.

In the year 1833, he was elected a member of Congress; at this period he was but twenty-nine, but he has always been chosen to office at a much earlier age than comports with general practice. And yet, for himself, he never aimed at public distinction, though always ready to step forward, when the welfare of his country might seem to be promoted by his doing so. Though his labors in Congress made but little noise and show, they were always directed to substantial objects, nor did they fail of success.

Even at this early period, FRANKLIN PIERCE's character began to be well understood by men of no small judgment. General Jackson once remarked to the Hon. Henry Hubbard, " You have a young man in your State, young FRANKLIN PIERCE, who will be, before he is

FRANKLIN PIERCE.

sixty years of age, a man for the Democracy, without the demagogue;" and Mr. Hawthorne tells us, when that eminent man was on his death bed, he remarked, as if with prophetic foresight of his young friend's destiny, that "the interests of the country would be safe in such hands." His whole conduct in the House of Representatives was such as to show a sound judgment, and the warmest patriotism; he was intent on the benefit of the whole people, and the preservation of the whole Union.

FRANKLIN PIERCE had scarcely reached the legal age for such an elevation, when, in 1837, he was elected a Senator of the United States, and took his seat at the commencement of the presidency of Mr. Van Buren. Here he was brought into contact with Calhoun, Webster, and Clay; here too, were Benton, Silas Wright, and Woodbury, with Buchanan and Walker,—men of eloquence and of vast power. Here he soon began to work, and proved that his public education had amply qualified him for high posts; and here, on many occasions, he displayed eloquence of a very high order. We should enjoy a high pleasure in detailing the services he rendered in the Senate for five years, but we are prevented for want of room. It is pleasant to know that they cannot be forgotten. In June, 1842, he signified his purpose of retiring from the Senate.

Mr. PIERCE had removed from Hillsborough, and taken up his residence at Concord, in 1838. On that occasion, the citizens of his native town invited him to a public dinner, in token of their affection and respect. In accordance with his usual taste, he gratefully accepted the kindly sentiment, but declined the public demonstration of it.

On retiring from the Senate, Mr. PIERCE returned to the Bar, and immediately started into full practice. Few lawyers, probably, have been interested in a greater variety of business than he, and few have met with greater success. No one ever showed more fearless independence; none ever devoted himself more earnestly to the interest of his clients; and no one has been more free from reproach, or more loaded with honors.

When he resigned his seat in the Senate, he did it with a fixed purpose never again to be voluntarily separated from his family for any considerable length of time, except at the call of his country in case of war; and on this account, when President Polk, in 1846, tendered him the office of Attorney General of the United States, he declined the proposal. He declined also the renewal of the honor of the Senate, and a nomination for the office of Governor of his native State.

NATIONAL PORTRAITS.

But the resolution of PIERCE to remain at home, could not be kept when, in 1847, the war with Mexico called forth his patriotism and his military spirit. Here, as in every other instance, he showed the possession of powers never developed till they were really needed. But to describe those powers, or to present a full view of his military knowledge, his deliberate courage, his benevolence, and his success, would in this place be impossible; suffice it to say, that he was all that a General of the United States Army ought to be, and that his soldiers and his enemies on the field, have alike borne testimony to his skill and his honorable conduct.

In the autumn of 1850, a convention assembled at Concord, for the revision of the Constitution of New Hampshire. By an almost unanimous vote, General PIERCE was elected its president, and his conduct as presiding officer was satisfactory to all parties. His powers of public speaking, his tact for business, and his never-failing courtesy greatly contributed to the regularity, unanimity, and results of the convention.

Immediately after the action of the State Convention which nominated him for the Presidency, General PIERCE wrote a letter to Mr. Atherton, declining to be a candidate for the Presidency, and declaring that the use of his name in any event before the Democratic National Convention would be utterly repugnant to his tastes and wishes. The strongest personal importunity of his friends could not dissuade him from the publication of this letter. The most earnest appeals to his State pride were made in vain. His invariable reply was, "No man can feel more grateful than I do for the high honor New Hampshire has conferred upon me. Her noble Democracy have stood by me always—but I must decline being considered a candidate for the Presidency. I can support most cheerfully either of the distinguished men who are mentioned in connection with the office. Let the Baltimore Convention designate the man, and the Democracy of the whole country will rally in his support."

Various movements took place before the Convention at Baltimore, all looking towards the nomination of PIERCE, but he remained immovable. At length the Convention met, June 12, 1852, and continued its sessions four days. But from the time the letter to Mr. Atherton was written to the day the news of his nomination by the Baltimore Convention was received, General PIERCE had been almost incessantly occupied with important professional engagements. Probably no prominent man in the country observed with less care the chances of the Presidential nomination than FRANKLIN PIERCE. The

FRANKLIN PIERCE.

letters he daily received from all sections of the country, predicting the necessity of his nomination as a compromise candidate, were regarded rather as the evidence of strong personal predilections and private friendship than as the prophetic predictions of a result so soon to be accomplished. It is a most beautiful example of "the office seeking the man, rather than the man the office."

It is too well known to make it needful to state here, that day after day did the members of the Convention ballot for various men without avail, except to prove that no one of the gentlemen prominent before the people would succeed in obtaining the two-thirds vote requisite for a nomination. Thus far not a vote had been thrown for General PIERCE, but at the thirty-sixth ballot the delegation from Virginia brought forward his name. Every ballot increased the number, till on the forty-ninth ballot there were two hundred and eighty-two for FRANKLIN PIERCE, and eleven for all other candidates. "Thus," as Mr. Hawthorne says, "FRANKLIN PIERCE became the nominee of the Convention; and as quickly as the lightning flash could blazen it abroad, his name was on every tongue, from end to end of this vast country. Within an hour he grew to be illustrious."

We are informed, that when General PIERCE received the news of his nomination, it affected him with no thrill of joy, but a sadness, which, for many days, was perceptible in his deportment. It awoke in his heart the sense of religious dependence — a sentiment that grew considerably stronger as all the toils and anxieties of the office presented themselves before him.

Such was FRANKLIN PIERCE, the fourteenth President of the United States, elected by a far larger vote than any of his predecessors. In private life, in the best sense of the word, he was a gentleman; in his legislative career distinguished for his ability; as a General he was crowned with laurels won by fighting the enemy, rather than improperly forced from the brows of other men; and he was elected by the popular voice the chief ruler of the most happy and honored nation on the earth.

The old people of his neighborhood, Mr. Hawthorne tells us, give a very delightful picture of FRANKLIN PIERCE, when he was some ten or twelve years of age. They describe him as a beautiful boy with blue eyes, light curling hair, and a sweet expression of face. In manhood he was about five feet nine inches in height, erect in his form, and slenderly built. He had not the breadth of shoulders, nor the depth of chest, which indicated a vigorous constitution. His face was thin, and his complexion pale; in a word, he was one of that

NATIONAL PORTRAITS.

wiry, active class of men, who are capable of enduring every sort of hardship. None knew him without admiring his unassuming and affable manners; always self-possessed and ready to converse with a true gentleman as well as a comprehensive statesman.

Shortly after his astonishing political success, a sudden and shocking calamity brought the deepest grief to himself and his wife, who was distinguished for her talents, amiableness, and piety. Having buried one son, there was only Benjamin left to address them as father and mother. This lad of thirteen years, intelligent, affectionate, and full of promise, was instantly killed in a car thrown off the track, when travelling with his parents.

President PIERCE was inaugurated on the 4th of March, 1853. His will ever be regarded as one of the great historical administrations of the government. In his inaugural address he denounced in strong terms the further agitation of the subject of slavery, and maintained that slavery was recognized by the Constitution, and that the fugitive slave law should be strictly enforced. He hoped that "no sectional, or ambitious, or fanatical excitement might again threaten the durability of our institutions, or obscure the light of our prosperity." The next year he signed the bill repealing the Missouri Compromise. An important treaty was negotiated with Japan through Commodore Perry—an achievement of benevolence toward that country, for so many ages exclusive and unapproachable. Still later came the excitements and disturbances in Kansas. The President held that the formation of a free-state government in that territory was a rebellious violation of the Kansas and Nebraska Act. The settlement of these serious difficulties was reserved for another administration.

After his retirement from office in 1857, Ex-president PIERCE travelled extensively in Europe, receiving attentions most gratifying to the American people, who regard their rulers as at least the equals of any foreign powers. At the beginning of the war in 1861, shortly after President Lincoln had called for 75,000 men to defend the government and to put down the Southern rebellion, Mr. PIERCE declared himself in favor of maintaining the Union against the confederacy of the Southern States, and he urged the people to give their cordial and vigorous support to the National Administration.

He now lives to rejoice in the success of the loyal arms, and to hope that, as four years of war have proved the strength of the government, the progress and prosperity of the future may prove her greatness and her glory.

BENJAMIN TALLMADGE

Benj. Tallmadge

BENJAMIN TALLMADGE.

The name of the subject of the present memoir, has been honorably mentioned in the histories of his time, as an active and enterprising officer of the revolution. It is in our power to give, from his own manuscript remains, some interesting details of his military life, and, from other authentic sources, the facts which will be necessary to complete our sketch.

BENJAMIN TALLMADGE was born at Brookhaven, on Long Island, New York, on the 25th of February, 1754. His father, the Rev. Benjamin Tallmadge, was the settled minister at that place; his mother, Susanna, was the daughter of the Rev. John Smith, of White Plains, West Chester county, New York. His mother died when he was fourteen years of age, but his father lived until after the revolutionary war.

He exhibited from childhood an eager desire for learning, and under the tuition of his father made such progress in his studies, that at twelve years of age he was examined by President Daggett, of Yale college, then on a visit at Brookhaven, and found to be qualified to enter that institution. His father, however, considered him entirely too young, and delayed the commencement of his collegiate course until 1769. In 1773, he graduated at New Haven, and was one of the public speakers on that occasion. He was soon after invited to become the superintendent of the high school at Weathersfield, which station he held until he entered the army.

When the legislature of Connecticut resolved to raise their quota of troops for the campaign of 1776, he accepted a commission as lieutenant, and received the appointment of adjutant, in Colonel Chester's regiment. After visiting his father at Brookhaven, he joined his regiment at New York, in June of that year, from which time until the end of the war, he was in constant and active service.

On the 27th of August, Lieutenant TALLMADGE was with his regiment engaged in the battle on Long Island, and was one of the rear guard when the army retired to New York from their lines at

Brooklyn. He was afterward engaged in several skirmishes on the evacuation of New York island by the American army; and on the 28th of October, he was with General Spencer's brigade, in the attack on the Hessians who were advancing from West Chester to White Plains.

When Washington commenced his retreat through New Jersey, the New England troops were left on the east side of the Hudson, to call the attention of the enemy to their posts at Kingsbridge and Harlæm, and to divert them from the pursuit of Washington and his broken corps. But the period for the discharge of this division of the army was at hand, as the year of their service was now near its close.

Before the regiment to which Lieutenant TALLMADGE belonged was discharged, he received the appointment of captain of the first troop in the second regiment of light dragoons. This was one of the new regiments which congress had authorized the commander-in-chief to raise for the war; and as this appointment was from Washington himself, he accepted it with great gratification, and immediately enlisted his troop from the Connecticut levies. The regiment was ordered to rendezvous at Weathersfield, where the winter was occupied in preparing for the campaign of 1777. As soon as the spring opened, Captain TALLMADGE, as senior captain, conducted a squadron of four troops of horse to head quarters at Middlebrook, New Jersey, where they were reviewed by the commander-in-chief. The varieties of active service, and numerous rencounters in which he was engaged with parties of the enemy, who made several attempts to bring on a general action, though extremely interesting in the personal narrative of Captain TALLMADGE, we must necessarily omit.

As the British general failed to draw Washington from his strong holds, he at length relinquished his efforts and embarked his army for their expedition up the Chesapeake. Washington then crossed the Delaware, and moved slowly towards Philadelphia.

At Coryell's ferry, the remainder of the recruits for the second regiment of dragoons joined the army, and Captain TALLMADGE was promoted to a majority. He now took his station as a field officer, and subsequently bore his part in the actions of Brandywine and Germantown, and in the sharp conflict with the advance of the British army under General Howe at White Marsh.

When the American army went into winter quarters at Valley Forge, late in December, 1777, Major TALLMADGE was stationed with a detachment of dragoons, as an advanced corps, between the two armies. This brought him into several conflicts with detachments of the enemy. In January, 1778, he removed with his regiment to Chatham, New Jersey, for winter quarters; and early in the spring, again took the field, and marched to King's Ferry on the Hudson, to which place also the main army proceeded after the battle of Monmouth, and the escape of the British army by sea.

In the course of this year, Major TALLMADGE opened a secret correspondence with some persons in New York, (for General Washington,) which lasted through the war. He kept one or more boats constantly employed in crossing the sound in this business. No important blow was struck by the main army during this campaign; but the light troops, being in advance, frequently came in contact with similar corps of the enemy.

On Lloyd's Neck, Long Island, on an elevated promontory, between Huntington harbor and Oyster bay, the enemy had established a strongly fortified post, with a garrison of about five hundred men. In the rear of the fort a band of marauders had encamped themselves, who, having boats at command, were in the constant practice of plundering the inhabitants along the opposite shores, and robbing the small vessels on the sound. This horde of banditti Major TALLMADGE had a great desire to break up. On the 5th of September, 1779, he embarked with one hundred and thirty men of his detachment, at Shipand point, near Stamford, at eight o'clock in the evening; and in about two hours, landed on Lloyd's Neck, and proceeded to the attack; which was so sudden and unexpected, that nearly the whole party was captured, and landed in Connecticut before morning. Not a man was lost in the enterprise, although the few freebooters who escaped fired on the party from the bushes while they were engaged in destroying the huts and boats.

In the campaign of 1780, the enemy extended their line of posts eastward on Long Island, for the double purpose of carrying on an illicit intercourse with the disaffected in Connecticut, and also to protect their foraging parties down the island. Major TALLMADGE, having constant intelligence from New York and all parts of Long Island, arranged a plan to break up the whole system, which he communicated to the commander-in-chief, who approved of it, and immediately gave him a separate command, consisting of the dismounted dragoons of the regiment, and a body of horse. With this body of troops, he took a position near the sound on the borders of Connecticut, where he had the best facilities of obtaining intelligence, either from the British lines, or across the sound. After some time was spent without an opportunity of effecting his purpose, he turned back towards the Hudson, and took a station on the lines near North Castle, the very day on which Major André had been captured. Soon after he had halted and disposed of his detachment, he was informed that a prisoner had been brought in, by the name of *John Anderson*. On inquiry, he found that three men, by the names of John Paulding, David Williams, and Isaac Van Vert, who had passed below our ordinary military patrols, on the road from Tarrytown to Kingsbridge, had fallen in with this *John Anderson* on his way to New York. They took him aside for examination, and discovering sundry papers upon him, which he had concealed in his boots, they detained him as a prisoner. Notwithstanding *Anderson's* offers of pecuniary satisfaction, if they would permit him to proceed on his course, they determined to take him to the advanced post of our army, near North Castle; and they accordingly delivered him to Lieutenant-Colonel John Jameson, then the commanding officer of the second regiment light dragoons. By an oversight the most surprising, the prisoner was sent, together with the particulars of his capture, to General Arnold at West Point, while the papers found on him were sent by express to Washington, then on his way from Hartford to West Point.

Major TALLMADGE, so soon as he learned the particulars, immediately intimated his suspicions to Colonel Jameson, and urgently recommended that the prisoner be promptly remanded, which with some difficulty was effected; but the Colonel insisted on his purpose to send forward the particulars of the capture to General Arnold, by which means he obtained information of his danger, and escaped on board the Vulture, a British sloop of war. Before the morning of the next day, the prisoner was brought back and committed to the charge of Major TALLMADGE, who was the first to suspect that under the assumed name of Anderson he was an important British officer. This opinion was formed from observing his military step as he walked up and down the room, and the precision with which he turned on his heel to retrace his course, together with his general manners, intelligence, and refinement. Up to the time of his execution, Major TALLMADGE had the charge of him; to him Major André delivered the open letter to General Washington, disclosing his real character; and with him he walked to the gallows. This intercourse, under such trying circumstances, awakened deep sympathy, and induced a strong attachment in Major TALLMADGE for Major André. His own remarks are, "that for the few days of intimate intercourse I had with him, which was from the time of his being remanded to the period of his execution, I became so deeply attached to Major André, that I could remember no instance when my affections were so fully absorbed by any man. When I saw him swing under the gibbet, it seemed for a time utterly insupportable: all were overwhelmed with the affecting spectacle, and the eyes of many were suffused with tears. There did not appear to be one hardened or indifferent spectator in all the multitude assembled on that solemn occasion."

In November of the same year, he resumed his scheme of annoying the enemy on Long Island. He directed his secret agents there to obtain the most accurate information of the state of a fortification called Fort St. George, erected on a point projecting into the south bay on Smith's Manor. This was a triangular enclosure of several acres of ground, strongly stockaded, with barricadoed houses at two of the angles, and at the third a fort with a deep ditch and wall, encircled by an *abatis* of sharpened pickets, projecting at an angle of forty-five degrees. Having obtained the necessary information, he communicated his project to the commander-in-chief, who considered the undertaking altogether too hazardous, and requested him to abandon it. Disappointed in his hopes at that time, he continued his inquiries, and at last determined to cross the sound and examine the post himself. He did so, and found that it was a depository of stores, dry-goods, groceries, and arms, whence Suffolk county could be supplied, and that "the works looked rather formidable." After much importunity General Washington authorized him to undertake the enterprise. With less than one hundred dismounted dragoons, he crossed the sound on the night of the 21st of November from Fairfield, and landed at a place called the Old Man's at nine o'clock. The troops had marched about five miles when the rain began to fall, and they were obliged to return and take shelter under their boats, which were concealed in the bushes, all that night and the next day. At evening the rain abated and the troops were again put in motion, and at break of day the attack commenced. The stockade was cut down, the column was led through the grand parade, and in ten minutes the main fort was carried by the bayonet. The shipping which lay near the fort loaded with stores attempted to make their escape; but the guns of the fort being brought to bear upon them, they were secured. The works, shipping, and stores were then destroyed; and while the troops were marching to their boats with their prisoners,—equal in numbers to themselves,—Major TALLMADGE with ten or twelve men, mounted on captured horses, proceeded to Coram and destroyed an immense magazine of forage, and returned to the place of debarkation just as his party with their prisoners had reached the same spot. Here they refreshed themselves for an hour, and before four o'clock in the afternoon were again afloat on their return. They arrived at Fairfield that night without the loss of a man. The commander-in-chief and congress returned their thanks for this achievement in the most flattering manner.

During that part of the campaign of 1781 in which the main army was in Virginia, Major TALLMADGE was left with the forces under General Heath in the Highlands on the Hudson; still, however, holding a separate command, he moved wherever duty or a spirit of enterprise dictated. In continuation of his former plan of annoying the enemy on Long Island, he marched his detachment to Norwalk; and as Fort Slongo at Treadwell's Neck was next in course to Fort St. George, he determined to destroy it. On the night of the 9th of October, he embarked a part of his troops under the command of Major Trescott, with orders to assail the fort at a particular point. At the dawn of day the attack was made, and the fortress subdued. The block-house and other combustible materials were burnt, and the detachment returned in safety with their prisoners and a handsome piece of brass field-artillery. He then returned to the neighborhood of White Plains, where he found full employment in guarding the inhabitants against the attacks of the Refugee corps, under Colonel Delancey, and the Cowboys and Skinners, who infested the lines.

When the campaign opened in 1782, there was a prospect that the toils and perils of war would soon be ended; but whatever might have been the private opinion of Washington in that respect, he inculcated upon the army the necessity of strict discipline. The army was reformed, many supernumerary officers were permitted to retire, and the veterans who remained in the field were organized anew. It now became an object of solicitude to come in contact with the foe; but as they kept very much within their lines, there were few opportunities afforded to reach them in combat.

In the course of the ensuing winter, Major TALLMADGE took his station on the sound, and arranged another plan to beat up the enemy's quarters on Long Island, but a violent storm prevented its being carried into effect. At this time he received information that an illicit trade was extensively carried on between the opposite shores of the sound, and this he determined to break up. He succeeded in capturing many of the vessels, and several cargoes of valuable goods were taken and condemned.

We have before alluded to the secret correspondence which was conducted by Major TALLMADGE, during several years, with persons within the British lines. When the American army was about to enter the city of New York after the peace, he entered the city before it was evacuated by the British, that he might afford protection to those who were the secret friends of their country, but who might otherwise have been exposed to ill treatment as Refugees or tories. On this occasion he was treated with great respect by the British officers, especially by General Carleton. He retired from the army with the rank of colonel. For several years afterwards he was the treasurer, and subsequently the president, of the Cincinnati society of Connecticut.

In March, 1784, Colonel TALLMADGE married Mary, the daughter of General William Floyd, of Mastic, Long Island, and shortly after removed to Litchfield, Connecticut; where he engaged extensively in mercantile pursuits, and resided the remainder of his life. Mrs. Tallmadge deceased June 3d, 1805, leaving several children, who are now living. Colonel TALLMADGE was married again on the 3d of May, 1808, to Maria, the daughter of Joseph Hallett, Esq., of the city of New York. This lady still survives.

It is not known at what period of life Colonel TALLMADGE became impressed with religious sentiments: it is probable, however, that the precepts and example of his pious parents never left their hold upon his mind. In his correspondence with Dr. Dwight, he says, "that he always determined at some time to become religious;" but it was not until 1793 that he publicly devoted himself to the service of God. From that period he exerted himself in the cause of piety and benevolence with as much zeal, earnestness, and perseverance, as had characterized his actions in early life.

Colonel TALLMADGE was chosen a representative in congress from Connecticut, in 1800. He was a firm and judicious member of that body, and watchful over the political interests of that country whose independence he had helped to win with his sword. His religious character while in congress was so well understood and so highly appreciated by the Christian public, that petitions involving religious interests were generally committed to him to be presented before the house. For a portion of the time of his service at least, the pious members of both houses held a stated weekly prayer-meeting, together with such of the members of their families as were present, of which Colonel TALLMADGE was an active and interested promoter. For eight successive elections he was returned as a member; and at the close of the last term, making a period of sixteen years' public service in this capacity, he declined a reëlection, and retired to private, but perhaps a no less useful life.

"To public objects of benevolence he gave *publicly* and *largely;* and in his private benefactions, there are those now living who were the almoners of his bounty to the poor and needy, who can testify to the distribution of *thousands* to those who knew not the hand from which they were relieved."

The influence of his example was felt in every good work, and all who knew him loved and venerated him.

His latter days were marked by an humble resignation to the will of God, accompanied with a joyful hope and Christian confidence. His death was tranquil and serene. On the 7th of March, 1835, "he breathed his last, and went to his reward." At his funeral might have originated those consolatory "Thoughts" which are to be found in the poems of our American *Hemans:*

> His was the upright deed,
> His the unswerving course,
> 'Mid every thwarting current's force,
> Unchanged by venal aim, or flattery's hollow reed:
> The *holy truth* walked ever by his side,
> And in his bosom dwelt, companion, judge, and guide.
>
> But when disease revealed
> To his unclouded eye
> The stern destroyer standing nigh,
> Where turned he for a shield?
> Wrapt he the robe of stainless rectitude
> Around his breast, to meet cold Jordan's flood?
> Grasped he the staff of pride,
> His steps through death's dark vale to guide?
> Ah no! self-righteousness he cast aside,
> Clasping, with firm and fearless faith, the cross of Him
>   who died.
>
> *Serene, serene*
> He pressed the crumbling verge of this terrestrial scene,
> Breathed soft, in childlike trust,
> The parting groan,
> *Gave back to dust its dust—*
> *To heaven its own.*

DANIEL D TOMPKINS

DANIEL D. TOMPKINS.

It is a pleasing task to sketch the life of such a man as DANIEL D TOMPKINS, and a proud one to a citizen of the great state which had the honor of giving him birth. It may be compared to a landscape, such as the eye delights to rest upon; not one of abrupt transitions from mountain to ravine, from "antres vast" to "deserts idle," but an open, expanded, and unbroken scene of refreshing and unfading verdure. And if the pleasure of contemplating it be not unmingled, it is because the sombre clouds of adversity began at length to hover round and darken its brilliant horizon.

Governor TOMPKINS seemed to embody within himself the peculiar characteristics of the citizens of his native state—activity, energy, and perseverance; and his talents, as constantly and variously as they were tried, were always found equal to any emergency. At the bar in the city of New York, during the early period of his life, he sustained an honorable rank; on the bench of the supreme court of the state, amid the bright constellation of judicial talent, learning, and eloquence, which then adorned it, he was conspicuously distinguished, while yet in comparative youth; and we venture to say, that no judge, since the formation of our government, ever presided at nisi prius, or travelled the circuit with more popularity. Dignified in his person, graceful and conciliating in his address, and thoroughly amiable in his character, he won the respect and confidence of the bar, and the admiration of the public. He was not one of those—for such have been—who "bullied at the bar, and dogmatized on the bench;" he was a man of warm and kindly feelings, and disdained to avail himself of the accident of official station, to browbeat or insult his inferiors.

The distinction which he gained in his judicial capacity, soon elevated him to a different theatre of action, the gubernatorial chair of his native state. He was put forward as a candidate by the most influential of the republicans of that day; and in the mode in which he administered the government, he did not disappoint their choice.

NATIONAL PORTRAITS.

Those were turbulent times in politics; but, like a skilful pilot, he safely and triumphantly weathered the storm—not only that which was raging within our own bounds and among ourselves, but a more fearful one which was pouring in upon us from a foreign foe. By his unwearied efforts, in repeatedly pressing the subject upon the attention of the legislature, slavery was finally abolished in the state of New York. In a message addressed to the legislature in 1812, he says, "The revision of our code of laws will furnish you with opportunities of making many beneficial improvements,—to devise the means for the gradual and ultimate extermination from among us of slavery, that reproach of a free people, is a work worthy of the representatives of a polished and enlightened nation;" and in 1817, he again submitted to the legislature, "whether the dictates of humanity, the reputation of the state, and a just sense of gratitude to THE ALMIGHTY for the many favors he has conferred on us as a nation, do not demand that the reproach of slavery be expunged from our statute-book."

The subject of public education and morals was always near his heart; and thus he invites to it the attention of the legislature, in one of his messages: "As the guardians of the prosperity, liberty, and morals of the state, we are bound by every injunction of patriotism and wisdom, to endow to the utmost of our resources, schools and seminaries of learning, to patronise public improvements, and to cherish all institutions for the diffusion of religious knowledge, and for the promotion of virtue and piety." How noble are such sentiments, and how different from the maxims of despots, who for the most part govern the world! Here is not recommended endowments for splendid seats of learning, for the instruction of a privileged class; to propagate and maintain an exclusive creed, or to uphold some corrupt establishment to make the rich richer and more powerful, and the poor poorer and more debased; to use the mind, the immortal part of our nature, as an instrument to be moulded and fashioned so as to subserve the selfish purposes of a lordly few; but, with a philanthropy without limit, it is pressed upon the legislature to cherish and promote *all* institutions for the diffusion of knowledge, virtue, and piety. When a chief magistrate speaks thus to his people, be they his masters or his servants, we may consider that governments are not always given to us as a "curse for our vices."

The benevolent feelings of Governor TOMPKINS prompted him to call the attention of the legislature, on repeated occasions, to the abolition of corporeal and capital punishments; and he at length happily effected that of the former: the latter still remain.

So early as 1811, we find him raising his voice in favor of the encouragement of manufactures. "Let us extend to them," he says, "the utmost encouragement and protection which our finances will admit, and we shall soon convince the belligerents of Europe, to whom we have been extensive and profitable customers, that their mad and unjust policy towards us will ultimately recoil upon themselves, by giving to our industry, our resources, and our policy, a new direction, calculated to render us really independent." He makes the question one of love of country and honorable pride, and does not even hint at any sordid calculation of profit. If he erred as a political economist, and in this respect there are those who will doubt, he at least manifested the generous purpose of a patriot.

In this brief sketch, it is not to be expected that even all the most prominent measures of Governor TOMPKINS' administration can be noticed; but there is one which must not be passed over in silence— we mean his prorogation of the senate and assembly of the state in 1812; and in reference we will briefly remark, in the language of another, "The legislature had lent a favorable ear to the petitions of various banking companies for incorporation; and a system had been projected and fostered by bribery and corruption, which threatened irreparable evils to the community. In his communication to the legislature, the governor dwelt upon this subject with peculiar force, and clearly and ably pointed out the inexpediency and danger of multiplying banking institutions; but such had been the gigantic strides of corruption, that the pernicious law would have been enacted, had not the governor exerted his constitutional privilege of proroguing the legislature."

The anathemas of party animosity came thick and heavy upon him, in consequence of this measure, which, although strictly constitutional, was stigmatized as arbitrary and despotic; but he breasted himself to the shock, and triumphed in the support of public opinion. Here he displayed, in a conspicuous manner, that moral energy of character which we have attributed to him, and crushed the hydra of corruption, which was beginning to rear itself in the sacred halls of legislation. "The measure," says the writer above quoted, "excited the astonishment and admiration of the whole United States."

We come now to the part which he bore in our late war with Great Britain, which embraces a most interesting period of his life. Whenever the history of that war shall be written for posterity, his name will fill an ample space in it. As governor of the state of New York, he had the direction of all her energies; and many and arduous were the duties which he was called upon to perform. But those who were conversant with the scenes of that period, will recollect the universal confidence which he inspired in every lover of his country.

The following letter, dated a few days after the declaration of war, will show the perilous situation of the state of New York at that time, the condition of the army, and the responsibility he assumed to meet the exigency.

"Albany, June 28, 1812.

"To Major General Dearborn,

"Sir,—Your letter of the 23d inst. has been received. I had anticipated your request, by ordering the detachments from Washington, Essex, Clinton, and Franklin counties into service, and have fixed the days and places of their rendezvous. Upon application to the quarter-master general, I find there are but 139 tents and 60 camp-kettles at this place, and even those I take by a kind of stealth. The deputy quarter-master general declines giving an order for their delivery, until he shall have a written order from the quarter-master general, and the latter is willing I shall take them, but will not give the deputy a written order for that purpose. Under such circumstances, I shall then avail myself of the rule of possession, and by virtue of the *eleven* points of the law, send them off to-morrow morning, without a written order from any one. You may remember, that when you were secretary of the war department, I invited you to forward and deposit in our frontier arsenals, arms, ammunition, and camp equipage, free of expense, to be ready for defence in case of war; and the same invitation to the war department has been repeated four times since. The United States have now from five to six hundred regular troops at Plattsburgh, Rome, Canandaigua, &c., where those arsenals are; and yet those recruits are now, and must be for weeks to come, unarmed, and in every respect unequipped, although within musket shot of arsenals. The recruits at Plattsburgh are within fifty miles of two tribes of Canadian Indians. In case of an attack upon the frontiers, that portion of the United States army would be as inefficient, and as unable to defend the inhabitants, or themselves even, as so many women. As to cannon, muskets, and ammunition, I can find no one here who will exercise any authority over them, or deliver a single article upon my requisition

DANIEL D. TOMPKINS.

Neither can I find any officer of the army who feels himself authorized to exercise any authority, or do any act which will aid me in the all-important object of protecting the inhabitants of our extended frontier, exposed to the cruelties of savages and the depredation of the enemy. If I must rely upon the militia solely for such protection, I entreat you to give orders to your officers here to furnish upon my order, for the use of the militia detachments, all needful weapons and articles with which the United States are furnished, and of which we are destitute.

"You may rely upon all the assistance which my talents, influence, and authority can furnish, in the active prosecution of the just and necessary war which has been declared by the constituted authority of our beloved country."

From the day of the declaration of war, the governor entered heart and soul into the prosecution of it, and so continued until its close. Most of the frontier troops, the first campaign, were militia, and many of them were marched several hundred miles. The quartermaster general of that day refused to make any advances to them. The governor was therefore placed in the dilemma of providing as well as he could for their expenses of every kind, or of permitting them to return home for the want of accommodation, disgusted both with the war and the government. He issued orders for raising a brigade of volunteers upon his own responsibility, which greatly distinguished itself on our Niagara frontier, and particularly at the memorable sortie from Fort Erie. The officers were all selected by Governor TOMPKINS, and their gallant conduct in the field showed his admirable discrimination in this respect. He had previously recommended to the legislature to raise volunteer regiments for the defence of our frontiers and the city of New York, but by a perversity which seems strange to us at the present day, his patriotic recommendation was rejected. A man of less firmness than Governor TOMPKINS would have quailed beneath the storm which was raised against him in Albany in the winter of 1813–14; and the consequence would probably have been, that the state would have been overrun by the foe. Not only was the whole western frontier in danger of invasion, but Sackett's Harbor, Plattsburgh, and the city of New York. But, regardless of censure or disapprobation, he called into the field large bodies of militia, and organized a corps of sea fencibles for the protection of the city of New York, consisting of 1000 men. In September, 1814, the militia in service for the defence of the city amounted to 17,500 men. He was even ready to despatch a force, under the lamented Decatur, for the assistance of Baltimore, which was then menaced with an attack; and had not the news of the enemy's retreat been received, the succor would have been upon their march to the relief of a sister state.

In 1814, from information received, and corroborated by the movements of the enemy, there are sufficient grounds of belief that one great object of his campaign was to penetrate with his northern army by the waters of Lake Champlain and the Hudson, and by a simultaneous attack with his maritime forces on New York, to form a junction which should sever the communication of the states. The exigency of the time, while it subjected the executive to great responsibility, admitted of no delay. To defeat this arrogant design, and save the state from inroad, it was necessary immediately to exercise fuller powers and more ample resources than had been placed in his hands by the legislature. He proceeded, therefore, to make such dispositions as were deemed indispensable to secure the exposed points against menaced invasion. To effect these objects, he found it necessary to transcend the authority and means vested in him by law, perfectly satisfied that the legislature would approve and sanction what he had done.

In October of this year, Governor TOMPKINS was appointed by the president to the command of the third military district. He acquitted himself of the command with great ability, and, on the disbanding of the troops, he received from every quarter letters of compliment and gratitude; and this was the only recompense for his services in this command which he ever obtained.

During the fall of this year, the general government was desirous of fitting out an expedition to dislodge the enemy from Castine, in the then province of Maine. They had applied to the governor of Massachusetts to raise the necessary funds for this purpose, but without effect. In this dilemma, the situation of the general government was hinted to Governor TOMPKINS, who, with his individual credit, and upon his own responsibility, immediately raised the sum of three hundred thousand dollars, which he placed at the orders of General Dearborn, then commanding in Massachusetts. This noble act of patriotism speaks for itself, and comment would be superfluous.

In looking over his military correspondence, it is surprising to see how watchful he was to foster a delicate and punctilious regard to the relative rank of the officers of the militia, so as to preclude every cause of jealousy or complaint. The officers were appointed by the council of appointment, which in the winter of 1813-14 was together with one branch of the legislature, opposed to the administration of the general government and to the prosecution of the war; and it is evident, from his correspondence at this period, that attempts were constantly made to create discontents, by the recommending of persons for promotion over the heads of those who were entitled to it by their previous military rank; and in turning back to his private correspondence from 1808 to 1811, we are struck with the continual annoyance experienced by him from the intrigues and slanders of political opponents, and at the same time with the indefatigable industry and noble frankness with which he counteracted and exposed them.

In the fall of 1814, Mr. Monroe having just been appointed secretary of war, President Madison requested permission to name Governor TOMPKINS to the senate as his successor. This offer of what is considered the highest office in the gift of the president of the United States, was declined.

In the spring of 1815, after peace had been proclaimed, he resigned the command of the third military district; and the president addressed to him a letter of thanks, for his "patriotic, active, and able support given to the government during the war."*

In February 1817, having received official information of his election to the office of vice president of the United States, he surrendered that of chief magistrate of the state of New York.

DANIEL D. TOMPKINS was born on the 21st of June, 1774, at Scarsdale, (Fox Meadows,) in the county of Westchester, N. Y. He was the seventh son of Jonathan G. Tompkins, one of the only three individuals of the town who advocated the cause of their country during the revolution. His ancestors had emigrated originally from the north of England during the time of religious persecution in that country, and landed at Plymouth, in the then colony of Massachusetts. After remaining there a short time, they purchased a tract of land in Westchester county, where they permanently settled. The father of the governor was a member of the state convention which adopted the declaration of independence and the first constitution of the state. He was a member of the legislature during the whole period of the revolution, also for many years first judge of the court of common pleas for the county; and on the institution of the university of the state, was appointed one of the regents, which situation he held until his resignation of it in 1808. He died after seeing his son elevated to the second office in the gift of his country

NATIONAL PORTRAITS.

Governor TOMPKINS was educated at Columbia college, in the city of New York, and received the first honors of his class. He was admitted to the bar in 1797; in 1801 was elected a representative of the city in the convention to revise the constitution of the state; in 1802 was chosen to the state legislature; and in 1804 was appointed a judge in the supreme court of the state, to supply the vacancy occasioned by the election of Chief Justice Lewis to the gubernatorial chair. In the same year he was elected a member of congress for the city, as a colleague of the late learned Dr. Mitchill. In 1807, when not thirty-three years of age, he was elevated to the chief magistracy of the state. He was also chancellor of the university, and in June, 1820, was elected grand master of masons in the state of New York.

In 1821, he was chosen a delegate from the county of Richmond to the convention for framing a new constitution for the state; and he was afterwards appointed president of this body. This was the last public situation which he held.

We still fondly turn our recollections towards him, as one of the most amiable, benevolent, and true-hearted men that ever lived. He bore the stamp of this feeling of kindliness towards his fellow-men in his open and frank countenance, in his easy and unaffected address, in the very tones of his voice, in his every-day intercourse with society. Upon every subject that comes home to "men's business and bosoms," his opinions were liberal and expanded; exclusiveness or dogmatism formed no part of his moral creed. He found, as all have found or will find who aspire to raise themselves above the level of their fellow-men, that envy tracked his footsteps, and calumny was always at hand to endeavor to throw a shade over his fame; and we regret to say that, during the close of his career, he suffered from pecuniary embarrassments, resulting from his multifarious services and expenditures, and assumed responsibilities during the war, and from—what must not be disguised—the tardy justice of the government. He came out of this ordeal, however, completely triumphant; but our limits forbid our entering into details.

We merely add the date of his decease, which melancholy event happened on the 11th of June, 1825, on Staten Island; but his remains are interred in the family vault, at St. Mark's church, in the city of New York.

WILLIAM GASTON, LL. D.

The name of Gaston is honorably associated in the annals of France, where the ancestors of the subject of this notice were zealous and distinguished adherents of the Huguenot cause, in the latter part of the seventeenth century. On the revocation of the edict of Nantz, they retired to Ballymore in Ireland, where Dr. Alexander Gaston, the father of the judge, was born. He was the younger brother of the Rev. Hugh Gaston, a presbyterian clergyman of great piety and learning, and the author of "Gaston's Concordance," a standard work in his church. Dr. Alexander Gaston was graduated at the medical college in Edinburgh, after which he accepted the appointment of surgeon in the navy, and attended the expedition which captured the Havana. The epidemic dysentery which prevailed with so much fatality among the troops, assailed even the surgeon; and with a constitution broken by disease, and daily wearing away from the exhaustion of a warm climate, he resigned his post and sailed for the North American provinces. He landed in Newbern, and after a residence of some years, during which he was engaged in the practice of his profession, was married, in May, 1775, to Margaret Sharpe, an English lady of the Catholic church. She had come out to North Carolina, on a visit to her two brothers, Girard and Joseph Sharpe, who were extensively engaged in commerce, and it was during this sojourn, that the gallantry of the young Irish physician, succeeded in permanently detaining her in Newbern.

William Gaston, their second son, was born on the 19th of September, 1778. His elder brother died very soon after he was born, and before he was three years old, the accidents of war carried off his father. The circumstances of the death of Dr. Alexander Gaston are too tragical and interesting to be omitted, and as they strongly illustrate the ferocity of the intestine war, that was waged between the whigs and tories of the south, we shall venture to detail them somewhat at length. Dr. Gaston was one of the most decided whigs in North Carolina, and as early as the month of August, 1775, was elected, by the provincial congress, a member of the committee of safety, for the district of Newbern. At various periods of the war he served in the army, generally as a surgeon, and once (in the spring of 1776) as captain of a volunteer band, that marched to the aid of Wilmington, on the approach of the armament of Sir Henry Clinton. By his zealous and ardent support of the cause of freedom, he acquired the confidence of the popular authorities, and was distinguished by the bitter hatred of the loyalists, who, though in a minority, were still numerous in that section of the state.

In the month of August, 1781, Major Craig, of the British army, whose head-quarters were at Wilmington, advanced at the head of a small detachment of regular troops, and a gang of tories, towards Newbern, with a view of occupying that city. The tories were several miles in the advance, and rapidly entered the town on the 20th of August. The whigs, thus surprised, had but little opportunity to make a regular stand, and after an ineffectual resistance gave up the contest. Dr. Gaston, however, knew too well the hatred and ferocity of his foes, to surrender himself into their hands, and hurrying off his wife and children, endeavored to escape across the river Trent, and thus retire to his plantation on Bryce's creek.

He reached the wharf, accompanied by his family, but before he could embark them in the light scow which he had seized, the tories in a body came galloping down, in their eager and bloody pursuit, and forced him to push off in the stream, leaving his wife and children unprotected on the shore. He was standing erect in the boat, which floated about forty yards from the shore, watching the situation of his wife, and while she, at the feet of his pursuers, with all the agony of anticipated bereavement, was imploring mercy for herself and life for her husband, a musket, levelled over her shoulder, was discharged and the victim sacrificed.

Mrs. Gaston was thus left alone in America. Her two brothers had died, and the inhuman murder of her husband left her no other objects of affection, save her son and an infant daughter. But she did not shrink nor despair amidst these multiplied disasters. Supported by her high sense of religion, and an admirable energy of character, she sedulously devoted herself to the arduous duties which now devolved upon her. The education and proper training up of her son, became the grand object of her existence, and whatever of good there was in him must be ascribed to the affectionate tuition and admonitions of maternal solicitude. Her strong feelings, her exquisite sensibility, her high integrity, and above all, her religion, she indelibly stamped upon his mind, and even at the most advanced period of his life, his character, admirable as it was, was nothing more than the maturity of the efforts of his mother.

While a school boy in Newbern, he is represented as having been very quick, and apt to learn; of an affectionate temper, but yet volatile and irritable. His mother used every means to correct his infirmities of disposition, and to give an aim to his pursuits—sometimes employing kindness, or mild but solemn admonition, and occasionally still stricter discipline. He continued under her guardianship and strict observation, until the fall of the year 1791, when he was sent to the college at Georgetown. The course of studies, though not very extensive, were rigorously enforced, and, as in all other catholic colleges, the ancient classics were long and painfully studied. In the spring of 1793 it was apprehended that the constitution of our student was sinking under a consumption. Accordingly he returned to his native climate, and there soon recovered his health, and renewed his studies. Determined to give her son every advantage of education which America afforded, Mrs. Gaston placed him under the direction of the Rev. Thomas P. Irving, and after a few months of preparatory instruction, he entered the junior class of Princeton college, in the autumn of 1794. In 1796 he was graduated with the first honors of the institution; and he was frequently heard to say, that it was the proudest moment of his life when he communicated the fact to his mother.

On his return from college he commenced the study of the law, in the office of François Xavier Martin, afterwards a judge of the supreme court of Louisiana. In 1798, when he was only twenty years of age, he was admitted to the bar, and in August, 1800, the first year after his coming of age, he was elected a member of the senate of North Carolina. In 1808 he was chosen by the Newbern district an elector of president and vice-president, and in the same year he drew up the act of the assembly *regulating the descent of inheritances*. In 1813 he was elected a member of congress, and continued in that body until 1817, when he retired to the more agreeable pursuits of domestic and professional life.

Judge GASTON carried into congress the zeal and independence of an upright politician, as well as the learning of a jurist; and on reviewing his congressional career, his friends will find no cause for chagrin or mortification, whilst those who differed from him in opinions, will at least acknowledge the invariable rectitude of his political course.

His first great effort on the floor of congress, was his celebrated speech in opposition to the loan bill, and on that occasion he appears to have acted as the acknowledged leader of the federal party.

In the early part of the year 1815, a bill was introduced to authorize a loan of twenty-five millions of dollars to the government of the United States. In opposing this bill, Mr. GASTON declared that if it could be shewn necessary to accomplish any purposes demanded by the honor and welfare of the country, it assuredly should meet with no opposition from him. It was, he said, avowedly not necessary, except to carry on the scheme of invasion and conquest against the Canadas; and to that scheme he had never been a friend, and to its prosecution at that time he had invincible objections, founded on considerations of justice, humanity, and national policy. In the course of this speech he took a very extensive view of the causes of the war, as well as the manner in which it had been conducted.

There is one sentence in this speech which we shall extract as a fair specimen of Judge GASTON's style of oratory. Mr. Calhoun had, in the course of his remarks, spoken with much warmth of the factious opposition to the administration, which he was pleased to say might be salutary in a monarchy, but was highly dangerous in a government so republican as ours. Judge GASTON concluded his reply to this remark in the following eloquent peroration..

"If this doctrine were then to be collected from the histories of the world, can it now be doubted, since the experience of the last twenty-five years? Go to France—once revolutionary, now imperial France—and ask her whether factious power or intemperate opposition be the more fatal to freedom and happiness. Perhaps at some moment, when the eagle eye of her master is turned away, she may whisper to you to behold the demolition of Lyons, or the devastation of La Vendee. Perhaps she will give you a written answer. Draw near the fatal lamp post, and by its flickering light read it as traced in characters of blood that flowed from the guillotine—'Faction is a demon—faction out of power is a demon enchained—faction vested with the attributes of rule, is a Moloch of destruction.'"

In 1816, Mr. Stanford, of North Carolina, moved to expunge "*the previous question*" from the rules of the house; and this motion, which was opposed by Mr. Clay, Judge GASTON supported in one of the ablest speeches ever delivered by him in the hall of the representatives. It contained more learning than we thought existed on the subject, and we doubt whether, at the present day, its history in the

English parliament, or the American congress, is any where so accurately and ingeniously discussed, as in this speech. It was entirely a new field, and we shall venture to ascribe as much genius in the ingenuity which selected such an occasion for display, as in the eloquent and vivid manner in which the orator set forth his store of learning. It is a studied and richly carved work, and had obviously occupied his attention for a long time. We have not space for more than a short extract from this speech, but commend the whole of it to the perusal of all politicians and statesmen. After a few introductory remarks, Mr. GASTON said :—

"And, sir, I rejoice equally at the opposition which the motion of my colleague has encountered. If this hideous rule could have been vindicated, we should have received that vindication from the gentleman who has just resumed his seat. (Mr. Clay.) If his ingenuity and zeal combined, could form for the previous question no other defence than that which we have heard, the previous question cannot be defended. If beneath his shield it finds so slight a shelter, it must fall a victim to the just, though long delayed vengeance of awakened and indignant freedom. If Hector cannot defend his Troy, the doom of Troy is fixed by fate. It is indispensable, before we proceed further in the consideration of this subject, that we should perfectly understand what is our previous question. Gentlemen may incautiously suppose that it is the same with what has been called the previous question elsewhere. This would be a most fatal mistake.

Our previous question is altogether *sui generis*, the only one of its kind; and to know it we must consider not merely what is written of it in our code, but what it has been rendered by exposition and construction. Our previous question '*can* only be admitted when demanded by a majority of the members *present*.' It is a question, '*whether* the question under debate should now be *put*.' On the previous question '*there shall be no debate*;' '*until* it is decided, it shall preclude all amendment and debate of the *main question*.' If it be decided negatively, viz., that the main question shall *not* now be put, the main question is of course superseded; but if it be decided affirmatively that the main question *shall* now be put, the main question is to be put *instantaneously*, and no member can be allowed to amend or discuss it. The previous question is entitled to precedence over motions to amend, commit, or postpone the main question, and therefore, when admitted, puts these entirely aside. This, according to the latest improvement, is now our rule of the previous question, and certainly in your patent office there is no model of a machine better fitted to its purposes, than this instrument for the ends of tyranny. It is a power vested in a majority, to forbid at their sovereign will and pleasure, every member, not of that majority, from making known either his own sentiments, or the wishes or complaints of his constituents, in relation to any subject under consideration, or from attempting to amend what is proposed as a law for the government of the whole nation."

After detailing the history of the previous question in the British house of commons, and in the American congress, and shewing that it was not considered a machine to close debate, up to the year 1808, he proceeds to say, "It was impossible that any rule could be more completely settled, both by uninterrupted usage and solemn, deliberate adjudication, than was the rule of the previous question in this house. It was a rule perfectly consistent with good sense, with the requisite independence of the members of the house, and with the right of the free people whom they represented. It preserved decorum; it had a tendency to prevent unnecessary discussions; it superseded unnecessary questions; while it left perfectly untouched the fundamental principles of parliamentary and political freedom. Thus, sir, it continued the more firm for the impotent attempt which had been made to prevent it, and the better understood from the blunders which its examination had exposed. Such was the state of things, when on the memorable night of the 27th of February, 1811, the monster which we now call the 'previous question,' was ushered into existence, and utterly supplanted the harmless, useless being whose name it usurped."

This speech, so profound and so violent in its character, was received by the house with astonishment and admiration.

There is always something remarkable in the speeches of southern orators. A striking similarity of manner and of language, which shews at once the "*latitude*" of the orator. Vehement whenever they condemn, enthusiastic whenever they applaud, they carry into political strife "the rancor of opposition, or the idolatry of love."

Something of this feeling may be observed in the speeches of Mr GASTON, which we have noticed, and which are among the finest specimens of southern eloquence. They contain a great deal of calm, weighty argument, but it is only when the orator turns to watch the position of his antagonist, that his language is fired by passion, and his denunciations are sent forth burning, and blazing, and "withering as they go."

WILLIAM GASTON.

After his retirement from congress, Judge GASTON frequently appeared in the assembly of North Carolina, and always as tne leader of what may be called the constitutional party. In that body many of his most splendid speeches were made. He framed the law establishing the present supreme court of the state; and the liberal basis upon which it is established, is to be ascribed to his zealous and efficient support. In 1828, he delivered a speech upon the currency of the state, which has been classed among his highest efforts. His defence of the constitution of North Carolina in 1831, will long be remembered. The constitution of the state is a venerable instrument. It came down to the present generation, from the sages of the revolution, and is loved and venerated in North Carolina for its very antiquity. It was a fit subject for the exhibition of his learning, eloquence, and patriotism, and those resources of his mind he poured forth with the most brilliant profusion.

Judge GASTON now became junior member of the supreme court of North Carolina. It was in the practice of his profession, more than in the legislative hall, where he acquired his great reputation as an orator. He was at all times remarkable for his steady adherence to the UNION, and distinguished himself for his zealous opposition to the doctrine of nullification, as set forth by some South Carolina politicians.

Although Judge GASTON was throughout his life, busily engaged in the discharge of professional and legislative duties, he yet found time, in the intervals of such labors, to keep pace with the literature of the day. It was his custom, in riding the circuit of his courts, to take with him the last new publication, and to peruse it as he rode along the road, and he was not unfrequently aroused from the enchantment of Scott, or Irving, by the upsetting of his sulky. His habits of study were always intense, and his habits of recreation, refined. His intercourse in the society of his friends, was marked with great mildness, affability, and occasional conviviality. In the narration of an anecdote, especially a professional one, he was unrivalled, and his manner of conversation was generally playful and easy.

Active as was Judge GASTON in political and professional pursuits, he was equally devoted to the performance of the duties of domestic life. It was in this sphere, to which by his moral and social qualities he was so well adapted, that he found the enjoyments—though often marred by the hand of death—in which he most delighted. He was three times married. On the 4th of September, 1803, he married Miss Susan Hay, (daughter of John Hay, Esq., of Fayetteville,) who died the 20th of April, 1804. On the 6th of October, 1805, he married Hannah McClure, the only daughter of General McClure, who died on the 12th of July, 1813, leaving one son and two daughters. His third wife, whom he married in August, 1816, was Eliza Ann, eldest daughter of Dr. Charles Worthington, of Georgetown, District of Columbia, who died on the 26th of January, 1819, leaving two infant children.

The education of his children, and the performance of his official duties, occupied the remainder of his life. He died at Raleigh, N. C., on the 23d of January, 1844, in the sixty-sixth year of his age. The excellence of his character, and the grief occasioned by his death, are impressively portrayed in the proceedings of the bar, and the court. "Struck down suddenly," say the members of the bar of the supreme court of North Carolina, " by the hand of God, in the midst of his judicial labors—dying, as he lived, in the enlightened and devoted service of his country—endued by learning, and adorned by eloquence, with their choicest gifts—ennobled by that pure integrity, and undeviating pursuit of right, which only an ardent and animating religious faith can bestow and adequately sustain ; and endeared to the hearts of all that knew him, by those virtues which diffuse over the social circle all that is cheerful, refined, and benevolent, he has left behind him a rare and happy memory, dear alike to his brethren, his friends, and his country."

"Whereupon, Chief Justice Ruffin, on behalf of the court, responded : The court unites with the bar, in lamenting the calamity which has fallen upon us; and is ready to concur in whatever may honor the memory of our deceased brother, or express a sympathy with his bereaved family. The loss, indeed, is that of the whole country ; and it will doubtless be deeply felt and more deeply deplored, by the whole country. But to us, who have been connected with him here, it is peculiarly severe. Having been closely associated in private intercourse, and in the discharge of a common public duty, for the last ten years, we have had the best means of knowing and appreciating his personal virtues, and judicial services. We know, that he was indeed a good man and a great judge. His assistance, in the discharge of our official duties, is cheerfully acknowledged by us, who have survived him. In our opinion, his worth, as a minister of justice, and expounder of the laws, was inestimable; and we feel that as a personal friend, his loss cannot be supplied."

WILLIAM RICHARDSON DAVIE.

WILLIAM RICHARDSON DAVIE was born in the village of Egremont, near White Haven, in England, on the 20th June, 1756. He was brought by his father to America soon after the peace of 1763, who, returning, confided him to the care of the Rev. William Richardson, his maternal uncle, a Presbyterian minister in the Waxhaw settlement, South Carolina, who, having no children, adopted him as his heir. He was sent to an academy in North Carolina, whence, on being prepared for college, he was removed to Nassau-Hall, in Princeton, New Jersey, where the Revolution found him ready to graduate.

The venerable Dr. Witherspoon, yielding to the solicitations of the students, permitted them to organize a company, and join the American army, then making its first campaign. W. R. DAVIE acted as sergeant of this gallant band. After serving a tour of duty in New Jersey and New York, he returned to college, and graduated with the highest honor of his class.

On his return home, young DAVIE, finding all the commissions for the troops just levied had been issued, determined to study law, and went for that purpose to Salisbury, North Carolina. The war continuing, DAVIE's devotion to the cause of freedom, and his ardent desire to bear his part in the glorious struggle, again induced him to abandon his studies. In order, as soon as possible, to accomplish his wish, he prevailed on a patriotic gentleman by the name of Barnet, too far advanced in life for military service, but of high standing and great popularity, to raise a troop of dragoons, by whose influence he obtained a lieutenancy in this troop. The captain immediately joined the southern army; resigning soon after, the command devolved on Lieutenant DAVIE, by whose request the troop was attached to Pulawski's legion. In this corps he rose to the rank of major. In a charge of cavalry at the affair of Stono, DAVIE received a severe wound, and was removed from the field to the hospital in Charleston, where he suffered a tedious confinement. On leaving Charleston, being lame from his wound and unfit for duty, he returned to Salisbury, to prosecute the study of law, and in the fall of that year received from the governor of North Carolina license to practise.

In the winter of 1780, he was empowered by the government of North Carolina to raise one troop of dragoons, and two of mounted infantry. To equip this force he expended the whole of the estate left him by his uncle. With it he protected the south-west part of North Carolina from the predatory incursions of the British and loyalists, and was constantly on the enemy's lines, performing a most important and hazardous duty.

Colonel DAVIE joined General Rutherford, and shared in the battle at Ramsours' mill, which eventuated in the defeat and dispersion of a large tory force. Shortly after this, he united with General Sumpter of South Carolina, and Colonel Irvine of North Carolina, in the attack on the British encampment at Hanging Rock, where they succeeded in destroying the British commissary's stores, capturing three companies of Bryan's regiment, and about sixty horses, and arms of all kinds.

"When Lord Cornwallis entered Charlotte, a small village in North Carolina, Colonel DAVIE, at the head of his detachment, threw himself in his front, determined to give him a specimen of the firmness and gallantry with which the inhabitants of the place were prepared to dispute with his lordship their native soil.

"Colonel Tarleton's legion formed the British van, led by Major Hanger; the commander himself being confined by sickness.

"When that celebrated corps had advanced near to the centre of the village, where the Americans were posted, DAVIE poured into it so destructive a fire, that it immediately wheeled, and retreated in disorder. Being rallied on the commons, and again led on to the charge, it received on the same spot another fire with a similar effect.

"Lord Cornwallis, witnessing the confusion thus produced among his choicest troops, rode up in person, and in a tone of dissatisfaction upbraided the legion with unsoldierly conduct, reminding it of its former exploits and reputation.

"Pressed on his flanks by the British infantry, Colonel DAVIE had ow fallen back to a new and well selected position.

"To dislodge him from this, the legion cavalry advanced on him a third time, in rapid charge, in full view of their commander-in-chief, and still smarting from his pungent censure; but in vain. Another fire from the American marksmen killed several of their officers, wounded Major Hanger, and repulsed them again with increased confusion.

"The main body of the British being now within musket-shot, the American leader abandoned the contest.

"That they might, if possible, recover some portion of the laurels of which they had this day been shorn, Colonel Tarleton's dragoons attempted to disturb Colonel Davie in his retreat. But the latter, choosing his ground, wheeled on them with so fierce and galling a fire, that they again fell back, and troubled him no further.

"It was by strokes like these that he seriously crippled and intimidated his enemy, acquired an elevated standing in the estimation of his friends, and served very essentially the interests of freedom. With the resolution of Sumpter, and the coolness and military policy of Marion, he exhibited in his character a happy union of the high qualities of those two officers."*

After being engaged in several minor actions, he was, on the fatal sixteenth of August, on his way to join General Gates, when he met our dispersed troops. Notwithstanding the defeat, he hastened forward towards the battle-ground, and by his prudence and zeal not only checked the pursuit, but saved several wagons, one of which most fortunately contained the hospital stores and medicine chest. Justly apprehensive of the danger to which General Sumpter would be exposed by this catastrophe, he instantly despatched a courier to that officer, communicating what had transpired, and advising him to retire to Charlotte.

Shortly after the appointment of General Greene to the command of the southern army, finding great difficulty in managing the commissary department, arising from the unsettled state of the country, its almost entire exhaustion by the interruption to agriculture, and the support of the English and American forces, he sent for Colonel Davie to his camp, and requested him to take charge of that department; adding, that he knew Colonel Davie was then in command of a veteran band, with which he had acquired much reputation as a partisan officer; and he was confident he would be unwilling to relinquish a command in which he was sure of high distinction, and accept one in the civil staff of the army. He then laid open to him the situation of the American army, assuring him they must disband unless *he* would undertake their support; that if he wished to save his country, he could in no way do it so effectually; concluding with this handsome compliment: "From the best information, I am con-

---

* Caldwell's Life of General Greene.

vinced that you alone, colonel, can save us." Thus solicited by that great and good man, he disbanded his volunteers, thereby giving up all chance of personal distinction for the public interest. From that time he was a member of the general's family, and was with him during his celebrated retreat through North Carolina. During this retreat, the American general had almost insurmountable difficulties to encounter, from the inclement season of the year, and the wretched condition of the troops, without blankets, shoes, or clothes. From the absence of Colonel Carrington at this time, Colonel DAVIE had the double duty of quarter-master and commissary to perform, while the rapid retreat of the army greatly augmented the difficulties of his situation.

The retreat terminated on passing Dan River, where Colonel Carrington joined the army, and personally superintended its passage across that stream, for which he had made the best possible arrangements. Colonel DAVIE remained with the army at the south till the exhausted state of the country induced General Greene to send him to meet the legislature of North Carolina, under the hope that he could prevail on that body to fill up their lines, and make some arrangements for the support of the army in South Carolina. On Colonel DAVIE's visit to Carolina, he was furnished with letters to Governor Nash, General Allen Jones, and M. Willis Jones, to whom he made a true statement of the necessities of the southern army, and succeeded in convincing them of the importance of energetic measures, and inducing them to exert their utmost influence on the legislature. It was this united influence which led them to pass a law, laying what was termed the specific tax. The legislature at the same time made Colonel DAVIE commissioner for its collection and distribution, which, involving important and multifarious duties, forced him to resign his situation as commissary to the southern army, an arrangement to which General Greene consented, as it placed all the resources of North Carolina at the disposal of an officer in whom he had the highest confidence. By this law a tax was laid on every county in the state, and a commissioner was authorized to receive the produce of the country, and apply the same as he deemed for the public good.

For this purpose Colonel DAVIE appointed a sub-commissioner in each county, whose duty it was to take charge of the tobacco, corn, pork, and beeves, which were collected at various depots, and held subject to the orders of the commissioner-general, who was to apply the same to the pay and support of the governor and the general assembly, and the balance to the support of the army. This was a law that imposed arduous duties on the commissioner, and seemed to involve an endless detail of barter, contract, collection, and distribution. It was first necessary to ascertain what a county could best pay; if in tobacco, this was considered almost as cash, it being always possible to barter it with the merchants; if in beeves, they were driven to some place where they could be most easily maintained, and, when necessary, killed and salted for public use, or driven to the army or legislature, as both were to be fed by the commissioner. The same course was pursued when the tax was paid in hogs; corn was collected in depots, and issued under orders of the commissioner. All troops stationed in the state, or marching through it, were supplied by the commissioner, so that he had accounts to settle not only with his own deputies, but with all the officers, civil and military; in addition to which were accounts with almost every merchant in the state. In time of peace, the duties of such an officer would require incessant application, and indefatigable industry; but war and general distress greatly enhanced the difficulties. In 1783, the law laying the specific tax expired, when Colonel DAVIE, having settled his accounts as commissioner, retired from public service, and with the peace commenced the practice of law. About this time he was married to Miss Sarah Jones, daughter of General Allen Jones of North Carolina, and selected the town of Roanoke for his residence.

During the revolution, business had accumulated on the dockets from the unsettled state of the country; and many, whose crimes had rendered them obnoxious to the laws, were now to be tried; among the first of these was the noted Colonel Bryan, of Rowan. This man had raised a force of seven hundred men, and with them joined the British army. These troops had been routed and cut in pieces at the battle of Hanging Rock. On his trial at Salisbury, he selected Colonel DAVIE as his counsel, although but just come to the bar. This trial excited much interest, from the previous good standing of the criminal, and the respectability of his connections. The effort made to save him soon rendered Colonel DAVIE the most popular advocate in the state for the defence of criminals; and during the fifteen years he practised at the bar, not a man was tried for a capital offence at any court at which he practised, whom he was not called on to defend. This high rank as a lawyer was united with equal standing as a gentleman, in consequence of which he was returned as a member to the legislature of North Carolina, from the borough of Halifax, for many years, without opposition. In that body he took an active and efficient part in all the important business which came before the legislature. The statute books of the state are records of his wisdom. The university of North Carolina constitutes one of the benefits resulting from his labors; for notwithstanding that institution was advocated by all the talent and worth of the state, yet its interests in the legislature were almost exclusively intrusted to Colonel DAVIE. Little experience is necessary to convince any man of the pertinacity with which ignorance and prejudice will oppose every attempt at the dissemination of knowledge. There is in all legislatures a certain set of politicians, who array themselves against all liberal measures, feeling that they must lose all consequence in the general diffusion of learning; these opposed every measure that was introduced for the benefit of the institution, and it required both talents and address to succeed against them; but he did succeed, and the friends of learning and virtue now view the institution with a just pride, as the honor and ornament of the state.

Colonel DAVIE was now appointed Major General in the militia of North Carolina.

When it became apparent to all that the old confederation was not calculated to advance the interest of the union, and that the blessings of the revolution were likely to be lost from the imbecility of the general government, the states determined to assemble a convention at Philadelphia to amend the constitution. General DAVIE was chosen a member of that convention from North Carolina, and made one of that venerable body whose joint labors produced the federal constitution. By an article in that instrument, it became necessary for the same to be ratified in each state by conventions called for the purpose. General DAVIE was again chosen a member of that convention. Here he was aided by the late amiable Judge Iredel, who rendered all the assistance that could be derived from worth, talents, and learning. Their united efforts proved vain, and the constitution was rejected. A second convention called to reconsider it, ratified the constitution, and North Carolina became a member of the union. It may afford matter for surprise that General DAVIE's name does not appear to that great instrument. Various reasons have been assigned, but it was simply this, that illness in his family called him home before the labors of the convention were concluded.

In the winter of 1799, General DAVIE was chosen governor of the state. He was not, however, permitted to remain long in that station; his country had higher claims on his talents and services. He resigned that office to proceed as minister to France, associated with

WILLIAM RICHARDSON DAVIE.

Oliver Ellsworth, Chief Justice of the United States, and W. V. Murray, Esq., our resident at the Hague.

They arrived in France shortly after the revolution, which placed all power in the hands of Bonaparte. Little difficulty was experienced in adjusting our differences with that government, excepting those that resulted from the absence of the first consul with the army, which for a time suspended all negotiations. Late in 1800, they concluded a treaty with the consular government of France, the negotiations of which were conducted by Joseph Bonaparte, Count of Survilliers, with Messrs. Rederer and Fleurieux.

General DAVIE contemplated the character of Bonaparte with great attention. He saw him often, and conversed with him freely. He considered him a man of first rate talents as a warrior, and of great reach as a statesman; but he regarded him also as a man of unbounded ambition, restrained by no principles, human or divine. On one occasion, after an interesting conversation, Bonaparte concluded by saying, that he considered power as the only foundation of right: "*Enfin, Monsieur, la force est droit.*" General DAVIE's opinion of him was afterwards verified by his assumption of imperial and despotic power.

Shortly after his return to America, General DAVIE lost his wife, a lady of lofty mind and exemplary virtues, to whom he was greatly attached; and soon after he removed to a fine estate at Tivoli, near Landsford, beautifully situated on the Catawba river in South Carolina, where he had long cultivated a plantation. As a farmer he was active and intelligent. Deploring the wasteful system of farming in the southern states, which exhausts the land without returning any thing to it, he endeavored to improve it by the use of manures, rotation of crops, and rest to the land. On the formation of an agricultural society at Columbia, he was appointed president, and delivered an address, which, for purity of style, sound observation, and clear exposition of the proper course of agriculture for this country, has never been excelled.

"Some years after General DAVIE's retreat to his farm, the belligerent governments of France and England, each of which had endeavored to involve our country as a party in their quarrel, multiplied their aggressions on the commerce of the United States to such an extent, as to furnish just cause of war against both; and it was even seriously proposed in Congress to declare war against both. Finding, however, that such a course would expose the commerce of the country to the rapacity of both nations, it was abandoned, but with strong declarations that the conduct of France and England gave us the right to choose our enemy. That choice was made, and it fell upon Great Britain. In the formation of the army for the defence of the country in this emergency, the government, laying aside party distinctions, selected General Davie as one of the officers best fitted to be intrusted with a high command. Though dissatisfied with some of the measures of the administration, he felt that as a citizen he was bound to defend his country whenever it was in danger, however brought on it. But the wounds received in the revolutionary war, and the rheumatism, which had become fixed on his constitution, incapacitated him for the exertions which his high sense of duty would have exacted from him as a commander. He, therefore, after much hesitation, declined the proffered honor."

General Davie continued to reside at his beautiful seat on the banks of the Catawba, to which travellers and visiters were constantly attracted by his hospitality, his dignified manners, and elevated character. He occasionally made excursions to the warm springs for relief from the harassing disease which afflicted and wasted him. On these visits he was greatly admired by the intelligent strangers who resorted there. The affability of his deportment gave access to all. But no person approached him, however distinguished by his talents or character, who did not speedily feel that he was in the presence of a superior man. The ignorant and the learned, the weak and the wise, were all instructed and delighted by the irresistible charms of his conversation.

"At home, General Davie was the friend of the distressed, the safe counsellor of the embarrassed, and the peace-maker of all. He had a deep and even awful sense of God and his providence, and was attached to the principles and doctrines of Christianity."

In person he was tall and finely proportioned, his figure erect and commanding, his countenance possessing great expression, and his voice full and energetic. He died in 1820, at the age of sixty-five, of cold taken on his return from the springs. He met death with the firmness of a soldier, and of a man conscious of a life well spent. The good he did survives him; and he has left a noble example to the youth of his country, to encourage and to stimulate them in the honorable career of virtue and of exertion. May it be appreciated and followed!

LUTHER MARTIN.

LUTHER MARTIN, a lawyer, distinguished alike for his eccentric habits, his powerful genius, and his vast legal acquirements, was born in New Brunswick, New Jersey, in the year 1744. His ancestors were natives of England. Two of their descendants, who were brothers, removed from New England, and established their residence in that section of the country adjoining the river Rariton, upon the east of New Brunswick, calling the township in which they had located Piscataqua, from the name of the town whence they emigrated. They were by occupation farmers, and having obtained large grants of land in New Jersey, removed their domestic establishment there when a greater part of the Colonial domain was a dense wilderness.

LUTHER was the third of nine children, and his time was generally divided, during his early boyhood, between the duties of his father's family and the acquisition of knowledge. In 1757, in the month of August, he was sent to a grammar school, where he learned the rudiments of the Latin language; and in September, five years after, he was graduated at Nassau Hall, Princeton, in a class of thirty-five, with the highest collegiate honors. At that institution he laid the foundation of his subsequent greatness, and with his other classical exercises pursued the study of the French and Hebrew languages.

Among his friends and associates in Princeton were J. Habersham, Esq., the Right Rev. Bishop Clagget of Maryland, the celebrated Pierpoint Edwards, and Oliver Ellsworth. His parents, however were indigent, and they were enabled, consequently, to bestow upon this son a liberal education only; "a patrimony," he remarks, "for which my heart beats toward them a more grateful remembrance than had they bestowed upon me the gold of Peru or the gems of Golconda."* As an equivalent for the additional labor which

---

* Modern Ingratitude, in five numbers, by Luther Martin, Esq. of Maryland. p. 134.

his two elder brothers had undergone for the support of his father's family while he was receiving the benefits of a liberal education, he conveyed to them, as soon as the laws permitted his disposition of the estate, a small tract of land which had been granted him by his grandfather for his own support.

Upon his graduation from college, having fixed upon the legal profession as his choice, against which, however, his family entertained the strongest prejudices, upon the second day after his commencement, and when he was scarcely nineteen years of age, determining to be no longer a burden to his family, he departed, in company with two or three friends, on horseback, and with but a few dollars in his pocket, for Cecil county, near Octorara Creek in the state of Maryland, in order to be employed as an assistant in a school, which he had learned was just deprived of a teacher, and which was under the management of the Rev. Mr. Hunt, to whom he carried letters of recommendation. Before his arrival the place was occupied. He was received with great hospitality by this gentleman however, who, conjointly with his other friends, advised him to proceed immediately to Queenstown, Queen Ann's county, where a vacancy had just occurred in the common school of that place. Carrying to that county letters of introduction to the board of trustees, among whom was Edward Tighlman, (father of the distinguished Edward Tighlman, Esq. of Philadelphia,) as well as to many of the most distinguished gentlemen in the neighborhood, he was engaged, after the ordinary examination, to take charge of the school.

His object in entering upon this employment was, to acquire a support while pursuing the study of the law. Here he remained in the capacity of a preceptor until April, 1770. During this period he made many valuable acquaintances, among whom was Solomon Wright, Esq., the father of the Hon. Mr. Wright, late senator of the United States, who gave him the advantage of his library, and received him in all respects as a member of his family. For several years he had little relaxation from the most vigorous industry. His means were scanty, as the meagre profits of his school were his sole support. His improvident habits of expenditure brought him eventually into debt; and upon his expressing his determination to relinquish the business of an instructor, and to devote one year exclusively to the study of the law, he was arrested upon five different warrants of attachment. In fact, a want of economy in his pecuniary affairs was prominent through life, and frequently brought upon him the most unpleasant consequences. On this subject he somewhat quaintly

LUTHER MARTIN.

remarks respecting himself—"I am not even *yet*, I was not *then*, nor have I *ever been*, an economist of any thing but time."*

In 1771, through the kind agency of George Wythe, the former chancellor of the state of Virginia, and the Hon. John Randolph, he was admitted to the bar, continued his legal studies until 1772, and then proceeded to Williamsburgh, where the general court was in session, and remained in that place until it terminated. Here he formed many valuable acquaintances, among whom may be mentioned Patrick Henry, the great orator of the Revolution.

He soon after commenced the practice of the law in Accomack and Northampton, in Virginia, and was admitted as an attorney in the courts of Somerset and Worcester, which held their sessions four times a year. He made his residence in Somerset, where he soon acquired a full and lucrative practice, amounting, as he informs us, to about one thousand pounds per annum; which, however, was after a period diminished by the disturbances growing out of the American Revolution. At this time he was occasionally employed in causes of Admiralty jurisdiction, involving interests of great magnitude, and also in some important appeals to the Congress of the United States. A Criminal court had just been established at Williamsburgh, and Mr. MARTIN was employed as counsel for thirty prisoners, twenty-nine of whom were acquitted. His talents were at this time fully appreciated, and he was regarded as one of the most able lawyers at the bar at which he practised.

In 1774, while attending the courts in Virginia, he was appointed one of a committee for the county to oppose the claims of Great Britain, and also a member of the Convention which was called at Annapolis to resist the usurpations of the British crown. He threw the whole strength of his manly vigor, courage, and iron firmness into the cause of American freedom, and opposed these claims with extraordinary boldness at a period, to use his own words, "throughout which not only myself, but many others, did not lie down one night on their beds without the hazard of waking on board a British armed ship or in the other world." When the Howes were on the way to Chesapeak Bay, they published a manifesto, or proclamation, addressed to the people of that part of the United States, against which they were directing their military operations. This proclamation was answered in an address to the Howes by LUTHER MAR-

---

* Modern Ingratitude, p. 138.

TIN. He also, about the same time, published an address, directed "to the inhabitants of the Peninsula between the Delaware river and the Chesapeak to the southward of the British lines," which was distributed among them in printed hand-bills.

Upon the 11th of February, 1778, he was appointed, through th advice of Judge Chace, Attorney General of the state of Maryland; in which office his remarkable firmness, professional knowledge, and uncompromising energy, were most strikingly exhibited in prosecuting the Tories and the confiscation of their goods. No other man, in fact, could be found at that time of sufficient hardihood and firmness to fill this office. LUTHER MARTIN was called upon at this crisis, and he met it with a manliness of decision and a determined power, which left no room for fear; coming down upon this class of men with an iron hand, and bringing to bear upon them all the powers of the government in order to effect their total defeat and overthrow. In performing the duties of his office in other respects, he exhibited the same vigorous and unquailing determination. On one occasion, for his promptitude in prosecuting a man of great respect, ability, and influence, who was indicted for the murder of an Irishman, he was voted, by the friends of the murdered man, a massive service of silver plate, which, from official considerations, he refused to accept.

He continued in the office of Attorney-General during a long period, constantly augmenting his reputation as an advocate and jurist. The office was conferred on him originally without his solicitation, and his commission found him at Accomack, giving directions to workmen who were engaged in the manufacture of salt.

As a demonstration of his powers of mind, as well as his great legal acquirements, it may be remarked, that he stood among the brightest and strongest at a bar, which numbered among its members a brilliant constellation, composed of such men as Harper, Winder, Chase, Wirt, and Pinkney.

In 1783 he was married to a Miss Cresap of Old Town in the state of Maryland, who was the grand-daughter of Col. Cresap, against whom the charge was brought by Mr. Jefferson of having murdered the Indian family of Logan. This charge originated a long controversy between the latter gentleman and Mr. MARTIN, which were carried on through divers inflammatory pamphlets.

During the whole course of his practice at the bar he was a violent politician, and wrote for the press several pungent essays against what was then denominated the Democratic party.

In 1804 he was engaged, conjointly with Mr. Harper, in the de-

LUTHER MARTIN.

fence of Judge Chase, then one of the justices of the Superior Court of the United States, who was impeached in the house of Representatives, upon eight articles, for malfeasance in office. After a powerful argument in his behalf, Judge Chase was acquitted; a constitutional majority not having been found against him upon a single article.

Aaron Burr, that able though ill-fated man, was at this period the personal and political friend of Mr. MARTIN. He had just broken away from his brilliant career, and public opinion had branded him as a traitor. In 1807, his trial for treason "in preparing the means of a military expedition against Mexico, a territory of the King of Spain, with whom the United States were at peace," occurred in the Circuit Court of the United States for the district of Virginia. Messrs Wickham, Wirt, Randolph, and MARTIN, were engaged upon this cause, which involved interests of vast importance, and principles of constitutional law of great magnitude. Mr. MARTIN appeared in defence of his friend, who, as every body knows, was acquitted. During the whole course of the trial Mr. MARTIN demonstrated himself to be the steadfast friend of Aaron Burr, and entered into a recognisance for his appearance, from day to day, before the bar of court.

In 1814 Mr. MARTIN was appointed chief judge of the Court of Oyer and Terminer for the city and county of Baltimore, and fulfilled its duties with considerable rigor, though with great success, until a new state law made it necessary for him to relinquish his seat upon the bench. In 1818 he was again qualified as attorney-general of the state and district attorney for the city of Baltimore; but his declining health prevented him from attending in person to his official duties.

From that period to the time of his death, his mind and body were gradually impaired by disease, and a paralytic stroke, with which he was soon after attacked, almost destroyed his physical and intellectual powers. Suffering in his old age under the goadings of penury, he removed to the city of New-York, to take advantage of the hospitality of his old friend and client, Aaron Burr, who faithfully paid him the last rites of kindness, in the imbecillity of his age, in return for the valuable services which MARTIN had rendered him, both in money and talent, when he was in the full vigor and glory of manhood.

LUTHER MARTIN died at New-York, from the mere decay of nature, on the evening of the 10th of July, 1826, aged 82 years.

NATIONAL PORTRAITS.

The information of his death having reached Baltimore, the bench and the bar immediately convened in the court house of that city; and on motion of the Honorable John Purviance, it was "*Resolved*, that we hear with great sensibility of the death of our venerable brother, the former attorney-general of Maryland, and the patriarch of the profession, LUTHER MARTIN; and that, as a testimony of just regard for his memory, and great respect for his exalted talents and profound learning, we will wear mourning for the space of thirty days."

As a lawyer, Mr. MARTIN was learned, clear, solid, and second to no man among his competitors. In fact he shone far above his contemporaries in the accuracy of his knowledge and the clearness of his forensic arguments. He had drawn his legal attainments, like Pinkney, from the great fountains of jurisprudence; and was content to exhibit them only in the light of that reason, which, Sir Edward Coke declares, " is the life of the law." Of his general powers at the bar, his unbroken success and his exalted reputation abroad, are plain demonstrations. His mind was so completely stored with the principles of legal science, and his professional accuracy was so generally acknowledged, that his mere opinion was considered law, and is now deemed sound authority before any American tribunal. His cast of mind was less brilliant than solid. He ordinarily commenced his efforts at the bar with a long, desultory, tedious exordium. He seemed to labor amid the vast mass of *general matters* at the commencement of his speeches, sometimes continuing for an hour in a confused essay, and then suddenly springing off upon his track with a strong, cogent, and well-compacted argument. His address at the bar was not good, nor was his voice agreeable; consequently the value of his forensic efforts is based more upon the *fortiter in re*, than the *suaviter in modo;* more upon matter than manner. The sensitiveness of his feelings frequently led him to acrimonious expressions against his antagonists. He was accustomed, from the fashion of the age, to use a considerable quantity of the stimulus ot ardent spirit; and we have been credibly informed that he has delivered some of his most powerful and splendid arguments under its strongest excitement.

He was a man of warm heart and generous feelings, and to prove this, numerous examples of his benevolence might be cited; but in the discharge of his official duties he was rigorous and unyielding.

Before closing this article, we must add that Mr. MARTIN was opposed to the adoption of the present constitution of the United States.

LUTHER MARTIN.

As a member of the Convention by which that instrument was framed, he combatted it in its earliest stages; and when it was committed to the states for their approval, he addressed a long argument to the legislature of Maryland, which was intended to dissuade the people of that state from adopting it. This argument concluded with the following words—"Whether, Sir, in the variety of appointments, and in the scramble for them, I might not have as good a prospect to advantage myself as many others, it is not for me to say; but this, Sir, I can say with truth, that so far was I from being influenced in my conduct by interest, or the consideration of office, that I would cheerfully resign the appointment I now hold; I would bind myself never to accept another, either under the general government or that of my own state: I would do more, Sir, so destructive do I consider the present system to the happiness of my country. I would cheerfully sacrifice that share of property with which heaven has blessed a life of industry. I would reduce myself to indigence and poverty; and those who are dearer to me than my own existence, I would entrust to the care and protection of that providence who hath so kindly protected myself, if on *those terms only* I could procure my country to reject those chains which are forged for it."* Mr. Martin's violent opposition to the proposed frame of government was unsuccessful, but it most probably caused a more deliberate examination and approval than might have been deemed necessary had it not been so powerfully assailed.

Mr. Martin's personal appearance, as well as his mind, were alike extraordinary. He often appeared walking in the street with his legal documents close to his eyes for perusal—wholly abstracted from the world and absorbed in his profession. He was little above the ordinary size of men, but strong and muscular, although not very broad, in form. He usually wore a brown or blue dress, with ruffles around the wrists after the ancient fashion, and his hair tied behind hanging below the collar of his coat.

Luther Martin was undoubtedly one of the ablest lawyers which our country has produced, and his name will descend to posterity among the brightest of those, who have gained their reputation strictly at the bar, and in connection with causes which can never be detached from our national annals; but there are others of the same profession with natural and acquired talents certainly not superior to his, whose

---

* Secret Proceedings and Debates of the Federal Convention, pages 93, 94.

fame will probably occupy a broader space, merely from the fact, that the stage on which they play their part is more conspicuous than that on which he acted his.

PHILIP SYNG PHYSICK.

Dr. PHILIP SYNG PHYSICK was born on the 7th of July, 1768, in Third, near Arch street, Philadelphia. His father, Mr. Edmund Physick, was a native of England; and his mother, Miss Syng, the daughter of a highly respectable citizen of Philadelphia, who was one of the early friends and companions of Franklin; and whose name appears on the register of the American Philosophical Society as one of its founders, and also connected with other undertakings of public utility at that period.

The celebrity of Doctor PHYSICK has been so general, that to the American reader it is almost superfluous to state that he was distinguished by a long and brilliant course in Surgery and Medicine; by a deep and universal conviction on the medical and public mind of this country in favor of his skill; and by traits of character so prominent and so peculiar, that the chances are very improbable of their being repeated in any other individual. Even if Nature should renew her production, the difference of circumstances in which it will be placed, from the immense changes constantly and rapidly occurring in our social state, will prevent the same mode and degree of development.

The subject of our memoir received his academic education from Robert Proud, in "Friends' Academy," and during the time lived in the family of Mr. John Tod, the father-in-law of the present Mrs. Madison. He then entered the classical department of the University of Pennsylvania, and obtained his knowledge of the languages from Mr. James Davidson, one of the best scholars of his day. No small fondness for these his earlier studies remained with him to the end of his life.

Having passed honorably through his college studies, he received the degree of Bachelor of Arts. His father now considered him ready to engage in the study of medicine, and placed him under the charge of the late Dr. Adam Kuhn one of the most learned and successful physicians of that day.

His first introduction to anatomy excited strongly his aversion and disgust to the profession of medicine—it was the boiling of a skeleton in the Medical College in Fifth street, now the Health Office. He returned home, and implored his father to change his destination; it was all in vain. Finding his father thus inexorable, he began his medical studies in earnest.

When twenty years of age, in 1788, his father took him to London, and succeeded in fixing him under the direction of Mr. John Hunter, the great surgeon of the day; and now looked upon as the first medical man that the British empire has produced, his posthumous reputation having gone vastly beyond any that he ever had, when alive.

Being placed in a dissecting-room, he distinguished himself in a short time by his assiduity, and by the neatness and success of his dissections; he became a favorite with Mr. Home, the assistant in the rooms, and also with Mr. Hunter. The confidence and partiality of the latter were exhibited in the year 1790, while he was still a student under him, by Mr. Hunter using great exertions, and successfully, to get him elected House Surgeon to St. George's Hospital.

In the year 1791 he received his diploma from the Royal College of Surgeons in London. After which he visited Edinburgh, and having spent a winter there, took out the degree of Doctor of Medicine in the University, in 1792. In the latter part of the same year he returned home, highly instructed in his profession; after having declined offers by his preceptor Mr. Hunter, of a promising and advantageous kind, for him to settle in London, this course was probably influenced in some degree by his health, which the climate and atmosphere of that metropolis did not suit.

The year 1793 brought him distinctly and prominently into public notice. The premonitory indications of a fatal epidemic being on the approach, were but too faithfully verified, when, on the 19th of August, the celebrated Rush announced to his fellow-citizens that a malignant and mortal fever had broken out among them. This startling intelligence, whereby the repose of the public mind was disturbed, was received with the agitation and surprise created by some unexpected convulsion of nature; by some it was discredited, and strong indignation expressed against its author. The celerity, however, with which the disease invaded the several walks of life, left no room for disputation, and all that remained to be done, was to make the best possible arrangements for its visitation. Among the measures of the

PHILIP SYNG PHYSICK.

day, recommended by the College of Physicians on the 27th of August, and carried into immediate effect, was the providing a large and airy hospital in the neighborhood of the city, for the reception of such poor persons as could not be accommodated with suitable advantages in private houses. The erection of the Bush Hill Hospital was the result of this recommendation; and Dr. Physick having offered his services, was chosen physician of the same. He left his lodgings in town, entered immediately upon his new duties, and continued in the exercise of them till the disease had passed away.

In the year 1794 he was appointed a prescribing physician in the Philadelphia Dispensary, and a surgeon to the Pennsylvania Hospital; the public confidence was also exhibited by his practice increasing with no ordinary rapidity.

A recurrence of the yellow fever as an epidemic, in 1798, led again to a performance of similar duties in the Bush Hill Hospital. The zeal and fidelity with which he went through these, were recognised in the presentation of some elegant pieces of silver plate. Their cost was upwards of one thousand dollars, and they bore the following inscription:—

" From the Board of Managers of the Marine and City Hospitals, to
Philip Syng Physick, M. D.
As a mark of their respectful approbation of his voluntary and inestimable services, as Resident Physician at the City Hospital
in the calamity of 1798."

On Sept. 18th, 1800, he married Miss Emlen, the daughter of a gentleman of learning, distinction, and wealth, and who belonged to the very respectable Society of Friends. She died in 1820, leaving four chidren now alive—two sons and two daughters.

In 1805, the chair of Surgery in the University of Pennsylvania having been made a distinct one, he was elected to it; the success of his operations and lectures in the Pennsylvania Hospital, is considered to have created and established this change.

In July, 1819, he resigned his chair of Surgery in the University of Pennsylvania, and was appointed to that of Anatomy, vacated, the preceding November, by the death of his nephew, Dr. Dorsey.

The latest of his appointments was in 1836, when he was elected an honorary fellow of the Royal Medical and Chirurgical Society of London, and soon after received his diploma; he is said to have been very much pleased with this mark of respect from a city where his early studies had been conducted.

The earliest commendatory notice of him is found in the Treatise on the Blood by his preceptor, John Hunter. The latter wishing to arrive at some general conclusions on certain phenomena of the blood, as to its coagulability and putrescence under several conditions named, performed experiments on the subject, which were rather incomplete and unsatisfactory to himself; to verify, however, what he had done, he says, " Many of these experiments were *repeated* by my desire by Dr. PHYSICK, now of Philadelphia, when he acted as house-surgeon to St. George's hospital, whose accuracy I could depend upon."

In 1793 he, in conjunction with Dr. Cathrall, made several dissections of persons dead of yellow fever, which proved its inflammatory character, and that its principal violence fell on the stomach. These observations were not absolutely new, because they had been preceded by similar ones by Dr. Mitchill, in his account of the yellow fever of Virginia in 1737 and 1741, and by corresponding ones in the West Indies. They had, however, an important local influence in correcting the prevailing notions of the disease, by proving, that so far from being one of debility, it presented the highest possible grade of inflammation,—one exactly similar to what is produced by acrid poisons, as arsenic, introduced into the stomach. The principle was thus established, that the reputed putrid phenomena were merely the expression of the gastric inflammation, and that the proper treatment was precisely the reverse of what had obtained.

To this advance in the therapeutic indications of a disease so fatal and so terrifying, was added one of a most important prophylactic or preventive kind. At a time when it was perilous to the practice, as well as to the reputation for sanity of any physician, to assert that the yellow fever was generated among us and not imported, he had the manliness and dignity to declare openly this obnoxious truth. He also admonished the people, that the true protection from such visitations, was not in establishing an empty system of quarantine laws, and thereby interrupting foreign commerce, but in cleanliness at their own doors and along their own wharves. These were the views taken and enforced at the same time, by the eloquence and fervor of a Rush To this idea, constantly urged upon public attention, are to be traced the very complete and effective arrangements for supplying the city of Philadelphia with water, by applying, if required, the whole current of the Schuylkill to the purpose.

To the walks of Surgery, however, we must look for the genius of PHYSICK in its most decided and extensive application. It is there that we find it exhibiting a series of triumphs over cases of dis ease which had baffled the skill of men only inferior to himself and it is there that it was most active in inventions to improve and to palliate established modes of treatment. His management of diseased joints by perfect rest, elevation, and diet, is a happy substitute for the errors generated under the use of the term scrofula or white swelling, and ending either by amputation or in death—sometimes in both. His treatment of the inflammation of the hip-joint in children (coxalgia), by a splint, low diet, and frequent purging, exhibits another of those successful innovations upon ordinary practice. His invention of an appropriate treatment and cure for that loathsome disease, artificial anus, which invention has been so unceremoniously modified and claimed by a distinguished French surgeon, the late Baron Dupuytren, is a proof of the activity and resources of his professional mind. Another invention, still more frequent in its employment, from the greater number of such cases, is the application of the seton to the cure of fractures of bones refusing to unite. Other inventions are found in the treatment of mortification by blisters; of anthrax by caustic alkali; the ligature of kid skin for arteries in excisions of the female breast. To him, also, we owe the original act, if not invention, of pumping out the stomach in cases of poisoning; also an improvement in the treatment of fractures of the condyles of the os humeri, so as to render the restoration perfect. We might in this way go on to enumerate many other points of excellence about him; but, however appropriate it might be to offer a complete exposition of them, the space allotted to a memoir of this kind must prohibit a more extensive and complete annunciation. Those who have had an opportunity of witnessing his practice extensively, will at least conclude with us in saying, *Nihil tetigit, quod non ornavit.*

With this great fertility in invention and ardor in the prosecution of his profession, his original papers, as published, are few, and they are also very short.

Lecturing for many years on Surgery, his chief organ of publicity was his class of students. The Elements of Surgery, published by his nephew, Dr. Dorsey, contain the most perfect account of his opinions and practice up to that period.

To the preceding claims to professional veneration, were united physical qualifications of the most perfect kind. He had a correct, sharp, and discriminating eye; a hand delicate in its touch and movement, and which never trembled or faltered; an entire composure and self-possession, the energy of which increased upon an unexpected emergency. He had a forethought of all possible contingencies and demands during a great operation, and therefore had every thing prepared for it; when performed, he entered upon a most conscientious discharge of his duty to the patient, and watched him with a vigilance and anxiety which never remitted till his fate was ascertained.

If to the foregoing brilliant qualities as an operator, and the loud plaudits which attended their exercise, we add a chastening of feeling which subdued every sentiment of vanity and regulated entirely his judgment; and that he had an invincible repugnance, a horror at engaging in dangerous operations through ostentation, and where the probabilities of cure were not largely in favor of the patient; we have in this summary the most perfect example of a surgeon which this country has ever seen. But as these great points and striking professional landmarks seldom come in clusters, it will probably be long in the course of Providence before there will be a re-union of all the same excellent qualities.

His operation for the stone on Chief Justice Marshall, in 1831, was the last of his great efforts. He anticipated it with much anxiety, but when brought to the point, he rallied finely—every thing was, as usual, in readiness. The unexpected turn given to the operation by the almost incredible number, probably a thousand, of small calculi which he met with, and their adhesion to the internal coat of the bladder, did not disconcert him in the slightest degree. He in a little time detected the existing state of things, and they were brought to a successful conclusion, being followed by a complete cure. This operation was the more interesting from the distinction of its two principal personages; the one, the acknowledged head of the legal profession, and the other of the medical; and both sustaining themselves, though in advanced life, by that tone of moral firmness and dignity which had advanced them from inconsiderable beginnings to the stations which they then occupied.

Dr. PHYSICK was of middling stature, and not inclined to corpulence even at his best periods of health. His bust was a remarkably fine one; he had a well-formed head and face, the expression of the latter being thoughtful and pensive, sometimes enlivened in conversation by a smile, but very seldom so spontaneously. His nose was aquiline and thin; and his eye hazel, well-formed, vivid, and searching—his gaze seemed sometimes to penetrate into the very interior of the body. His eye acquired additional effect from his pallid, fixed, and statue-like face. His hands were small, delicate, and flexible. He dressed with great neatness: his clothes being put on with an exact attention to the process, and being from year to year of a uniform cut Many, no doubt, remember the very admirable and characteristic appearance imparted to his physiognomy and head by the use of hair powder, and how this almost solitary remnant among the gentlemen of Philadelphia, of an ancient fashion, seemed to be in entire harmony with his own individuality of mind and of reputation.

Dr. PHYSICK's traits as a teacher corresponded with other points in his character. His course of Surgery, upon which his reputation was founded in an especial manner, was eminently practical and instructive. He did not pretend to range over the whole field of this science, but limited himself to topics of daily occurrence, or at least such as might be expected in the practice of any medical man. Relying upon his own experience and habits of observation, he had but little to do with the opinions of others; he quoted them rarely, and never in such a way as to leave the point unsettled by an array of opposite authorities. His opinions were for the most part founded upon deep reflection, and were decided in one way or another; he never leaned to one side and inclined to another, so as to neutralise his weight; he either admitted entire want of information, or considered himself in possession of the requisite degree of it. This tone of sentiment pervading his lectures, they were most eminently didactic, and were listened to with a thorough conviction of their correctness; indeed, such was his authority, that it was held almost indisputable—to oppose it, was to brand one's self with folly.

He decidedly preferred studying every thing for himself in the laboratory of Nature, beginning his analysis of the human machine in a dissecting-room, and solving the problem of its disorders and their cure in a hospital. The proposition in every disease he considered as limiting itself to the positive experience of what had done good and what had done harm. His consultations always assumed this character.

As his opinions were, for the most part, formed with deliberation, so they were retained with firmness; and they, like his habits, were durable to an extreme. This we may account for, inasmuch as they were never taken up on capricious grounds, but always upon the most scrupulous examination of proof. He required, too, personal proof, such as would satisfy his understanding, through his eyes, his ears, and his touch. Naturally exact, systematic, and persevering, these traits were fully developed by his education and training.

Not being given to expressions of sentimentalities, his cold and steady manner was mistaken by some for apathy: he felt, however, acutely, when not the slightest external indication of it appeared. He was always anxious and excited when preparing for a great operation, and when it was finished, spent sometimes the remainder of the day in bed, in order to recover and tranquilize himself. The death of patients not unfrequently laid him up, from the excess of his sensibilities.

Having undergone a protracted illness, which reduced him to a most suffering and debilitated state, he died on the 13th of December, 1837, being in his seventieth year. He was interred in Christ Church burying-ground, corner of Fifth and Arch streets, Philadelphia, with the strongest expressions of public respect.

JAMES BUCHANAN.

"PENNSYLVANIA'S Favorite Son," as Mr. BUCHANAN has been affectionately breveted, was born at a picturesque spot called Stony Batter, in the immediate vicinity of Mercersburg, in Franklin County, Pennsylvania, April 23, 1791. From his earliest youth he evinced a degree of mental and physical vigor, which gave the happiest promise of future extensive usefulness and distinction.

His father was one of the pioneers of Western Pennsylvania, an Irishman by birth, and a person of strong sense, great integrity, and indomitable energy. He married Elizabeth Speer, daughter of a respectable farmer in Adams County, who was distinguished for her intellectual superiority and earnest piety. In 1798 the family removed to Mercersburg, where their son, JAMES BUCHANAN, received his early education, in English, Latin, and Greek.

At the age of sixteen he entered Dickinson College, Carlisle, where he graduated with the highest honors in 1809. Having determined to adopt the law as his profession, he commenced the study of it with Judge Hopkins, of Lancaster, and was admitted to the bar, November 17, 1812. Here he speedily attained a degree of eminence rarely enjoyed by youthful devotees of that exacting mistress, and, after only four years of practice, he was called upon to defend before the Senate of Pennsylvania, during the session of 1816–17, a distinguished judge, who was tried upon articles of impeachment. This he did with brilliant success, unaided by senior counsel. His practice, and his reputation, increased with almost unprecedented rapidity, and at the age of forty, when he gracefully retired from his profession, his name had occurred more frequently in the "Reports" of the State, than that of any other lawyer of this period.

Once only, after his retirement, did Mr. BUCHANAN appear in court, and then in a cause which did his heart, as well as head, so much honor that we cannot refrain from mentioning it. A poor widow, whose little all was in imminent danger from an action of ejectment, appealed most urgently to him for professional aid. in a case made almost hopeless by the technical difficulties which surrounded it. Acting upon the scriptural injunction, to "comfort widows in their distress," he undertook the cause with such earnestness and ability as to overcome all opposition, and establish the poor woman's undeniable title to the property in question. Thus did Mr. BUCHANAN give, in public, evidence of that kindness of heart so obstinately denied him by those who, unable to find a flaw in his moral character or political integrity, assail him in those points only defensible by *friends*, who have had the privilege of knowing and appreciating his many acts of graceful and unobtrusive benevolence.

The military episode in Mr. BUCHANAN's life must not be forgotten. During the War of 1812, when the British, after destroying the public buildings of Washington, threatened an attack upon Baltimore, a public meeting was held at Lancaster, to obtain volunteers to march to the defence of their sister city. With words of stirring eloquence, Mr. BUCHANAN addressed his fellow-citizens, appealing to their patriotism, to expel the intruders from a soil made sacred by the blood of their forefathers; and then, proving his sincerity by his actions, he registered his name at the head of the enrollment-list as a private soldier. His example was followed by many gallant spirits, and the company, commanded by Judge Henry Shippen, marched to Baltimore, and served under Major Charles Sterret Ridgeley, until they were honorably discharged.

Mr. BUCHANAN then evinced his devotion to his country no less decidedly in the Legislative Halls of Pennsylvania, where, when Philadelphia was in danger of an attack, he made the most urgent appeals to the Legislature to adopt measures for her protection. On being re-elected, in 1815, he gave his ardent support to the bill, appropriating three hundred thousand dollars, as a loan to the Federal government, to pay the State volunteers and militia for services to the United States. In 1820 he was elected to Congress, and soon took a position among the most able debaters in that body.

The second speech which Mr. BUCHANAN delivered, in this new arena, was upon a bill to establish a general system of Bankruptcy. Mr. Lowndes, one of South Carolina's most gifted and cherished statesmen, whose health, at that time fast failing, prevented him from speaking on a subject which he considered so important, selected, with prophetic foresight, Pennsylvania's young representative, to express his views and convictions, in which (as he was aware) he fully sympathized. This Mr. BUCHANAN did in a manner that excited the admiration and attention of the country, and gave him at once a reputation for eloquence and statesmanlike ability, which he has always sustained unquestioned. An instance of his magnanimity,

JAMES BUCHANAN.

which occurred in connection with this event, may not be out of place here. Not many years since, an old friend of his was alluding to this speech, and mentioning the admiration it excited, and the predictions of future distinction to which it gave rise, when Mr. BUCHANAN, with noble frankness, disclaimed all right to any credit for a speech which was really, he said, that of Mr. Lowndes, and merely delivered by him. Such an avowal, made so long after that distinguished statesman had passed away, shows a degree of generous candor rarely met with.

We cannot, in this brief sketch, attempt an account of the various occasions on which he distinguished himself whilst a member of the House: abler pens have already described, with graphic power, this portion of his career. One event, however, in which he was associated with, and opposed to, some of the ablest and most prominent men in the country, must not be passed unnoticed. This was the trial of Judge Peck, of the District Court of Missouri, against whom articles of impeachment were passed, upon which he was tried before the Senate. The circumstances were these. In December, 1825, the claims of the widow and children of one Antoine Soulard, to lands in Missouri and the then Territory of Arkansas, were decided upon adversely by Judge Peck. One of the prosecuting counsel, Luke E. Lawless, of St. Louis, wrote a respectful article for a newspaper, in which he pointed out the errors into which he conceived the Judge to have fallen. Upon this the Judge had him summoned, and, after depriving him of the right to practise his profession, committed him to prison. Mr. Lawless then appealed to the House of Representatives, and his memorial was referred to the Judiciary Committee, of which Mr. BUCHANAN was chairman. The committee reported, *unanimously*, articles of impeachment against Judge Peck, which were adopted by the House, and presented to the Senate, upon which that body resolved itself into a court of impeachment for his trial. Five managers were chosen, by ballot, on the part of the House, to conduct the prosecution: they were JAMES BUCHANAN, of Pennsylvania, Henry P. Storrs, of New York, George McDuffie, of South Carolina, Ambrose Spencer, of New Jersey, and Charles Wickliffe, of Kentucky. The counsel for the defendant were William Wirt and Jonathan Meredith. The case was opened, on the part of the prosecution, by Mr. McDuffie in a speech of great power, and closed by Mr. BUCHANAN, who, confining himself closely to the legal and constitutional questions involved, presented an argument so eloquent, and so convincing, that, although the Senate refused, by a vote of 22 to 21, to punish Judge Peck, it passed, a short time after, *unanimously*, an act, obviating the technical objections which had prevented his conviction, and so framed the law that no Judge could again venture to commit a like offence.

Mr. BUCHANAN retired voluntarily from Congress at the close of his fifth term, and was almost immediately after appointed, by General Jackson, envoy extraordinary and minister plenipotentiary to Russia. He remained there two years, in which time he concluded the first commercial treaty between the United States and Russia, which secured to our merchants and navigators important privileges in the Baltic and Black Seas. His personal popularity at the court of the Czar contributed not a little to this result, and the impression which his dignified courtesy and attractive social qualities made upon all who were there associated with him, was most pleasingly described by his successor.

Upon his return, in 1833, he was elected to the United States Senate, which had, during his absence, been the scene of one of the most violent struggles our country has ever witnessed. A rupture between General Jackson and Mr. Calhoun had led to a dissolution of the Cabinet; a new tariff had been enacted, and the battle against a renewal of the charter of the United States Bank had been fought, and won by the administration party. In this position, Mr. BUCHANAN displayed the same profound ability, calm judgment, and statesmanlike qualities, joined to the never-failing courtesy which had distinguished him in the Lower House, and took from the first a prominent part in all subjects which arose for discussion and disposal at that eventful period. At no time in our country's history, or at least since the courtly days of the First Congress, has the United States Senate presented such an array of varied and distinguished talent.

There was Calhoun, always imposing, enthusiastic in his devotion to the interests of his beloved Carolina, and never failing to command admiration even from his opponents; Daniel Webster, whose giant intellect was acknowledged and deferred to even in the Parliament of Great Britain; Henry Clay, the trusted idol and fearless champion of his party; Silas Wright, the model statesman, whose uprightness and consistency, together with a vigor and perspicacity of mind which never failed to elucidate any subject which he undertook, and whose gentler qualities endeared him to all who ever knew him; Thomas H. Benton, whose mental power and untiring industry enabled him to master a subject however abstruse, and handle it with telling effect; John Forsyth, the graceful and ready debater, whose quickness and skill in parrying attacks made upon the administration during the contest in 1831 and 1832, was compared to a triumph of small-sword exercise.

With such men did Mr. BUCHANAN take a position confessedly second to none in ability and learning. To the various subjects which were acted upon during the ten years that he was in the Senate, we shall merely allude: the French Indemnity bill, which he warmly advocated; the attempted agitation of the question of slavery, by the introduction of a bill for abolishing it in the District of Columbia, which was opposed by Mr. BUCHANAN as an unwise and inflammatory measure; the Texan Revolution, in which he evinced always a deep interest; the naturalization question, in favor of which he took strong ground; the debate on expunging the resolutions of censure upon the gallant old soldier, whose fearlessness and inflexibility had carried him triumphantly through a political contest as fierce and desperate as the military one in which he won the laurels that gave him a place in the foremost ranks of his country's heroes. Here Mr. BUCHANAN spoke *con amore*, and, the vote being taken immediately after he had concluded, the objectionable resolutions were expunged from the records of the Senate. The Sub-Treasury bill, also, was defended by him with ability and earnestness. Passing on to the Tyler administration, we find another attempt being made to re-charter the United States Bank, which was vetoed by the President, whose action in the matter was warmly sustained by Mr. BUCHANAN. The question of the annexation of Texas next came up, and was eloquently advocated by him, as he had from the beginning shown a kind and active interest in the young State. The bill passed only a few days before the inauguration of Mr. Polk, upon which Mr. BUCHANAN left the Senate to take the chair of Secretary of State. In this department, he had many important and delicate subjects to meet and dispose of. The Oregon question, which had been pending during the previous administration, had now assumed a position of critical importance, which demanded prompt and decided action. A proposal had been made for its adjustment by Mr. Tyler. by fixing the line of latitude at 49° N. This was accordingly renewed by Mr. BUCHANAN, in his first protocol to the British Minister, Mr. Packenham, but immediately rejected by him, without reference to his government. Mr. BUCHANAN then replied, in a state paper of great power and elaborate detail, in which he exhibited the claims of the United States to the whole territory, and proved that the compromise proposed was an exhibition of great generosity on the part of our government, proceeding from a desire to avoid a rupture between two countries, to whose welfare mutual friendliness is so essential. He concluded by formally withdrawing the proposition, which decided the fate of the controversy, and took the matter out of Mr. Packenham's control.

The spirited and determined tone of this despatch satisfied the British Cabinet that our government was resolved to maintain its rights, and produced, very soon, a proposal from them to settle the boundary according to the offer made by Mr. Polk. This it declared was its ultimatum. In the dilemma, the President determined to submit the matter to the Senate, which was then in session, and, that body having recommended an acceptance of the proposition, it was so settled.

Our relations with Mexico began now to assume an angry aspect; in truth, our forbearance towards that government had been trifled with to a degree that rendered armed remonstrance a positive necessity. Our troops having advanced to Corpus Christi, the Mexicans crossed the Rio Grande, and, without awaiting the form of a declaration of war, commenced open hostilities. Under these circumstances, there was but one course to pursue, and Congress declared war, and passed a bill authorizing the acceptance of a volunteer force of ten thousand men; upon which fifty thousand pressed forward, eager for the glory of defending their country's rights.

The history of this war (where the unparalleled success of our noble little army, in numbers a mere handful compared to the force to which they were opposed, seemed at the time, and appears on retrospection, almost miraculous) is too well known, and too proudly recorded in our country's annals, to need more than a passing allusion. Our troops, whose chivalric gallantry, high honor, and generous humanity, not less than their unfailing courage and strategic skill, shone never more brilliantly than during this campaign, performed prodigies of valor, and, aided by our no less efficient naval forces, proceeded uninterruptedly upon a series of victories which resulted in unfurling from the enemy's capital the stars and stripes of our glorious republic. During this time, Mr. BUCHANAN was ever on the alert to seize the fitting moment to terminate, by an honorable and advantageous treaty, a contest so fortunate in its results to us, and so disastrous to our antagonists. The terms proposed by our government were, in point of generosity, unequalled in the history of nations

JAMES BUCHANAN.

To our country, however, the acquisition of California, and the peace which enabled us at once to profit by the wealth resulting therefrom, more than compensated for any additional advantages of territory which, as some suggested, might have been obtained; but only, as they did not consider, by an unwarrantable sacrifice of life and money. In this negotiation, Mr. BUCHANAN especially avoided European intervention, and instructed our minister to Mexico, Mr. Slidell, emphatically to decline all such offered mediation.

In 1849, at the close of Mr. Polk's administration, Mr. BUCHANAN retired to private life; but even then his watchful eye was still upon the ship of state, and his far-seeing sagacity appreciated, while yet but a speck in the political horizon, the storm which was gathering, and which, unless prompt and vigorous precautions were taken, would bring destruction upon the vessel which had already met and weathered so many dangers. The slavery agitation was spreading with fearful rapidity and violence in the North, whilst a spirit of determined resistance to what they deemed an unwarrantable interference with the rights of property, was equally strong in the Southern States. Our veteran statesmen were reduced to a little band, who had thought to enjoy tranquillity and freedom from care in their declining years, but who found themselves again called upon to aid their country in her need. Clay, Webster, and Cass in the Senate, and Mr. BUCHANAN in his own State, (where his voice was all-potent,) brought forward conciliatory resolutions and suggestions, like oil upon the troubled waters of the opposing factions, "saying to the North, give up, and to the South, keep not back," until finally, by the united efforts of these devoted patriots, aided by the "good men and true" from both sections of the country, the compromise measures of 1850 were passed, occasioning a jubilee long to be remembered throughout the Union. The broad national ground taken by Pennsylvania throughout this memorable contest, gave her a new right to the proud title of the Keystone State, in which she has always gloried.

Mr. BUCHANAN now gave himself up to the calm pleasures of country life, at his beautiful home near Lancaster, where he dispensed a Southern-like hospitality to all who came within its limits, and where he himself, always genial and agreeable, was the very life of the home circle. This was composed of the charming niece, whose beauty, and grace of manner, and peculiar conversational attractions were as remarkable in the then school-girl, as now they are in the hostess of the Executive mansion; and of two nephews, with the almost constant addition of visitors of all ages.

NATIONAL PORTRAITS.

Notwithstanding any fatigue he might have undergone during the day, Mr. BUCHANAN always devoted his evenings to the family, who eagerly anticipated the rich treat afforded by his inexhaustible variety of anecdotes of people and events in this country, as also in Russia, which were told with a spirit and interest indescribably fascinating. These were always cheerfully contributed to the entertainment of the little circle, and a participation in any social game merrily and cordially acceded to. It is in his home-life that Mr. BUCHANAN should be seen and known by those who doubt his possession of those genial qualities which so adorn it.

From this quiet happiness, he was summoned, in 1853, by President Pierce, to represent our government at the court of St. James. This mission he reluctantly consented to accept. The Central American difficulty was at that time under discussion, and Mr. BUCHANAN'S despatches to Lord Clarendon on the subject are considered models of concise simplicity and ability. The question had, however, been complicated by previous negotiations, and still remains unsettled. In March, 1856, Mr. BUCHANAN resigned the position, and returned home to a welcome so cordial and demonstrative, as to prove most satisfactorily how fully he and his services were appreciated by his countrymen. He was unanimously nominated the June following (by the Democratic Convention assembled at Cincinnati) for the Presidency, and, despite a twofold opposition, triumphantly elected.

On the 4th of March, 1857, he was inaugurated as the President of the United States. Great difficulties were before him. There were international variances with Spain and Central America to be adjusted; but the most serious troubles rose out of questions pertaining to slavery in Kansas. The North and the South were becoming involved in contentions that threatened the Union. Mr. BUCHANAN sought to be a peace-maker. He gave the South a fair representation in the Cabinet. He signed the bill, passed by Congress, submitting the whole question of slavery indirectly to the people of the Territory. Kansas became a Free State. The South was not satisfied. Sectional jealousies were excited. The Southern Confederacy was organized in spite of all Mr. Buchanan's efforts to allay the rebellion. Scarcely had he retired from office in 1861, before the war was opened. He returned to Wheatland to pass the rest of his days in private life. History will assign him a position among the distinguished men of America.

www.ingramcontent.com/pod-product-compliance
Lightning Source LLC
Chambersburg PA
CBHW022139300426
44115CB00006B/261